Coppola's Monster Film

Coppola's Monster Film

The Making of Apocalypse Now

STEVEN TRAVERS

McFarland & Company, Inc., Publishers
Jefferson, North Carolina

LIBRARY OF CONGRESS CATALOGUING-IN-PUBLICATION DATA

Names: Travers, Steven, 1959– author.
Title: Coppola's monster film : the making of Apocalypse now / Steven Travers.
Description: Jefferson, N.C. : McFarland & Company, Inc., Publishers, 2016. | Includes bibliographical references and index.
Identifiers: LCCN 2016024255 | ISBN 9781476664255 (softcover : acid free paper) ∞
Subjects: LCSH: Apocalypse now (Motion picture)
Classification: LCC PN1997.A653 T73 2016 | DDC 791.43/72—dc23
LC record available at https://lccn.loc.gov/2016024255

BRITISH LIBRARY CATALOGUING DATA ARE AVAILABLE

ISBN (print) 978-1-4766-6425-5
ISBN (ebook) 978-1-4766-2449-5

© 2016 Steven Travers. All rights reserved

No part of this book may be reproduced or transmitted in any form or by any means, electronic or mechanical, including photocopying or recording, or by any information storage and retrieval system, without permission in writing from the publisher.

Front cover: Francis Ford Coppola (at right) working on *Hearts of Darkness: A Fimmaker's Apocalypse*, a 1991 documentary about the making of the film *Apocalypse Now* (Showtime/Photofest)

Printed in the United States of America

McFarland & Company, Inc., Publishers
Box 611, Jefferson, North Carolina 28640
www.mcfarlandpub.com

*To Tim Silano,
film editor extraordinaire*

SC is the West Point of Hollywood. —John Milius

Table of Contents

Introduction   1

1. Kurtz   7
2. Godfather of 'em All   15
3. Protégé   24
4. "The End"   41
5. Zen Anarchist   50
6. "University of Northern California Graduate Film School"   58
7. Shooting Star   69
8. *Patton*   74
9. "That was like raising a red flag in front of a young bull"   83
10. *Hubris*   95
11. Ordeal in the Jungle   104
12. "I was going to the worst place in the world"   114
13. "Kill ... gore"   120
14. "He's not dead unless I *say* he's dead"   124
15. "I felt like von Rundstedt going to see Hitler"   129
16. Prima Donna   139
17. "He took a face from the ancient gallery"   148
18. "Apocalypse When?"   155
19. "It's not about Vietnam—it *is* Vietnam"   164
20. Triumph   167
21. The Milius Screenplay   190
22. "I've been blacklisted as surely as anybody in the '50s"   198
23. Postscript   202

Chapter Notes   215
Bibliography   221
Index   229

Introduction

*Coppola's Monster Film: The Making of **Apocalypse Now*** is a sweeping epic covering an era dominated first by John Wayne, finally by George Lucas. It explores each of the characters and their backgrounds intimately, and details the unique educational experience of the great film schools, then and now. It is a portrait of America and its great, unique art form, cinema, and its meaning as art, entertainment, propaganda, and business.

* * *

In 1968–69, Hollywood's movers and shakers were given a proposal. America was deep in a quagmire against Communism in Southeast Asia at the height of the Tet Offensive. A handful of scruffy, long-haired twenty-somethings from the two burgeoning California film schools, USC and UCLA, had no military experience, but had recently watched a *cinéma vérité* movie called *Medium Cool*, which sent actors and a partial screenplay to the Democratic National Convention in Chicago. The actors, playing journalists, moved around on camera along the periphery of the worst riot in American history, mouthing scripted words mixed with "reality TV" response to the violence about them.

The young California film graduates proposed something similar. They would fly ten thousand miles to the 'Nam with cameras and a few actors, who would "mingle" with the soldiers amid actual combat, and produce their *cinéma vérité*, putting viewers smack dab in the middle of the great conflict of their times.

* * *

Perhaps never before in history, at least outside of pre-revolutionary Enlightenment Paris, has so much sheer talent and hubristic vision come together in one place at one time as in the confluence of the emerging film schools USC and UCLA, in the greatest of all Los Angeles decades: the '60s.

Two University of Southern California film students: John Milius and George Lucas; a UCLA film school graduate, already working in Hollywood: Francis Ford Coppola; the fourth, a drifter from Florida, whose father was a Navy admiral in charge of all U.S. operations in Vietnam, the man who carried out President Lyndon Johnson's orders to "give me my damn war" at the Gulf of Tonkin, a UCLA film school drop-out-turned-rocker named Jim Morrison.

Add to the mix a USC editing genius named Walter Murch and a tormented UCLA screenwriter named Paul Shrader. Finally, a young Arizonan turned down by both schools. Steven Spielberg hung out with Lucas and Milius so much at USC that most assumed he went to school there, not at Cal State, Long Beach. Beyond that, a bevy of young writers, would-be directors, producers, editors, cinematographers, most of whom would become world renowned in the decades that followed.

Out of this ether of youth, talent, testosterone, and drugs emerged the nexus that would create Hollywood's greatest decade, the 1970s, and in the last year of that decade, it's most monumental epic: their *cinéma vérité*, rejected by the Pentagon, now called *Apocalypse Now*.

* * *

Our story begins in 1966. It is the opening game of the 1966 college football season. The Southern California Trojans are in Austin to play the Texas Longhorns. The night before the game, former Trojans football player John "Duke" Wayne gets rip-roaring drunk and begins to spout off about how the United States is gonna "bomb those piss-ant Commies back to the Stone Age" in Vietnam. Nearby sits a writer, perhaps opposed to Wayne's jingoism, with a history of run-ins with the Duke. An argument ensues, in which Wayne may or may not have taken a full swing at the writer, Harley "Ace" Tinkham, missing by inches.

The next day, still drunk, Wayne makes an incendiary, war-like speech to the USC team. Sitting in the room are assistant coach Marv Goux and student manager Ron Schwary. Goux was once a gladiator in *Spartacus* whose own fiery speeches to the players are borrowed from Kirk Douglas's speech in the Stanley Kubrick classic. Schwary is a film student.

Upon returning to L.A., Goux begins to "channel" Wayne, using military jargon like "we're gonna go through those bastards like crap through a goose" and "no bastard ever won a game by getting injured, he won it by laying out the other poor, dumb bastard." According to the theory, Schwary tells his friend, John Milius, about Goux's speeches.

Milius grew up a huge John Wayne fan who watched *The Searchers* "hundreds of times." He is a Right-wing conservative who wants to join the Marines so he can "kill Commies" in Vietnam, but has asthma and is declared 4-F. He decides instead he will make pro-military movies. Perhaps Schwary sneaks him into the old gym at USC, where he hears Goux channel Wayne in a pre-game speech. He is told by Schwary, Goux has gotten the idea of his speech from Wayne's speech to the 1966 Trojans. Milius begins to research John Wayne.

Speaking to other USC film school students, he begins to hear "rumors and random intelligence" that Wayne nearly punched Soviet Premier Nikita Khrushchev in 1958, and that he is slated to play the role of General George S. Patton in an upcoming bio-pic to be produced by Darryl F. Zanuck and Twentieth Century–Fox, the character and the film modeled in part on Wayne's performance in *The Longest Day* (1962). The film, however, is on hold because the Patton family will not cooperate with Zanuck, thinking liberal Hollywood will not be fair to his memory. By 1966–67, however, Zanuck has enough juice to get the film into development even without the family's permission. He hires Francis Ford Coppola to write the screenplay. Coppola is a close friend of Milius. Then Zanuck's own son, Richard, forces him out in a political move.

Milius, perhaps, interjects, giving Coppola "advice" on the screenplay. Coppola is at this time researching George S. Patton. But Coppola is adamantly opposed to the Vietnam War and writes an anti-military script, bent on making Patton look crazy. He does this, perhaps, by infusing the screenplay with Marv Goux's rhetoric to the USC football team, fed to him by Milius. To Coppola, this is a way of making Patton look crazy. To Milius, it makes Patton look ... like Patton. When Wayne sees the screenplay, he decides it is not patriotic enough for him, it is not a "John Wayne story," so he drops out. Rod Steiger, having won an Oscar in *The Heat of the Night*, is offered the role, but he sees it differently: it *glorifies* war. He, too, drops out, for opposite reasons. Enter George C. Scott, ex-marine. He believes Coppola has written Patton's character as a crazy, unhinged general, but sees a spark, a way to channel that energy into a positive performance.

Then Franklin Schaffner, fresh off the success of *The Planet of the Apes*, is brought in to direct. He will not make an anti-Patton film. He served under Patton in North Africa and admires him.

Coppola turns in his script and gives up on Hollywood, moving to San Francisco to make independent films and documentaries for a fledgling company he hopes to turn into a "counter-cultural M-G-M." It is called American Zoetrope. One day he gets a phone call from Twentieth Century–Fox. He has invented an editing machine that has broken down. Only he can fix it. Will he come to L.A. to repair the machine?

While repairing the editing machine he looks up and sees dailies on a screen. It is George C. Scott playing Patton. Then—and only then—does he realize his screenplay is being produced.

The film, *Patton*, debuts in 1970. Reaction to it is amazing. The Patton family, with a lawsuit ready to file against the studio, actually loves the film. Scott has infused the character with charisma, and turned the words of Coppola, maybe channeled by John Wayne then by Marv Goux then by John Milius, into an Academy Award–winning performance. The lawsuit quietly disappears.

At a movie theatre in Birmingham, Alabama, the USC football team sees *Patton* the night before a game with Bear Bryant's Crimson Tide. Their reaction? *Patton sounded just like John Wayne ... no, Patton sounded just like Coach McKay ... no, man, Patton sounded just like Coach Goux.... YEAH, THAT'S IT! Patton sounded EXACTLY like Coach Goux!*

Marv Goux has been giving the speech made by George C. Scott at the beginning of *Patton* for *three years before Patton has even been released*! But that is not all. There is a scene at the end of the movie in which Scott-as-Patton tells a Russian general, "I have no desire to drink with him, or any other Russian son of a bitch."

A search of Patton's 1963 biography, *Patton: Ordeal and Triumph* by Ladislas Farrago, reveals no evidence that the real Patton ever made this exact speech, or said quite those words to the Russians after the fall of Nazi Germany. Neither the film's advisor, then-retired General Omar Bradley, or his screenwriter wife, advised the filmmakers that Patton spoke quite like this.

The "Patton speech" is based on John Wayne and Marv Goux! The scene with the Russian general is based on Milius hearing about Wayne practically slugging Nikita Khrushchev in 1958!

Francis Ford Coppola could not care less; he is out of the business practically, laboring in San Francisco obscurity.

Somewhere, John Milius smiles.

* * *

We now flash back to the mid–1960s. The USC and UCLA film schools are both considered second rate, classes offered in Quonset huts and old World War II military barracks.

Anybody can get in. It is not considered real academia, like business, journalism, law, or science. But it is the '60s, and the times they are a-changin'.

We learn of a Calvinist from Pennsylvania named Paul Shrader, who is tortured by the belief that his destiny either as a saved Christian or a damned sinner has been pre-ordained by God. Looking for an outlet for his emotions, he enters the UCLA film school, where he befriends Francis Ford Coppola and his coterie of film protégés. Through his art, he begins to find rest, but his tortured persona will pour out in later years when he pens *Taxi Driver*.

Jim Morrison is a Navy brat who has lived all over the world. His father is an admiral, in charge of Naval operations at the Gulf of Tonkin, which started the Vietnam War. He, too, has found his way into the UCLA film school. There he meets John Densmore and Ray Manzarek. Frustrated by the negative reactions to their student films, they drop out of school and form a rock band called The Doors. One night Coppola journeys to the Sunset Strip to hear them play. He is mesmerized by the lyrics of one song in particular: "The End." He foresees that these are the lyrics of a movie he wants to make about a "desperate land" call Vietnam.

In 1966–68, Coppola is working in Hollywood. He is taking film stock and equipment from his employers, handing it out to his friends, John Milius and George Lucas of USC, and their pal from Long Beach, Steven Spielberg, promising that when they all make it, they will "make it together."

Coppola's vision from Morrison's "The End" meshes with an idea by Milius and Lucas for a docudrama about the Vietnam War ... *in Vietnam, using actors mingling around combat zones*. Milius is challenged by a USC film professor named Irwin Blacker that "nobody could ever tackle Joseph Conrad's *Heart of Darkness*. It ruined Orson Welles." Brazenly, he decides to write a screenplay, basing it in Vietnam. He calls it *Apocalypse Now*, but nobody wants to make a Vietnam movie while men are dying in Vietnam.

* * *

Coppola has formed American Zoetrope Studios in San Francisco's north beach neighborhood, home of Jack Kerouac and the Beat movement. He has no desire to return to Hollywood, but he cuts a revolutionary deal with Warner Bros., who fund the development and eventual production of a slate of upcoming movies. One of these is *Apocalypse Now*, but first they shoot and distribute Lucas's original student film classic, *THX 1138*. It is such a disaster that Warners pulls the plug on Zoetrope. They want their money back. *Apocalypse* is shelved along with a host of other scripts and projects.

Enter legendary film producer Robert Evans, who has been tasked with making Mario Puzo's *The Godfather*. He wants an Italian-American director who will make a movie so realistic you can "smell the spaghetti." He is unimpressed with Coppola's artsy persona and anti-war attitude, as well as his vision of mob life as a "parable for capitalism," but he is the only Italian-American film director available. He hires him. The shoot is a disaster, and in 1971 he will fire "the prince of Napa Valley" from *The Godfather*. Just before that, however, Coppola is a sudden hot property when he wins the Academy Award for his *Patton* screenplay. Evans cannot fire an Oscar winner. Coppola finishes the film, and it is an instant classic. For decades, filmgoers have reported that when Al Pacino asks Diane Keaton, "Do you like your lasagna?" they get hungry!

After a successful sequel, flush with glory and money, Coppola now embarks on his *magnum opus*: *Apocalypse Now*.

* * *

George Lucas has also moved to his native Northern California, where Coppola helps him fund a pet project filmed in Marin County called *American Graffiti*. A key character, John Milner, is based on Milius. The film's success is largely credited with spurring the independent film movement. The old studio system is now dead.

Meanwhile in Los Angeles, Jim Morrison soars to great success in rock music, only to die of a drug overdose in 1971. It appears The Doors are gone, and forgotten.

At weekend parties at actress Margot Kidder's house in Malibu, gather the inhabitants of young Hollywood, the Baby Boomers who have disdained the studio system and given the business a youthful new flavor. Among her regular guests are Spielberg, Shrader, Milius, and Marty Scorsese.

Meanwhile, up the road in Beverly Hills, Robert Evans and his wife, actress Ali MacGraw, are hosting parties for the "in" crowd at his Woodland estate. Guests include Clint Eastwood, Warren Beatty, Jack Nicholson, Dustin Hoffman, and Steve McQueen. McQueen will steal Ali from Evans!

The partygoers at Kidder's and Evans's homes have made such classics as *Rosemary's Baby*, *The Odd Couple*, *Love Story*, *Butch Cassidy and the Sundance Kid*, *The French Connection*, and *Chinatown*.

But Lucas and Spielberg are about to change the very nature of box-office expectations in Tinseltown. Milius wrote *Dirty Harry* and *Magnum Force*, but is facing resistance to his conservative politics from liberal Hollywood. *American Graffiti* has made Lucas a hot commodity. Coppola is the biggest name in the game, and is telling his friends they need not play by the old studio rules. They can fund their own pictures and paint their own vision of the world. Spielberg is the last to break through, but when he does it is a game changer. *Jaws* breaks all box office records. Then Lucas's *Star Wars* creates a new genre: the "pop corn movie." Many have never forgiven these two for what they did to the so-called "character-driven story," overshadowed by computers and technical wizardry.

* * *

In 1975, flush with money and fame from two *Godfather* epics, Coppola goes to the Philippines to film *Apocalypse Now*. His co-producer is George Lucas. The screenplay has been written by John Milius. The original script is a jingoistic vision of how U.S. Special Forces take guerrilla war tactics to the guerrillas, thus winning a war many felt was unwinnable. Absent Milius, Coppola scraps much of the premise, including a victorious ending.

Harvey Keitel plays his main character, Captain Willard. The Colonel Kurtz character from Conrad's novel is played by an overweight Marlon Brando, who requires a huge, budget-busting salary, but can only film for a few weeks, which must somehow fit into the schedule. The Marcos government promises Coppola use of their helicopters, but at the last minute they are diverted to the hinterlands to fight Communist insurgents. Typhoons and rain seem to fall every day ... for four years. Keitel is fired, replaced by Martin Sheen, who has a heart attack. Coppola films for years ... without an ending. The shoot threatens to be the greatest disaster in movie history. Finally, Milius is called back in to punch up the script and give it life. After four years they call it a wrap. Back in California, Coppola has a stroke of genius. The opening song will be "The End" by The Doors, and Morrison's singing from live concerts on the Sunset Strip, which inspired Francis thirteen years earlier, will be interspersed throughout the movie.

Apocalypse Now becomes one of the great films of all time. It revives the music of Jim Morrison, elevating The Doors to Hall of Fame status. Milius makes *Red Dawn*, the quintessential anti–Communist screed of the Cold War era, but the future belongs to Lucas and Spielberg. Their "cartoon" movies are the wave of post–'70s Hollywood. The last great film of the "1970s" is *Raging Bull* (1980) by Scorsese and Shrader, but the disaster of *Heaven's Gate* a couple years later brings down United Artists, changing the film industry forever. A new business model is hatched. Rogues like Francis Ford Coppola will not be allowed to run amok, allowing budgets to skyrocket beyond control. After the Reagan years, Milius will be marginalized more and more by the Left. The kind of art he, Coppola, and Jim Morrison once produced will not be seen again, either.

1

Kurtz

While *Apocalypse Now* was released in varying forms, starting at the Cannes Film Festival in the spring of 1979, to a "general" release in the late summer of that year, the majority of Americans who saw it for the first time viewed it with the ending eventually settled on by director Francis Ford Coppola over the Christmas holidays, 1979.[1] In this respect, *Apocalypse Now* represents the end of an era, one written extensively about by Peter Biskind in his seminal telling of Hollywood tales from the late 1960s to the early 1980s, *Easy Riders, Raging Bulls: How the Sex-Drugs-and-Rock 'n' Roll Generation Saved Hollywood*. *Apocalypse Now*'s release coming in the final year of a decade makes it symbolically convenient, although Biskind's title suggests that a "golden era," roughly in confluence with the end of the old studio system, starts with *Easy Rider* (1969), and ends with *Raging Bull* (1980). *Heaven's Gate* (1980) is viewed as the film that "brought down" a Hollywood that has not been seen again.

Apocalypse Now was released to great fanfare, terrific buildup, and overwhelming negativity. The buzz, however, was on par with previous blockbusters such as *Gone With the Wind* and, of course, both of Coppola's *Godfather* epics. Those films were viewed as masterpieces before the general public ever saw them. *Apocalypse Now* was as much a curiosity as a huge, interesting film. Many went to see it because they thought it might be a spectacular train wreck, the burning of *The Hindenburg*.

Moviegoers had been reading about the film in the trades, on entertainment television programs, in *People* magazine, and in newspapers. The buzz equaled anything seen in the subsequent Internet age, although not all of it was positive; most, in fact, was negative or semi-negative. People arrived at theatres curious, but like highway "rubber neckers," they could not resist looking.

For a film to truly succeed, indeed to reach blockbuster status as Coppola's Vietnam epic needed to do in order to earn his money back and save him from financial—and professional—ruin, it must achieve "pop corn" status, in that its audience cannot be sustained merely by a cult, by engaged film students, by art house aficionados, or industry insiders. It needs average high school and college students; guys and girls on dates; the kind of people who like shoot-'em-ups and disasters, and are not there to have their art spoon-fed to them. They just want to be entertained.

Many of those who ventured into movie cineplexes—a relatively new movie theatre trend spurred by the success of Coppola and two protégés, Steven Spielberg and George Lucas—were young men and women who in recent years had attended American high schools, where one of their required classes had been a rote course roughly described as "literature." For most, it was boredom city, required reading of novels they neither had the time nor the enthusiasm to read cover to cover. Many looked at enough of the words on the pages of the required books to remember a few details, enough to pass and move on.

Some of the books taught in public schools in the 1970s included *The Old Man and the Sea* by Ernest Hemingway and, after much controversy over content, in more liberal areas of the country, *The Catcher in the Rye* by J. D. Salinger. For many, their first impression of *Apocalypse Now* was a name that rang vaguely familiar: Kurtz.

For Western educators of the 1960s and 1970s, Joseph Conrad's *Heart of Darkness* was perfect fare for public school education. The novel, completed in 1899 and published in 1902, was by then a classic along with Conrad's other, similar tale of journey and redemption, *Lord Jim*, which had been made into a very fine film, if not a highly commercial success, in the 1960s, starring the estimable Peter O'Toole.

Heart of Darkness is almost a novella, in that it is short, making it easier for high school students to read. But it is by no means light. It is dark and heavy, far beyond the normal bounds of teenage intellect. What made it appealing to an increasingly liberal education class reacting to McCarthyism was its indictment of the West as, essentially, the rapist of the dark-skinned peoples of the Third World, most notably the Africans, the sacred cow of victimhood. While average students would not likely grasp this indictment, left-leaning teachers would, allowing them the perfect platform to espouse the general, growing view that the white man, Western Civilization and—in the Vietnam era increasingly—the United States of America, was the focus of all evil; the source of all problems in the world. These young people, wracked with white guilt gleaned from the lesson of books like *Heart of Darkness*, would therefore go forth and change the world in a kinder, more liberal image.

Conrad's own background played into this narrative in a small way. Born in Poland, he moved to France to join the merchant navy before eventually settling in London, westernizing his name and establishing himself as a writer penning works in his third language. *Heart of Darkness* is based on Conrad's own experiences as a merchant seaman in the Belgian Congo, mostly in 1890.[2]

The history of the Belgian Congo and the role of King Leopold II of Belgium has been papered over by 20th Century history. Belgium is seen as a poor little country, its strategic geography making it the awful victim of German invasion in World War I, then some of the heaviest fighting of World War II. But in the late 1950s and early 1960s, its colonial past became a symbol of the de-colonization movement marking the end of the British Empire, in accord with an agreement between President Franklin Roosevelt and Prime Minister Winston Churchill, to bring a form of "democracy" and "freedom" to the former European colonies in the wake of World War II political settlements.

International Communism seized on the Third Word as its great prize, playing on age-old resentments by blacks, Arabs, Muslims, Latinos, Orientals, and the dark-skinned people of the Earth, who historically had been conquered, raped, pillaged and kept down by white militaries from England, France, Germany, Spain, Belgium, and other European nations. The fact that the United States had hardly participated in this kind of colonized subjugation—its role in the Philippines, Cuba, Hawaii, Puerto Rico, and a few other protectorates was not comparable to 19th Century colonization—meant nothing to liberals and Communists. The U.S. had ascended in a short time to a power and reach above all previous world empires. The fact that she was the one spearheading *de-colonization*, not the further subjugation of native people, was immaterial. She was the symbol of capitalism, of greed, of exploitation, and white racism. This narrative fit perfectly with the times: the Civil Rights Movement, and a re-examining of America as a slaveholding country. The fact that slavery, a thriving institution for time immemorial, needed to come to America in order *to die*, was also immaterial, but if educators were to look for books about the Civil War, it would force them to teach kids that *hundreds of thousands of whites died for black freedom*. That was not acceptable.

Liberal educators were hard-pressed to find books actually describing American "atrocities." Cuba might have been a good subject, since greedy capitalist mobsters had turned the island into a veritable casino/whorehouse, but Fidel Castro's takeover and subsequent killing of some 1 million people made it hard to be a sympathetic country. The Philippines might have been an easy target, except Douglas MacArthur had talked FDR into rescuing it from the Japanese, who were engaged in atrocities there rivaling Auschwitz. When people thought of Puerto Rico, they thought of great baseball stars like Roberto Clemente, who found success and respect in the U.S. Hawaii could not so easily be viewed as a victim, since its citizens had, after being bombed by the Japanese, overwhelmingly sought statehood and were now reaping the great benefits of American citizenship.

So, American educators needed to look elsewhere to find stories of white racism in literature. A novel like *Heart of Darkness* seemed perfect. It was considered a great work, and sufficiently European to appease conservatives who saw in *The Catcher in the Rye* a call for rebellion against American traditionalism. But the Belgian Congo was the perfect subversive setting.

King Leopold and the Belgians who ruled the land were among some of the most vicious, violent and oppressive of the white colonialists. Their treatment of the local populations was certainly worse than English treatment of the Indians or other colonized people, and arguably more heinous than what the Germans, French—or even the Spanish—did to people under their respective thumbs.

By the 1960s, this history was in the news since the Congo had rebelled, kicked out the Belgians, and taken up Communism. This caused the CIA to more than likely—it has never been fully proven—assassinate a suspected Communist revolutionary, Patrice Lumumba, and install an authoritarian government that was committing atrocities against its own people that made what the Belgians did pale in comparison.

Liberals like Norman Mailer and George Plimpton papered this over, in fact practically glorified Zaire (the nation's new African name), in their descriptions of the 1974 Muhammad Ali-George Foreman "rumble in the jungle," held in a stadium literally holding tortured political prisoners under the boxing ring. This was overlooked as it was during the Church hearings, when decades of CIA secrets were revealed to the public.

* * *

Heart of Darkness went against type in its own time. It was the age of British Empire and muscular Republicanism embodied by President Theodore Roosevelt. Writers like Rudyard Kipling glorified imperialism. Autocratic royal families, who viewed their positions as ordained by God Himself, largely ran European governments. The colonized were viewed by a strange combination of Greek philosophy and social Darwinism. Plato, Socrates, and Aristotle argued that slavery was "natural." The natives were not officially slaves, anyway, but rather seen as the weakest link of humanity, like little children to be taken care of by their educated betters. This thinking would give rise to the abortion and eugenics movements, which emphasized that some people—the dark-skinned, the lame, the stupid, the homosexual—should be "humanely" put to sleep rather than burden society. The result: Adolf Hitler, Joseph Stalin, Mao Tse-tung, and the death, mostly by pure murder, of some 250 million human beings.

Written as a frame narrative, the novel is about Charles Marlow's life as an ivory transporter down the Congo River in central Africa. The river is "a mighty big river, that you could see on the map, resembling an immense snake uncoiled, with its head in the sea, its body at rest curving afar over a vast country, and its tail lost in the depths of the land," wrote Conrad.[3] During the river journey, Marlow hears about an ivory trader named Mr. Kurtz. The more Marlow hears about, and contemplates, what he hears about Kurtz, the more obsessed he becomes with who, and what—and why—he has apparently become a malevolent figure.

The story's premise is to delve into what 19th Century Europeans considered to be civilized, as compared to what was thought to be barbarian. In so doing, it explores themes of racism that many had never contemplated. This was the direct result of Conrad's own experience when he sailed in the Congo and, in so doing, saw things that disillusioned him with imperialism. These included acts of cruelty and racism that compelled him to challenge the conventional view of who was civilized and who was the barbarian after all.

In this respect, *Heart of Darkness* is far more than a novel about 19th Century colonialism and cruelty, but delves into man's very soul, and the nature of what Christian theologians call Original Sin. All men are created equal, and Satan corrupts all people. While the book was well received critically, it was not a big success. After two world wars killing mass millions, however, people wanted to understand themselves better; what made us capable of such barbaric acts? Conrad provided some of the answers.

The Kurtz character appears to be a composite of historical imperial figures of the era, and is also a reversal of sorts from the image of the Welsh explorer Henry Morton Stanley (who asked, "Dr. Livingstone, I presume?"), which fit in with the self-serving white narrative promoted by Albert Schweitzer, the kindly father figure who brings civilization to central Africa.

Conrad himself described his work as "a wild story of a journalist who becomes manager of a station in the (African) interior and makes himself worshipped by a tribe of savages. Thus described, the subject seems comic, but it isn't ... an anecdote of a man who went mad in the Centre of Africa."[4]

Aboard a trawler called the *Nellie*, Charles Marlow describes the passage from the heart of civilization itself, the Thames River, London, and subsequent voyage to Africa, where he describes scenes of devastation and human suffering; the detritus of an empire. For later readers, this may well be the first impulse to compare what Marlow sees with the American experience in Vietnam. It certainly is the first time Marlow experiences disillusion. Properly prepared to expect the worst in man, he then is told of a "first-class agent" named Kurtz.

Moving into the jungle, Marlow finds his steamboat has been wrecked and needed by Kurtz, who is ill. There are numerous delays and, during this time, Marlow hears reports of Kurtz's poor behavior. As they approach Kurtz at his Inner Station, a thick, white fog envelops the boat. From the riverbank they hear a very loud cry, followed by a discordant clamor. A few hours later, as safe navigation becomes increasingly difficult, the steamboat is hit with a barrage of sticks—small arrows—from the wilderness.

The crew fires into the wilderness and the helmsman is impaled by a spear, falling dead at Marlow's feet. Conrad then uses a device, which is to flash forward to a report Kurtz wrote, urging, "Exterminate all the brutes!" Marlow thinks Kurtz must be dead and the native attacks the result of a lack of white authority. The crew wants to turn back but Marlow has a strong desire to confront whatever it is that awaits them upriver.

Finally they arrive at the station where a harlequin Russian figure, familiar to the Polish-born Conrad, escorts them and describes Mr. Kurtz, whom Marlow identifies as a wanton figure, perhaps maniacal or insane. The natives have not turned from white authority. The opposite has occurred. They worship Kurtz as a pagan idol. The Russian calls him a poet filled with admirable qualities. One of these qualities, very Nietschean in its historical influence on the Nazis, the Soviets and Red China, is Kurtz's willingness to exercise his power. Marlow suggests that Kurtz has gone mad.

From the steamboat, through a telescope, Marlow observes the station in detail where he sees a row of posts topped with severed heads of natives. From there he sees Kurtz, carried on a stretcher, while the natives ready for a confrontation. A beautiful woman also appears, possibly Kurtz's lover or one of his harem. Marlow learns that Kurtz had ordered the attack in which the helmsman was speared to death.

Finally, Marlow confronts Kurtz and they clash. Over time, both men become increasingly ill. It is revealed that Kurtz was a man of high ideals. He may symbolize the white man, the doctor, the missionary who originally engages the natives with the hope of helping them, but ends up hurting them. In the novel, Kurtz assumes the full power of his authority until the tribe's people worship him like a god. This is his ultimate downfall, a message that might have Christian overtones, although not espoused by Conrad; all men are corrupt and must bow before God. Satan, as the Bible points out, wanted to be God, thus ensuring the downfall of man.

Eventually, Marlow is ready to return after his boat is repaired. Kurtz gives him a packet of papers and, as he dies, whispers, "The horror! The horror!" Marlow does not tell anybody but a "manager's boy" appears and announces, "Mistah Kurtz—he dead." The next day Marlow pays little attention to the pilgrims as they bury "something" in a muddy hole. Marlow falls very sick, himself near death. Finally he returns to Europe.

Embittered by the experience and the role of "civilized" countries in the dark jungles of native lands, Marlow gives some of the papers Kurtz wrote of the "suppression of savage customs" to a journalist, hoping the truth of what happens in these faraway places can be exposed. He finds Kurtz's fiancée and lies to her, telling her his final words were not "The horror!" but rather her name.

Harold Bloom wrote that *Heart of Darkness* was the most analyzed work of literature in universities and colleges, which he attributed to the author's "unique propensity for ambiguity," but it was not successful during Conrad's life.[5] One critic felt it was an "incomprehensible mystery." Conrad was not impressed with himself.

Interestingly, the book re-emerged not as an indictment of white colonization, but when a Nigerian post-colonization writer named Chunua Achebe called it "racist."[6] The argument was that its depictions of backwards black savages played to the white racism of the civil rights era. It was the defense of Conrad that made the novel an educational tool in schools and colleges.

Both liberals and conservatives can argue their points. The liberal would say that the

Kurtz parable symbolizes white greed and exploitation; this history is the reason white power structures "owe" the dark-skinned peoples for the crimes of their forefathers. The conservative would argue that Kurtz represents the liberal high-mindedness of the welfare state, and stands as an example of how harmful their "help" is.

While such examples and allegories with the Great Society are worth exploring, the role Kurtz ultimately stands for is of civilization and advancement. This is an endless argument of history, but when the dust clears it emerges as a clash of civilizations with an inevitable result based on human nature that would have happened no matter how much historical revision is applied.

This marks the history of the world, one aspect of which is written about by Conrad via Marlow's musings about the Roman Empire's conquest of pre–Christian Britain. England is the ultimate symbol of European civilization, yet at one time was a desolate island occupied by native people subjugated to Roman rule. Since time immemorial, man has militarized, expanded his base geographically, and subjugated the peoples he comes across. Even the Earth itself has aided in this advancement, as tectonic shifts of land mass enabled certain peoples to move from continent to continent.

The Persians, the Egyptians, the Greeks, the Arabs, the Muslims, the Israelites, Genghis Khan, the Spanish Inquisition—all mark the inevitable military conquest of one people by another, often until another military power comes along and conquers them. England's victory over French Naval forces at Trafalgar opened the spice trade to India, and was followed by the Industrial Revolution. European nations needed natural resources. Africa, the Orient, and other unmined territories had what they needed. They went in and took what they needed, calling it progress. Natives who stood in their way were slaughtered. The United States was not innocent of this historical fact. The American West offered some of the greatest natural resources on Earth, which included oil, and the native Indians who lived there were displaced to make way for U.S. advancement to the Pacific.

When the U.S. defeated Germany and Japan in World War II, for the first time a conquering empire that had defeated its adversary and occupied its territory, gave it back to its citizenry, thus ensuring a new kind of empire, an empire of ideas and democracy, this one greater, more widespread and more influential even than the Romans or the British before them.

But the great argument, engendered by works like *Heart of Darkness* and any impartial view of history, ultimately comes down to whether the white man was right to do what he did, whether the natives ultimately benefited, and whether there was any alternative. The third plank of this thesis is the most compelling. If, for instance, modern man were able to create a time machine and go back centuries to do it all over again, this time sparing the natives agony, which today has so paralyzed and split apart politics, could this be accomplished? One imagines sending a team of good liberals, politically correct "do gooders," and military men given orders not to use their weapons. One further imagines the white man, thus unwilling to assert his authority, slaughtered before any "progress" can be made.

Kurtz, in fact, represents this very man, the idealist who will use his intellect to spread civilization to the natives, until he takes the slippery slope of establishing his dominance in order to "force" reason upon the savages. Cut some heads off, put them on sticks to scare the brutes, and only then will their hearts and minds see reason! Conrad thoroughly refutes the logic of this idea.

But as with all history, the long view must be our ultimate window. If, for instance, the white man had chosen not to interfere with the native populations, to just leave them alone, at some point whites would have been accused of racism for *not offering* their inventions to the natives. Railroads, medicine, hospitals, cures, automobiles, air travel, education, protection from Communism, Christianity; are these not benefits of society that modern "natives" are happy to have and would surely never give up?

Christianity is, of course, a source of great controversy. The atheist will argue that to "subjugate" the "masses" to its tenets is to deny them their traditions. If one actually believes in God, however, and—to extend that further—knows that Satan exists and is constantly at war with Him, using man as his proxy, then one understands that despite all the horrors, the "subjugation" that ultimately led billions of "heathens" to the Lord Jesus Christ is "God's work," and in so doing was hated by the devil, who, as Norman Mailer once wrote, thought all these people of the Third World to be merely his "fodder." One can use the example of China in examining this philosophy, through the lens of *Time* publisher Henry Luce, who grew up the child of Christian missionaries in pre–Maoist China. When China went Communist, Luce saw it as metaphorically going to hell. An estimated 70 million were subsequently murdered. The Chinese would have benefited from some authoritarian white Christians saving them from this horror; far more than those victims of their same race who murdered them in numbers only Satan could envision.

Thus the great argument engendered by Joseph Conrad and others who philosophize over Europe's role in history remains a conundrum for the ages.

* * *

Orson Welles adapted and starred in *Heart of Darkness*, part of his popular CBS Radio broadcasts of the late 1930s, made most famous by his incredible description of *War of the Worlds* on *The Mercury Theatre on the Air*, which was so realistic listeners panicked, thinking it a real newscast of an alien invasion.[7] In 1939, Welles adapted *Heart of Darkness* for his first film for RKO Pictures, writing a screenplay with John Houseman. The project was never realized. Welles held out hope he could still produce the film when he presented another radio adaptation of the story as his first program as producer-star of the CBS radio series *This Is My Best*.

Welles scholar Bret Wood called the broadcast of March 13, 1945, "The closest representation of the film Welles might have made, crippled, of course, by the absence of the story's visual elements (which were so meticulously designed) and the half-hour length of the broadcast."[8] Ultimately, the film's projected budget, what with an elaborate boat trip, jungle conditions, and period costumes, was deemed too costly and Welles made his masterpiece *Citizen Kane* instead. There were various stage, operatic, and TV adaptations, but the general impression was that Conrad's *Heart of Darkness* could not be made, that Welles, one of the great masters, could not "lick it," and, like other epics such as Ayn Rand's *Atlas Shrugged*, it could never be brought to the big screen. (In the case of *Atlas Shrugged*, an American film version of the Rand novel was ultimately released in two parts: the first in 2011; the second in 2014.)

* * *

John Milius was a self-described "bad kid" who, at age seven, moved with his family from a "normal" environment where it "snowed in the winter," St. Louis, to Los Angeles in the 1950s.⁹ The family was affluent. They lived near the posh Bel-Air Country Club, one of the ritziest neighborhoods not just in L.A., but in the world. His family enjoyed the country club lifestyle, but Milius rebelled. An indifferent student, he found solace at the nearby beaches, where he fell in with a surf crowd.

This infuriated his father, who saw no value in surfing or beach life. When Milius was seventeen he was sent to Colorado to get him away from the beach. A rugged outdoorsman, he took to mountain life with the same fervor he had taken to the ocean. Determined to "become Jim Bridger," he became a gun aficionado, a hunter, a trapper. He lived not like a modern American teenager but a mountain man of the early 19th century.

While young Milius had rebelled against the social conventions his family expected of him, he always had a thirst for knowledge. Today, Ritalin, liberal academic control, "smart phones" with mind-numbing "games," and the endless drone of texts, tweets, and techno-garbage would likely have ruined John Milius. Spurred by super-violent content put out by Hollywood, TV, and video games, he might have turned his love of guns into a violent confrontation with the authorities he always romanticized opposing as an amorphous "other," a Big Brother. Absent these terrible influences, he turned to classic books, and in Colorado, without television, drank even more deeply from them.

He read Homer, George S. Patton's biography, Edward Gibbon's *The History of the Decline and Fall of the Roman Empire*, Shakespeare, and all the great works. Living in a cabin out in the woods, he read *Heart of Darkness*. He described the experience as if "in a dream," relating the solitude of Marlow on the boat, traveling upriver, surrounded by jungle and nature, with his own rural surroundings.[10] He began to imagine dangers behind every tree, as he imagined Kurtz had used his fear to turn into mastery of his jungle surroundings, and the jungle people. Milius mastered the mountain woods, becoming one with nature.

A few years passed and Milius tried to channel this experience into something positive in his life. He returned to L.A., where he attended junior college. He made a surf Mecca visit to Hawaii, where he wandered into a movie theatre showing Akira Kurosawa movies. He wanted to join the Marines and fly missions in Vietnam, but "washed out" due to asthma. He determined to do the next best thing; if he could not be a military commander, he would become, like Kurosawa, a film director. Thus, he entered the University of Southern California to study film.[11]

At USC he took a screenwriting course from an old Hollywood veteran named Irwin Blacker. Milius asked Blacker about making *Heart of Darkness* into a movie. Blacker said it could not be done, that Welles had tried and failed, that it was too ponderous and weighty and fraught with peril.[12]

2

Godfather of 'em All

Francis Ford Coppola was born in 1939 to first-generation Italian-American immigrants, Carmine and Italia Coppola. The Coppolas had three children; two were given Italian names (August, born five years before Francis, and Talia, born five years after him). Francis got his name from his grandfather, Francesco Pennino, and from a radio show (*The Ford Sunday Evening Hour*) his mother was employed by at the time. Later, his parents regretted Americanizing his name, but it would be Francis who would most identify with his Italian heritage.[1]

His was an artistic family. Italia was an assistant conductor and musical arranger. Francesco was a musician and songwriter. He also opened movie theatres in New York. Augusto Coppola, Francis's paternal grandfather, taught his children a love of music. Carmine Coppola played the flute and studied at Julliard. He was a noted musician but his life was marked by frustration, in that his true break, in which his great talent could lead to fame and fortune, came only when his son became famous and employed him.

But the Coppola family were not merely erudite *artistes* and musicians. Like so many Italians they immigrated through Ellis Island around the turn of the century. Family lore was rife with stories of "wise guys" and "honor slayings" associated with the Mafia. In many ways, the Coppola household in which Francis grew up resembled his *Godfather* movies: a combination of mob influence and Italian opera music. Many of the family stories and anecdotes inspired scenes from Francis's movies.[2]

But it was a middle-class existence. They were comfortable, although not wealthy. Money was always an issue, especially when Carmine invested a large sum of money in the Tucker, an ambitious new style of automobile coming out of Detroit. The car failed and never produced returns on his investment.[3]

Older brother Augie was the great hope of the family. "He was the star of the family, and I did most of what I did to imitate him," recalled Francis. Augie was a talented writer, and his younger sibling tried to emulate his story telling prowess, sometimes to the point of plagiarizing them in his own schoolwork.[4] A bout with polio threatened Francis's health, possibly his life, but he miraculously made a full recovery. The experience may have helped formulate his creative mind.

A similar experience occurred to Jim Murray, a Connecticut youth who was hospitalized with a childhood disease. Murray spent hours reading books about history and literature, and even wrote letters to political leaders. This helped him formulate his style as a legendary sports columnist for the *Los Angeles Times*.[5] Similarly, young Coppola used his recovery as time to formulate stories, often told to a tape recorder, and even used a 16mm film projector given him by his grandfather Pennino. His obsession with gadgets influenced his career and his films, finding its way into movies like *The Conversation*. He would invent editing machines that nobody else knew how to use, adding greatly to his early success.

Augie was the writer. Francis, after spending countless hours working on gadgets during his recovery from polio, was to be the engineer. Augie entered UCLA to study philosophy, although his initial plan was to advance to medical school. He decided in midstream to become a professional writer. Francis became absorbed by reading the classics and playing the tuba at a tough all-boys military academy in upstate New York. He then announced his intentions to go into the theatre, and spent a summer living with Augie in Los Angeles. Upon his return, he spent a great deal of time knocking around New York City, which he described as duplicating the adventures of Holden Caulfield, the central figure of *The Catcher in the Rye*.[6]

The family moved to Great Neck, out on Long Island, and after graduating from high school Coppola entered the local college, Hofstra University, on a partial scholarship to study theatre. But he loved movies and gravitated toward them. His politics were largely shaped by Sergei Eisenstein's *October* (1928), a loving portrait of *Ten Days That Shook the World*, John Reed's book on the Russian Revolution, which papered over the genocide in favor of the idealized lie of a "workers' paradise." It also transformed Francis's career aspirations.[7]

"On Monday, I was in the theatre," he said. "On Tuesday I wanted to be a filmmaker."[8]

Still, he studied theatre, realizing it would help his filmmaking later. He directed an acclaimed production of Eugene O'Neill's *The Rope*.[9] He was known as being brilliant as well as arrogant.[10] He sometimes hid his foibles behind his arrogance, but was known to be friendly. He started to make small student films. His final, grand success was in directing a production of Tennessee Williams's *A Streetcar Named Desire*. He graduated in 1960 and prepared to follow his brother's footsteps to UCLA, where he would pursue his master's degree in their film school.

Francis Ford Coppola had already spent a summer in Los Angeles. His second "arrival" came at a key point in the city's history. L.A. was once extremely conservative to the point of evangelical Christianity. The city he would later be far more associated with was San Francisco, some four hundred miles north, up the coast; a more cosmopolitan area featuring New York–style architecture and less rigid moral codes.

But the film industry was in L.A.; if one wanted to make it in the movies, they had to be there. Highly successful Broadway actors and directors were occasionally whisked off to the West Coast, where they struggled in this strange new environment. Some made it. Many returned to New York and London, embittered by the experience. But Coppola wanted to attend film school in the city where film was king, and that was Los Angeles. Both NYU and Columbia offered film training, but even if one made it through those programs, eventually the day would come when they would either make it or break it in Hollywood.

Los Angeles was dominated by the Chandler family, owners of the Republican-friendly *Los Angeles Times*. The Chandlers represented San Marino society, which was somewhat Southern in its sensibilities, to the point of militarism in a horse cavalry sort of way.[11] General George S. Patton had come out of San Marino. The city was largely Protestant, churchgoing and industrious. But after World War II, so many people moved to L.A. that it lost any single identity—Southern, evangelical, Republican—and became a truly diverse melting pot.

It was no "minor league" town anymore. Hollywood had put L.A. on the map after World War I. Movies were invented by the French, but the early film industry was centered in New York in the East, and San Francisco in the West. After the Great War, the wide boulevards, easy access, good weather, and diversity of both architecture as well as scenery made L.A. the natural home to a film industry; it was also far removed from the monopoly of Thomas A. Edison, Inc.'s film patents and its litigious attempts to preserve it. Most of the early movie producers were Jewish businessmen, gambling on something that had no template for prior success. It was the ultimate endeavor for those who had failed on one coast, only to re-invent themselves on another, as so many had during the Gold Rush.

But it was the move by the Brooklyn Dodgers to Los Angeles in 1957, with the building of Dodger Stadium a few years later, which truly made it a "big league" city. Two Californians, Earl Warren and Richard Nixon, had been Republican vice-presidential running mates, with Nixon elected along with President Dwight Eisenhower before losing by a tiny margin to John Kennedy in 1960. California was electoral-rich.

Aviator-industrialist Howard Hughes helped create the so-called Military Industrial Complex, largely located in west L.A. stretching from Santa Monica Airport to the Long Beach shipyards. By 1960 the city was threatening to overtake New York and Chicago in terms of economic, political, and cultural impact. Rival San Francisco's reputation was of an older, more sophisticated city. Los Angeles's "plasticity" was embodied in the term Tinseltown.

Growing up side by side with Hollywood, equally important to the development of Los Angeles, were the two great universities, the University of California, Los Angeles (UCLA), and the University of Southern California. USC was older and more traditional. UCLA was the "second school." It began in 1919 in Westwood, a remote section of Los Angeles. People said nobody would go to school "way out there," west of Western Avenue, a sort of city "border." The only people who went that far west were the wealthy owners of beach cottages in Santa Monica, but a nascent film industry was being built. The *nouveau riche* preferred building their own community, rather than trying to fit in with the established wealth of Hancock Park and San Marino. They began building mansions in nearby Beverly Hills and Bel-Air. Within a short period of time, the Westside was where the action was.

UCLA started as a commuter school but built its football team into a powerhouse on the strength of enlightened recruitment of African-American stars such as Jackie Robinson. A decade before Robinson's breaking of baseball's color barrier in 1947, battles between the integrated USC Trojans and UCLA Bruins, played before 75,000 fans at the L.A. Memorial Coliseum, were the greatest social statements made to date.

UCLA thought of itself as more egalitarian, a public school far friendlier to L.A.'s Jewish population. And, as many Hollywood films shot on location there after World War II often featured surfing and bikinis, it was also something of a party school, located just a few miles from the Pacific Ocean, featuring handsome beach boys and classic California blondes.[12]

In the 1950s, with the publication of *On the Road* by Jack Kerouac, a growing "beatnik" movement began to form at UCLA. This sort of "fuzzy" character was generally rejected by USC, which went beyond conservatism and was downright right-wing, virulently anti–Communist and supportive of Richard Nixon.[13] But the beats had formed a "headquarters" of sorts in San Francisco's North Beach, fanning out from there to the University of California, Berkeley, across the bay, then other college campuses.

The influence of the counter-culture grew so fast at Berkeley that the school largely rejected some of its most traditional concepts, such as football.[14] Once a national powerhouse in all sports, in the 1960s Cal became something of a laughingstock, while both USC and UCLA enjoyed their greatest glory. Largely because of athletic success, UCLA became a national brand. Once called the Southern branch of the University of California system, Rose Bowl victories and NCAA basketball titles established them as UCLA once and for all.

UCLA's presence in the film industry was ephemeral. Many scenes were shot on its picturesque campus, and many of its beautiful coeds sought and sometimes found modeling and acting careers in *ingénue* roles. Blonde bombshell Jayne Mansfield went to UCLA. Famed quarterback Bob Waterfield, who went from UCLA to the Los Angeles Rams, dated Jane Russell.[15] Another Bruin football star, Woody Strode, later acted in movies. Comedienne Carol Burnett had also gone to UCLA.

But training in its film school was no easy pathway to a career in the movies. There was a scattering of UCLA Bruins working in the industry. Some were agents and producers. By and large, the sons of successful Hollywood career people got in because of connections.[16] Francis Ford Coppola had no connections. One advantage of the school, however, was its location.

UCLA was and is located in the Westwood section of west Los Angeles, neatly tucked into a corner adjacent to Sunset Boulevard and the San Diego (405) Freeway. Directly west, hugging the Pacific Ocean a few miles away, is the industry town of Santa Monica, then to its north Brentwood, Pacific Palisades, and Malibu, home to many film industry power players. When departing the campus on the Sunset Boulevard side, one is across the street from the famed Bel-Air Country Club, and in the hills rising above that the posh L.A. enclave of Bel-Air, a major center of film industry *glitterati*. To the east, traveling by car along the winding curves of Sunset Boulevard is Century City, Beverly Hills, and then, of course, Hollywood proper, its legendary Hollywood Hills the home of movie star mansions and the iconic Hollywood Sign.

To attend UCLA was to be in the middle of a working movie town. Aside from rubbing shoulders with the offspring of famed actors and directors, film notables were always spotted in local restaurants, bars, and just walking the streets. But for Coppola and other UCLA students interested in the movies, the greater advantage was the existence of art houses all over L.A. County. These theatres played foreign films, old silent movies, and independent films. They held symposiums and seminars featuring the work of great, but sometimes obscure, directors. Long before video or the Internet, these art houses offered a look into movies found only in a handful of other cities in the world. The most popular art house was—and remains to this day—the Nuart on Santa Monica Boulevard, an easy jaunt from the UCLA campus.

Despite any vestige of L.A.'s colloquial past—it's evangelical Christian and Midwestern/Southern roots, its Republican voting patterns—it was the entertainment capital of the world. In addition to the film industry, the music industry induced creative, artsy people from all over the world to come there. Some of them were a little on the bearded side, readers of Kerouac, beginning to find an identity for themselves somewhat from the jingoistic, John Wayne patriotism that marked World War II and the subsequent 1950s. This was Francis Ford Coppola's generation.

Coppola never considered any future other than filmmaking. He was one of the first of a new breed of educated people of immigrant stock who possessed some vague sense of American entitlement. His family was not rich, but they were artists who never lived hand to mouth, either. There was money for college, money for a middle-class existence.[17]

The UCLA that Coppola entered was the "cinematic equivalent of the Paris writers' group of the 1920s," wrote film writer Dale Pollock.[18] It was an extension of what Time-Life publisher Henry Luce called the "American Century."[19] Not only had victory in World Wars I and II made the U.S. the most powerful empire ever, it had unleashed the American culture. That culture found its voice first in the "Great American novel," when writers from Mark Twain to Ernest Hemingway were producing the most influential literature. Next came the "great American art form," film. The Soviets and the Nazis used film as propaganda tools in the 1930s, but there was no comparison to the star power of Hollywood. The "studio system" refined it into a combination of creativity and business model with no previous example.

Coppola's timing was perfect, because for the first time, film students were beginning to be taken seriously. "For a while, film schools seemed to have a stigma," remarked Martin Scorsese, who would shortly enter the cinema program at New York University. "A few reviewers would write, 'His work is full of student pretensions.'"[20]

Coppola was disappointed at first. He imagined a happy group of young artists hanging out and making movies with communal purpose. "There was none of the camaraderie I imagined when I was in college," said Coppola. "All they know is to criticize the lazy ways of Hollywood film producers, implying that only they could be capable of directing great films."[21] Most filmmakers "get so hung up—handling film is so much fun, so exciting—that they tend to bypass content and acting, the other things which eventually the film will make use of. They go into it with just technique."[22]

Eventually, UCLA developed a style to accommodate this way of thinking. The UCLA method involved an organic interaction between the film school and the drama department. Future directors and writers met and became associated with future actors.

"They provide a terrific stimulus, a chance for young people to meet someone—a teacher or another student—who can influence them," said Coppola. "And secondly, they let you get your hands on real movie equipment. You can't do that anywhere unless you're rich enough to go out and buy your own."[23]

Prior to Coppola, filmmakers generally started as assistants, grips, maybe camera operators. Over time, after working on enough films and getting to know enough people, they might be given a chance to direct, and if what they did was relatively impressive or even successful, they were given more opportunities. The key was getting into a trade union, which usually required a sponsor. In other words, they needed to know somebody. Unlike athletics, in which African Americans demonstrated skills that opened doors for them, the Hollywood guilds, like most unions, were not friendly to minorities.

Hiring a film graduate was irregular, but by Coppola's time veterans of the industry increasingly populated the faculty at UCLA. They had contacts and could make introductions. Over time these students befriended the children of movie bigwigs, allowing greater association with influential people. The program Coppola studied included film history, directing, some acting, and the technical aspects of animation and editing. They worked with 8mm or 16mm cameras, and were tasked with operating within a theorized budget. Even more important than classroom instruction were the long "bull sessions" between students and professors; the exchange of ideas and theories.[24]

Coppola was on the cutting edge of an exciting time, which he would help create. In 1960, however, UCLA was not quite what he had hoped it would be and he considered a return to the theatre.[25] For one thing, the film school was separated from the rest of the university, a sort of stepchild located in a wood building behind the main campus. Classes were held in several Quonset huts left over from World War II.

Many students were older and viewed Hollywood negatively, believing they would not be given the chance to really test their abilities professionally. They were iconoclasts who looked down upon the jocks and beach babes who dominated the UCLA social scene.[26]

"It was highly competitive and ego-driven," recalled Carroll Ballard, a fellow Bruin who would direct *The Black Stallion* (1979) for Coppola. "Everybody thought of themselves as the next Kurosawa. I don't remember it being all that congenial. What was good about the film school itself; it was the enthusiasm of so many young people who had the same dreams, and how that kind of cross-fertilized. The academic aspects of it were a snore and a waste, as far as I was concerned. I felt the film school should be run like a body shop: you had to learn to bang out those fenders and do all this stuff. No amount of talk is really going to do it."[27]

Film students of the 1950s and 1960s were thought to be "slackers and shirkers," to use a term of the day; "ghettos" for unserious college students.[28]

"In those years, it was unheard of for a young fellow to make feature films," said Coppola. "I was the first one!"[29]

While still a student, Coppola made in-roads in the growing independent film movement. "Francis was known to be the big man on campus across town at UCLA, which is to say we were at USC," recalled Matthew Robbins. "He had made quite a splash, and was the first person we'd heard of in the film community who'd had serious beginnings."[30]

Only two student films were actually funded each year. Students were not given enough film, enough equipment, or enough time. Coppola managed to make two shorts, *The Two Christophers* and *Aymonn the Terrible*. The first concerned a boy plotting to murder another boy of the same name; the second was a kind of *Picture of Dorian Gray*, a narcissistic sculptor who wishes only to re-create himself. Coppola was lauded for these films, which he made sometimes by hook or by crook, talking his way onto Forest Lawn Cemetery to shoot a replica of Michelangelo's David.[31]

"Who *was* this guy?" recalled Ballard, adding that he had "everybody working for him like a bunch of slaves.... It was incredible, what an operator he was."[32] Coppola's arrogance, even his sense of entitlement, would rub people the wrong way, but they ultimately worked for him; Francis was the man who got done what others could not.

"I had this overwhelming urge to make films; not to read about them or see them, just to make them," Coppola recalled. "All I lacked was the opportunity."[33]

So he started making nudie flicks. Perhaps because of this, UCLA would come to be regarded as more *avant-garde* than USC; the place that tended to show topless or bikini-clad beach girls under the guise of art. Coppola's first employer, Russ Meyer, was not much of an artist. His films were pure sexploitation, basically considered pornography at the time.³⁴ Coppola directed a movie called *The Peeper*, about a voyeur who discovers an apartment where pin-up photo sessions are taking place, and goes to great lengths to observe the action. Meyer was famous, or infamous, for his portrayal of women with enormous breasts, but Coppola had great trepidations.³⁵ His mother was emphatic that women be treated with respect. L.A. was still run by moral crusaders, and was not nearly as capricious as San Francisco. Vice cops regularly busted women for going too far in strip clubs, and making movies for Meyer was somewhat perilous. Coppola did not do it for the money, though; he did it for the experience and the connections.³⁶

From Russ Meyer he made his way to another entrepreneur of the business, whose B-movies were barely a cut above Meyer's semi-pornographic pictures. Roger Corman made cheap movies with just enough flair to attract just enough audience to make just enough profit, which added up since he mass-produced so many films. After years of cheap Westerns, Corman was making more ambitious films, including some commercially successful Edgar Allan Poe–inspired classics like *The House of Usher* (1960), *The Pit and the Pendulum* (1961), and *The Raven* (1963), all starring actor Vincent Price.

Dorothy Arzner, a pioneering female director whose career spanned the late silent era through the early 1940s, was by this time a teacher at UCLA. It was she who recommended Coppola to Corman. By the time he was hired for editing work, money was becoming an issue and the $250 pay check was much needed.³⁷ "It felt as if I had got started at last," Coppola said.³⁸ Coppola impressed Corman, always operating on shoe-string budgets, by finding ingenious ways to save money during shooting. Coppola developed sub-skill sets, such as editing and set creation, and got the chance to work with Vincent Price.

There was jealousy at UCLA, where some said he "sold out" by working with cheesy B-movie directors such as Meyer and Corman, but his student films were accorded great acclaim.³⁹ He was quickly viewed as the star of the UCLA film program. He won $2,000 in a screenplay contest. From there he was hired as the sound technician on a Corman movie shot in Europe, *The Young Racers*. Coppola helped him save enough money to shoot a second film on location.⁴⁰

Coppola then engaged in some very ingenious bookkeeping. Given a blank check of $20,000 by Corman, Coppola approached an independent British film producer, saying he had financing and needed it matched.⁴¹ It was, and now he had $40,000 to direct a "feature" film, *Dementia 13*. Then Coppola did something that he would be noted for, and which would have a profound impact on the movie business. He wrote a series of letters to fellow film students at UCLA, telling them he was directing *Dementia 13* and wanted them to come to England and work on the crew.

"I had hoped that one of them, John Vicario, would be the camera operator," Coppola said. "He mentioned that he hoped his girlfriend, Ellie Neil, could come as well."⁴²

Eleanor was three years older than Coppola. A Los Angeles native and a talented artist, she had a degree in applied design from UCLA and was immediately attracted to Francis when she first set eyes on him, hammering out the *Dementia 13* screenplay in a farmhouse operating as the film's headquarters. "I was struck by his intensity and energy," she recalled.⁴³

He was also the first Italian-American she had ever met, and was struck by his emotional expressiveness and affectionate nature. As she enthused, "I found him thrilling."⁴⁴ The relationship flowered into romance, but by summer's end Ellie needed to return to UCLA, where she was teaching a class. Corman then dispatched Coppola to Yugoslavia to shoot another film for him. Eventually, he returned to Los Angeles, and married Eleanor in 1963. *Dementia 13* received weak reviews, but Coppola did not care; he had gained experience.[45]

"I very much wanted a wife, a family, and children when I was young," said Coppola.[46]

Having won acclaim at UCLA, and experience with Roger Corman, Coppola also won the prestigious Samuel Goldwyn Award. Universal Studios offered him a job, and he seemed to be on his way, but he had a fierce independent streak. He turned down Universal because he felt he would be pigeonholed in their TV division.[47] Instead, he took a job writing the screenplay "Reflections in a Golden Eye" for Seven Arts Productions. Coppola's script was eventually set aside, but it had a big effect on his career. John Huston liked it and the studio thought it excellent.[48] Now Coppola had a reputation in the business and would be sought out as a scriptwriter.

That said, it was a period of frustration for Coppola. While he found work as a writer, much of his work was changed and re-written by others. "The position of the screenwriter is an absurd, ridiculous one," he said. "He earns a great deal of money but has no say whatsoever about the film, unless he is one of the famous screenwriters. This is particularly true for young authors."[49]

Coppola studied the French New Wave, which considered directors to be *auteurs*, a holistic approach to filmmaking in which a single artist is thought to be responsible for the entire content of the production. This concept was years from coming to fruition in American cinema. Next, Coppola was hired to write *This Property is Condemned*, a Tennessee Williams play Coppola directed at Hofstra. Like *Reflections in a Golden Eye*, it was re-written and the 1966 film, starring Natalie Wood and Robert Redford, was completely unlike the Coppola version. Despite that, Coppola's reputation as a brilliant, although independent, artist was growing. He needed the money he was paid but turned down larger paydays rather than sell out his filmmaking vision, because the many variations of script and cast of *This Property is Condemned* was a hard experience for him.[50] Money would always be an issue throughout his career, and this would always be the main reason.

Screenwriting jobs followed. The pattern began to establish itself. He would write a script, it would be considered excellent, but perhaps too artsy. Most were not produced. "What's a real pity is I've seen scripts of Francis's that never got made—scripts that were some of the best stuff that he ever did," remarked Coppola's Hofstra classmate Joel Oliansky.[51] Included were adaptations of Budd Schulberg and F. Scott Fitzgerald that never came about. Not everything was classic and literary. Coppola saw a future in which popular TV programs like *Batman* would be made into motion pictures. By the mid–1960s, produced or not, Coppola was getting $1,000 a week, making him one of the better-paid screenwriters in the industry.[52] He moved his family (son Gian-Carlo was born in 1963) into Mandeville Canyon, a ritzy area perched on a hill between Bel-Air and Pacific Palisades with sweeping ocean views. He bought a Jaguar. His goal was now to direct a feature motion picture, and not a Roger Corman B-movie. He had saved $20,000 and was already thinking about financing films on his own to avoid studio control. Unfortunately, a bad investment landed him nothing and his savings were gone.[53] It was a pattern that would repeat itself, and become a large part of the Coppola legend.

Coppola was then sent on a "working vacation" to Paris with his family. Seven Arts wanted him to contribute to the screenplay for *Is Paris Burning?* It once again left Coppola quite sure that screenwriting was a soul-depleting experience.[54] He needed to direct, and to have enough power to gain a semblance of autonomy. This led to a rupture in his relationship with Seven Arts. His son Roman was born in 1966 and Coppola needed money.[55]

Coppola turned twenty-eight in 1967. He was a hefty five feet eleven, bearded, wore horn-rims with glass-brick lenses, and was terminally rumpled in what Peter Biskind wrote was his "Fidel Castro phase."[56] To complete the look he wore fatigues, boots, and a cap, often a beret.

Then Jack Warner, one of the venerable old lions who had built Hollywood, offered Coppola a chance to direct *Finian's Rainbow*. It was not an easy choice for Coppola.[57] He had family responsibilities and a good life to support. It was a big studio and a chance to direct. It was a successful Broadway musical, and it would star the great Fred Astaire. But it was a *bourgeoisie*, formulaic studio product. He had vowed not to participate in this form of capitalism disguised as art.[58]

But he accepted the offer because "my family would be impressed," he reasoned. "I could see how it worked, and how the film director was a cog in the machine, but really it was hard to hold out for any vision you might have."[59]

While filming *Finian's Rainbow* on a practically abandoned Warner Bros. lot—old man Warner was selling to corporate interests and the place was practically out of business—Coppola met a young USC film student who had been awarded an ignominious "scholarship" to study the filmmaking process ... at a studio now more resembling a ghost town. His name was George Lucas.

"George told Francis he was doing it all wrong, and Francis likes that kind of chutzpah," recalled Lucas's USC classmate, Walter Murch.[60]

Lucas did not bow down before Coppola's star like so many other admiring film students did in those days, although another film student did. "Coppola at that time was my shining star, because here was a student from UCLA, who was writing professionally, who was making a living from his writing, and just starting out as a director with Roger Corman, I think about '67 or '68," recalled Steven Spielberg.[61] Spielberg was studying at California State University, Long Beach, but he might as well have been attending the USC film school. When not hanging out with George Lucas and John Milius at USC, he was checking out student films at UCLA.

"So, in a way Francis was the first inspiration to a lot of young filmmakers, because he broke through before many others," he added.[62]

Frustrated by the experience on *Finian's Rainbow*, Coppola took his family to Denmark, but if he thought he would find meaning there it did not happen.[63] When he returned, however, his agent gave him the news that would change his career, and his life. It would, in fact, change Hollywood, the studio system, and the nature of movie-making.

Would Francis Ford Coppola write the screenplay for the movie *Patton*?

3

Protégé

Nineteen sixty-two remains one of those years that seem to stand out in the romantic imagination, along with years like 1927, when Babe Ruth hit sixty homers and Charles Lindbergh crossed the Atlantic. Whereas 1962 is not a year of extraordinary national triumph, like 1918, 1945, or 1989, for some reason it resonates. John Glenn circled the Earth in outer space. John F. Kennedy stared down Nikita Khrushchev during the Cuban Missile Crisis. It also represents a kind of final innocence before JFK's assassination, followed by Vietnam and Watergate.

But 1962 also presents itself as a coming-out party for the state of California. The Los Angeles Dodgers and San Francisco Giants, both finally ensconced in brand-new stadiums, carried on one of the all-time great pennant races, resulting in a final play-off reminiscent of Bobby Thomson's "shot heard 'round the world" eleven years earlier in New York. The USC Trojans, a major football power in the 1920s and 1930s, returned to glory by going unbeaten, and capturing their first national title in twenty-three years. Television shows were being broadcast in color, and the splashy images of Rose Bowl games, played in glorious sunshine on New Year's Day, captured the attention of cold weather denizens across the country. Otis Chandler was by now publishing the *Los Angeles Times*, quickly turning it from an ultra-partisan Republican newspaper into one of the greatest papers in the world. Music and beach movies were establishing California in the national mind as a land of beautiful women, hot night life, and surfing.

Ultimately, however, one of the reasons people over the years would ask, "Where were you in '62?" revolved not around baseball, the Trojans, or the Beach Boys. Instead, the California image of hot girls and hot rods was being developed in the mind of a young man actually living the experience in a dusty San Joaquin Valley town called Modesto.

Entering Modesto today is not unlike the experience of entering the small farming community in 1962. Life has changed some, but not all that much. A large sign welcomes visitors with the proclamation, "MODESTO: WATER WEALTH CONTENTMENT HEALTH." George Lucas would put it on the map.

"Even though it's California, it was a quiet Midwestern kind of upbringing," he said.[1]

It took several hours to drive to San Francisco or Sacramento. Fresno, farther away to the south, could be traversed using a one-lane road. Los Angeles seemed to be in another country. Modesto was not close to the 101 Highway, which hugged the coast traversing motorists between San Francisco and L.A. Interstate 5 had not yet been built, and making it to L.A., first on country roads, then crossing the Tehachapi Mountains, seemed a daunting task, reminding people of the Donner Party's perilous trek west during the Gold Rush.

Lucas had what he called a "Norman Rockwell upbringing." He was only five feet seven inches and was frequently picked on by bullies. His younger sister would chase them away. His father was a rock-ribbed Republican who grew up during the Great Depression. He ran an office supply store and thought of his kid as a slacker, calling him a "scrawny little devil."[2]

Lucas graduated from high school in 1962. He was eighteen years old, the son of a successful small businessman. He had little idea what he wanted to become. He was an indifferent student, interested mainly in cars and rock music. The temperatures in central California approached 110 degrees on June 12, 1962. Lucas was studying for his final exams at Thomas Downey High School, but his mind was on a trip to Europe his dad promised him as a graduation present. That and his car, a Fiat Bianchina also purchased by his father, which he had been too young to drive legally at first.

He souped it up and put it through the paces, drag racing it on the outskirts of town, always one step ahead of the local law. Seven of his schoolmates died doing the same thing, but he ignored the danger.[3]

Around five o'clock P.M., he tired of his books and decided to drive home. The late afternoon sun was bright and he did not see a Chevy Impala, driven by another teen, barreling down the road. The two cars crashed into each other, the Impala impacting the driver's side of the Fiat, which was totaled. Miraculously, he survived and the other driver was unhurt. But Lucas was badly injured. He spent the summer trying to recover, and for the first time began to contemplate his life and what he would do with it. In this respect, the experience was similar to Coppola and Jim Murray, both of whom spent a long period of their youth convalescing, using the time to read and philosophize.[4]

Lucas had dark hair and a small frame. Although not gifted with athletic ability, he thought the ticket out of Modesto would be a college education. He liked comic books and began to draw. He enjoyed watching TV. He fell in love with the Flash Gordon character. When Disneyland opened, his father took the family to Southern California on a vacation. He was quiet, something of a recluse, retreating to his room to listen to Elvis Presley or Chuck Berry.

He began to grease his hair with Vaseline, affecting a juvenile delinquent's attitude. Finally, he had a car. "I had my own life once I had my car," he recalled. "Along with the sense of power and freedom came the competitiveness." He began to hang out with a "bad element" of car crazies in town. His only "skill" was photography, but he lacked ambition. His older sister, Kate, called him "a total loss." He began to think of a racing career; that is, until June 12, 1962.[5]

During his immobilization, his dad gave him an 8mm movie camera. He started reading books and going to the movies. When he recovered from the accident, he enrolled in Modesto Junior College, where he was a decent student, improving upon his high school grades.

Lucas was a child of TV. "Movies had extremely little effect on me when I was growing up" he said. "Television had a much larger effect."[6] While at Modesto JC, however, he started going to San Francisco to see art movies.

A friend told him the University of Southern California offered film school classes. It was not a popular major and much easier to get accepted in than business or other majors for which USC was known.

"We had a couple theatres in Modesto," said Lucas. "They'd show *The Blob* [1958] and

Lawrence of Arabia [1962] and things like that, but no foreign films came there. Once I started driving, I'd go to San Francisco on the weekends and occasionally see a foreign film or other kinds of films. There was a group called Canyon Cinema, which did *avant-garde* underground movies. There were a few little theaters where they'd hang a sheet on a wall and project a 16mm movie onto it. I liked the more *avant-garde* films, the ones that were more abstract in nature."[7]

His acceptance to USC surprised him, but his father was unsure. Los Angeles was "sin city," a place where his son could easily get in trouble. But the young man had few other opportunities, and his father agreed to fund his education, although he predicted he would be back in Modesto "in a few years."

"I'll never be back," George shouted, "and as a matter of fact, I'm going to be a millionaire before I'm thirty!"

"My best friend was going down to USC to go to the business school and he wanted me to go with him," Lucas recalled. "But I said, 'What am I going to do down there?' He said, 'Well, if you go down there, they have a school of cinema-photography, which is like photography, and I know you like photography.' I thought this seemed close enough to art school, and I really wanted to go to art school. So we drove to Stockton and took the test—the entrance exams. And I applied. I didn't think I'd get in because even though my grades had come up considerably in college, I didn't think they were good enough.'"

In the summer of 1964 Lucas worked a local race car circuit. "I met George in the race car pits," Haskell Wexler recalled. "I got to know him through our mutual interest in automobiles. My friend, the mechanic, came up to me and said, 'Is there anything you can do to help? He's bugging the hell out of me!' George wanted to get into USC." Wexler helped with his successful application.[8]

Founded in 1880, the University of Southern California was the first private university in the West. Originally offering Methodist religious instruction, it was the wealthy home to the elites of Southern California, including the San Marino crowd. It was dominated by conservative WASP fraternity life and football; the Trojans were one of the great grid powerhouses.

John Wayne had played football at USC in the 1920s, but it was his work as an assistant to director John Ford that opened doors for him. Wayne, still known as Marion Morrison, arranged for the Trojans football team to train all the way to Annapolis, Maryland, so Ford could film them as stand-ins for the naval academy in *Salute*, an early talkie about Navy's team. That gave Morrison/Wayne, and USC, a foothold in Hollywood. A film school began and the school was the preferred destination for the children of famed movie stars and producers.

Morrison had come to USC in 1925, a heralded football star out of Glendale High School. He played for legendary coach Howard "Head Man" Jones, whose "Thundering Herd" Trojan teams would win four national championships between 1928 and 1939. Prior to his sophomore year in 1926, Morrison made a trek to Newport Beach to body surf the wild waves that have come to be known as "the Wedge." One of those breakers caught him and pounded him on the ocean floor, dislocating his shoulder. When football practice began, he was unable to block.

Although the facts are sketchy, Morrison's injury may have cost him his starting job in favor of a teammate named Brice Taylor, who was a mix of black and American Indian, and, incredibly, had use of only one hand. Taylor would go on to become the first All-American football player in Trojans history, cementing the school's reputation as a place of opportunity for African Americans.

For Marion Morrison, his injury meant football ignominy. It also meant his scholarship, directed only to the starting players, was rescinded. He quickly fell into debt with his Sigma Chi fraternity brothers. Coach Jones had already set up his players for summer employment with the nearby movie studios, a major recruiting inducement. Morrison had spent the previous summer "training" the actor Tom Mix so he would be in shape to ride horses in his next Western. One rumor has it that famed "It Girl" Clara Bow, who hosted wild parties at her Hollywood home, was "gangbanged" by the entire Trojans football team, including Morrison. Apparently, the story was complete fiction, made up by one of Bow's disgruntled ex-employees.[9]

Morrison knew there was work at nearby Fox Studios. He left school and went to work, a sometime extra and worker on John Ford movies. Ford, a former football player, knew of his USC football background and through that connection a friendship began. Then one day Ford tasked Morrison with the role that would change his life and career. It was not an acting part.

Ford wanted to make *Salute*, a tribute to the Naval Academy football team. He planned to film it on location at Annapolis, Maryland. In 1928, Southern Cal won the first of their eleven national championships. They were the toast of Hollywood and much of America. Ford wanted to use USC players in the football scenes, and publicize the film so that everybody knew they were actually watching the national champions onscreen. He wanted to bring a large group of players to Annapolis for the summer, but needed them available before school was set to let out. He went to Morrison and asked him to arrange all of this with the school.

It was a major challenge for Morrison, who had lost his scholarship, was a drop-out, and by no means a prominent university alumnus. But Morrison's fraternity brother was Rufus von Kleinsmid's son. He arranged for Morrison to meet his father, the president of the university. Morrison made a strong case to let the players go, arguing that it would be great publicity and fanfare for the school and the football program, while extolling the educational virtues of a summer near Washington, D.C., a kind of "exchange student" program popular today. Dr. von Kleinsmid agreed. This was a huge feather in Morrison's cap. Ford now loved him and owed him.

The players took a train to Maryland and Morrison befriended another USC player, Ward Bond. Ford saw something in their camaraderie; future scenes, often of barroom fights with the two making up over a shot of whiskey, which certainly played out in many films over the decades. *Salute* was a big hit upon its release in 1929, one of the first "talkies." Morrison had a small role onscreen but, of course, a huge one offscreen. When they returned to Los Angeles, Ford recommended Morrison to director Raoul Walsh to star in his epic *The Big Trail* (1930). His name was changed to John Wayne. His booming voice was perfect for the new medium, and the film launched him towards stardom.

At the time of Lucas's arrival, the USC Division of Cinema at the School of Performing Arts was thirty-five years old. The film school, the first of its kind anywhere in the world, had started under President von Kleinsmid in 1929. He was influenced in large measure by Duke Wayne.

Dr. von Kleinsmid, seeing the obvious connection between USC and the film industry, agreed to begin a study of film as part of the university curriculum. Over the next three decades, however, it did not produce a lot of directors or screenwriters. Most USC students who made it in the movies were like Wayne and Bond—athletes cast as actors, such as Olympic swimming champion Johnny Weissmuller, made famous as Tarzan, or a baseball player named John Berardino, who had a long-standing role on *General Hospital*. Football stars like Nate Barrager, Russ Saunders, and Aaron Rosenberg became successful movie and TV producers, but it was their sports connections—more than any affiliation with the USC film school—that opened doors.

USC was always and continued to be the preferred school where famed Hollywood heavyweights sent their children. "USC was the most popular school, where everybody wanted to go," recalled Woody Strode, a groundbreaking African American athlete at crosstown rival UCLA, where he was a football teammate of Jackie Robinson's.[10]

Strode would clash on occasion with Duke Wayne, ostensibly when their horses would run into each other, causing the Duke to take a fall, but just as likely the result of the Trojan-Bruin football rivalry. But Strode would be part of a film that inadvertently gave impetus to both the USC and UCLA film schools of the 1960s.

Even though the director, producer, screenwriter, or above-the-line talent were not Bruins or Trojans, all the gladiators in famed director Stanley Kubrick's classic *Spartacus* (1960) were USC and UCLA football players. The six-foot-seven-inch Strode played the key role of Draba, a black gladiator who sacrifices his life so that Spartacus (Kirk Douglas) can live and eventually lead the slave rebellion against Rome.

USC would eventually place more emphasis on production and photography than they did when George Lucas arrived. It was a wealthier school, more business-friendly, and this would produce more producers and agents who helped more technical people make their way in the business.

UCLA was "artsier," a little more *risqué* when it came to female nudity, and meshed the film school with the drama school so directors and actors would get to know each other, then connect later as professionals. USC would create a producer's division. This meant many creative types would know agents and producers who understood the business end of filmmaking, with excellent results in the real world.

Lucas's father liked the idea of his son attending a prestigious college like USC, but did not like the fact that he would be in Hollywood, which the elder Lucas equated to Babylon. He would shave George's hair in boot-camp style. Lucas's move to Los Angeles was as much escape from his dad as it was an opportunity. Many felt his eventual relationship with Francis Ford Coppola was his seeking a parental relationship.

Oddly, the father instilled an anti-authoritarian instinct into George, who was repressed and angry, yet this played out in his movies as their greatest theme. But many values like hard work took root, and he identified money with power. After he was accepted, Lucas lived in a house on Portola Drive, a sublet he rented with Randal Kleiser. "George spent most of his time upstairs in his part of the house, at his drawing board," recalled Kleiser.

His desire was to "chase girls and hang out." Lucas was an innocent, very much a product of his Modesto upbringing, but he had already developed artistic concepts that he would explore at film school.

"I discovered the school of cinema was really about making movies," he recalled. "I thought this was insane. I didn't know you could go to college to learn how to make movies. But once I got there, I fell in love with it and just decided this was it for me. It combined my interest in social issues with my interest in art and drawing and photography, and it was a whole new medium that I didn't know anything about. So I really fell into it by accident."[11]

But prior to George Lucas's arrival at USC, aside from Francis Ford Coppola at UCLA, neither of the school's film programs were producing any large number of identifiable Hollywood players. It was still all about connections. USC students, whether in the film program or some other major, were more likely to break into the business because they were the son of somebody famous, or knew the right people. It was an extremely incestuous business, not the sprawling industry it is today. A typical example was Alan Ladd, Jr., the son of a famous actor. Baseball player Bill "Spaceman" Lee recalled Ladd driving around in an expensive sports car, which he used to "snake my girlfriend away from me."[12]

Lloyd Robinson was another student on campus who had the right pedigree. His grandfather had once been the vice-president of Universal Studios. Robinson graduated from USC and its law school before embarking on a long career as a talent agent.

There was an average student at USC in the 1960s who later achieved great success in Hollywood. Ron Schwary would go on to win Academy Awards for *Ordinary People* (1980) and *Tootsie* (1982). However, it again was football and connections that opened the door for him. He held one of the most important positions at USC, student manager of John McKay's football powerhouse, which won two national championships in the decade. So important was he to McKay that the legendary coach gave him a scholarship. In that role, he was on hand one extraordinary weekend in 1966, tasked with taking care of the needs of the great alumnus John Wayne during a football weekend at the University of Texas. They became friends, Wayne was impressed, and eventually the Duke helped pave the way for Schwary in show business.

USC was a school of great wealth and privilege, but always there were "scholarship boys," athletes or deserving lower income students, a fair number of them African American or from other countries.

This created a certain divide. Many international students would study at the Von Kleinsmid Center, while the fraternity and sorority members "studied," or socialized, at Doheny Library. USC was heavily centered on Greek life. Frat boys were generally handsome S*Cions* of USC alumni. Sorority girls were beautiful blonde Newport Beach and San Marino "daddy's girls." Still, the shared experience, particularly football, bonded all who went to the school.

"I didn't have a pot to piss in," recalled All-American football star Mike Battle. "But I'd go on ski trips with [fellow All-American] Tim Rossovich with all these rich kids to Tahoe and we'd all get along."

"You could be sitting in a class room with the son of a famous producer, but we were all the same at USC," recalled another All-American grid star, Adrian Young.[13]

Around the world, young hopefuls aspired to Hollywood success as actors, but few saw directing, writing, or producing as a future. Directors were culled from Broadway, England, or the German film industry. A director might be an actor who had made enough films to gain the experience to direct, or some longtime assistant deemed capable. Screenwriters were already famed as playwrights in New York or the London stage, or were established novelists such as F. Scott Fitzgerald. Many found work in Hollywood soulless and produced less-than-stellar work.

The Blacklist of the 1950s had robbed the industry of some of its best talent, producing a series of dreary films. In addition, talent agents were becoming powerful, just as the old studio system—wealthy moguls who ruled major studios with an iron fist—was beginning to break down in favor of young stars with new visions.

All of this was just beginning to create opportunities for those lucky enough and talented enough to be in just the right place at just the right time. George Lucas was in the right place at USC at just the right time, although he did not realize it at first.

Lucas was twenty years old when he arrived in Los Angeles in the fall of 1964. It was hot, smoggy, and crowded. Big business was everywhere, and plans were in the works to create a skyline of office towers matching New York. The city had room to expand, however; business centers were growing in Beverly Hills, the Westside, and in Newport Beach.

Los Angeles had been built on oil wealth. Oil was found under the ground and offshore mostly in Southern California, not in Northern California. This profoundly shaped the political differences between the regions. Environmental concerns were far more prevalent in the Bay Area. Weapons of war, many of mass destruction, as well as tools of the space race, were being built in factories west of the San Diego Freeway stretching twenty-plus miles.

The Dodgers were the reigning World Series champions and the place fancied itself the "sports capital of the world," which did not interest Lucas one bit. That fall Coach McKay's Trojans won one of their greatest victories, a come-from-behind 20–17 triumph over rival Notre Dame at the L.A. Coliseum. It was truly a golden era at USC. The football team was in the early stages of a two-decade run between 1962 and 1981 that saw them capture five national titles, five Heisman Trophies, and likely achieve the greatest dominance over a sustained time in collegiate football annals.

The baseball team had won the national championship in 1963. Lucas entered USC the same year as another young fellow from the San Joaquin Valley, Tom Seaver, who would go on to a Hall of Fame career with the New York Mets. Another young athlete at USC during those years was Tom Selleck, who played baseball and volleyball before a stellar career in Hollywood. A few years later, an African American junior college transfer from San Francisco would arrive on campus. His name was O. J. Simpson.

Between the Hollywood standouts who would emerge from USC during this era, and the sports stars who brought NCAA titles and glory to Troy, USC probably enjoyed its Camelot era.

George Lucas did not care about sports glory or even Hollywood. "My choice in the end was to go off to San Francisco State and be an anthropology major," he said. "I *really* wanted to go to the art center and become an illustrator. I ended up going to USC because I thought I was going to a photography school, but it ended up being a movie school. I had no idea you could learn how to make movies in school, but I thought that would be fun, and I got there and fell in love with it."[14]

He certainly did not identify with the region's politics, which he rejected as too closely paralleling his father's. That fall, the Democrats swept to overwhelming victories, but Southern California—particularly Orange County—was dominated by the John Birch Society and virulent anti-Communism. Lucas certainly rejected USC's politics, which was dominated by Young Republicans. USC was the most Republican campus in the nation and had been since John Wayne's undergraduate days. In fact, it was not just Republican, it was downright right-wing.

A number of USC graduates during these years, including Dwight Chapin, Ron Ziegler, Donald Segretti, and Gordon Strachan, among others, would go to work for Richard Nixon and become embroiled in the Watergate scandal. H. R. Haldemann had attended USC before graduating from UCLA. He hired several of these USC Republicans when he ran the J. Walter Thompson advertising agency in Los Angeles, the perch from which he used to launch Nixon's post–vice-presidential political career.

The movie industry was still being run by the studios. Independent filmmakers like Orson Welles had been practically driven out of the business. The Vietnam War was only just beginning, and was enthusiastically supported by the American public. It had certainly not shaped politics in Hollywood. There was little evidence of the counter-culture in Tinseltown or anyplace else outside of San Francisco's North Beach, Berkeley's University of California campus, or New York's Greenwich Village.

But there were small indications of change in the movie industry. The Blacklist had been a reaction to Soviet infiltration of Hollywood, as well as other institutions, in the 1930s, 1940s, and 1950s. U.S. Senator Joseph McCarthy (R.-Wisconsin) had led the charge in uprooting the conspiracy, but his alcoholism and headstrong tactics were carried too far. He was disgraced, and Hollywood began what would be a long campaign to discredit the Blacklist. One of the first chinks in the armor occurred with the production of *Spartacus*. Stanley Kubrick's classic starring Kirk Douglas and Laurence Olivier was written by a blacklisted Communist, Dalton Trumbo. It was the first time a member of the Hollywood Ten was given screen credit; many wrote under aliases until then. Trumbo's script was masterful in its subtlety and subversion, describing an all-conquering Roman Empire meant to remind people of modern America. One controversial scene reflected Olivier inquiring whether a servant, played by Tony Curtis, preferred snails or oysters, meant to reflect a preference for straight or homosexual sex, with either choice given equal moral weight.

Rod Serling's TV program, *The Twilight Zone*, explored deep questions of national morality and purpose, such as race relations, nuclear weapons, and femininity. In 1962, Darryl Zanuck produced *The Longest Day*, an unflinchingly patriotic portrayal of American heroism on D-Day, starring John Wayne. It would be the last of its kind. John Frankenheimer's *The Manchurian Candidate* (1962) was an explosive psychological thriller starring Frank Sinatra that explored the depths of moral depravity amid the Cold War. Serling's *Seven Days in May* (1964) openly flaunted the possibility, based on actual events of 1934, that right-wing militarists could take over the U.S. government. Stanley Kubrick's *Dr. Strangelove or: How I Learned to Stop Worrying and Love the Bomb* (1964) made fun of military officers and fear of the Soviet nuclear threat. Sidney Lumet's *Fail-Safe*, also released in 1964, warned the world just how easily we could blow *ourselves* up. By 1966, Hollywood was changing and a liberal like Francis Ford Coppola would be offered the opportunity to write the screenplay about the ultimate symbol of American military might, General George S. Patton.

When George Lucas entered USC, the studios were producing a steady stream of old-style musicals and family fare like *Mary Poppins* (1964) and *The Sound of Music* (1965), or epics like *Cleopatra* (1962) and *The Bible* (1966). Younger audiences were turned off and the studios, already reeling from the effect of television, were losing money. In 1966, Paramount was practically bankrupt. Its corporate owner, Gulf+Western, hired a young producer named Robert Evans to take over.

George Lucas eventually chose to live near the beach instead of the gritty downtown neighborhood in which USC was located. South-central Los Angeles was dirty and crime-ridden. A year later it would explode in flames when riots broke out in Watts. Lucas lived with a couple of friends in Malibu. He painted pictures of sad-eyed surfer girls in order to pay the rent. His dad gave him $200 a month for expenses, and expected that he make good grades. He looked for work in Hollywood. He also took English, astronomy, and history.

"I had to take my film writing classes, but I suffered though them," Lucas recalled. "I had to go into the drama department and do drama and stage work, but I hated getting up and acting. I really wanted to be in a real situation with a camera on my shoulder following the action."[15]

"USC was a good school, but it needed people," said fellow film student Robert Dalva. "So we all got in. The way USC was organized at the time was that if you had the drive to make a film, then you got to make a film. Of the eighty or so people who took the classes and made the department function, there were eight or ten of us who ended up making movies while we were there. It was an incredible group."[16]

"We were a loose confederation of radicals and hippies," Lucas said.[17]

USC's film school was in an old stable. Fellow Trojan film students of Lucas's era included Hal Barwood, Caleb Deschanel, Willard Huyck, Howard Kazanjian, Randal Kleiser, Christopher Lewis, Charles Lippincott, Basil Poledouris, Walter Murch, and John Milius. All would go on to success, some to great acclaim, as directors, writers, producers, cinematographers, or editors. Actor Henry Winkler later attended USC during the era. The school itself became part of movie lore when iconic scenes of Dustin Hoffman and Katharine Ross were filmed on campus for *The Graduate* (1967).

"Even though I was going to go into completely abstract filmmaking, I got involved in all kinds of filmmaking," Lucas said. "And the great thing about being in that film school was that there were filmmakers that were interested in [Jean-Luc] Goddard, there were filmmakers that were interested in John Ford, and there were filmmakers that were interested in commercials and surfing movies. And we all got along together."

Slavko Vorkapich, a renowned Serbian montagist, had been the dean of the USC film school from 1949–51. His colleague, Sergei Eisenstein, pioneered film editing in the 1920s, juxtaposing related images. Lucas's group studied these filmmakers. USC was one of the first American institutions that broadened their expanses to European art conceptions.

"Vorkapich's influence was everywhere at the school," said Lucas. "We focused a lot on filmic expression, filmic grammar. I was not into story telling. I was into trying to create emotions through pure cinematic techniques. All the films I made at that time center on conveying emotions through a cinematic experience, not necessarily through the narrative. Throughout my career, I've remained a cinema enthusiast; even though I went on to make films with a more conventional narrative, I've always tried to convey emotions through essentially cinematic experiences."[18]

"It wasn't considered a serious major," recalled Willard Huyck. "You'd be walking by the film school, they'd grab you and say, 'You want to be a filmmaker?' It was very easy to get into."[19]

"We had all gone to film school because we were interested in film, but it was also this bubble of refuge from being drafted," said Walter Murch.[20]

"When I went to film school, the other students said, 'You really can't make movies here,'" recalled Lucas. " 'They don't give you enough film, they don't let you keep the camera for very long....'

"Well, I made eight films at USC.... It was difficult, and there were lots of barriers, but it wasn't impossible....

"The department never taught us that much, other than the basics. They opened the door, but we had to go inside and find out for ourselves.... Whenever I broke the rules, I made a good film, so there wasn't much faculty could do about it."

"The first day that we all got together, the head of the camera department surveyed us with a baleful eye, and said, 'My advice to you, is quit now,'" said Walter Murch. "Get out fast. Don't continue with this because you all have expectations that are not going to be fulfilled."

"At USC, we were a rare generation because we were open-minded," Lucas recalled. "We had guys there who did nothing but Republic serials and comic books. I was being exposed to a whole lot of movies you don't see every day. I don't know how else I could have learned so much."

One of his first assignments came from instructor Herb Kossower, who tasked his animation class with creating a one-minute film. Lucas used thirty-two feet of film to create *Look at Life*, which consisted of shots from *Life* magazine, including an equal number of violent and peaceful photos. It was brilliantly edited and won some awards. Some years later the Alan J. Pakula film *The Parallax View* (1974), starring Warren Beatty, featured a similar montage of photos used to determine the psychological reliability of potential assassins.

"I realized that I'd found myself," Lucas recalled. "I took the bit and ran with it. I was introduced to film editing ... and I think ultimately that film editing was where my real talent was."[21]

The USC credo was experimental and hands-on, reflecting the culture of the school in a way; conservative, business-oriented, preparing students for real life rather than academic theory. Lucas was learning skills the movie industry could use and would hire him for. But he was not merely an expert editor; he was becoming an artist who used his ability to express emotions on screen. He quickly discovered that his vision was a popular one that resonated among others. He was not Fellini-esque (as in Federico Fellini), creating abstract images confusing people.

Like UCLA, USC's cinema school was separated from the main campus, although USC was much smaller than UCLA, especially in the mid–1960s. It was an exclusive little private college despite its world-wide reputation and the TV exposure its football team garnered. It was the size of a high school, with Greco-Roman architecture surrounded by trees and lawns. The baseball and practice football fields were located almost in the middle of the campus. The Los Angeles Memorial Coliseum and Sports Arena were located directly across the street, so close they practically were part of the campus, but officially were operated by the city of L.A. These structures and parking lots were as big as the actual USC campus at that time.

Huge additions such as Howard Jones Field, Dedeaux Field, the Galen Center, Heritage Hall, the McKay Center, the modern School of Cinematic Arts, parking garages, and other buildings did not start to expand—much of it replacing old residential homes—until the 1970s. The 1984 Olympic Games also created major additions. The building continues to this day, much of it funded by the likes of George Lucas himself.

But on a campus filled with sports stars and right-wingers, the film geeks were "looked at as a weird group," recalled film student Howard Kazanjian. "It was mostly guys at the time. Very few women."[22]

All the talent at USC initially intimidated Lucas. Film students came from all over the world to study there, to be within the glow of Hollywood. He came from a one-movie-theatre cow town. When great *auteurs* like Jean-Luc Goddard, Federico Fellini, and Orson Welles came up in discussion, he was unsure what to say about them. His great interest had not been films, *per se*, but photography and comic-book-inspired serials. USC showed Akira Kurosawa movies, which Lucas studied as well as disparate filmmakers such as John Ford, William Wyler, and Fellini. Lecturer Arthur Knight interviewed celebrities for his "Thursday Night at the Movies." These included Ford, George Cukor, Alfred Hitchcock, David Lean, Sydney Pollack, King Vidor, and Robert Wise. Most of his fellow students felt Lucas would make documentaries.

USC's legendary beautiful blonde coeds were attracted to handsome jocks or wealthy S*Cions* of industry studying business. The film students got no love from them. Somewhat separated from campus life, the film students developed cliques. One group began calling themselves the "dirty dozen," from the 1967 film about a group of convicts who take on a dangerous mission against the Nazis; a movie that broke from traditional type in its depictions of valor and race.

Lucas joined a group that would grow beyond his college years, and would include Randal Kleiser (future director), John Milius (future writer-director), Walter Murch (future editor), Howard Kazanjian (future producer), Chuck Braverman (future producer), Robert Zemeckis (future writer-director), Ronald Schwary (future producer), and Willard Huyck (future writer-director). This intellectual clique began to attract attention beyond USC's borders. Francis Ford Coppola befriended some of them, including Lucas. A young film student from Cal State, Long Beach, who had been turned down by USC, practically "attended" the school, he was there so much hanging out with this group. His name was Steven Spielberg. Other young Hollywood hopefuls started to spend time with them, collaborating on ideas. These included Brian De Palma and Martin Scorsese.

Eventually, Lucas began to stand out among the "dirty dozen." His greatest asset was not merely talent, but a capacity for good old-fashioned hard work, a trait he inherited from his businessman father (who was surprisingly pleased to see his once-listless son find his calling). Young George had what President Richard Nixon called "an iron butt," which was the ability to sit for hours without break while working on his editing machine. It was time-consuming and tedious, but it absorbed him. While others were daydreaming of wide-angled shots and high-blown concepts, he stuck to the task at hand, consuming candy bars and cookies, breathing the fumes of the splicing glue.

"I'm gonna shoot my film in color," he told Howard Kazanjian. "I'm not going to be limited to the footage I'm given or limited to the length of my completed film."

Lucas met Chris Lewis, the son of actress Loretta Young, a lifelong friend of John

Wayne. "It was exciting for us to meet a real star, and Loretta couldn't have been friendlier," said Kleiser. "Chris, George, and I formed a filmmaking partnership called Sunrise Productions, with offices on Sunset Boulevard."

They made one movie called *Five, Four, Three*, a spoof on beach movies. Then Lucas made *Freiheit* ("freedom"), which was about East German Communism. The theme was "Freedom is definitely worth dying for." *Freiheit* dealt with a student's attempt to escape from Communist East Germany to the free West Germany. The student is shot and killed. The soldier who kills him stands over his body.

"Without freedom, we're dead," he says, a statement twisted with irony. It is ironic on several other levels. "*Arbeit macht frei*" ("work makes you free") was the sign hanging over the Nazi death camps.

Lucas disagreed with American policy in Vietnam, which by 1966 was escalating and starting to look like a quagmire, yet he chose escape from Communism—the driving force of the South Vietnamese people—as the subject of *Freiheit*.

In 1965, *Look at Life* animation tutor Herb Kosower gave him a minute's worth of 16mm black-and-white film images from *Life* magazine with tranquil guitar music playing, while a young victim of war peers through a gap in a broken fence followed by jarring images of survival. This formed the core of *Freiheit*. Then came *Herbie*, inspired by jazz impresario Herbie Hancock.

Mathew Robbins arrived at USC in 1965. "George had already started his meteoric rise as superstar film student," he said. "I was just amazed by his work; we all were. He could take almost anything and make a movie out of it. And he was very resourceful. He always would find a way to get what he needed in terms of equipment and bodies to put together a crew. He was highly regarded by all the students and a source of puzzlement to much of the faculty."[23]

"I thought I was going to be a documentary filmmaker," Lucas reiterated. "I came at it from a visual side. The first thing I did was in animation. I started out as a cameraman, and then became fascinated by editing. *Cinéma vérité* was just coming in at that point, and the school was very influenced by the French unit of the Canadian Film Board, so we studied that a lot."

He did a student film on race car driver Peter Brock called *1:42.08*. "It's a visual tone poem," Lucas said of the color film.[24]

The USC campus was practically devoid of any real protest against the Vietnam War. The Free Speech Movement, begun at the University of California, Berkeley, in 1964, had morphed into full-blown anti-war protest by 1966. Protest was gaining momentum at Columbia University in New York, with such traditional campuses as the University of Wisconsin and the University of Michigan soon following suit; beyond that most of the campuses would erupt in one form or another.

UCLA remained relatively quiet, not becoming particularly radical until late in the war. John Wayne, a former USC football player, spoke at his alma mater in 1965. An outspoken supporter of the Vietnam War, his observation of a Marine heckled by anti-war activists on the campus spurred his production of *The Green Berets* (1968). When introduced by comedian Bob Hope during a fundraiser, he was met by signs and hecklers, but he forcefully advocated his position and, according to those who were there, turned the tide of sentiment in his favor. An anti-war protester peripatetically known as "Brother Lennie" tried to rally the campus but was told to "get yer ass outta here" by fire-breathing Trojans assistant football coach Marv Goux. The *Los Angeles Times* featured letters and op/eds for a week, both favorable and critical of Goux, but coach John McKay and university president John Hubbard backed Goux without recourse.[25]

The politics of USC was a conundrum of sorts. This was a college coming to be known as *USCinema* and "Hollywood's school." It would come to dominate the TV and film industry, creatively and from a business perspective, above any other. Hollywood, already becoming increasing liberal in the wake of the Blacklist, would turn more and more to the left over succeeding decades. While USC today is not nearly the hard right atmosphere it was in Lucas's day, it remains one of the most traditional colleges in America. The conundrum is that the greatest influx of talent and artistic conception ever in Hollywood, responsible for its best decades critically and financially, came from a Republican enclave!

"What we had in common is we grew up in the '60s, protesting the Vietnam War," said Lucas. "We were gonna take over the world. The other thing that we were passionate about was movies. We never thought we were going to make money at it, or that it was a good way to become rich and famous. It was like an addiction. We were always scrambling to get our next fix, to get a little film in the camera and shoot something." (Lucas's remark that he never believed he would "make money" contradicts his statement to his dad when he left for L.A. that he would be a millionaire by age thirty.)[26]

While Lucas was a liberal, he was a relatively moderate one. His work ethic showed in his passion toward the craft of editing. Most of the "dirty dozen" opposed the war, but not all. The USC group reflected the school to one extent or another, and was far more conservative than the free-wheeling students at the UCLA film school. One USC student of Lucas's vintage, John Milius, was not merely conservative or even right-wing; he bordered on militaristic to the point of bloodthirstiness, and his politics showed in much of his work. Milius and Lucas, as well as others who opposed the war, agreed to disagree and remained more than amicable; they were close friends whose associations would shape the industry.

Lucas's graduation in 1966 came at a bad time, in that the war was escalating and he faced the draft. He decided, again ironically, to join the U.S. Air Force. He was told of a photography unit within the air force and hoped to become an officer, which, strangely enough, would keep him out of combat. However, he had gotten so many speeding tickets tooling around Modesto that the air force rejected his application. He thought about deserting to Canada, but was too far-sighted to do something with such drastic repercussions.

Faced with no choice, he went for his army induction, only to be rejected as diabetic, possibly brought about by his consuming of so many candy bars while editing at film school. His older sister, Kate, was married to a doctor, who confirmed he was diabetic, albeit mildly so. He could control it through diet and medication.

Armed with a legitimate résumé of film school work, he looked for jobs in the industry, leading to veteran film editor Verna Fields. Lucas worked, ironically, on documentaries Fields made for the United States Information Agency, explaining the presence of the U.S. in Southeast Asia. He also taught a course for U.S. Navy cameramen at USC.

"These veteran Navy cameramen had been taught to shoot film by the book," Lucas said. "The Navy wanted them to loosen up a bit, so they decided to send them back to school. This class obviously had lots of film and a lot of cameras because it was sponsored by the Navy. I had to train the Navy guys to shoot using available light, to think about composition, and to try to get them to make a movie in a different way."[27]

He became employed as a cameraman for Saul Bass, one of several interesting jobs he had right out of school. In 1967, Lucas returned to USC as a teaching assistant to Gene Pedersen, who ran the cinematography program. During this time, Lucas met Marcia Griffin, who worked in the industry. Her father was in the military so she moved around a lot. She had lived for a time in Modesto, but had mostly grown up in North Hollywood. Painfully shy, Lucas did not know how to speak to her. He was so reticent that Marcia could not even get him to tell her he was from Modesto. Even when he asked her out, to the screening of a friend's film, he hardly spoke. "It wasn't a real date," she recalled. They attended many movies together, which became "dates," and eventually were married.[28]

Lucas decided to concentrate on his first would-be feature, *THX 1138:4EB (Electronic Labyrinth)*. Now enrolled in the master's program at USC, he used his position and the film school's resources, to create and edit the film. It was a de-humanizing look at a robotic science fiction future, stark and antiseptic in its context.

Steven Spielberg went to UCLA's Royce Hall in 1967 to watch a series of USC and UCLA student films, including the film school version of Lucas's elaborately titled film. Spielberg was transfixed. Lucas used navy equipment to shoot the original student version of *THX 1138:4EB*.

The movie "absolutely stopped the festival," said Spielberg. "I thought some Hollywood genius had slipped something in and that it should be disqualified for its sheer professionalism." He was "jealous to the very marrow of my bones," he said. "I was eighteen [actually twenty] years old and had directed fifteen short films by that time, and this little movie was better than all of my little movies combined. No longer were John Ford, Walt Disney, Frank Capra, Federico Fellini, David Lean, Alfred Hitchcock, or Michael Curtiz my role models. Rather, it was someone nearer my own age, someone I could actually get to know, compete with, draw inspiration from."[29]

Spielberg was an overachiever at ill-equipped Cal State, Long Beach. "I met George that day, and I realized that there *was* an entire generation coming out of NYU, USC, and UCLA, and I was kind of an orphan abandoned in Long Beach at a college that didn't really have a film program. So I even redoubled my efforts [at] that moment to attend those two [California] universities. And every time I went in with my application for transfer, they kept saying, 'No, your grades aren't high enough.' I remember one teacher at USC said, 'You're probably going to Vietnam anyway....'

"I had never seen a film created by a peer that was not of this earth—*THX* created a world that did not exist before George designed it," he added. Lucas reminded him "of Walt Disney's version of a mad scientist."[30]

George, Sr., and his wife, Dorothy, drove down from Modesto for a screening, sitting in a theatre with long-haired college kids. "Every time one of George's films would come on, the kids would whisper, 'Watch this one, it's George's film,'" George, Sr., recalled. "We went out to the car and all over campus all they were talking about was Lucas's films! Now I had been against this thing of his going to the cinema school from day one, but we guessed he had finally found his niche. As we drove home, I said to Dorothy, 'I think we put our money on the right horse.'"[31]

His older sister, Kate, who once thought George to be "a total loss," was overwhelmed.

"He's a great example for parents not to lose their cool," she said. "I'm just amazed that a person that was so un-together could turn out to be so together."[32]

THX:1138, *Freiheit*, and *Marcello, I'm So Bored* made the student film festival tour and also played at L.A.'s Fairfax Theatre in a retrospective of USC student films.

"I didn't know anything about movies before I started film school," said Lucas, "but as soon as I made my first film, I thought, 'Hey, I'm good at this. I know how to do this.' From then on I've never questioned it. Everything I've done since then I've felt confident about—even when I didn't pull it off!"[33]

In 1967 he was given a major break when he was selected along with some other USC and UCLA student filmmakers for a Columbia Pictures scholarship, co-sponsored by producer Carl Foreman. The students were tasked with making a promotional short for the upcoming film *MacKenna's Gold*, to be shot in Utah and Arizona. He and his friend Walter Murch also had applied for a Warner Bros. scholarship, which would amount to six months studying and working in a studio atmosphere. The two agreed that whoever made the first real breakthrough would help the other do the same.

Lucas's independent streak shone through in the way he handled his "promotional" film for *MacKenna's Gold*. The other student filmmakers all diligently showed the film being shot; behind-the-scenes footage, cast and crew busy handling their duties, the producer on the job. Lucas, however, was very unimpressed by the inefficiency, the amount of time and money wasted. He went out into the desert and shot a "visual poem" intended as an ode of love to his girlfriend Marcia, waiting for him in Los Angeles.

Back in L.A., *THX* won top prize for drama in the National Student Film Festival. His desert poem, titled *6.18.67*, won for experimental film. USC classmate John Milius won for best animated film, *Marcello, I'm So Bored* (edited by Lucas).

"There were walls up in Hollywood then, and the place was very cliquish," said Milius. "Movie deals were made at parties.... There were parties for people on the A list and for the less important ones on the B list."[34]

Milius and Lucas were on neither list ... yet. "The credo of film school that we had drilled into us every day," recalled Lucas, was that "nobody would ever get a job in the industry. You'll graduate from film school and become a ticket-taker at Disneyland, or get a job with some industrial outfit in Kansas. But nobody had ever gotten a job in Hollywood making theatrical films."

Prior to the scholarship, Lucas shared an iconoclastic vision of Hollywood with his classmates, which was also shared by Coppola, who may have been working in the "system," but was increasingly disenchanted with its politics.

"We hadn't been around such opulence, zillions of dollars being spent every five minutes on this huge, unwieldy thing," recalled Lucas of the *MacKenna's Gold* set. "It was mind-boggling to us because we had been making films for $300, and seeing this incredible set—that was the worst of Hollywood." Lucas usually wandered off the shoot to film desert images. Upon his return to Los Angeles he learned that USC had short-listed Walter Murch and him as potential scholarship recipients of the Samuel Warner Memorial Scholarship.

"It was a big deal," said Lucas. "One student who'd gone to the story department wrote a screenplay and sold it." Despite star status at USC and the scholarship to film *MacKenna's Gold*, film students were not yet seen as viable directors. The industry was still relatively closed.

"I hit every two-bit movie company on Ventura Boulevard, a thousand of them, going from door to door," said Lucas. "I said I was looking for a job and I'd do anything. No luck."

But one film student *had* made it: Francis Ford Coppola. Coppola made a film called *You're a Big Boy Now*, which was distributed by Warner Bros. in 1966. This was a notch above his screenplay-for-hire or script-doctor work. Warners was as big a studio as there was and they were distributing this young director's film in theatres. Lucas's classmates paid attention to Coppola's progress.

Just as Coppola was the star at UCLA and had used his position to break into the movie industry, Lucas hoped to do the same thing. His experience on the *MacKenna's Gold* set convinced Lucas he could do it better. His main goal by then was to figure out how to develop independence, which is another way of saying he needed to figure out how to get his movies financed. Orson Welles was practically ruined when he tried to buck the system. There were few independents in those days. The talented actor John Cassavetes was making in-roads, and some, like Clint Eastwood, were working with the Italians, or the French, but this was a long shot.

Lucas decided to go along to get along, one time at least, when he accepted the Warners scholarship. His arrival, an act of cosmic Hollywood irony, came the day Jack Warner, the personification of the studio system, retired and left his family company. Lucas described the lot as a "ghost town." Lucas figured he would study how Bugs Bunny was made, only to discover the building was empty. He then wandered to a back lot, and saw his friend Howard Kazanjian working as a second assistant. The film was the only one being shot at the time on the Warners lot. It was *Finian's Rainbow*, directed by Francis Ford Coppola. Lucas and Coppola had briefly made their acquaintance earlier. Lucas would become his protégé.

"I was in admiration of him because he was the first film student to break into the film industry," said Lucas. "At that point, film students just didn't make it into the film industry. You had to be related to somebody or know somebody; the idea that you could get there with an education and knowledge and skill and talent was unheard of. Francis was the first one to break through, so all of us students were very much in awe of him. When I first saw him on the set, we rekindled our acquaintance."[35]

At that point Lucas was souring on Hollywood, thinking of returning to San Francisco to do commercials and educational films after getting his master's degree at USC. Coppola was struggling with *Finian's Rainbow*; it didn't look like much fun. But Lucas in essence had to be there, so he watched and learned. Coppola agreed to help Lucas make *THX:1138* into a commercial movie. They were opposites who attracted, and Coppola thought of him as a "brother."

"I was about twenty-eight, and very young to direct a Hollywood film," said Coppola. "I was feeling a little engulfed by the studio personnel and what have you. One day I noticed this skinny kid wearing a college sweater. Someone told me he was a student observer from USC. I went over to him and said, 'See anything interesting?' He shook his head and waved his hand, palm down. 'Nope. Not yet.'"[36]

Also on that set, along with Howard Kazanajian, was Carroll Ballard from UCLA. Lucas was twenty-three when he met Coppola. He wore the same outfit every day: jeans, white T-shirt, button-down collar, tails out. Later, Lucas took Spielberg to see Coppola during his Warners internship.

"Because of his personality he actually succeeded in getting his hand on the doorknob and flinging open the door," Murch said of Coppola, "and suddenly there was a crack of light, and you could see that one of us, a film student without any connections to the film business, had put one foot in front of another and actually made the transition from being a film student to being somebody who made a feature film sponsored by one of the studios."[37]

"Francis had this closet in the producer's building," said John Milius. "He was stealing film stock and equipment and putting them in there. He said, 'Someday when they finally throw me out of here, we'll have enough and we can make another film.'"[38]

4

"The End"

On August 2, 1964, the destroyer USS *Maddox*, while performing signals intelligence operations patrol as part of DESOTO operations, engaged three North Vietnamese Navy torpedo boats of the 135th Torpedo Squadron. A sea battle began, and the *Maddox* proceeded to expend heavy ordnance while four USF F-8 Crusaders strafed the torpedo boats. There was minimal damage to the American boats and planes. The North Vietnamese sustained more severe damage while suffering four killed and six wounded. There were no U.S. casualties.

This battle began the Vietnam War. It is steeped in controversy to this day. A second event, called the "Tonkin Ghosts," was claimed to have been "staged" two days later. The exact motivations of the event are still shrouded in some mystery. Many believe that President Lyndon B. Johnson, hoping to provoke war in Vietnam, had his military force the episode in order to give him the excuse he needed to escalate the conflict.

No matter what the truth is, it began a war that *did* escalate, beginning in 1965, and did not end until 1973, by which time some 58,000 Americans and more than 1 million Vietnamese had died.

Admiral George Stephen Morrison, a Naval Academy graduate and World War II fighter pilot, had taken command of the *Essex*-class *Bon Homme Richard*, flagship of a 3rd Fleet Carrier Division in the Pacific based out of Alameda, near San Francisco. Admiral Morrison was in command of the carrier division during its pivotal role in the Gulf of Tonkin incident.

Back in the United States, Admiral Morrison had a family. His wife, Clara, had given him three children. They included a daughter named Anne Robin, a son named Andrew Lee, and an eldest son, born in 1943 in Melbourne, Florida. His name was James Douglass Morrison.

He was known as Jim Morrison.

Young Jim was four years old when his father transferred to Albuquerque, New Mexico. His father was training in Pensacola, Florida, when his first son was born. He served in the Pacific during the war, was given stateside duty in Washington, D.C., after it, and was assigned to New Mexico to work as an instructor at an atomic weapons facility.

During the drive, having crossed into New Mexico on the highway towards Santa Fe, the child experienced "the most important moment of my life."[1] The family car came upon an overturned truck, where they all plainly saw injured and dying Pueblo Indians lying where they had been thrown on the asphalt, waiting for medical help.

Jim began to cry. His father, who went by his middle name of Steve, stopped the car to help and dispatched another onlooker to call for help. Jimmy, as his folks called him, stared at the scene with rapt attention. When Steve returned to the car, Jimmy sobbed, crying, "I want to help, I want to help...."

His mother cradled the little boy. "It's all right, Jimmy, it is," she told him.

"They're dying! They're dying!"

"It was a dream, Jimmy, it didn't really happen, it was a dream," his dad told him.

Sobbing, Jimmy stared out the back window as the car pulled away. According to Jim Morrison, the soul of a dead Indian passed into his body where it would remain all his life.[2]

In 1955, when Jim was twelve, he was riding a toboggan down a snowy mountain with his younger brother and sister. According to his siblings, Jim frantically pushed the toboggan until it reached dangerous speeds, did not stop it when they screamed for him to even though he had the ability to, and forcibly prevented both of them from escaping what they thought would be violent injury or death when it crashed. It was as if Jim was pushing the bounds of death, trying to break through to the other side. Steve Morrison finally managed to somehow pull it to a stop, and, when questioned, Jim, looking quite pleased with himself, replied, "We were just havin' a good time."[3]

Over the next decade, the Morrison family moved to different locations in America, including Florida, Virginia, and California, while the father moved inexorably up the chain of command, ultimately attaining the rank of admiral. It was the apex of the Cold War, a time when the United States resembled Rome after the defeat of Hannibal. Steve Morrison symbolized American Exceptionalism: handsome, Christian, a commanding presence, demanding respect from his family and accorded total obedience from those serving under him.

Jim Morrison was essentially raised by his mother while his father was serving the country. She did the best she could, adhering to a "wait until your father comes home" line, in which the arbiter of all dilemmas was the paternal figure. Jim was different from his siblings and his classmates: good-looking but a loner, not intimidated by girls but not a lothario, either. He was not athletic despite a strong build. His solace was literature.

The family moved to Alameda, home of a major naval air station located directly across the bay from the glittering lights of San Francisco. That was where he read *On the Road* by Jack Kerouac, which was largely devoted to events in the City, as locals referred to it, and was promoted most vociferously by the beat movement that grew there.

Morrison read anything and everything, devouring Shakespeare, Irish poetry, French and German philosophy, and music. He was most likely a genius, possibly possessing a photographic memory. He would invite friends to his room, which was filled with books. Morrison would close his eyes and ask his friend to pick any random book from off the shelf and read from whatever passage they happened to turn to. Invariably, he could finish the passage and tell the other person the name of the book and its author.

Morrison made excellent grades but rebelled against his father's rigid militarism. He enrolled at Florida State University, drank heavily, and took road trips. In January of 1964, he transferred to the UCLA film school. Before enrolling in classes, however, he visited his father, now captain of the *Bon Homme Richard*, a 3,000-man ship docked at Coronado, near San Diego. He was forced to cut his hair short in order to conform to the visit, then made the drive some 100 miles north to Los Angeles, where he started taking classes. That was the last time he wore his hair short.

"Unlike her older sister university in Berkeley, UCLA was virtually apolitical," wrote Morrison's biographers, Jerry Hopkins and Danny Sugarman in *No One Here Gets Out Alive*. "The students were tanned, athletic and pleasing to look at, and their attire was casual, classless."

But the film school was entering "what the professors call the Golden Age," they continued. "The faculty included some of the top directors—Stanley Kramer, Jean Renoir, and Josef von Sternberg among them. The students themselves counted among themselves a score of brilliant and volatile personalities, including the young Francis Ford Coppola. Perhaps most important, the division had an exhilarating near-anarchic philosophy...."

"The good thing about film is that there aren't any experts," Morrison later wrote. "There's no authority on film. Any one person can assimilate and contain the whole history of film in himself, which you can't do in other arts. There are no experts, so theoretically, any student knows almost as much as any professor."[4]

Morrison assimilated in this eclectic environment, soaking in the city of Los Angeles and Southern California landscape as much as his formal education. During Easter vacation he and two classmates—a somber, bearded New York intellectual and an older Irish girl—spent three drunken days in Tijuana. He read voraciously and sometimes went to the Lucky U., a Mexican restaurant near the Veterans Hospital, located about a mile from the UCLA. Some of the crippled vets would drink there and get into scrapes, which he found amusing.

On weekends he hung out at Venice Beach, L.A.'s version of San Francisco's North Beach, where the beatniks were. Poets, painters, musicians, and students lived cheaply in a ramshackle, bohemian tradition. He began to study shamanism, a mystical religion of the American Indians, trying to grasp what he believed was the soul of the dead Indian who, he said, "leapt" into his body during the road trip through New Mexico when he was a child.

Jim was in advanced placement and quickly adopted his literary likes to film. One of his favorites was *The Doors of Perception* by Aldous Huxley. "Huxley wrote that Los Angeles was like Venice during the Renaissance—an independent city-state that had funneled the riches and wisdom of Asia to Europe," wrote Stephen Davis in *Jim Morrison: Life, death, legend*. He lived on Goshen Avenue near campus and scored a part-time job at Powell Library, where he sometimes got drunk while reading in the stacks, and then tried to pick up coeds.

"*Film student* was considered synonymous with goofball, slacker, draft dodger," wrote Davis, echoing Steven Biskind's description of the same in *Easy Riders, Raging Bulls*.

While USC was oriented towards getting kids technical jobs in the movie business, UCLA was more New Wave, focusing on *auteur* theory, *avant-garde* and underground experimental movies. The saying went that at USC they read *Variety* and at UCLA they read *Cahiers du Cinéma*. Their film culture emulated Jean-Luc Godard, Francois Truffaut, Norman Mailer, John Cassavettes, and Andy Warhol.

Morrison was very influenced by director Josef von Sternberg, who was on the faculty. His German expressionist roots would later highly influence The Doors. Morrison listened to Bob Dylan and read esoteric novels. A group of fellow existentialists hung out together at the Lucky U. Mexican restaurant.

It was at UCLA that Morrison met fellow film student Ray Manzarek. Manzarek lived in Manhattan Beach at the time. He had enrolled in law school, dropped out, and transferred to film. His girlfriend was an exotically stunning Japanese-American named Dorothy Fujikawa. He played with Rick and the Ravens, a local bar band.

Manzarek was a fan of Ingmar Bergman and Michelangelo Antonioni. His student film featured Dorothy showering in the nude. Ray refused to cut it and won the right to show it uncensored. Morrison appeared in a party sequence of the film's introduction.

Fellow student Felix Venable was "credited" by Stephen Davis with turning Morrison into an alcoholic. He might have given him LSD. He did give him lots of beat and Dylan Thomas poetry. Morrison developed a persona then and there: the Irish poet. The Irish drank. It was a holistic, lifestyle approach in which Morrison's habits and haunts were part of who he was, an artist, a poet. He studied Arthur Rimbaud.

Venable and Morrison went to the desert together. According to Davis, Venable may have arranged for Morrison to meet Mexican writer Carlos Castaneda, whose psychedelic, peyote-inspired stories were very appealing among the young anarchists of the 1960s, and also influenced much of Morrison's musical work. Morrison, a "crap disturber" to rival William Shakespeare's Iago, would shout "nigger" after getting drunk, just to get a rise during UCLA's "freedom summer" of 1964.

"As a conservative Southerner, Jimmy seemed to have a racist fear of black people that unfortunately surfaced when alcohol impaired his ability to control himself," wrote Davis.

He began to hang out at the Whisky a Go Go, just up the street from the UCLA campus on Sunset Boulevard in West Hollywood. The Whisky in the 1960s was one of the most storied night spots of all time. A playboy baseball player with the expansion Los Angeles Angels, Bo Belinsky, regularly hung out there. A "kiss and tell" artist like none other, he regaled all within earshot with stories about picking up young lovelies from the Whisky, until gossip columnist Walter Winchell actually assigned a photographer to capture him in action, complete with juicy columns in the next day's papers. Every day stories of Bo squiring *Gilligan's Island* beauty Tina Louise, *Carnal Knowledge* star Ann-Margret, busty beauty Mamie Van Doren, or any of dozens of other starlets, made Bo and Winchell infamous. Bo once played pool with Morrison there.

The Whisky drew Steve McQueen, Natalie Wood, Warren Beatty, Julie Christie, and most every celebrity of note into its fabled doors. *Life* magazine did a spread on it. Jack Paar broadcast *The Tonight Show* from there. Cary Grant would drop by, lending it a sense of class. John Lennon and Paul McCartney were chauffeured there along with Jayne Mansfield. Jack Nicholson showed up.

Morrison's old high school girlfriend Mary Werbelow was a go-go dancer at Gazzari's, located just up the Sunset Strip from the Whiskey. She was named "Miss Gazzari's of 1965."

Morrison wanted to make a film of Friedrich Nietzsche's descent into drooling insanity. Morrison took film from a friend's training department film of psychology; of couples massaging each other, and cut it to make it look pornographic. "He cut this footage real fast," recalled film student Phil O'Leno, "so it looked like there was a lot more going on. A *lot more*.... But that would be like him, to make controversy out of something that he could use. Everyone was screaming at him, especially all the faculty."[5]

He wrote a poem about "super people" called "the Lords," who "saw things as they were." This derived from *Nova Mob* by William Burroughs.

"Jim was a very talented and brilliant person," O'Leno said. "But he was a little too young to be wise."

A sense of mysticism made its way into the film school philosophy. "Part of the vague philosophy of the UCLA film students was you blur the distinction between dreams and reality," recalled one of Morrison's classmates, John DeBella.[6]

"Dreams beget reality" was a catch-phrase among them. Many studied Carl Jung. Life was not as romantic as they wanted it to be, so they set out to portray it according to their vision on film. This was similar to the experience of young Jim Murray, an aspiring writer who went to see Babe Ruth play at Yankee Stadium, expecting to experience what legendary sports columnist Grantland Rice had told him it would be like. When Ruth hit a home run there was little fanfare. Murray realized it was the writer's descriptions of the "mammoth swat" that gave it real color.

Morrison, who had the looks of a movie star, was becoming a wild partier and womanizer bent on outlandish public acts. His films were filled with images of horror, lust and sex, tempered by Jungian philosophy us well as themes of Sigmund Freud and Nietzsche, whose "will to power" is often seen as the motivating force behind the atrocities of both Adolf Hitler and Joseph Stalin. "The appeal of cinema is the fear of death," he wrote,[7] echoing a theme recurring throughout his life; from the Indian "leaping" into his soul, his seemingly trying to drive his siblings to their death in a toboggan; undoubtedly exacerbated by the fact that his father made a living preparing to deliver mass destruction. His writings became increasingly poetic, as well. He tried to find meaning in horror, such as John Kennedy's assassination.

Morrison's favorite instructor was Ed Brokaw, who tended to outrageousness himself. "Brokaw would've been drawn to Jim's destructiveness," said Colin Young, head of the film division. That was where Brokaw found "real talent."[8]

In May of 1965, some forty or fifty film students presented their films, the best of which were selected for showing at Royce Hall. Everything came to a head when Morrison finally produced his movie, which was held in a raucous atmosphere that could be compared to a modern version of the gladiatorial games. To fail meant to do so publicly amid humiliation.

Drawing on Nietzsche's "will to power," Morrison used friend John DeBella's beautiful blonde German girlfriend Elke as a *faux* dominatrix-stripper, cavorting in sensuous lingerie above Morrison, as he stares at her in wonder. But the film was fraught with problems, not the least of which was that it kept breaking in the projector. Most of the films were heavily influenced by Truffaut, Chris Market, and Andy Warhol. Jim's was one of the last shown and the crowd was antsy.

"When the film starts," Jim later said, "the screen is black and you hear noises—a mixture of a record called 'Erotica' and a tape of a priest and some children chanting something back and forth from a Catholic catechism hour on the radio. It sounded like something primitive, out of the jungle."[9]

Then a fuzzy test-pattern, like the one from the television show *Outer Limits*, cuts into the film's crew smoking cigarettes and theoretically getting ready to film a stag movie. Then hand puppets and *Playboy* centerfolds appear over Navajo chants. Then darts are thrown at the centerfolds. A woman disappears into an elevator. Morrison puffs from a joint, then an atomic bomb explodes while he winks to the camera. Then Elke, in bra, panties, garter belt and stockings, parodies the Blue Angel dancing on top of a TV, images from the set seeming to emanate from between her legs. Then the TV show *Victory at Sea* morphs with Nazi storm troopers. Themes include masturbation, and eyeball licking, meant to represent the cleansing of one's sight after having viewed pornography or obscenity.

"Porn, Drugs, Television, Nazis, Sex, Music, Irony," is how Stephen Davis described it.[10]

When the film concluded the class sat in horrid silence. One close friend confided to Morrison that he "got it," but that was all. The overall conclusion was that Jim Morrison was a disturbed human being, a "chaotic guy," wrote Davis. This confirmed it. Some faculty called it the worst student film ever. Women hated it. "Jim, I'm terribly disappointed in you," Brokaw said.[11] Some students howled and mocked the effort. Another called it degenerate. What happened next is debatable. Some say they saw Jim cry. He did become petulant and defensive. Morrison, a lifelong academic and sparkling student, received a D. He decided to quit. Colin Young talked him out of it, but before picking up his diploma he disdained it, choosing to smoke dope at Venice Beach instead.

"Jim just put a lot of things he liked into the film," recalled Ray Manzarek in *Eye* magazine. "It didn't have anything to do with anything. Everybody at UCLA hated it, but it was really quite good." A vocal few called it "non-linear."

"I'd say it was less a film than an *essay* on film," Morrison himself said of it.[12]

Jim had a UCLA degree in cinema, but having skipped the June 1965 graduation, his diploma was mailed to his mother in Coronado. The film was lost to the trash and had to be re-created by Oliver Stone for his 1991 movie, *The Doors*.[13]

Jim Morrison admired Ray Manzarek because he refused to cut film of his girlfriend in a nude shower scene. Nudity was almost *de rigueur* at UCLA. Manzarek's band, Rick and the Ravens, performed at a place called the Turkey Joint in nearby Santa Monica. It was with this band that Morrison made his singing "debut." Drunk, he was invited on stage with others there to see Manzarek, and they all sang a boozy rendition of "Louie, Louie."

Shortly thereafter, Manzarek's band got a gig to back up Sonny and Cher at a high school graduation dance. One of the band members quit and Manzarek was told if he did not produce six musicians as contracted, they would not be paid.

"Hey, man, wanna play a gig with us?" he asked Morrison when he ran across him.

"I don't play anything," Morrison replied.

"That's okay, all you have to do is stand there and hold an electric guitar," Manzarek replied. "We'll just run the cord behind one of the amps. We won't even plug it in."

That was Jim Morrison's first professional "performance."

Shortly thereafter, Morrison told one of his friends he wanted to start a rock group called The Doors. "There's the known. And there's the unknown," he said. "And what separates the two is the door, and that's what I want to be. Ahh wanna be th' dooooorrrr...."[14]

Asked if he could sing—he had no training on any instrument—he replied, "I can't sing."

But he could write. His poetry began to take on a more lyrical, musical quality. One day, sitting on the beach, a young, thin black girl "insinuated" her way toward him. He was inspired to write a song called "Hello, I Love You." It was a brilliant, beautifully simple song that animated a vision of the girl walking, and the environment reacting to her in organic manner.[15]

He wrote song after song, an entire concert playing in his head. Many songs were drawn from the Venice experience, but others played to deeper visions of death, philosophy, morality, and fear. They were significantly different from anything being played on the radio in 1965.

The American sound had morphed into different regional variations. Elvis Presley had combined black jazz rhythms with Southern rock 'n' roll. There were the "Philadelphia" and "New Jersey" sounds of crooners like Frankie Valli, which were more traditional variations on singers like Frank Sinatra. In Morrison's California, the Beach Boys were all the rage with their tunes of girls, cars, and surfing. The British Invasion was under way, with English rebels singing against authority, breaking away from their World War II past.

Morrison's poems and songs had no sound yet, since he had no band, but they were dark and foreboding, yet alive at the same time. Morrison was staying with a friend named Dennis Jacob. Two months after holding an un-plugged guitar with Ray Manzarek's band, Morrison ran into his old film school pal at Venice Beach.

"Hey, man."

"Hey, Ray, how ya doin'?"

"Okay. I thought you went to New York."

"No, I stayed here. Living with Dennis on and off. Writin'."

"Writing? What'cha been writing?"

"Oh, not much. Just some songs."

"Songs? Let's hear 'em."

Morrison squatted on the sand and sang a little ditty called "Moonlight Drive," a magnificent, visually evocative depiction of a car riding along the coast, a swim in moonlit waters, all encompassing the cityscapes that connect Los Angeles to the Pacific Ocean.[16]

Ray Manzarek stared in amazement and declared those to be the "greatest" lyrics he had ever heard. "Let's start a rock 'n' roll band and make a million bucks," he declared.

"Exactly," Jim replied. "That's what I had in mind all along."

Manzarek, the more promising filmmaker at UCLA, was an intellectual from Chicago. He was inspired, like John Milius, by Japanese filmmakers. Manzarek earned his master's degree in film from UCLA, but was disappointed in his efforts to get hired by studios.

When he and Morrison began working on music, their shared intellects created unusual musical imagery totally different from anything playing in the mid-1960s. Morrison's reading of Aldous Huxley's *The Doors of Perception* inspired an early song, "Break on Through." They added a drummer named John Densmore and began to take acid to expand their minds. They also added a guitar player, another UCLA student, this one named Robby Krieger. The band started practicing in Venice and taking local gigs.

Morrison, who had been chubby as a youth, ate so little and lost so much weight that his body took on a lean, sexual vibrancy. He grew his hair, often went shirtless, and looked like a Greek statue. His appeal to women was irresistible, and it became obvious to the band that he was their front man, the key to their success.

The group made its way to the desert to drop acid and contemplate existence. At some point Morrison, exploring some caves, had visions that reminded him of the dead Indian who "leapt" into his soul in New Mexico. He began formulating the experience into "weird scenes inside the gold mine," of a snake who was a metaphor for life or the devil, or death, and how fear or lack of fear of the creature was the meaning of existence.[17]

Eventually, the band started playing on the famed Sunset Strip, which at the time was the apex of rock 'n' roll, a golden era never seen before or since. On any given night in any given club rock fans could see some of the greatest performers in history just a year or two from becoming world-famous bands. The most famed of the clubs was the Whisky a Go Go.

It was at the Whisky in 1966 that The Doors entered the pantheon of myth and legend, at least in the re-telling. They were in the middle of their set, playing a series of songs, mostly classics by other groups, like "Louie, Louie" and "Gloria," plus a few that would later be their early hits. Crowds were beginning to come see them, especially horny young girls enchanted by Morrison in skin-tight leather pants.

The Whisky featured go-go dancers, *faux* strippers in high heels, mini-skirts and bare midriffs, writhing around, throwing their big hair around in sexy poses. Then The Doors began to play a song they had not played before. It was a song written by Morrison about faded, unrequited love, but his experience walking around the cave in the desert on acid resonated in him and found its way into the song.

The music started. It was not the usual peppy rock 'n' roll songs they were known for, which had the dancers flailing away, the dance floor filled. It began slowly, Morrison approaching the microphone in dark chino pants and a T-shirt, hair curling to his collarbone, "an unshaven Botticelli face, he lurked around the kinetic flash and shadow of the Whisky a Go Go dance floor," wrote Hopkins and Sugarman.

Morrison stopped to look at the dancers in their glass cages. Manzarek's organ was mournful, full of churchy soul. Morrison hung on the microphone, head tilted back. He planted a boot on the base of the mic stand and began a recitation. The song includes mournful evocations of "the end," which originally stood for the end of a love affair, but quickly expand into something deeper, the end of "elaborate plans." The song is not about Vietnam, but nevertheless its imagery of a "stranger's hand" in a "desperate land" indeed does conjure the thought of U.S. troops in Southeast Asia at that very time.

The music was hypnotic, Morrison's voice "plaintive, threatening," wrote Hopkins/Sugarman. The organ was skipping "heartbeats," mixed with a "sudden ejaculation" from Densmore's drums, and Krieger's guitar sounded like a sitar. Morrison moved through the song using words with precision, like bullets. Anticipation began to build in the crowd as he intones of "danger" on the "King's highway," of "weird scenes" inside the gold mine emanating from his acid experience in the desert, now vaguely Dante-esque.[18] The lyrics reflect Morrison's visions from the desert cave. The "highway west" could symbolize his personal journey to California, the edge of a continent, the New Rome. Much of this verbiage was added from its origin in the Venice studio, turning it into a song about much more than lost love, but something far deeper ... and darker. All the other band members had not heard it in its entirety and were as stunned as was the crowd.

The dance floor stopped moving, people swaying shoulder to shoulder. Bartenders stopped taking drinks, and nobody was ordering. There was silence outside of the singing and the hypnotic music. The waitresses stood, staring in awe. The dancers came to a halt in their glass cages as Moirrison described a snake at an "ancient lake." The "blue bus" has been said to refer to LSD. The snake is Morrison's ancient version of humanity, the duality of good and evil, our reaction to it—fear or ecstasy—the test of one's soul. Morrison looked out, convinced he had the audience right where he wanted them. The haunting music continued as backdrop. His eyes now opened, he entered pop mythology, Morrison describing a "killer" who takes a "face from the ancient gallery," girds for his mission, and advances to a room where he announces his intent to have sex with his mother and kill his father. The crowd gasped. These lyrics were both personal and philosophical, as well as obscene to the point of sacrilegious. There seems little doubt by those who knew of Morrison's deep resentment of his father and lack of respect for a mother who bowed down before him that they were not merely Freudian fantasy, but real desires. He sings of his brother and sister, whom he apparently spares, then of the "door" that he always wanted to be and inspired the band's name.

The audience slowly recovered from the shocking display, the song concluded, and then ... all hell broke loose. Phil Tanzini, the Whisky's owner, possibly connected to the mob, called Morrison a "foul-mouthed son of a bitch" and fired the band.

Morrison later explained that the song referred to Nietzsche's *The Birth of a Tragedy*, with roots in Greek poetry, with Oedipus "the most sorrowful figure ... the type of noble man who despite his wisdom is fatal to error and misery, but who nevertheless, through his extraordinary sufferings, ultimately exerts a magical, healing effect on all around him, which continues even after his death."

The song may have gotten them temporarily fired from the Whisky a Go Go, but it would garner them attention that would lead to a major record deal, which in turn would lead to fame and fortune. But the Greek and Nietzchean metaphors and overtones of "The End" would be heard from a fellow UCLA film school alumnus, who would hear in it an explanation of sorts for why the United States was fighting in Vietnam, already raging heavily at that very time, and how it could help explain a mad man who thought he had the answer the nation sought in its quest for victory. Francis Ford Coppola filed "The End" away in his fertile mind, to be pulled out and used when appropriate.[19]

5

Zen Anarchist

Born in 1944 in St. Louis, John Milius—in response to a critic's accusation that he was a "Fascist," replied that he truly was a "man of the people" and a "Zen anarchist."[1] Milius's father was a successful businessman who was fifty-eight when John was born. He retired and moved the family to Los Angeles, where they joined the elites of society at the posh Bel-Air Country Club. Young John never conformed to that environment, preferring to hang out at the beach and develop into an excellent surfer. He claimed his family was "dysfunctional," that he and his two siblings were "always trying to kill each other." He was a "bad kid" bordering on juvenile delinquency, and the "black sheep of the family," but that did not stop him from a voracious reading habit.[2]

It was in great books that he drank deeply. He read the classics: *Moby Dick*, *The Iliad* and *The Odyssey*, *Heart of Darkness*, Ernest Hemingway, and especially books on war and history, from the Persians to the Greeks to the Romans to George S. Patton. His political hero was President Theodore Roosevelt. He came of age in the 1960s, at the height of the Vietnam anti-war protest movement, but was a total reactionary. When the counter-culture was turning to the left, he made a hard right turn, saying since his father was fifty-eight when he sired him it made him feel that he had been born a century too late. He had a truly oppositional personality who found romance in the notion of revolution, not just the American Revolution, but revolution against conformity, to sameness. He endeavored to be, and utterly achieved, the quality of uniqueness.

A photo of the teenaged Milius, shirtless and at the beach, shows a young, sturdy, handsome man with a face that seems to belie his youth. It is the face of a turn-of-the-century ballplayer, a farmer working the Oklahoma land grab. It is not fresh and innocent. It is the face of toil, of experience. It is a face of pain, of a fellow who has disappointed his elders and is an outcast, yet the surf scene is telling. It was at the beach where he found a home. Despite the athleticism of surfing, he developed girth at a young age, which along with a beard, a leather jacket, and penchant for both motorcycles and guns, gave him a certain personality that made people stand up and take notice. He was a ... searcher, looking for something at which he could excel.

"I had a paper route, and for an entire week after I finished I went to see *The Searchers* every day," Milius recalled of the early influence of John Wayne and his 1956 John Ford-directed classic, along with the "incomparable Gene Autry," on his life. "I didn't see it again until I got one of my first writing jobs, and they let me get a film to watch," he said. "I was sure that I had imagined this film. I was enormously relieved to find it was better than I'd remembered it."[3]

He read *The Decline and Fall of the Roman Empire* by Edward Gibbons, and the works of H. G. Wells; he did not understand F. Scott Fitzgerald's *The Great Gatsby*. "I read everything that Hemingway and Faulkner ever wrote. I was obsessed with Herman Melville and *Moby Dick*. To this day I still think we need no other novel. It's the greatest work of art. I would rather have written *Moby Dick* than painted the Sistine Chapel or made *Citizen Kane*, or made *Citizen Kane while painting* the Sistine Chapel! I would rather have written *Moby Dick* than walked into the Mother Ship at the end of *Close Encounters*, which is really going far because everyone wants to walk into that Mother Ship and walk off with Rick Dreyfuss. I was always interested in history and got good grades in it. I loved the idea of history because it was like stories being told around a campfire. Even if you had a bad history professor and he required you to read *Plutarch's Lives*, what a wonderful thing to do! I couldn't imagine how anyone could *not* read *Plutarch's Lives*."[4]

It is difficult to imagine today how a young fellow who loves classic books could be considered some sort of problem child, but that was how Milius's parents looked at him. He did not conform. He did not want to follow in the father's footsteps or work in the family business. He was not an entrepreneurial businessman in that regard, although his politics, already well formed, were very supportive of capitalism. It was the era of Ayn Rand's conservative anthem *Atlas Shrugged*, but Rand's Objectivist philosophy was creating a cult of personality around her. John Milius was never a man to follow a cult of personality, on the right or on the left.

His time spent at the beach disturbed his Midwestern father. He could not understand the lifestyle, being one with nature, the very *Zen* of surf riding. It was a spiritual experience for his son, but all Mr. Milius saw was cheap arcades, slackers, and slutty girls in bikinis enticing young men to no good. So he shipped John to Colorado to get him away from the Pacific Ocean "because I was a juvenile delinquent." Milius started to write short stories. "I had learned very early, to write in almost any style. I could write in fluent Hemingway, or in fluent Melville, or Conrad, or Jack Kerouac, and whatever." He was also influenced by the oral story telling of surfers at the time, who had a beatnik tradition.[5]

Instead of becoming a "fish out of water," he completely adapted to his mountain surroundings. He hunted, fished, and trapped game. He challenged himself against the elements, just as he had with big wave riding. He read all about Jim Bridger and Western history, and imagined he was an early pioneer. It was the perfect environment for his personality.

"I was always kind of a loner ... outcast," Milius said. He read Joseph Conrad's *Heart of Darkness*, likening his own surroundings to the jungle threats described in the novel.

He knew what he wanted to do. He wanted to be a fighter jock like his hero, test pilot Chuck Yeager, "because he broke the sound barrier," he said. The Vietnam War was just heating up. John Milius wanted to fly missions over North Vietnam. Years later he told actor Charlie Sheen it was his "fantasy to come in low over tree tops and drop fire on children."

How serious he was—he broke into a disarming grin as soon as he said it—can only be speculated on, but his desire to fly combat jet aircraft in a war in which those jets were dropping fire on the North Vietnamese Communists, some of whom were indeed children, was very real.

"I didn't plan on coming back," he said. "I was gonna be a Naval aviator and I planned that I probably wouldn't live past twenty-six, because I didn't see any point in it." Milius may not have been realistic about his chances of becoming an aviator. By the 1960s, the U.S. Air Force, Navy, and Marine Corps all required pilot-candidates to have college degrees. Milius did attend Los Angeles City College, but beyond that his academic record was not outstanding. It was not like World War II, when a desperate Army Air Corps needed pilots so badly they accepted high school kids, or even Korea, when the need was great enough to force retired Reservists to re-up and learn new jet technology. But the prospects of Milius moving on from L.A. City College, then graduating from a four-year college, were not beyond reason. After that, he would face a rigorous challenge just to get accepted to flight school, then make it through the training program, which had a tremendous "wash out" rate. Asked who the "best pilot" he ever saw was, a marine fighter pilot of the era, Frank McCormack, said flatly, "All of 'em." Asked what he meant, he said that the standards were so high only the elites ever even earned their wings. All the "mediocre" fighter pilots, as the old joke went, never became fighter pilots.

"They went over to Pan Am," McCormack joked.[6]

Milius looked into the Marine Corps and was immediately crushed long before he ever had a chance to test himself. He had asthma and "washed out. It was totally demoralizing. I missed going to my war. It probably caused me to be obsessed with war ever since."

He turned to the ocean for solace, making a pilgrimage to Hawaii's North Shore. Once a surfer has been to Sunset Beach, he said "you can never look at anything the same way again."

During that time he made a discovery that changed his life and eventually made movie history. "I walked into a movie theatre in the depths of depression," he recalled. "When you're eighteen, you're always either exhilarated or depressed. I don't think I had enough girls or *a* girl. Just one, that would have been enough. So I made a pilgrimage to the famed Sunset Beach in Hawaii to surf and noticed that the local Japanese art house was showing a week of Akira Kurosawa movies."

Every day Milius sat for hours in that dark theatre until he had seen every one of them, now totally absorbed in the riveting Samurai action, the heroes' journey, and the warrior code that marked Kurosawa. "It just blew me out," he stated. "I said, 'This is what I have to do.'" He could not have a military career, but "being a director is about the next best thing...."

But the prospects for an unknown with no contacts of getting into the film industry, and becoming a director, were beyond dire at that time. "You had to know someone to get in," said Milius. "At that time, really, you had to be born in Hollywood. When I saw those Kurosawa films I was determined to die trying to assault the walls of whatever establishment there was." Kurosawa's were "the finest movies that have ever been made and as far as I can tell ever will be made."[7]

"He reached that point in his life where he realized how unimportant he was in the world; he hadn't done anything," said his daughter, Amanda.[8]

Getting into the University of Southern California business school, or pre-dental program, or trying to land a spot on one of their national championship athletic teams, was a daunting task likely to be met with stiff competition, but at that time the USC film school was literally looking for people. John Milius, self-described "bad kid" as a teenager, sent to exile in Colorado by his father, had his junior college transcripts sent over and—just like that—he was a Trojan.

"SC is the West Point of Hollywood," he said, but it was what men like John Milius would accomplish in subsequent years that would give resonance to that statement. Milius, influenced by classic books and novels, was already a writer of great skill.

"He may have been trained in that, but it was in him, it just came naturally," said his son, Ethan Milius, a Los Angeles district attorney.[9]

"There just aren't that many people who are natural writers that can really write," Milius said.

Milius joined an eclectic and exceedingly talented group of young film hopefuls at USC, training to be directors, cinematographers, editors, but "I was always known as the writer." He was the "story guy."[10]

"The 'USC Mafia'—who also included such other future Spielberg collaborators as John Milius, Robert Zemeckis, Robert Gale, Hal Barwood, Mathew Robbins, Gloria Katz, and Willard Huyck—were unwilling to settle for such limited dreams," wrote Joseph McBride of their collective mindset in *Steven Spielberg: A Biography*. "The funkier UCLA film school—whose most prominent students from that period included Coppola, writer-directors Paul Schrader and Colin Higgins, and director Carroll Ballard—encouraged its students to take a more personal approach to filmmaking. USC's Milius defined the difference between the films made at the two schools."

"Ours were trying to be professional and imitative of Hollywood," said Milius. "Theirs always had beautiful naked girls running through graveyards.... They were, I guess you could say, more left-wing, a little more far out. They used more powerful chemicals and they smoked stronger things."[11]

His influences—he watched John Wayne in *The Searchers* over and over again, "hundreds of times"—was far more conservative than George Lucas or many of the others, who were attracted to the French New Wave and *avant-garde*, but his talent was undeniable.[12]

"Francis couldn't tell a story like John," said Steven Spielberg. "George is a great story teller, [but] he couldn't tell a story like John. None of us [could]."[13]

Spielberg himself was unable to gain entry into either the USC or UCLA film schools, where he desperately wanted to study. He was forced to matriculate at nearby California State University, Long Beach, and stayed with his father, who lived on L.A.'s Westside.

He attended the school's film festivals and became friends with George Lucas and John Milius. He spent so much time at USC with them, in and around the film school, that for all practical purposes he *did* study movies there. Cal State, Long Beach, had a communications/media department, but it did not fit the needs of a dedicated film student like Spielberg.

"I think at that point there were only three film schools in the United States," recalled fellow student Walter Murch. "It's hard to imagine that today. There was NYU in New York, USC and UCLA."[14]

"What USC is now is a lot different than what it was then," recalled another contemporary, Randal Kleiser. "They were working out of these small shacks which had been converted into classrooms and a production stage. Now it's harder to get into the film school than medical school."[15]

"There were just a handful of us," recalled Lucas. "There were a dozen or so. We were part of that group."[16]

This included the likes of Caleb Deschanel, Basil Poledouris, Don Glut, William Phelps,

Willard Huyck, Ronald Schwary, Lucas, Kleiser, Murch, and Milius. Robert Zemeckis was younger and was not yet at USC, but he was following their progress and would be part of the next wave of Trojan film stars.

The standouts among them were undoubtedly Lucas and Milius. As talented as Lucas was, however, Milius was seen as the most promising young filmmaker among them. This was his desire from the very beginning. Murch said he first met Milius "in the dark" at a student film screening when he heard a loud, authoritative voice (Milius) announce, "This film doesn't have enough *moxie*."

"He's created this persona," Lucas said of him.

"He wanted to make himself into a legend," is how Kleiser put it. Lucas's student film was said to be so much better than everybody else's, the instructor refused to show it because "it would be an embarrassment to them," said Lucas, who then said Milius punched the teacher. They were on opposing film units, yet Milius felt the need to stand up for the high quality of the competition.

"*Esprit de corps* is very important to John," said Lucas.

"I'm not sure he's a big brother or crazy uncle," actor Harrison Ford said of Lucas looking up to Milius, on their shared history and loyalty to each other

"It was George and John," recalled Spielberg. "It was just that group. All the names are kind of bunched up."

"It was obvious this was a guy with an enormous talent for dialogue," William Phelps said of Milius.

Lucas's *THX 1138* was considered the most outstanding film produced among these *wunderkinds*, followed closely by Milius's animated short *Marcello, I'm So Bored* (1967, edited by Lucas), which won an international student film award. Milius added to his legend by appearing for the screening wearing a huge, oversized sombrero, adding to his girth, overbearing manner, loud voice, and dominant persona. His main character says, "I want to be *big*! I want to be really *big*!" That was John Milius in a nutshell.

"We won a lot of us stuff with those films," Milius said of the sweep of national student film awards he and Lucas garnered at USC. "That and *THX*; we papered the walls with those two movies."

Marcello screened around the country in various festivals and was praised by Vincent Canby of the *New York Times*. Milius received a job offer to work in animation but he was not interested in that field as he could not see himself "sitting there drawing cel after cel."

Milius was thought to be the more "conventional" filmmaker. Lucas was an iconoclast who never aspired to the mainstream; he saw himself as a documentarian, still a photographer more than an *auteur* director. He was not a great writer and was more influenced by the *avant-garde*, while Milius, the fan of John Wayne, was the superior writer-storyteller and traditional American director. Lucas, the Northern Californian, had no desire to stay and struggle in mainstream Hollywood. Milius, who grew up, albeit as an outcast, in Bel-Air, wanted to make it in the studio system, even though it was rapidly changing in those years.

"When he was coming up, of all of them John was considered the shining star," said Huyck. "He was considered the most talented, and the one who was gonna be the great director."[17]

Steven Spielberg, the man who spent so much time at USC with Lucas and Milius he is practically considered one of the USC film students of the 1960s, said he is not one of them because he went to Cal State, Long Beach. He does say, however, "I think I'm among the maybe five or ten individuals that helped prime the target.... I didn't know anybody then except George Lucas—and I only met George at a USC retrospective of all the student projects of that year. I knew John Milius very early, because John was in that USC group. Just a year down the line I met Hal Barwood and Matthew Robbins. Mathew was AFI, and Barwood was USC."[18]

Milius's politics were already posing a potential problem for him. It was the late 1960s and even though USC remained relatively immune from campus riots, especially among the artful film community, liberalism was the order of the day. It was the preferred "morality" of their films, yet here was a guy who loved Theodore Roosevelt and wanted to espouse TR's muscular Republicanism, reflected in America's defeat of Spain in the Spanish-American War, its "colonizing" of the Philippines, and desire to "walk softly and carry a big stick" while asserting itself as a "modern power" in the years prior to World War I.

"John's point of view was considerably different from people's point of view at the school there," said Lucas.

"Hippies used to wear buttons that said, 'Nirvana now' and had a peace sign on them," recalled Milius. "I modified it to read 'Apocalypse Now' with a mushroom cloud and a B-52. Let's get it over with."

He told Murch he was really a hippie "if they'd elect him King, 'and I wanna be King.'" Milius certainly wanted to move beyond the social isolation he had felt since his rebellious youth, when he found solace in the ocean and in the mountains. "We would sit on the grass and try to hustle the girls as they went by," Milius recalled.[19] They found little of interest in the scruffy film students, preferring instead hotshot football and baseball studs.

In 1968, the world began to take notice of USC and UCLA, opening the doors for the big breakthrough in which talent and perseverance could win one a place in the pantheon, not just "knowing somebody" or being "somebody's kid." *Time* magazine ran a story called "The Student Movie Makers." Kids were "turning to films as a form of artistic expression.... The reason for this celluloid explosion is the widespread conviction among young people that film is the most vital modern art form. Jean Cocteau believed that movies could never become a true art until the materials to make them were as inexpensive as pencil and paper. The era he predicted is rapidly arriving."

This foreshadowed video, digital media, and the Internet, while mentioning as the leading lights of this new charge Francis Ford Coppola (UCLA), Martin Scorsese (New York University), Lucas and Milius (USC).

"My ambitions stopped at B Westerns ..." said Milius. "I thought that was a good life. I never wanted to be Hitchcock or some big mogul, I didn't want to be Louis B. Mayer. I wanted to be, I don't know what, Budd Boetticher or something.... John Ford, that's who I wanted to be."

Milius almost left the business before he got started, however. "I quit, actually. I decided to go back to being a lifeguard.... I was irresponsible. I got a job as a story assistant to Larry Gordon at American International Pictures. Willard Huyck and I lasted two weeks. I was fired for insubordination and he was fired for surliness."[20]

Gordon was initially turned off by the two brash young Trojans. Milius "was a big guy with a lot of fire and BS," he said.[21]

Gordon decided they were too talented to be let go. He hired them back. "After that we wrote a script for AIP, *The Devil's Eight*," recalled Milius. "I always had good writing jobs after that." Milius also did an uncredited rewrite of *Little Fauss and Big Halsy* (1970). Rising talent agent Mike Medavoy read the *Time* magazine piece and decided to represent Milius, whom he called "a bad boy mad genius in a teenager's body, but he was a good and fast writer with original ideas."[22] He called his friend, producer Al Ruddy, and asked him to hire Milius, stating that if he did Medavoy would owe him a big favor in return. Ruddy drove to his small apartment and saw "this huge bear of a guy."[23] Milius agreed to write Ruddy's screenplay if Ruddy would take his large Rhodesian ridgeback dog off his hands as part of the deal.

Milius wrote *The Texans* for Ruddy and Paramount, followed by *Truck Driver*. "I didn't do a good job and I realized the reason I didn't do a good job was because in both cases I was influenced by the people who had hired me," said Milius. "They said put this in and put that in, and I went along with it. Every time I went along with something in my whole career it usually didn't work. Usually there's a price to pay. You think of selling out, but there is a price to pay. Usually what people want you to do is make it current. They want you to make it relate to people in 2000."[24]

Actor-producer George Hamilton hired Milius to write a screenplay about the motorcycle daredevil Evel Knievel, and it was during this time that the Milius legend grew exponentially. Hamilton arranged to have some of the hottest young screenwriters meet with him, among them Terrence Malick, Willard Huyck, and Milius. When he told Milius about Kneivel, who thrilled crowds while challenging death with impossible motorcycle stunts, Milius became orgasmic with excitement, declaring, "That's … just … GREAT!" In this respect, his fascination with death-flirtation was similar to Jim Morrison.

"He just got it," said Hamilton. "He could just see that this was Americana."[25] Hamilton had a place in Palm Springs for Milius to research and write the script. Milius "couldn't wait" to get down there. When asked what he wanted as compensation, Milius told Hamilton, "I want girls, gold and guns." Hamilton agreed and threw in some motorcycles for Milius to ride around in for good measure. He paid Milius handsomely and asked a friend to get "some of those piston-sprung hookers" that hung around Hollywood.

Milius thought he was in paradise, living large in Palm Springs, partying with the girls, and tooling around the desert on a motorcycle, shooting his new weapons. After a week or so went by Hamilton called one of his assistants who was "attending." He asked how it was going and was told "not good," Milius had not written a page yet. He had an earlier script written by some Englishman, which Milius deemed so bad he threw it into the swimming pool and "drowned" it with a paddle. The rest of his time was spent with the girls, spending the gold, riding bikes, firing guns, and living the high life.

Hamilton then had his assistant tell Milius that "this is from me, there would be no more gold, no more guns, and the girls won't mount up if you don't come through."

Hamilton was staying at one of the top New York hotels when, a week later, he started getting telegrams. It was the Evel Knievel screenplay, coming in one telegram at a time. Hamilton liked what he saw and knew he had his screenplay.

"After that he was a terror," he said, laughing.

While Lucas had earned a Warners scholarship, he had not yet really broken into the mainstream Hollywood film industry. Milius was USC's Coppola, the first from their film school to break through on merit without knowing somebody or getting lucky. John Wayne, Ward Bond, and Johnny Weissmuller, among others, were Trojan athletes who used that platform to vault into acting. Most others were like Alan Ladd, Jr., wealthy and connected people who had the skids greased for them. Even Ron Schwary would benefit from his role as student manager of the USC football team, where his encounter with Wayne opened doors for him.

But Milius's quick ascension of the ladder marked a larger change, spurred largely by the end of the old studio system. The retirement of Jack Warner, Darryl Zanuck's eventual loss of control at Twentieth Century–Fox, Paramount's sale to Gulf+Western, along with other changes—star salaries, powerful agents, a younger audience—ushered new blood into an old industry. Robert Evans was taking over at Paramount. Independent films like *Easy Rider* (1969) were surprise hits.

Randal Kleiser and his USC classmates were astounded when they actually read Milius's name in the trade magazine *Hollywood Reporter*. "There was a kind of changing of the guard in the industry, and John was at the forefront, because his name was in the *Hollywood Reporter*," noted Kleiser.

"Nothing was working in Hollywood," said Peter Bart, whose article in the *New York Times* vaulted Bob Evans at Paramount, where Bart and Evans then helped build it back into a juggernaut after many down years. "The audience had basically abandoned the movie business. The star system had broken down and all the studios were basically going down."

Warner and Zanuck were retiring and selling their studios to big corporations "who didn't know much about making movies," said Lucas.

"People like Milius, and George Lucas and Coppola all were lucky to come along at that time," said director Michael Mann, adding that, the way "people get out of slumps is to make radical choices."[26]

"They fought their way out of the trenches and into public sight," said Harrison Ford. "Man, we were there at the second California Gold Rush. We were there at the biggest moment in movie history."[27]

By the end of the 1960s, John Milius was the hottest new screenwriter in the industry, constantly in demand, and well paid.

"John was definitively as a writer valuable to the studios," remarked Francis Ford Coppola. Years later, Milius would insist on casting Arnold Schwarzenegger in *Conan the Barbarian*. He told the Italian producer Dino DeLaurentiss, "If we don't hire him we'll have to invent him."[28]

6

"University of Northern California Graduate Film School"

Film, moving images, actually was developed in France. By the mid-1910s, silent movies were a popular form of entertainment. What many people do not realize is that San Francisco, not Los Angeles, was the center of the budding movie business.[1] Frank Capra originally made movies in San Francisco, where he lived after serving in WWI, before moving to Hollywood. The movie industry gravitated towards Los Angeles for a number of reasons. While San Francisco was unquestionably *the* West Coast city from the Gold Rush until the Great Earthquake of 1906, the Rose Bowl and the building of the Los Angeles Aqueduct gave rise to Los Angeles. The 1932 Olympics cemented L.A. as the predominant California city.

But practical reasons pushed movies to the Southland. San Francisco was colder, rained more, was windier and foggier, making for more challenging outdoor film shoots. While the Bay Area has magnificent vistas, views, mountains, lakes, and scenery that could enhance any scene, its greatest attribute, a huge bay stretching some 90 miles north to south, was one of its greatest hindrances to movie companies. To transport a cast, crew and equipment to many of its magnificent sites meant, prior to the building of the Golden Gate and San Francisco-Oakland Bay Bridges, a boat trip. Los Angeles, on the other hand, rarely rained, offered great outdoor weather year round, and was in the middle of a giant basin absent a body of water, easily accessible by roads that connected film crews to vistas largely as spectacular, or almost as spectacular, as San Francisco's: ocean, beach, mountain, desert. It was a big enough metropolis to present "city life." Its corrals and canyons, found right there within city limits, could be replicated into realistic Westerns. Its deserts could resemble Pharaoh's Egypt.

So, the world flocked to Hollywood. By the mid-1920s, the studio system was in place, while San Francisco remained a place where the occasional filmmaker came for beautiful visuals, particularly Alfred Hitchcock, but the movie industry located itself in Los Angeles: Universal (Universal City/North Hollywood), Columbia (Gower Street, in Hollywood), Warner Bros. (Burbank), Metro-Goldwyn-Mayer (Culver City), 20th Century Fox Film Corporation (Edendale), and Paramount (Melrose Avenue, in Hollywood proper) among the major players.

But the great studio system of Darryl Zanuck, the Warners, Louis B. Mayer, Harry Cohn, David O. Selznick, Irving Thalberg; that was cultivated mainly after film went to "talkies" in the late 1920s and early 1930s. Before that, during the 1910s and early 1920s, for a few years artists themselves ran Hollywood. They even called themselves United Artists: Charlie Chaplin, Douglas Fairbanks, D. W. Griffith, and Mary Pickford. There was a sense of egalitarianism; Chaplin was a Socialist, Pickford a woman of power in a male-dominated society, but eventually their dream came to an end, via attrition as much as anything. By the 1930s, the great studio honchos ran their empires unfettered. It is surprising to many that Hollywood was dominated by conservative Republicans like Mayer, who ran M-G-M as a veritable wing of the GOP. The moguls supported the anti–Communist efforts of Joseph McCarthy and instituted the Blacklist on their own, not by government order. There was resentment and little sympathy for them among liberals when corporations began buying them out, via anti-trust court decisions separating the ownership and power of studios, movie houses, agents and producers in the 1960s.

Francis Ford Coppola came out of UCLA and endeavored to break into a rigged game—the Hollywood system. While he was granted grudging access due to his obvious talents, he was never an insider. He resented the studios and always wanted to break from them. His ultimate dream was to create a "counter-culture M-G-M." He wanted out of the stifling grip of Los Angeles; its traffic, its smog, its plasticity and endless meetings with Beautiful People and power players, none of whom could be trusted. He endeavored to move to the relatively virgin territory of San Francisco and make independent movies. He wanted to control his own destiny.

San Francisco was a dynamic city that had undergone an enormous change since World War II. L.A. was still a Republican town, the town of reactionaries like Ronald Reagan and Sam Yorty. Its economic wealth was rooted in oil and defense. Northern California did not sit on top of oil, and its citizens were not enamored of its riches. There was a military presence in the Bay Area, but it was oriented more towards technology than missiles, and would some day give birth to the Silicon Valley.

Culturally, it had always leaned towards the outrageous and the *avant-garde*, going back to its Barbary Coast roots right after gold was discovered in the Sierra foothills of 1848–49. There was an Old World elegance and sophistication in the City, as its citizens referred to San Francisco, and this served Coppola's New York style, his love of opera and the theatre. While this world was conservative by nature, it was not uptight. In its midst grew an entirely different culture. First came the beats of the 1950s. On the strength of Jack Kerouac's *On the Road*, a book highlighted largely by its descriptions of San Francisco, came Allen Ginsberg and the poets of North Beach, an Italian enclave (home of Joe DiMaggio) giving way to a youth movement.

The Free Speech Movement at cross-bay University of California, Berkeley, begat the Anti-War Movement when troop strength escalated in Vietnam, 1965–66. In 1967, the rock 'n' roll revolution was in full swing, when Jimi Hendrix "went electric" at Monterey and the flower children poured in for the infamous Summer of Love. By the late 1960s San Francisco, at least the Haight-Ashbury district, Golden Gate Park, and certain eclectic night spots like the Fillmore West, where live music by The Grateful Dead, Jefferson Airplane, and other Sausalito houseboat bands rivaled what was happening on Sunset Boulevard, barely resembled what many of its native citizens recalled of their childhoods.

Coppola appeared almost a Bolshevik in full beard some five years earlier when he met Frank McCarthy, who hired him to write *Patton*. He felt at home in the City. *Finian's*

Rainbow was the "last straw" for him. It had been a huge Broadway hit, it starred the legendary Fred Astaire, dancing, yet it did not resonate with the hipster audience of that era.

By 1969, the prospects for a film student in Hollywood were considerably better than they had been five, and certainly ten, years earlier. That said, it was slow going. Steven Spielberg and John Milius had landed steady work, but George Lucas was turned off by the industry, figuring he would go to San Francisco and make documentaries. In 1969 he did just that, capturing the infamous Rolling Stones debacle at Altamont that eventually became the documentary *Gimme Shelter* (1970).

Brian De Palma, from Columbia, and Martin Scorsese, from NYU, were completely off the radar. Francis Ford Coppola was still the lone film student who had made it in any sense of the word. While he had directed several films, the single truly exceptional achievement Coppola could hang his hat on was his screenplay for *Patton*, which, in 1970, would be a smash hit, and, in 1971, would earn him his first Academy Award.

"He was like the golden child of student filmmakers, because at that point nobody from film school had actually broken into the film industry, but he had won an Academy Award for writing *Patton*, and he was only five years older than I was," said Lucas.[2]

But *Patton* had not yet been released in the winter of 1968–69. Despite "success" in an anticipated mainstream production from the venerable Twentieth Century–Fox, Coppola did not trust that this was the path towards his goals. He was determined to fully break from—and possibly *actually break*—the studio system. The idea of independent films was not new.

Harry Belafonte made some groundbreaking independent movies in the late 1950s. He was very left-wing, a protégé of the black Communist Paul Robeson. So, too, was Sidney Poitier, who relied on his acting career, whereas Belafonte could fall back on his music and did not have to have Hollywood's approval. Poitier turned away from Robeson and Belafonte, at least publicly, and made a string of hits that made him a beloved star. But over time liberalism became secular religion in the entertainment industry, with the exception of country music, which remains Christian and Republican. In 1960, John Cassavetes made *Shadows*.

By 1969, John Wayne was out and liberalism was in, finally, after domination by Louis B. Mayer and the right. The Blacklist had rotted the industry from within. Prior to this era the general apprentice system consisted of sons of union members waiting to get their shot.

The early art of Chaplin, Pickford, Fairbanks, and D.W. Griffith had long been lost to the studios, which were producer driven. Directors were often of the stage, selected as technocrats, skilled in technique, not story. Coppola was part of a new age of young directors that included Stanley Kubrick, Norman Jewison, Mike Nichols, and Robert Altman, all of whom were changing this.

"I've had it with these big Hollywood movies; I don't want to do this," Coppola told George Lucas. "I've got this plan to do a tiny movie with just a small group of people, a bit like making a student film. I'm going to start in New York, get in a truck and drive across the United States, making a movie as I go. No planning, no nothing—just do it...."[3]

Coppola's vision was democratic and not physically located in L.A. Actors, writers, directors, and editors all meshed together as "filmmakers." "My fantasy was you're working on the films and drinking wine at night, and there are beautiful girls who are working on the films and you're all in it together," he said. The first movie that embodied this philosophy was *The Rain People* (1969), which was no masterpiece but did help launch the careers of two great stars of future Coppola epics, Robert Duvall and James Caan. The experience of shooting a road movie enthused Coppola. Lucas worked with him on that shoot, and they decided they wanted to go into business together.

"We thought that we could go to San Francisco and produce new cinema of contemporary stories, with more ambitious themes, shot with tiny and mobile crews, and making use of the new technology," said Lucas.

The Rain People was based on a quarrel Coppola's mom had with his dad. She spent two days in a motel. "To have had the guts to have plunked down $20,000 of his own was astonishing," said Walter Murch of *The Rain People*. "That has been part of Francis's genius all along, to walk not only out on the gangplank, but off the edge of it and seemingly not fall down but sort of hang in there in space while the sharks are nipping at his heels, and he's saying, 'Come on out, it's great.'"

"Francis just didn't want to be part of that Hollywood scene," said Lucas. "He wanted to be more independent. We were more anti-establishment than ever because it was the '60s. We didn't want to be part of the establishment. Francis wanted to be doing more artistic films, and not be forced to make commercial films. I was still interested in doing *avant-garde*, non-story, non-character films. I grew up knowing the underground of Scott Bartlett and Bruce Connor and the whole gang of underground filmmakers in San Francisco. So, for me, it was great. That was the sort of world I wanted to come back to."[4]

"We could make movies anywhere in the world," Coppola said to Lucas after shooting *The Rain People* cross-country. "We don't have to be in Hollywood."[5]

Lucas, who was from Northern California, had little professional association with the industry beyond a Warners scholarship that he found of dubious value, and was even more determined than Coppola to be a San Francisco filmmaker. He wanted to make documentaries and *cinéma vérité*. They went to San Francisco and met Bay Area filmmaker John Korty, who had a nice, self-contained little studio in Stinson Beach. This was the inspiration for American Zoetrope. Coppola began looking for a mansion in Marin County in which to move the operation. Lucas opened the company's first office in Mill Valley. Coppola put his Los Angeles home on the market, intent to pour his profits from the sale into a company called Zoetrope, and went to Europe, largely to buy cheap film equipment, and learn how to use it so he would not be dependent on the industry.

Coppola acquired a Keller three-screen editing table, the only one of its kind in the U.S. "I became a sort of mini expert on this stuff by really trying to find out about it," said Coppola. "It's like taking a guy who flies a bi-plane and showing him the controls of a 707. He's going to say, 'Aw, I can't fly this.'"

"Like Preston Tucker, his old idol, he would have the design but lack the wherewithal to bring it to fruition," wrote Michael Schumacher in *Francis Ford Coppola: A Filmmaker's Filmmaker*.[6]

Lucas and his wife, Marcia, were already expert editors. When Coppola returned, Zoetrope moved to 827 Folsom Street in San Francisco. They called Walter Murch, Lucas's USC classmate and a sound-editing genius, to help run it.

Coppola wanted to call his new company Trans-American Sprocket Works, but settled on Zoetrope (composed from the Greek root words for "life" and "turning"), a cylinder-shaped gadget that, when spun, projected a moving image. He then called it *American Zoetrope* so it would be prominently listed on the New York Stock Exchange.

Rolling Stone magazine moved into nearby 625 Third Street. Their legendary scribe, Hunter S. Thompson, was already capturing the vibe of San Francisco with his wild descriptions of the Summer of Love and the Oakland-based Hells Angels. Zoetrope was at the epicenter of the counter-culture.

"San Francisco was more radical than any other part of the country, which suited us fine, because we wanted that," said Lucas. "I think we felt more secure in that kind of environment because we really wanted to shake up the status quo in term of the aesthetics of how movies were made and what they were about. We did not want to fall into the corporate reality that was creeping ever more oppressively into the Hollywood mainstream."

Lucas said that since he was "raised sort of on the San Francisco idea of pure cinema," he "wanted to make those kinds of abstract films."

"San Francisco had always been a Mecca for poets, and a tradition that always favored the arts," said Coppola, adding that it was "hospitable to the oddball, or the person who didn't fit in."[7]

Coppola originally told Lucas he would give him a job if he would come up with one good idea per day. "I thought he was a really bright kid and I would say to George, 'You can stay here and observe me, but all you have to do is come up with one great idea a day,' and he began to," said Coppola. He made Lucas vice-president. Then *Easy Rider* came out and spurred this way of thinking to many more people across the spectrum.

"Francis could sell ice cream to Eskimos," Lucas remarked. "He has charisma beyond logic. I can see now what kind of men the great Caesars of history were; their magnetism."

"The system will fall by its own weight!" Coppola said, prophetically, of the studio system at the time. "It can't fail to!"

"Francis saw Zoetrope as a sort of alternative *Easy Rider* studio where he could get a lot of young talent for nothing, make these movies, hope that one of them would be a hit, and eventually build a studio that way," recalled Lucas. "It was very rebellious. We had very off-the-wall ideas that never would have been allowed to infiltrate the studios. Zoetrope was a break away from Hollywood. It was a way of saying, 'We don't want to be part of the establishment, we don't want to make their kind of movies, we want to do something different.' To us, movies are what counts, not deals and making commercial films."

"Francis was going to become the emperor of the new order, but it wasn't going to be like the old order," said John Milius. "It was going to be the rule of the artist."[8]

Eleanor Coppola did not want to raise a family in Hollywood. "I think Francis left L.A. because he didn't want to be a small fish in a big pond," said Marcia Lucas. "I think he wanted to be a big fish in a small pond."[9]

At first, in 1969, Zoetrope was south of Market Street; a gritty neighborhood known as SoMa that has since been transformed, first by tech wealth, then by the building of Pacific Bell (now AT&T) Park in 2000. American Zoetrope operated out of a run-down warehouse on Folsom Street. Hippie carpenters, some stoned on acid, laid sheetrock that had to be ripped out. Francis's first office was Swedish-modern; Mylar cases, Eames chairs, gold-covered rug.

Lucas was the V.P. There was one rule. "No drugs," said Murch. Coppola made himself an expert machinist and could fix the machines and consoles when they went down.

"He was not somebody who said, 'Let's bring in an expert to fix it,'" said Murch. "You had to admire a guy who not only wrote, produced, directed, but was able to figure out what was wrong and patch it up, which was beyond my ability, even though I was the sound mixer."

"George was not a writer, and it was Francis who made him write, who said, 'If you're gonna be a filmmaker, you have to write,'" said Marcia Lucas. He practically handcuffed George to the desk.

"If you're going to be a director, you've got to be a writer, for your own protection," Coppola told Lucas.

Coppola wanted to create a "counter-culture M-G-M," wrote Peter Biskind, but "all George wanted was a roof over his head where he could gather his friends and re-create the USC experience."[10]

"My life is kind of a reaction against Francis's life," said Lucas. "I'm his antithesis."

They handled money differently and dealt with actors differently. Coppola delegated. Lucas was a control freak.

"All directors have egos and are insecure," said Lucas. "But of all the people I know, Francis has the biggest ego and the biggest insecurities. "

"George was like a younger brother to me," said Coppola. "I loved him. Where I went, he went."[11]

Coppola always professed to be an anti-capitalist, at least at some level, yet he liked money and sought money. He was married and started a young family. He had been well paid for his work in the 1960s. He had a great reputation as a screenwriter, less so as a director, but everybody agreed he was brilliant. His style was to spend the money he had at his disposal immediately. He was not a saver or planner. When he was paid handsomely by studios he lavished nice things upon himself and his family: a beautiful home on L.A.'s Westside, a Mercedes-Benz. He was happy to project American Zoetrope as a publicly traded stock.

He was willing to use the studios, to take advantage of them. When he opened Zoetrope's doors in 1969, he immediately joined forces with the "enemy," Warner Bros. Perhaps Coppola felt that Jack Warner's retirement meant a new direction that would be more favorable to his view of what the movie business should be, but the studio had been sold to the Kinney National Service Corporation, who ran funeral parlors and parking lots. It was an incongruous partnership and not likely to see it Francis's way, unless he could pull the wool over the old caretaker's eyes!

Ted Ashley was appointed to run Warner Bros., which was also partnered with Seven Arts, with whom Coppola had a previous relationship. Ashley was bright and a smart film man. He was one of the new breed of Hollywood power players who hoped to capitalize on whatever *Easy Rider* had somehow capitalized on, a youth market or whatever *zeitgeist* it might be. He saw in Coppola and Zoetrope potential, but in doing business with them, Coppola was veering away from his view of himself as independent of Hollywood. He could be four hundred miles to the north, grow his beard and smoke dope with the hippies, but his money, at least initially, was coming from an old source.

Warner Bros.-Seven Arts gave Zoetrope $600,000: $300,000 for equipment; the other half to develop six scripts, one of which was *Apocalypse Now*. Aside from Murch, a large number of their old classmates and colleagues from USC and UCLA moved to San Francisco to work for them. Lucas invited John Milius, Willard Huyck, Matthew Robbins, Hal Barwood, and Gloria Katz to come work at Zoetrope. Coppola was hoping to develop something for Carroll Ballard from UCLA, whose talent he admired as much as any of this group. For Lucas, it was a gas. A lonely, introspective "car crazy" from Modesto, he had found his niche at the University of Southern California. It was a community, a family, a tribe. Now he was able to do something very few college graduates get to do, which is to keep the "old gang" together after college and hold on to the fantasy of a frat house existence well into adulthood. That he was able to induce these young movie hopefuls to move *away from Los Angeles*, to join him in his favorite city, was a fantasy almost too good to be true, but here he was, livin' the California Dream.

There was something fantastic about all these Southern Californians transported to Northern California. In this collegial atmosphere, Zoetrope seemed to be like a graduate film program. It could have called itself the University of Northern California (UNC) Graduate Film School, but they had $600,000 from Ted Ashley and it was not play money.

"American Zoetrope was organized as an extension of our film school experience, and it was organized in such a way that you would bring your friends together the way you had in film school, where everybody would help each other out, and we brought Carroll Ballard from UCLA and George bringing Matthew Robbins and Walter Murch and John Milius and people like that," recalled Caleb Deschanel.[12]

"It seemed like a fantastic opportunity to continue to make 'student' films with students, which we all were—ex-students—except it would be on a larger canvas," said Murch.

"Francis was able to talk anyone into anything," said film editor Robert Dalva, one of the USC crew.[13]

They certainly knew they were in serious business when Zoetrope began fielding calls from heavyweights like Stanley Kubrick, John Schlesinger, Mike Nichols, and Orson Welles. In 1970, *California Living* magazine, a supplement of the *San Francisco Examiner*, featured Lucas on its cover: "NEW AGE FILM-MAKER GEORGE LUCAS: Turning the Tables on Hollywood."[14]

Warner Bros.-Seven Arts did deals with American Zoetrope to make some low-budget movies: *The Conversation*, Carroll Ballard's *Vesuvio*, and *Apocalypse Now*. They agreed to lend Coppola $300,000 plus an additional $300,000 for script development for even more pictures. The money immediately went into more equipment. Coppola, an expert on editing machines, knew how to make use of all the equipment on a shoot.

"So he came back and he said, 'Okay, I've made a deal for my film *The Conversation*,'" said Lucas. "'I made a deal for your film, *THX 1138*. I made a deal for *Apocalypse Now*, and I made a deal for four other films.'"

But the marquee first pick-up of the Zoetrope launch was Lucas's *THX 1138*. He would re-shoot his famed USC student film, this time with professional actors, a crew and Warner Bros.-Seven Arts money behind the project. *THX 1138* seemed a natural at the time. Ever since the dropping of the atomic bomb in 1945, jet aircraft, the breaking of the "sound barrier" (by John Milius's hero, Chuck Yeager, in 1947), followed by missile technology, nuclear weapons, and the "space race" between the United States and the Soviet Union, space, technology and the future had fascinated the public.

Science fiction cartoons and movies were all the rage in the 1950s. After the successful Mercury space program (leading to America landing on the moon in 1969), interest reached its peak. Television shows like *Lost in Space*, *The Outer Limits*, *Star Trek* and *The Twilight Zone* explored themes of space exploration and futurism, often asking ethical questions about where technology would lead mankind. Alvin Toffler's *Future Shock* became a documentary shown at high schools, exploring the reality of these themes. "Futurism" became a legitimate social science, relied on by the government and the military as part of game theory. *The Planet of the Apes* (1968) was a recent huge hit.

THX 1138 was a challenge for Lucas. He was not a great writer or even a "story guy" like John Milius. His original student film had wowed everybody with its mood, its editing, and tone, but if it was to be a successful feature it needed a real screenplay. Coppola was really on Lucas to write, which was not his natural talent.

"Francis forced me to write the screenplay," Lucas said. "I wanted somebody else to do it, but he said, 'Look, if you're going to become a good director, you're going to have to learn to become a writer.' So he coached me on writing and forced me through a few drafts of the screenplay."[15]

Warner Bros.-Seven Arts had invested some money, but it was a relatively small amount. Ted Ashley seemingly had done it almost as a dare, just to see if Coppola and his motley crew of San Francisco Trojans and Bruins could actually put up ... or shut up. Finally Lucas completed his screenplay, a hard task for him. Had Milius written it he probably would have given it an NRA theme, with the oppressed futurists fighting back like John Wayne against space Indians, but Milius did not write *THX 1138*.

"He pushed Warners into giving us the go-ahead to make the movie," Lucas said of Coppola, who ran into resistance when Warners read Lucas's depressing, iconoclastic script. Coppola figured they would just start shooting and all events would fall into place—his normal, optimistic style. Finally, Coppola put up some of his own money, too, then flew to L.A. and read Warners the "riot act" for dragging their feet.

They eventually put up the money. Lucas directed his first feature, starring young Robert Duvall, who had starred in *The Rain People* (he was also Boo Radley in the 1962 film version of Harper Lee's *To Kill a Mockingbird*).

"Every shot was about craft ... it was a combination of all the crafts," said Steven Spielberg of *THX 1138*. "It was, to me, one of the greatest science fiction movies I'd ever seen."[16]

"As it turned out, he had to fight for that vision," said Matthew Robbins. "He did make a film that was highly personal to him, but it was highly personal in a pop culture way, like *American Graffiti*. It was not as if he went out and started making Doris Day films."[17]

Ted Ashley oversaw the project for Warners and forced Lucas to make numerous changes in the script, cutting to pieces the final version, which Lucas still believes was the movie's ultimate downfall. When *THX 1138* was done, they screened it in Mill Valley to a less-than-enthusiastic response, including Marcia Lucas, who did not like her husband's movie.

THX 1138 screened before the "suits" in 1970. Ashley, John Calley, Frank Wells, Richard Lederer, and even Coppola, all hated it. "This is either going to be a masterpiece or a masturbation," Coppola had told Murch as they were mixing it. He told Lucas "it would be crazy to think we're going to hit the bull's-eye the first time." Coppola surely had not in the 1960s. Coppola tried to play both sides down the middle, telling Warners he would supervise Lucas while telling him to "do your own thing."[18]

Fred Weintraub re-edited it, changing it drastically. Even Marcia said *THX* "left me cold." Coppola flew to L.A. to pitch *The Conversation*, *Vesuvio*, *Atlantis Rising* by Steve Wax, *American Graffiti* by Willard Huyck and Gloria Katz, and *Apocalypse Now*. The Warners brass all hated *THX 1138*, and in one fell swoop turned down the other projects. Coppola returned to San Francisco with his tail between his legs. They nicknamed it "black Thursday" (November 19, 1970).

It was bad enough that Warner Bros, a corporation now literally and actually owned by a funeral parlor company, did not wish to fund their ambitious agenda of future films; they *wanted re-payment of the loan*. Coppola was suddenly, overnight, half a million dollars in debt. Warners told Francis to pay the money back or buy back his scripts.

Coppola, who was never a businessman and always played fast and loose with money, either had not made a good contract or loosely considered it less than a binding agreement, but there was small print spelling out Warner's prerogatives and ability to call in the "loan." Coppola felt it was a solid multi-picture deal. "Loans" for equipment were "investments," or so he thought. Scripts optioned were bought and paid for, not on margin that could be called if the stock price went too far down.

The only thing keeping him above ground was the success of *Patton*, which hit movie theatres hot and heavy in 1970, but if there was money from that coming to Coppola, it was not enough to pay off Warner Bros.-Seven Arts.

Warners told him, "This doesn't look like what we want," so "they just gave us the axe, and the whole group with them," said Coppola. At one point Coppola was "staving off the sheriff from putting the chain across the door." Film executive John Calley got a telegram from Coppola in San Francisco. "Shape up or ship out," it read.[19]

"They hated it, and canceled the deal and forced Francis to buy all the scripts back," said Lucas.[20]

"That was the beginning of the end of the original alliteration of American Zoetrope, and the beginning of the end of the original visions of what the Northern California film scene might be," said Matthew Robbins.[21]

"Francis was in debt about $300,000," said Lucas. This was an enormous figure. There probably was only a handful of professional athletes in America making as much as $100,000 per year in 1970.

"My enthusiasm and my imagination far outpaced any kind of financial logic," said Coppola. "I wasn't associated with anyone who was the businessman of the group. It was all me, and I was forging ahead without looking back and seeing whether we could afford this or that."

The good employees of Zoetrope responded by trying to unionize, as if there was some prescription in such ridiculousness. Like all utopian visions, Zoetrope quickly frayed. It was the death knell for Zoetrope in its original form. Coppola, the silver-tongued devil, tried to rescue his company. The only thing Warner Bros. liked at all was the screenplay for *Apocalypse Now*, but Vietnam scared them away. Then they turned down *The Conversation* script.

"Okay, we have a deal, you're running Zoetrope?" Warner Bros. head honcho Frank Wells said.

"Yeah, I'm running it," replied Coppola.

"But you're fucking up."

"I'm an artist."

"But you said you were an executive."

"What are you talking about, I'm a fucking artist, you're the Philistines!"

"You're humping us...."[22]

Coppola's "megalomania" was his only asset; *hubris* in the face of great odds. The truth is, Coppola wanted to take over the studio system and make it radical.

"I'm not the oldest of the young guys, I'm the youngest of the old guys," he said.

"Calley and Ashley had decided that they didn't want to be in business with Coppola," said Jeff Sanford, a young executive at the time.[23] They turned down future projects and kept insisting they get $300,000 back.

"That's when the shit hit the fan," Lucas said. "We were rising, and suddenly it was the crash of '29."

A source said that "they had gotten on the wrong side of somebody who turned out to be a wonderful filmmaker."[24]

"They had turned down what became the whole '70s cinema movement," Coppola said.

Lucas did not speak to Ashley for a decade. Ashley bad-mouthed him on *American Graffiti* and had to apologize when he bid for *Raiders of the Lost Ark*, which he did not get anyway. Coppola and Lucas rarely worked for Warner Bros. again. Oddly, their good friend John Milius would build his career as their star screenwriter. Haskell Wexler had given Coppola $27,000 to buy equipment, but it never arrived. There were hard feelings all around.

The entire episode strained the Lucas-Coppola friendship, which was a real shame. They were as close as brothers, two immense talents who had vowed to help each other, and while they would, it was never according to the original, naïve vision they shared when Lucas came off the USC campus and saw Coppola directing *Finian's Rainbow* on the Warners lot. At this point Marcia's editing gigs provided the family with much-needed money. Lucas ran up a $1,800 bill on the Zoetrope phones calling to get Marcia editing jobs.

Lucas had to get money from his father to pay the bill, but Coppola later was mad that his assistant confronted Lucas on the matter. "I always believed that that incident was one of the things that pissed George off and caused a breach," said Coppola.

"I needed to go and develop another project; I couldn't rely on Zoetrope to do that for me," Lucas said. "It fell apart."

"I had always regarded George as my heir apparent," Coppola stated. "He'd take over Zoetrope for me while I went out and did my personal films. Everybody utilized Zoetrope to get going, but nobody wanted to stick with it."[25]

"We were gonna be the new Godards and Kurosawas," said Milius. "Francis was gonna lead us. He wanted to ride in the car, but he still was at the head of the parade."[26]

Bob Evans is a man for whom Francis Ford Coppola has no love. Their rivalry, arguments, even wars, are legend in Hollywood circles, the stuff of best sellers and documentaries, the back story for some of the greatest and most controversial movies ever made. But a decision Bob Evans made in 1969 saved Francis Ford Coppola's career, kept him financially solvent, allowed American Zoetrope to live to see another day, and ultimately allowed *Apocalypse Now* to be made. Coppola would dispute much of this, but had Evans not decided in 1969 he needed an Italian director—Coppola was the only one working at the time—then the first seed the director needed to grow his career and company after Warners uprooted it, likely would have withered and been tossed, as the Bible calls it, "to the wayside."

Evans had been made the head honcho at Paramount, and had saved it from oblivion. His option of a little novel made into a small movie starring two unknown actors—Ryan

O'Neal and Ali Macgraw—would become *Love Story* (1970), a cultural phenomenon of the "sexual revolution."

After the failure of *THX 1138* (which was released to theatres in 1971), Zoetrope seemed in big trouble but Coppola told Lucas that Evans offered him to direct *The Godfather*, which he called a $3 million "potboiler" based on a lascivious best seller by Mario Puzo. Lucas told him he had "no choice" but to do it, for him and to save the dream of American Zoetrope.

This premise itself was quite noble and unique to the film-school-ethic Coppola, Lucas, Milius, and the others who had formed in the 1960s, a "one for all, all for one" mentality that is nothing less than quaint in today's world, when actors are paid $20 million for a few months work, when a star athlete unblinkingly leaves his teammates and the dynasty they built together in order to cash in on free agent bucks with a rival team.

For George Lucas, *The Godfather* meant his mentor could funnel money back into his projects. For Coppola, it would have been easy, stars in his eyes, to go off and accept the praise and riches of fame; indeed he did, but to his great credit it was always with the goal of getting back to American Zoetrope and the movies he, Lucas, Ballard, Milius, and others wanted to make together. It would happen in ways that could not be predicted, but Coppola did not abandon his friends. There would be a falling out, some recriminations, some hard feelings, but ultimately he was true to his word.

"He had no way to pay that back, so he took a job directing this Hollywood film called *The Godfather*," said Murch.

"I was offered the possibility of directing *The Godfather* as much as anything because I was young and possibly could do it very cheaply and possibly because I was Italian-American, and when I first read *The Godfather* I thought it was kind of this salacious Irving Wallace or even a Jackie Collins book, and at the bottom didn't have that kind of heart in it, and I didn't want to do it," Coppola said.

Coppola felt it was beneath him, not to mention somebody else's material. "I was into the New Wave and Fellini and, like all the kids of my age, we wanted to make those kinds of films," he explained. "So the book represented the whole kind of idea I was trying to avoid in my life."[27]

With Evans literally coming to the phone Coppola shouted to Lucas, "Should I do this?"

"I don't see any choice here, Francis," Lucas told him. "We're in debt, Warners want their money back, you need a job. I think you should do it. Survival is the key thing here."

"For him, it wasn't really, *Should I do this movie?*" Lucas recalled. "It was, *Can I really accept the fact that the dream of Zoetrope, of this alternative studio, all this stuff we'd been talking about for the last two years—failed*? Because at that point, Zoetrope fell apart.

"Francis was very disappointed when the whole thing collapsed, but he had to pay his debt back."

"It was George Lucas who kept saying, 'Francis you have to do this, we have no money, they're gonna chain up the doors of Zoetrope and we're all gonna be out the door on our ears, and you have to do it,' recalled Coppola.[28]

So Francis Ford Coppola agreed to direct *The Godfather*. Eventually it was Warner Bros. who were paid by Paramount out of *The Godfather* profits, but the good news was that all the scripts Zoetrope developed reverted back to Coppola.

This included *Apocalypse Now*.

7

Shooting Star

Both UCLA and the University of Southern California film programs of the 1960s would produce famed Hollywood legends. Before any of them were household names, however, a film school "failure," Jim Morrison, would ascend to great heights before the world knew the names of any of the others.

Despite the poor reception of his thesis student film, Morrison was awarded a degree from UCLA, although he did not attend the ceremony. His goal to become a director was thwarted by the criticism he received, so he moved to Venice, where he lived a bohemian lifestyle on the "roof top" of Dennis Jacobs's house. There he sat and wrote poetry. Enamored of Irish poets, he continued to drink, often to excess, thinking that was simply what Irish poets do. He wandered by day on the shores of Venice Beach, where beautiful, bikini-clad California girls pranced and tempted countless young beach boys.

This was where Morrison ran into his friend from UCLA, Ray Manzarek, in the summer of 1965, and at Manzarek's urging "sang" his poem "Moonlight Drive," which Manzarek immediately recognized as the best lyrics he had ever heard. Manzarek formed a band with drummer John Densmore, guitarist Robby Krieger, Manzarek on keyboards, and Jim as the vocal front man. A common thread among this group was Transcendental Meditation (TM), popularized at the time by Mahareshi Mahesh Yogi, who would be made famous by The Beatles. Morrison moved in with Manzarek and Ray's girlfriend Dorothy.

The band, named after Aldous Huxley's *The Doors of Perception* (and a William Blake quotation) quickly rose up the ladder on the Sunset Strip musical circuit, until they drew long lines at the Whisky a Go Go. Morrison's incredible good looks—he resembled a Greek god—long flowing hair and seductive voice made him especially popular with young girls. Shy at first, he sang with his back to the crowd and needed to be coerced into facing them, but the reaction of women was immediate and inspirational.

The Doors also made some short films, utilizing their music. Morrison was a prolific poet, most of which was formed into early, original songs. In 1966, two long, mesmerizing songs in particular left audiences spellbound, although they were "strange," making their initial commercial appeal questionable. "When the Music's Over" was long and sensuous, with disturbing lyrics that practically pleaded God to send the singer to the "house of detention," a veiled reference to hell. The go-go dancers would stop gyrating, softly swaying as if in a trance, until the song exploded in an almost violent eruption of Morrisonian exhortation.

Even more disturbing, of course, was "The End" in its final version. Originally a song about the end of a love affair, Morrison's experiences with psychedelic drugs while traipsing around the Southern California desert transformed it into a mournful ode to death, in which Morrison brings the long, tempting lyrics to a heated pitch declaring an Oedipal desire to kill his father and then have sex with his mother. Again the dancers and audience would quiet down, the teeny-boppers would stop grabbing for Jim's body, and all eyes would be on Morrison as he grabbed "a face from the ancient gallery...."

Some of the "gin joints" on the Strip still had mob affiliation, going back to the days of Mickey Cohen and Bugsy Siegel. The Sicilian Mafia is oddly familial and Catholic, a contradiction with their violent methods, but Morrison's exhortations on mounting his own mother was too much. When Whisky owner Phil Tanzini heard it loud and clear he went ballistic.

"You are one foul-mouthed son of a bitch and you are fired!" he screamed at Morrison. "All of you! And don't bother to come back."[1]

It did not matter and The Doors would not have come back even if Tanzini begged them too, because Elektra Records owner Jac Holzman and producer Paul Rothschild offered them a record deal that sent them on their way to fame and fortune.

While Morrison was their main songwriter and front man, The Doors vaulted to the top of the charts on the strength of a fairly light, commercially appealing song written by Krieger called "Light My Fire." Their 1967 debut album remains one of the great debut albums in rock history. It was not just popular commercially, but was received as an anthem of counter-culture angst, a new Los Angeles sound after years of light Beach Boys fare, a worthy follow-up to the British Rock Invasion, which beginning in 1964 had vaulted The Beatles, The Rolling Stones, The Who (and later Zed Zeppelin) to the very heights of musical stardom.

"Light My Fire" led to appearances in San Francisco, which was at the height of the Summer of Love, and New York, where the group played the vaunted *Ed Sullivan Show*. One of the show's producers asked Morrison not to use certain lyrics which connoted drug usage. Morrison refused, emphasizing the word, which led the producer to have a backstage fit declaring the band would "never play *Ed Sullivan* again."

Morrison was a chubby teenager, but after graduating from UCLA and moving to Venice Beach, possibly because he lacked much money and ate little, he lost weight. After the band started, he became vain about his appearance and actually started working out on the "monkey bars" at Venice's famed Muscle Beach outdoor gym.

A fit Morrison posed for a series of iconic, shirtless photos, emphasizing his lean physique, lion's mien of hair, and angelically handsome face. Those photos, today emblazoned like Che Guevara's on T-shirts and imagery worldwide, were as responsible for his mythic place in history as almost any other factor, including their amazing music.

Aside from "The End" and "Light My Fire," an early hit was "Break on Through (To the Other Side)," which audiences took to be a rambunctious, fast-paced rock song when in fact it was based on Morrison's morbid fascination with death, that being the "other side." Nevertheless, it was energetic enough to be considered a dance song that was also highly popular with soldiers fighting in Vietnam. The Doors' 1967 album *Break on Through* was advertised on a huge billboard above the Sunset Strip. "THE DOORS: Break on Through with an electrifying album" read the first rock sign ever on the Strip.

Morrison called himself the "Lizard King," a reference to "the snake" in "The End" that might be viewed as the devil, or God; man's eternal struggle between good and evil. He explained that man must approach the snake, whose scales represent the history of the world, without fear, in order to attain nirvana; to fear the creature would result in its instantly swallowing up the approaching mortal, presumably resulting in death and, possibly, damnation.

"I've always been attracted to ideas that were about revolt against authority—when you make your peace with authority you become an authority," he said at the time. "I like ideas about the breaking away or overthrowing of established order—I am interested in anything about revolt, disorder, chaos, especially activity that seems to have no meaning."[2]

While John Milius and even Ronald Reagan, at the time the controversial reactionary governor of California, held political/cultural views that seemed the polar opposite of Morrison's, both were revolutionaries, even radicals at least within their own spheres. Milius was a huge fan of Morrison's, noting that soldiers—not hippies—were his most loyal audience. He did not sing of love and peace, but rather, as he stated, of "revolt, disorder, chaos." This desire led Morrison, along with other members of his band, to dark explorations of Satanism, which many felt was inculcating itself into rock 'n' roll in that era. The Rolling Stones' "Sympathy for the Devil" and later songs like AC/DC's "Highway to Hell" were very disturbing to Christians. "When the Music's Over" referenced a minister's daughter who was in love with "the snake," which added to other rock band's general imagery of hell as a place where the hot chicks, the best musicians, and the strongest drugs could be found. It was not, to these New Age people, a place of sinful regret and certainly not of fiery torment.

Morrison, raised largely in the Bible Belt, rejected that from an early age and now, with fame and fortune, lacking moral boundaries, he began to flame out like a proverbial "shooting star." He told the press his parents were dead and when his family came to see him perform, he refused to see them.

He had a regular girlfriend who would be considered his common-law wife, Pamela Courson. She was the daughter of a conservative Orange County, California, school principal, but she, too, became embroiled in Morrison's world of drugs and decadence. Morrison had an unending supply of gorgeous women throwing themselves at him. He indulged this activity with enthusiasm, along with bountiful quantities of drugs and alcohol. He lived off and on in a seedy motel, a short, steep hike south of Sunset Boulevard, called the Alta Cienega.

After their first hit album, The Doors produced more popular songs and successful albums. "Back Door Man," an old blues tune, was modernized to emphasize Jim's urge for anal sex with women. "Five to One" referred to the number of anarchic protestors living in the city limits of Los Angeles, compared to the number of people with guns who were prepared to use them when a civil war, ostensibly a race war, would inevitably begin. This dark vision was also the impetus for Charles Manson's ordering of the slaughter of innocents in 1969, in order to start just such a "war."

Most of the work did not quite reach the level of their early music. This was partly due to Morrison's Ruthian appetites for life. He became self-indulgent and petulant, and the band argued. By 1969 he had grown a full beard and was overweight. He no longer posed as the sexy front man. In a concert held in Miami, Florida, Morrison arrived in a highly intoxicated state. Amid much angst and internal arguments, Morrison finally appeared before a huge, impatient crowd and began to pepper them with insults based on his unhappy personal memories of growing up in Florida.

He interrupted several songs and finally harangued the crowd with threats that he would expose himself, and finally—maybe—took the dare. To this date, whether Morrison exposed himself or not is in dispute, but he was arrested for indecent exposure and charged by the Dade County prosecutor. He was eventually convicted and sentenced to six months in jail, which was suspended pending appeal. This sentencing would hang over his—and the band's—head until his death.

Incredibly, The Doors made a magnificent comeback with "L.A. Woman" (1971), which featured two of the band's most famed songs, "Riders on the Storm" and "L.A. Woman." Both songs reflected deep aspects of The Doors' persona. "Riders" again explored dark philosophical questions, using the metaphor of picking up a hitchhiker as a choice between life and death, just as the fear or lack of it in facing "the snake" in "The End" determined one's eternal destiny.

"L.A. Woman" sounded to many people like a hard rock, post–California Girls *paean* to slutty Sunset Strip sex dolls, but it was not. Inspired by Morrison's Apocalyptic vision of Los Angeles when he returned from a trip, only to see the Hollywood Hills ablaze, it was based partly on the 1969 Manson family murders, with Morrison wailing on about the changing of the mood from "glad to sadness." Over time, this has become the parable ending of the 1960s, when love and freedom seemed possible, only to end in the spread of HIV. The Who's "Won't Get Fooled Again" was a direct reference to the failed promises of the 1960s, based on their bad experience at Woodstock.

The final lyrics are his ode of love to his adopted hometown, which he saw as a lonely, desperate, painted woman he loved no matter how much she cheated, or let him down; no matter her faults, he would be loyal to Los Angeles.

While this song lacks the sentimentality of Frank Sinatra singing "Theme from New York, New York" or "My Kind of Town (Chicago Is)," or of Tony Bennett crooning, "(I Left My Heart) In San Francisco," it remains a song not only symbolic of rollicking L.A., but even forms, along with the movies and The Beach Boys in some minds, with the building of the Rose Bowl, the Coliseum, the arrival of the Olympics, the Dodgers and Dodger Stadium, as a sign that this was now a "Major League" city.

With "L.A. Woman" still selling well and playing on the radio, Morrison and Pamela left for Paris, where the poet/singer planned to write and devote himself to the classical arts that he had gravitated to in his youth. Then, in July of 1971, Morrison died in his Paris bath tub. The cause of death was never officially determined, as Pamela refused to allow an autopsy of his body. It could have been a heroin overdose, a heart attack, or just his body giving out under years of alcohol and drug abuse. He was twenty-seven.

Morrison's death culminated in a tragic threesome, coming on the heels of drug overdoses by Janis Joplin and Jimi Hendrix. It symbolized rock excess. There was a certain amount of "glamour" associated with dying young. Morrison joined the likes of James Dean and Marilyn Monroe, those who left beautiful corpses behind, captured only by iconic poster images.

But The Doors had no future without him. They tried to keep the band together for a few years, but without Morrison they were just three more musicians. The great English bands—The Stones, The Who, Zeppelin, Clapton, and others—dominated music into the 1970s. American music changed, the era of "day on the green" concerts played in huge multi-sport stadiums now featuring Aerosmith, The Eagles, Van Halen, and the like.

Sales for Doors songs plummeted. The band became relegated to a second tier of excellent but nostalgic musical groups such as The Byrds, Buffalo Springfield, and Steppenwolf.

Like a shooting star, Morrison had flamed out and died. "Jim Morrison's death in Paris in July 1971 was the *coup de grace* for the American '60s," wrote Morrison biographer Stephen Davis. "'Let's change the mood from glad to sadness' had accurately predicted the fading of communitarian '60s ideas—protest, reform, emotional intensity, the intransigence of nature, the expansion of consciousness—into the harsher realities of the '70s."

But Morrison's music was not to be forgotten. It was remembered by Vietnam veterans, who favored it above all others when they did their tours "in country." It was remembered by John Milius, who knew many of those veterans and heard them talk about listening to The Doors. Finally, it was remembered by Francis Ford Coppola, a fellow UCLA film student who still wanted to make a Vietnam movie, and needed the perfect theme to capture its meaning.

8

Patton

Because John Milius was such a war hawk, a conservative patriot through and through, who was highly influenced in his youth by General George S. Patton's autobiography (*War As I knew It*), based on his voluminous wartime diaries, it would seem a natural that it was Milius who wrote the screenplay for *Patton* (1970). It was not. It was instead a dove, a liberal, who wrote it as an anti-war screed. That writer was Milius's good friend Francis Ford Coppola.

The film, however, is anything but an anti-war screed. It is considered a favorite among military officers, shown regularly at West Point, at boot camps, wherever the "gung-ho" gather, and each Memorial Day weekend. How did it go from what Coppola originally intended to what it actually became?

The answer to that question may not be entirely known, but the recollections of a USC football player named Charles "Tree" Young leads one to an exploration with threads tying it to John Wayne, a Trojans assistant football coach named Marv Goux, USC film student Ron Schwary … and maybe, just maybe, John Milius.

General George S. Patton was America's most flamboyant and controversial general. A West Point graduate and decorated World War I hero for his actions on the battlefields of France, he was the honored protégé of General "Black Jack" Pershing. But after the war, General Douglas MacArthur rose to the greatest prominence in the peacetime army. His protégé was Dwight Eisenhower. Eisenhower and General George C. Marshall were favored, especially by liberal elements, after the election of President Franklin Roosevelt. Patton was a conservative Republican of Southern aristocracy, although he was born and raised in Southern California. He despised, and warned of the threat, of international Communism.

In World War II he achieved stunning victories in North Africa, Sicily, France, the Battle of the Bulge, and in the drive straight into the heart of Nazi Germany. He quarreled with Eisenhower, had a rivalry with British general Sir Bernard Law Montgomery, was disciplined for slapping a soldier, and outraged Democrats with his stance against Soviet Communism.

The press loved him and the American public adored him, but he was killed in a questionable auto accident in 1945, leading to endless speculation that the U.S. or the Soviets killed him because of his desire to defeat the U.S.S.R. in another war, and end Communism forever.

A former military officer, Frank McCarthy, became a Hollywood producer and desired to bring Patton's story to the big screen, but the Patton family resisted, feeling liberals would destroy his reputation. They refused to cooperate. Twentieth Century–Fox honcho Darryl F. Zanuck wanted to make the film, but without the family's blessing the project stalled.

Finally, in 1962, Zanuck produced *The Longest Day*, a successful depiction of the Normandy invasion, and landed its star, John "Duke" Wayne, to play the Patton role. The success of *The Longest Day* and involvement of the world's most popular movie star gave Zanuck confidence that the film could be made even without the family supporting it. McCarthy originally hired novelist Calder Willingham, who had worked on two war films from 1957: Stanley Kubrick's *Paths of Glory* and David Lean's *The Bridge on the River Kwai*. He was given *Patton: Ordeal and Triumph*, a recently written biography of the general by historian Ladislas Farago, which was under option. Patton's own autobiography was not used, as it, along with the Patton family's consent, legal or otherwise, was not obtained. There were, however, some legal problems with Farago's book, delaying the project. Zanuck wanted hot director John Frankenheimer (*The Manchurian Candidate*, *Seven Days in May*), but Willingham's screenplay made up too many facts, especially in the early North Africa scenes that were key to developing who the man was and what kind of challenges he and the nation faced in the early days of the war. He missed the deadline, delaying the project further.

"There is no story in Farago's book and there are not any dramatic scenes in it," Willingham wrote in a memo to McCarthy. "The truth is that the studio is paying Farago for a very high-class research job; there is no 'property' in this book, and there is no picture in it—you have only two raw materials of a property and a picture."[1]

Willingham's treatment had many imaginary scenes that set the basis for the general theme of a feature, but McCarthy, who knew Patton's story well, rejected many scenes as overly dramatized events. He felt the truth of Patton's huge victories in battle, combined with actual depictions of his swagger, were enough and did not need to be falsified. Willingham, the novelist, argued that he was an "artist" and had "license" to make up scenes based on his personal vision; that a movie like a painting was not a slave to historical fact as was Farago's rather dry biography.[2]

McCarthy decided to hire another writer. Willingham seemed relieved not to have his option renewed. McCarthy and Zanuck struggled to find a screenwriter who could capture Patton's unique blend of swagger and religious ethics.

They eventually settled on Francis Ford Coppola, who only recently had come out of the UCLA film school, to write a new version of the screenplay. He had won a Samuel Goldwyn Writing Award at UCLA and had written unproduced scripts for Seven Arts Productions, but had been hired to direct a war film called *Is Paris Burning?* (1966). McCarthy thought his time in France developing that movie gave Coppola some sense for war in Europe.

He had never served in the military and had no military background or affinity for war, but this was seen, in a move that hindsight revealed to be brilliant, to be a plus. If John Milius or some "gung-ho" screenwriter had tackled this project, it would have been jingoistic and "rah-rah." McCarthy and Zanuck wanted patriotism, but they wanted Patton's flaws and unique traits, such as his fascination with reincarnation, to give nuance to his character, rather than portray him as a comic book-type hero.

"He arrived with a full beard," McCarthy said of meeting Coppola. "I wouldn't say exactly a hippie. He had more of a Bolshevik look than anything else." In the early 1960s, beards were thought of as beat symbols, something out of Allen Ginsberg and the San Francisco North Beach scene to which Coppola gravitated. Coppola was twenty-six years old in 1965. He chose to watch Sergei Eisenstein's *October: Ten Days That Shook the World* (1928), based on John Reed's admiring description of Soviet Communism, as his "inspiration" for Patton. This was certainly a strange inspiration, considering his subject was a virulent anti–Communist, but Coppola seemed to sense right away the man he was writing about was multi-dimensional and needed to be approached that way. McCarthy called him "the most impressive young writer I have met in years," adding, "He is standing on the edge of a great screenwriting career. Of all the writers [with whom] I have discussed Patton, he impresses me as having the best potential."

Coppola was given *Patton: Ordeal and Triumph* along with lengthy material, which he worked on closely with McCarthy. Farago's book was no more dramatic for Coppola than it was for Willingham, but Coppola was a much more talented and intuitive screenwriter than the novelist.

"We had a history lesson every day," said McCarthy. He also gave Coppola an article Major General James Gavin wrote about how General Eisenhower had to hold both Patton and General Bernard Montgomery back, and was not able to give either one all the resources they wanted.

General Omar Bradley also began to emerge as a hero. McCarthy admired him and liked this approach. Slowly, but surely, began the formation of a more colorful, and highly interesting, portrait of the general as a man and commander: the rivalry with the Englishman Monty; Patton's enigmatic personality; his strained relationship with Dwight Eisenhower, the younger man who found need to discipline him; his odd, yet effective, collaboration with Bradley; and his admiration of George Marshall, who is never actually shown.

At the core of Coppola's study of his subject was Patton as a "war lover." In this regard, he saw Patton as unbalanced. Coppola wanted to undermine the idea of war. America was now knee-deep in the rice paddies of Vietnam, and he wanted to create a polemic that would make audiences sit up and say, "Hey, let's give peace a chance." On the other hand, Patton was an odd relic of American history, the sort of "trigger happy" militarist the nation kept in the closet, but trotted out and told to save its behind—like William Sherman and U.S. Grant before him—when the rubber hit the road and he was needed, as when Adolf Hitler tried to take over the world.

"I said, 'Wait a minute, this guy was obviously nuts,'" recalled Coppola. "If they want to make a film glorifying him as a great American hero, it will be laughed at. And if I write a film that condemns him, it won't be made at all."

Coppola was paid $50,000 to write *Patton*. He worked on it for six months. The key scene was the opening monologue, well known to film buffs, in which a be-medaled Patton stands before a huge American flag and delivers a stirring address to unseen troops before a battle that is not identified.

"I wrote that first scene by combining several of Patton's speeches," said Coppola. "At first, some of the executives at Fox thought the script was too 'strange,' and they objected to that opening, among other things."[3]

Zanuck figured on cooperation from the United States Department of Defense (DoD). *The Battle of the Bulge* was playing in theatres and doing well, but not very well. They wanted something beyond the run-of-the-mill war picture.

Coppola left the project in February of 1966. By then John Huston was discussed as director. John Frankenheimer had left. Huston wanted to do a rewrite. Coppola was offered to direct *You're a Big Boy Now*. McCarthy and Zanuck agreed to release him. In later years Coppola said he was fired, but this was not so. He claimed the opening sequence was the reason.

> Now, all you young people bear note that the things that you are fired for are often the things in later life that you are celebrated and given lifetime achievements for.
>
> That's one of the things that made me realize that things that get you in trouble are usually things you are remembered for. They brought in another writer—a fine screenwriter named Edmund North—but he pretty much added some additional battle scenes and didn't change the strange parts that *Patton* is remembered for, such as the beginning and the ending.
>
> I had nothing to do with evolving the character the way George C. Scott played him. The script I wrote was very much like *parts* of the film. You know the beginning, which was sort of more stylized with this character way out in the foreground. That was the opening of the original script, but more of my script was that way....
>
> I wrote the first scene by combining several of Patton's speeches. The first draft was more "bloodthirsty" than what audiences saw.[4]

"At the time, the speech was not a matter in dispute," wrote Nicholas Sarantakes in *Making Patton*.

"He wrote a very imaginative script," said McCarthy. "He really wrote a wonderful script."

Zanuck felt it was "sprawling, at times confusing," but "very promising ... a remarkable first draft."[5]

As Coppola developed the screenplay and the producers began to see a more fully developed characterization, the film, long on the back burner, began to build momentum towards actual production. The family was still not on board, but a key element was added when the cooperation of Omar Bradley was obtained. Bradley's character was a very prominent aspect of Coppola's script. He was portrayed in a positive light. He had written a book, *A Soldier's Story*, and had worked more closely with Patton than any other World War II commander, including Eisenhower, Marshall, or Montgomery.

Getting rights to *A Soldier's Story* in addition to *Patton: Ordeal and Triumph* gave Twentieth Century–Fox greater legal claim to Patton's story rights, and less need to obtain his family's permission. Bradley's wife was a screenwriter, so he had tangential association with the film industry, anyway. He was still alive, of course, and able to do publicity to promote the film. His imprimatur as a bona fide war hero with a reputation as a sensible, levelheaded general, would give great credence to the movie. His own relationship with Patton somewhat mirrored the complicated narrative Coppola painted. He certainly admired General Patton, and considered him a friend, but they had sparred, he had disagreed with him, and they did not see eye to eye on war. This is exemplified by a classic scene in which Patton invites Bradley to accompany him so they can bathe in the glory of a hard-fought victory in Sicily. Patton, against Bradley's advice, sent his troops into a major fight resulting in heavy casualties. Patton sees only the victory; Bradley sees the cost. "There's one big difference between you and me, George," Bradley says. "I do this job because I've been trained to do it. You do it because you LOVE it."

McCarthy and Zanuck discussed Bradley as a narrator. As Bradley's influence began to deepen, other changes began to come into play. First, John Wayne dropped out of the project. Wayne said the role was "too tough" to get a handle on Patton's character. Wayne was still a star, but much had changed since 1962, when *The Longest Day* glorified D–Day. The United States was now in Vietnam, and public opinion about war was changing greatly. Certainly, Wayne's version of patriotism was becoming diluted by Vietnam and reaction to the Blacklist, when the Duke played a major role in uprooting communists (and alleged communists) in the movie industry, to great resentment by liberals. These forces were prompting him to plan his own film, *The Green Berets*, which he would produce and direct in 1968. That film was a box-office hit, but critics hated it as pure jingoism. It certainly does not stand the test of time as does *Patton*. It is obvious, therefore, that Wayne was not the right man to play the general.

McCarthy and Zanuck then went after Burt Lancaster. This seemed to make sense, especially since they wanted John Frankenheimer to direct. Lancaster had starred as a general some might have compared to Patton in Frankenheimer's 1964 classic *Seven Days in May*. He was certainly more iconoclastic and character-driven than Duke Wayne. Lancaster had originally liked Willingham's script, although when he met with Coppola he was impressed with the young screenwriter, too. The Lancaster-Frankenheimer involvement had the effect of pushing *Patton* to the front burner after years of languishing in what is called "development hell" at Twentieth Century–Fox.

But movie politics continued to rear their head. Lancaster wanted more say in the film, a producer's credit not just in name but in influence. His friend Kirk Douglas had produced the highly acclaimed *Spartacus* (1960), and Lancaster wanted that kind of power for himself. Lancaster also wanted his title role heightened at the expense of Bradley's character, although he did want Bradley to weigh in. Bradley himself wanted to influence the film to his liking, as a protector of history and his own sterling reputation.

But terms could never be agreed to with either Frankenheimer or Lancaster. Both dropped out of the project. A director was found, however, who seemed perfect for the subject. Franklin Schaffner, a genteel, old school fellow, had directed the highly successful *The Planet of the Apes* starring Charlton Heston. On top of that, he had served in an operation under Patton in North Africa. He admired Patton and was no Hollywood liberal. No matter what undertones Francis Ford Coppola might have subversively written into the screenplay, Schaffner *was not* going to make an anti–Patton picture.

But the entire project was turned on its head when Zanuck was essentially fired by his own son, Richard, as head of Twentieth Century–Fox. This was the frenetic late 1960s, when Gulf+Western bought Paramount, when Warner Bros. went corporate, and now one of the great moguls ever lost a struggle with his own son. It could be viewed as the end of the studio system.

Finally, and unexpectedly, came the last and most important piece of the puzzle: George C. Scott. Scott himself was as complicated as Patton. He was certainly not the seemingly impenetrable American hero John Wayne was. He was an ex-marine who considered himself a pacifist. He was a raging alcoholic who had physically beaten Ava Gardner, with whom he had an affair, on the set of *The Bible*. He was utterly brilliant as General Buck Turgidson in *Dr. Strangelove* (1964), but that was a comedic role. In later years people could see much of the Patton character in Turgidson; his voice and bombastic personality, but at the time this was not how people thought of George S. Patton. The real Patton's voice had a lilting Southern quality to it, despite his California upbringing. It was almost squeaky.

But Scott identified with Coppola's screenplay. Young Richard Zanuck's vision was on par with Scott's and Coppola's. Scott decided to make him a "man out of his time, a pathetic hero, a Don Quixote figure...."

"The people who wanted to see him as a bad guy could say, 'He was crazy, he loved war.' The people who wanted to see him as a good guy could say, 'We need a man like that now.' And that's exactly the effect the movie had, which is why it was so successful."[6]

That and incorporation of Bradley's book, giving the film a life Farago's tome did not, are credited with turning it into a classic, but above all other factors is Scott's magnificent opening scene, as iconic a movie image as anything before or since, including the likes of Vivien Leigh being spurned by Clark Gable, or Marlon Brando yelling, "STELLA!"

Incredibly, it almost never happened. Scott objected to it, saying it took all the drama out of the picture. It was a huge, powerhouse scene filled with mental war imagery and patriotic fervor, but he thought it should come at the end; it would suck all the energy out of subsequent scenes, none of which could match it. Coppola did not write the script that way. His screenplay called for something that was the opposite of Roman glory, a great processional with the victorious commander laden with praise. Instead, his Patton is quietly relieved, says goodbye to his aides, and walks into the sunset while quoting an ironic Latin phrase: "All glory is fleeting." Eventually, Scott was talked into doing it at the beginning.

"I was playing with a presentational style—the idea that you have a character just stand in front of the audience for five minutes, and the audience would know more about him just by looking at him than if you went into his past and told about his family life," Coppola recalled. "That's why the best part of that film, in my opinion, is the ending scene. It was the best scene in my script too."

Scott "worked six months on that script," said Coppola. "It was a pretty definitive script. But there was a big time lag.... They had re-written my script many times and thrown it out and got different writers." Scott "remembered my script and told them that he would do it if they could use the old script. Scott is the one who resurrected my version."[7]

Indeed, while Coppola's screenplay was considered brilliant and gave momentum to the project, he had been removed from the process and, after several unsuccessful directorial efforts, moved to San Francisco to form Zoetrope and make independents away from the meddling influence of Hollywood studios. However, his skills were still needed, in an unexpected way.

Growing up, Coppola had always worked with electronics. He loved technology. As he went through UCLA and then worked on films, he always involved himself in every aspect of filmmaking: editing, camera work, acquiring knowledge of the equipment needed to make a movie. Over time he had developed a special editing machine. He learned how to make it while attending a film seminar in Europe, and created a machine he could use at Zoetrope, instead of buying expensive equipment from studios.

Now, Twentieth Century–Fox was using one of his editing machines. With *Patton* in post-production, the machine broke down. Nobody knew how to fix it. A call was made to San Francisco. Coppola agreed to fly to Los Angeles and fix the machine. He arrived at the editing bays and started to work on the machine. On a screen overhead footage from *Patton* played; George C. Scott in uniform, bellowing orders and so forth. This caught Coppola's eye. He recognized the dialogue and asked somebody what it was. He was told it was *Patton*, slated for a 1970 release as one of the studio's big upcoming pictures.

So far had Francis Ford Coppola removed himself from the doings of big Hollywood, not to mention how little influence the screenwriter is allowed to have unless he directs, that he did not know until then this movie was being made for sure.

For Twentieth Century–Fox, the Zanucks and Frank McCarthy, having labored since 1952 to get *Patton* made, the timing of its release might have convinced them they were cursed. It could not possibly have been released at a worse time. Richard Nixon had been elected President in 1968 by promising a "secret plan" to end the Vietnam War, but by 1970 it was still raging, the anti-war protestors were out in force, calling it "Nixon's war," and there was no end in sight. Support for the war, the kind of people who might look at a film such as *Patton* and declare, "That's the kind of man we need in Vietnam," was dwindling to the point where they were much less likely to believe *anybody* could turn that quagmire into victory.

If indeed Coppola wrote a subversive anti-war screed, Schaffner, McCarthy, and Edmund North added enough admiration for Patton and American patriotism that it could not succeed as an anti-war box-office smash like *MASH*, which came out the same year. They were releasing, not a pro-war movie, but a film that dared to admire the traits of military valor that were being spit upon by protestors at that very time.

That was not all. Despite buying books by Farrago and General Bradley, plus securing Bradley's cooperation with publicity, the Patton family prepared a lawsuit, which they were prepared to file the day after the film premiered. But the movie's trailers were very compelling and the film more so; audiences formed lines all across the country to see it, it immediately drew raves, and the next day the Patton lawsuit was quietly removed. They had gone to a theatre, saw it, and loved it like everybody else.

Scott gave one of the finest performances in screen history and the movie was immediately declared the best war picture ever; better than *From Here to Eternity* or *The Longest Day* or any other contender. To this day most experts would still rate it at this level; it has never lost its attraction or audience, and is one of those films that people see while channel-surfing, then just put their device away, settled in with their entertainment for the evening. It won eight Academy Awards, and its musical theme, composed and delivered by Jerry Goldsmith, an alumnus of the University of Southern California, was without competition among stirring movie sounds.

"The North African tank battle is surely the finest battle featuring mechanized weaponry ever put on the screen," wrote Robert K. Johnson in his 1977 book, *Francis Ford Coppola*.

"McCarthy and Schaffner had either presence or blind luck.... They commissioned a screenplay by Francis Ford Coppola and Edmund H. North that emphasizes the contradictions of their hero," wrote Stanley Kauffman. Famed critic Rex Reed said Patton "was religious yet profane, brutal yet he easily moved to tears. He was so flamboyant and theatrical that he even went so far as to design the uniforms of his tank crewmen ... he firmly believed he was reincarnated." Reed then added, "fortunately, the script for *Patton* is so well-researched and brilliantly thought out that it examines both the faults and the virtues of the man without leaning too heavily in either direction."

"The movie ... is huge, initially ambivalent but finally adoring," wrote Vincent Canby of the *New York Times*. "[It is a] pop portrait of one of the most brilliant and outrageous American military figures of the past 100 years."

Joseph Morgenstern wrote, "Though seductive and constantly entertaining, it is the muddled glorification of a madman." He added: "Time and again Patton is portrayed as a deceitful, self-justifying megalomaniac, who can't follow orders. Yet the movie makes shrewd, sentimental capital of the soldier-slapping incident and Patton's subsequent fall from favor.... The closer Patton comes to lunacy, the more the movie encourages us to laugh at him as a lovable, irascible old coot who can't understand politics and can't keep his tactless mouth shut."[8]

* * *

Marv Goux was one of the gladiators in Stanley Kubrick's *Spartacus*. Every gladiator in that film was either a USC or UCLA football player. The tragic Draba character was played by ex-UCLA receiver Woody Strode. Goux himself had played at USC before becoming an assistant coach on John McKay's staff, effectively ending his "acting" career.

But Goux "kept his hand in" by paraphrasing Kirk Douglas's speech in that film ("I'd rather be here, a free man among brothers, facing a long march and a hard fight ... than live as a slave") in fiery pre-game speeches to the Trojan football team.

Around 1966 he started to change his speech. His players became very familiar with it. Goux also took the team to movies the Friday night before games. Coach McKay told him he did not want the guys seeing *Easy Rider*, he preferred John Wayne Westerns and war pictures. In 1970, Goux took the team to see *Patton*.

One of those players was Charles "Tree" Young, an All-American tight end who is in the College Football Hall of Fame and played with Joe Montana on the 1984 Super Bowl champion San Francisco 49ers. After the film, Young looked at some of his teammates with a funny expression on his face. Among them was wide receiver Bob Chandler, running back Sam "Bam" Cunningham, and lineman Allan Graf, today a respected second-unit director known for his work on football movies like *Any Given Sunday* and *Friday Night Lights*.

"Am I crazy, or did the stuff that cat Patton was saying sound like what Coach Goux has been saying to us for the past two or three years?" Young asked the group.

The others looked at one another and lights seemed to turn on in their heads. *Yes*, that was *exactly* what Marv Goux had been saying to them for several years now. Sure, Coach Goux had paraphrased Kirk Douglas from a movie he had personally appeared in, but how did he know what George C. Scott was going to say in the opening monologue of *Patton* ... prior to the release of *Patton*?

Goux had used phrases like "going through the enemy like crap through a goose," and "using their living guts to clean our cleats," and "putting your hand in some blood where your teammate had fallen, and then you'll know what to do." All of this anticipated Scott's opening speech. Had he seen Coppola's screenplay and memorized it? Was this just coincidence?[9]

Well, after starring for Darryl Zanuck in *The Longest Day*, Wayne was slated for the lead in *Patton*, which was delayed largely due to legal issues with the Patton family. It stands to reason that Wayne studied and researched George S. Patton. This specific language is not found in Farrago's book or Patton's diaries. Francis Ford Coppola claimed it was found in various speeches he made, but the evidence to support this is sketchy at best.

At some point, Wayne dropped out of the *Patton* project and concentrated on making *The Green Berets*. Whether this decision had been made in September of 1966, when USC played Texas, is uncertain, but would not matter; he would have been researching the general and either found the language in his research or come up with it on his own.

Around nine o'clock the USC coaches, including John McKay and Marv Goux, returned from a movie, reportedly *El Dorado* starring the Duke, and met Wayne in person at the party. It is distinctly possible that Goux heard this war language directly from Duke.

The next day, Coach McKay asked his student manager, Ron Schwary, to attend to Wayne's needs as he spoke to the Trojans before the game. There are differing reports on whether he used the war language in this speech or not, but Goux was definitely there. USC won the game, and afterward Wayne came through on a promise he made to Schwary, a film student himself, to help him break into the business. He later won Academy Awards for producing *Tootsie* and *Ordinary People*.

So how does this get into Coppola's screenplay? Schwary was friends with John Milius, a USC film student in 1966. Milius was a self-professed right-wing conservative, a huge John Wayne fan who saw *The Searchers* "hundreds of times," and was a war buff who had read everything he could get on George S. Patton since his youth.

Did Schwary tell Milius of John Wayne's fiery speech, and did he further tell him that Marv Goux was "channeling" Wayne in Friday speeches to the USC football team? Did he, as student manager, sneak Milius into the old gym on campus to hear Goux's speeches with his own ears, and take notes?

If so, then what? Well, Milius knew Francis Ford Coppola. He, Lucas, and Coppola would shortly team up to try and make *Apocalypse Now* as *cinéma vérité* in Vietnam, then with Zoetrope. Could Milius have told Coppola something like, "Hey, I heard Marv Goux make these great war speeches he heard from John Wayne, who may have come up with it while researching George Patton … and you should put it in your *Patton* screenplay"?

Reportedly, by 1966–67, Coppola was finished writing *Patton*, was on to directing films like *Is Paris Burning?*, *You're a Big Boy Now*, *The Rain People*, and *Finian's Rainbow*, but could he have done a last polish and given it to Frank McCarthy? Or could Milius, who, by the late 1960s, was firmly established as a young screenwriter in the industry, have given the language to somebody involved in the project? After all, he was never given credit for *Dirty Harry* despite writing some of its best lines, including, "Do you feel lucky?"

Finally, one last thread. In 1958, John Wayne, at the request of President Dwight Eisenhower, attended a U.S.-Soviet "friendship conference" in which he actually *got drunk* with Soviet Premier Nikita Khrushchev, and threatened to slug the Communist for offering a toast to the "domination of the world by the Soviet Union." The interpreter told Wayne he could not tell Khrushchev, whom Wayne called "Mr. Iron Curtain Pants," that Wayne was threatening him. Fans of *Patton* read this and immediately identify its similarity with a scene at the end of *Patton* when Scott's character tells the Russian, "I do not care to drink with him, or any other Russian son of a bitch." Only this time he insists the interpreter tell the general this "word for word."[10]

Again, this scene is not in *Patton: Ordeal and Triumph*, nor in any other known research. Coppola has never really stated where he got it. Was it artistic license? Or did somebody, like John Wayne or John Milius or Ron Schwary, come upon Wayne, a USC alumnus who may have spent time researching the subject at USC and also at the USC film school, hear the Khrushchev story, and get it to Coppola to use in his script?

The threads are too numerous and, frankly, almost make sense, but the mystery remains. It is, however, a fascinating bit of Hollywood trivia that could make a worthy movie or documentary on its own merit.

9

"That was like raising a red flag in front of a young bull"

Joseph Conrad's *Heart of Darkness* was published in 1902. It was based on his experiences working for a Belgian company, in which he managed a boat that operated on a river in the Belgian Congo, ferrying the goods harvested from the jungle for trade. Belgium was still a royal European power at the height of the Industrial Revolution. Most major European countries had colonies in Africa and around the world.

Conrad's novel was unusual at a time in which most writers were pro-establishment colonialists. Rudyard Kipling was a cheerleader for the British Empire. There were exceptions. Fyodor Dostoevsky's works were considered subversive by the Russian monarchy. Charles Dickens bridged social sensibilities. Mark Twain took a stance against racism. Upton Sinclair advocated Socialism.

Conrad was Polish but had learned to write in English. His book, a very short novel, earned some early praise but was not a huge success. It was somewhat esoteric. In essence it was the first-person observations of Charles Marlow, mostly in anticipation of his meeting with Mr. Kurtz, an ivory trader of high ideals, stationed at the end of the river. Kurtz's intellectualism and humanity, meant to enlighten the native population, backfire and he turns to pagan savagery. Like F. Scott Fitzgerald's *The Great Gatsby*, its meaning and message was not plainly spelled out, certainly not the way Dickens advocated Christian love of his fellow man, Sinclair for government regulation of commerce, or Twain's common sense.

Like *The Great Gatsby*, *Heart of Darkness* gained a following over a period of decades and was aided by two world wars in which large numbers of servicemen of different nations needed something to read. They liked its short length. After World War II, its anti-colonialist message was well received. Liberal educators and classicists thought it a telling tale of white racism that needed to be taught.

In 1938, Orson Welles did *Heart of Darkness* for his famed *Mercury Theatre on the Air* radio broadcasts. Welles read Conrad's words, dripping with drama and heavy anticipation of the confrontation with Kurtz, complete with harrowing sound effects depicting the jungle savagery. Conrad's allegories were masterful, captured perfectly by the eleoquence of Welles.

> Imagine the feelings of a skipper of a fine frigate or a boat; a civilized man, traveling to the very end of the world, in a swamp, march in the woods, and in some inland post feel the savagery, the utter *savagery*, that stirs in the forest, the jungles, in the hearts of wild men.
>
> It's like traveling back to the earliest beginning of the world, when vegetation rioted on the Earth, and the big trees were kings. Millions of trees; massive, immense, running up high and at their foot, running up against the bank against the stream, in the river, the begrimed steamboat, like a sluggish beetle, crawling on the floor of a lofty portico … for me, it crawled toward Kurtz.

> The river, crowded with memories of men and ships, hunters of gold and treasures of fame, greatness has not flowed on the ebb of that river to the mystery of an unknown origin. The dreams of men, the seed of commonwealth, the germs of empires. The river is black tonight my friends. It seems to lead into the heart of an immense darkness.[1]

"In 1939 Orson Welles planned to make *Heart of Darkness*, his first motion picture," said Eleanor Coppola on her acclaimed 1991 documentary, *Hearts of Darkness: A Filmmaker's Apocalypse*. "*Heart of Darkness* is the story of a ship captain's journey up the Congo River to find Mr. Kurtz, an ivory trader stationed deep in the jungle. A brilliant man of high ideals, he intends to enlighten the natives, but succumbs to the primal temptation of the jungle, and goes insane. Screen tests were done with Welles as Kurtz. But the studio backed away from the project, fearing the elaborate production would go over budget. Welles made *Citizen Kane* instead. *Heart of Darkness* was abandoned in pre-production."

Made famous by his *War of the Worlds* broadcast that had many in New Jersey thinking a real Martian invasion was taking place, Welles was in demand by Hollywood. The costs of an extravagant river and jungle set proved daunting, so his first project, *Heart of Darkness*, was deemed too expensive and difficult. Capturing the essence of the novel's allegories and messages was thought too hard for a movie, as was the feeling for *The Great Gatsby*. After it was scrapped Welles concentrated on making *Citizen Kane*, based on controversial publisher William Randolph Hearst.

Other producers proposed a film adaptation, but always they were told no, that it was too ambitious a project and would land the filmmakers in an allegorical jungle. One of Francis Ford Coppola's classmates at UCLA, Carroll Ballard, contemplated trying to write and direct *Heart of Darkness*, and even joined the American Zoetrope crew, but it was nothing more than an idea in his mind. Applicable copyright laws had expired, making it easy enough to adapt the novel without paying Conrad's heirs or estate.

Enter John Milius. A loner and misfit, he spent his life reading the classics. He loved solitary, spiritual endeavors like surfing. When his father sent him to a Colorado high school to get him "away from the beach," he took to the mountain life with full force.[2] It was during this time that he read *Heart of Darkness*. He identified with the jungle, which he came to see resembled the mountains and forest he was living in at the time. He viewed the story as one of man vs. nature, and of man vs. his own sinful nature.

He entered the University of Southern California film school, where he was quickly recognized as a talent with special emphasis on writing, especially character and dialogue. He took a screenwriting class from a crusty old Hollywood pro named Irwin Blacker, who told old film tales. Blacker was very tough on his students, wanting them to recognize the rejection they certainly would face in the business, but Milius was his favorite. He saw great promise in him.

"That started at cinema school," Milius told John Andrew Gallagher in *Film Directors on Directing*, of *Apocalypse Now*. "Lucas and I were great connoisseurs of the Vietnam War. As a matter of fact, I wanted to go to Vietnam but I had asthma and couldn't get in anything. I was the only person I knew who *wanted* to join the Army. George and I would talk about the battles and what a great movie it would make. He loved it because of all the technology, the helicopters, air strikes by Phantoms, the night vision scopes and devices to detect people walking around at night, and I loved the idea of a war being fought that way. Of course, we hadn't lost it then, so it was a little easier to be interested in it. We wanted a scene where the guys are doped out of their minds and they call in an air strike on themselves. We'd come up with all these things. They'd filter into my head and we always wanted to do it. I had the title, *Apocalypse Now*, because the hippies at the time had these buttons that said 'Nirvana Now.' I loved the idea of a guy having a button with a mushroom cloud on it that said 'Apocalypse Now.' You know, let's bring it on, full nuke. Ever hear the Randy Newman song, 'Let's Drop the Big One Now?' That's the spirit that it started in right there."[3]

One day Milius asked Blacker if anybody had ever tried to make *Heart of Darkness*. No, the professor said, it had never been made because it was impossible to make. Orson Welles had tried. Others had tried. It was too daunting, too expensive to re-create the jungle, to shoot on a moving boat on water, or capture the story's essence. Milius recounted,

> I was going to USC, and I was the guy who wrote everything in my class. I knew I was gonna be a writer. And I remember all the while the war was going on I kept thinking what a great movie this would make, and this kind of thing. My number one writing class, there was a real tough old guy, Irwin Blacker, and Mr. Blacker would teach you the forms, where the text went before the day, and if there was any mistake in the form, if you didn't say where the text was, he'd flunk you. If you made one mistake in the form he'd throw it in the waste basket. He was right because he was saying, "I'm gonna treat you like professionals." The least you're gonna get when you come out of this class is you're gonna know how to write a screenplay. It may have nothing to say, but …
>
> He was one of the few teachers who had actually worked in Hollywood and would tell these great stories, like lunch with Loretta Young. He told us nobody had been able to lick *Heart of Darkness*. That was like waving a red flag in front of a young bull, and I immediately set out to write *Heart of Darkness*.
>
> I had read Conrad when I was seventeen, and I read it once. I didn't want to go back and read it again because it had so impressed me that it felt like other things, that I had dreamed it, and I had a vision, and I didn't want to go back and then have to say, "Well, this is what really happened." I had my own kind of vision of it.
>
> It's a pretty obvious story. There were things I put in like the Dennis Hopper character, although there is a character similar to that in *Heart of Darkness*, this Russian guy who's sitting there talking to Kurtz, but I sort of envisioned this crazy photographer, who's running around.... I didn't want to get it exactly right, but I wanted to call him Colonel Kurtz, so you knew who it was and it was *Heart of Darkness*, "The horror, the horror."[4]

Naturally, Milius decided it would be the very first screenplay he would write and try to actually get made by Hollywood. Milius, being a hardcore right-winger, also saw a completely different message in the Conrad novel than the liberal educators teaching the book as a cautionary tale of white racism and colonialist imperialism. To Milius, it was the story of an idealist liberal, Kurtz, sent into the real world to bestow upon the "great unwashed" the fruits of civilized society. When his practices and theories are actually put into place, however, Milius feels it is like the Great Society, then a hot topic. It backfires, and the opposite of its well-intended consequences become what actually happen.

That made it a juicy apple to pick from the tree. Milius's decision not to re-read the novel before writing the screenplay, viewed from the prism of his time in Colorado, was almost transcendental, a period of mountain Zen in which he set traps, hunted, fished, fired weapons, and lived off the land. Reading Conrad in that environment was organic to his surroundings. The book seemed almost a dream, and he wanted to keep it that way, instead of letting too many details in the re-reading force him away from his vision.

At the time, George Lucas thought of their "Vietnam movie" as a black comedy like *Dr. Strangelove*. Someone suggested the movie be along the lines of *Catch-22*. Milius was too gung-ho for that in 1968. He sought out soldiers returning from the war. USC was a popular destination for returning veterans attending college on the G.I. Bill. He heard wild, disturbing stories from soldiers, including surfing during firefights. After *Heart of Darkness* and Irwin Blacker's admonitions, this became early, added inspiration to write a screenplay, set in Vietnam, called *Apocalypse Now*. He would also base it on Homer's *The Iliad* and *The Odyssey*, somehow updating the Homeric traditions with surfing as a way of "tricking" the Cyclops.

"Joseph Conrad's allegorical novella had always been a kind of Everest to filmmakers—Orson Welles had been obsessed with making a movie out of it, only to give up on the project—and superimposing the Vietnam War on the Conrad story complicated the task exponentially," wrote Francis Ford Coppola's biographer, Michael Schumacher.

"In 1968 Francis founded American Zoetrope, a company for filmmaking outside the Hollywood system," said Eleanor Coppola. "One of their first projects was 'Apocalypse Now,' a Vietnam war story based loosely on *Heart of Darkness*. The screenplay concerns a Captain Willard on his mission to assassinate a Green Beret colonel named Kurtz. Kurtz has gone insane and is conducting the war on his own terms in Cambodia. George Lucas was to direct John Milius's screenplay."[5]

Milius recalled, echoing Blacker:

> Francis said that *Heart of Darkness*, which had been one of the favorite things I've ever read, he said it had been tried and no one could lick it. He said that Orson Welles tried it and he couldn't lick it. Richard Brooks I think or someone else, and that's the best thing to tell a young writing student, that no one can possibly write this, and that was the first thing I tried.
>
> The war was raging then, and everyone was getting set to go to Canada or get out of it or whatever they were gonna do, and we prepared a whole method of doing this thing in Vietnam. We were gonna do it in 16mm in Vietnam, to avoid the war you know, we were willing to go to Vietnam....
>
> We would have been over there right on time for Tet probably, and whatever, and all these people, that were in school with me and done terrible things, and were planning to go to Canada or do something as drastic as getting married, they didn't care, they wanted to carry lights, and sound equipment and do it....
>
> George and I had a much different plan. We wanted to go to Vietnam and make the movie in Vietnam, because there had been movies made like that. There'd been a movie called *Medium Cool* [1969], which had been filmed during the riots of the [1968] Democratic Convention, and we wanted to go to Vietnam, there were people in our group who'd sooner go to Canada than be in the Army, really rash things like get married, but were perfectly willing to go make a movie in Vietnam, to make their way through the trip wires and snakes and tigers and stuff to make a movie, which was really interesting.[6]

They wanted to bring actors and a film crew *to Vietnam*. Once "in country," as the soldiers referred to the 'Nam, they would intersperse scripted and improvised scenes of performers interacting with real action and soldiers. Bombs would be exploding. Real people would be fighting. Anything could be happen. It would be dangerous.

"John is very good at being grand," said Lucas. "I would have been the one who went over there."

"George wanted to make it in Stockton on 16mm with a couple helicopters and basically do it in kind of a 'pursuit of documentary' documentary style," said Coppola.[7]

"He wanted to copy *The Battle of Algiers* [1965, Italian-Algerian pseudo documentary], which is an interesting idea, but looking back on it, we believed in *cinéma vérité* then, but now you look back on it and you realize you can't sustain that for more than about half an hour," said Milius.

Milius and Lucas were by far the two great stars of the USC film school, and were already fielding significant attention from the industry proper. It was appearing more and more likely that they could get a movie made, an unheard-of dream just a couple years earlier. Milius would write it. Lucas would direct it. That was the plan, but the original idea was far, far from what the film eventually became, at least in Lucas's view.

Haskell Wexler, who would win an Oscar for Best Cinematography on *Bound for Glory* (1976), directed *Medium Cool* (1969). For the latter he employed actors and took them on location to Chicago during the 1968 Democratic National Convention. In Goddard style he filmed them, often without script, sometimes improvising, intercutting them with documentary footage of the riots that ensued. It remains today a very interesting, provocative, and visually entertaining movie. Coppola's *The Rain People*, filmed in black-and-white, tried to capture the vibe but was not as striking. This was the original impetus of the Milius-Lucas vision, whether filmed in Vietnam or Stockton.

"When I was at cinema school I became obsessed that this war was raging on, and I thought this was a very colorful place to have a war, but I figured I was going to go, and I was looking forward to it, a military career, and it would end shortly, and I wanted to fly F-4s, and I washed out because of asthma," Milius reiterated. "I didn't think that was fair.... It made me reconfigure my whole life; I wasn't gonna be killed in Vietnam and I'd live past twenty-six, which I'd not planned on, and I had to think differently, so in 1968 I wanted to do something about this."[8]

In 2010 Milius recounted *Apocalypse Now*'s genesis in a sit-down interview conducted by Francis Ford Coppola himself.

> George, me, Randal Kleiser, Basil Poledouris; George and I would sit at the old stables at USC, the area with grass ... and discuss movies ... everybody loved *Dr. Strangelove* ... which had a profound influence on *Apocalypse Now* ... but my writing teacher Irwin Blacker really liked me, and was tough on you, he would destroy the confidence of most students. He'd say, "I'm bored, I'm gonna make arrangements to play tennis," and some girl would cry and he'd say that wouldn't do you any good out there, you'll deal with rude, illiterate people, and tell Hollywood stories.... We discussed *Heart of Darkness*. He said it had beaten Orson Welles, he could not do it, it had been attempted many times, various other people had failed; it's one of the great stories of all English literature, and it's tempted every great writer. Ben Hecht, Ernie Lehman, all these fabulous writers. It was like waving a red flag in front of a red bull.
>
> I read it when I was seventeen in Colorado. I was sent away to get me away from the beach. I immediately became a mountain man, I had a trap line and was hunting and I'd become Jim Bridger, so reading *Heart of Darkness* was wonderful in the middle of winter. It's in Africa, and the Congo, and I'm surrounded by snow, but it had the same kind of feeling like mountain men, so the whole theme was the jungle as a force in itself, it corrupts you by fear, primeval fear, give yourself something simple but your being afraid of dark subjects, yourself are in the darkness, and you go as deep as you can in the jungle, so you're no longer afraid of the jungle, you put on war paint and you become a creature of the jungle, howling like a wolf. I did all this in Colorado, convinced a yeti was on the side of the tree, I'd take my rifle and say this is a primeval spirit. I can't really deal with it with my rifle so I have to learn to speak with just my knife, and finally I stick the knife in a tree, and you give yourself to that anger, that's exactly what *Heart of Darkness* is, and Kurtz had become part of that. He's given himself to these forces, he's befriended them. When I read that, I was more transformed by it than any literature I ever read.... I knew I had to put something down and start thinking about it.
>
> I had a number of friends just coming back from Vietnam and they talked about it a great deal.... I started finding anybody I could find to talk about it. I found a couple of surfers, but there were very few surfers who actually went, because most surfers figured out how to get out of the draft.
>
> Maybe it was George who said, "You should write this down." Nobody else wanted to be a writer, and when it came time to do it, I thought of *Heart of Darkness*, and to use it in Vietnam, as an allegory. I thought I should go back and read it, but then decided I didn't want to, because I remembered it as if it was a dream, and I wanted it always to be that dream. If I go back and see it exactly, I'll probably screw it up.
>
> The PBR was just me. George just said, "Put all the neat stuff in it." It was always the idea George would do it. I never thought I'd be a director, I'd not been in it to be a director and thought a director was Kurosawa or John Ford. Not 'til I got into Hollywood did I realize how bad the directors were....[9]

Apocalypse Now might never have gotten off the ground but for a series of odd twists of fate. That is not to say it was dead in the water. Lucas would become rich and powerful; after *Star Wars* he would have had the clout to get it made. Milius would become the hottest screenwriter in the business, and in the 1970s was a successful director. He might have succeeded where Orson Welles failed. Lucas never directed after *Star Wars*. He might well have hired Milius to make *Apocalypse Now*. He might have hired Francis Ford Coppola to direct it.

Coppola and Milius met on the set of *The Rain People* along with Carroll Ballard. Milius had not written a complete *Apocalypse Now* screenplay in earnest when Coppola got the Zoetrope deal.

"But I'd written scores of notes and scenes," he stated.

"Others called it 'Psychedelic Soldier,' but I always called it 'Apocalypse Now,'" added Milius.[10]

"Hippies were good and bad. I loved beatniks. Hippies would have a peace sign say 'Nirvana now,' why wait, take a chemical that will help you reach that, you don't have to study Zen. Me being contrasting and a war-like individual anyway, so I converted it into a 'beehive' with missiles and a tail and wrote 'Apocalypse Now,' with a B-52, and carried it around and everybody liked that....

"We all figured if we were gonna work in the business at all, it was gonna be at some art house, so the idea that you conned them into bringing this motley entourage over there, that we'd actually be employed by a real fucking studio.... By that time I was kind of the second guy out, I was so far behind you I couldn't find the marks on the trees."[11]

The "first guy out," Francis Ford Coppola, had always promised to help his friends when he made it. He would steal film stock from the Warner Bros. supply room, waiting for the day when he would be fired and go out on his own. He had written *Patton*, which was not released yet but insiders raved about his writing. He was considered a future star, albeit an iconoclastic, bearded one. Coppola would hire his film school pals and help them break into the business. He wanted to do more than that; he wanted to create a new business model, a modern paradigm in the post-studio system. He broke from Hollywood, but only to some extent. In forming American Zoetrope in San Francisco, he was largely funded by Warner Bros., now a corporate entity in the wake of Jack Warner's retirement from the studio. Ted Ashley now ran Warners.

Coppola talked John Calley into $300,000 for a series of films to be made by Lucas, Willard Huyck, Carroll Ballard, Matthew Robbins, Hal Barwood, and himself. *Apocalypse Now*, the joint creative idea of both Lucas and John Milius, was slated third, to be directed by Lucas. Barry Beckerman was assigned by the studio to "babysit" Coppola. "Francis had this Mansonesque effect on all of us," said Becker. "If he'd told me to stab Ashley, I probably would've stabbed Ashley. As Francis always said, it takes no imagination to live within your means."[12]

"We moved to San Francisco and I took the money and divided it up between you and George, and Carroll Ballard and Willard Huyck," Coppola said to Milius in the 2010 YouTube.com symposium shot at Coppola's wine country estate.

"You came to me and asked me, 'How much do you need to live for a year?' and I was very bold and I said, 'fifteen grand,' and you said, 'I think I can get it for you,'" recalled Milius. "I couldn't believe it."

Coppola's original concentration was on his collaboration with George Lucas on *TXH*

1138. "George kept telling me to do it, he'd say 'Tell me about it,' but I don't think he read any of it until I was about sixty pages into it," said Milius.

"There were about six guys writing scripts in this mini studio ..." said Coppola. "You had all the key ingredients in that first script, the helicopter battle, and I think a Colonel Kharnage, and always Colonel Kurtz."

"I wanted the moment when he said, 'Colonel Kurtz, he dead ...'" said Milius of adapting the screenplay to Conrad. "Once I knew I was headed upriver, I let the river just carry me...."[13]

Ultimately *Apocalypse Now* went past a treatment and an idea, becoming a bona fide film project, during the early American Zoetrope deal with Warner Bros. Lucas still planned to film it in 16mm *cinéma vérité* style, shot with real soldiers and recruits mixed with actual news footage. It was estimated that the cost would be $1.5 million to $2 million

"When George got to make *THX 1138*, Francis made his American Zoetrope deal with Warner Bros.," said Milius. "Part of the deal was to develop projects and they gave me money to write *Apocalypse Now*. It was a big turning point in my life, because just before that I had been offered a chance to go to work for Universal for seven years as a writer. The two people they were taking in on their seven-year program were Spielberg and me. It worked for Steve because he got the chance to learn how to direct. It would have destroyed me writing television, and I didn't do it. I was very lucky Francis gave me the opportunity to write what I wanted to write. I thought it would be interesting to do Conrad's *Heart of Darkness* in Vietnam because it made a statement in itself. I felt it was interesting to take Conrad's idea of the end of the 19th century with merchants selling Christianity to the heathens and setting themselves up as god, and equate it with Special Forces units being dropped in and sent up to the river to sell democracy to the heathens, again setting themselves up as god. I worked from there. I don't think the script was ever political really. I think Francis had sentiments about the war and how horrible it was as someone who lived in San Francisco and listens to the political ramblings of the people around him. When Francis started talking to the people who'd been there, the soldiers who fought in the war, he began to study the war very thoughtfully. He took more of an historian's attitude."[14]

Milius was offered $17,000 to rewrite *Skin Game* (a 1971 comedy starring James Garner and Lou Gossett, Jr.) when Coppola made a counter-offer of $15,000 to write *Apocalypse Now* for Zoetrope.

"He offered that wonderful fork in the road where I could go do my own thing rather than just rewrite some piece of crap that would probably be re-written by somebody else," said Milius. "That was the most important decision I made in my life as a writer. That sort of steered me onto the path of doing my own work and being a little more like a novelist.... I tackled an unpopular subject that no one was going to make a movie about where the chances were really slim that I could pull it off. There was no book, nothing but me and the blank page. And that was wonderful because I had followed my heart. One of the nicest times in my life was writing *Apocalypse Now*."[15]

Milius built on the notes and treatment he previously wrote, with Kurtz from the Conrad novel, but changed Charles Marlow to B. L. Willard, a captain of the Airborne. Kurtz is modernized from a 19th Century ivory trader stationed deep in the African jungle—a man of high ideals—into a brute, worshipped by the natives because his brutality commands their respect; he is bold enough to seize and handle power that few can handle. The *Apoc-*

alypse Kurtz is a demented Special Forces character, based on accounts Milius heard from veterans. Some boy told him of the Viet Cong hacking off the arms of children after they had been immunized for smallpox, and he heard stories about surfing in the 'Nam. This was all in the original screenplay.

For some strange reason, the Department of Defense nixed the idea of filming in the 'Nam, and the intrepid group of USC and UCLA film students, most of whom (except for Milius) had gone through every gyration to avoid military service, never got to carry sound equipment or utter heroic lines or theoretically fight the actual VC. But that was beside the point.

Milius wanted *Apocalypse Now* to be a helicopter journey. Lucas wanted it to be a boat ride. It was to be about "surfing and bombs," said Gary Kurtz, who had done marine photography in Vietnam. An early inspiration was Akira Kurosawa's *Hidden Fortress* (1958).

Then *THX 1138* bombed.

Ted Ashley told them to pay the money back. "But they sold us completely down the river," Lucas said.[16] Warners pulled the plug. Zoetrope ran out of money, but Warner Bros. hard-lined Coppola, demanding a substantial sum they gave him to develop "Apocalypse Now," "The Conversation," and a string of other scripts, be paid back. Coppola, as was his style, spent the money freely and was broke.

"Warner Bros. finally backed off of it 'cause they figured one of us would end up being killed," said Milius. "Because we were so stupid, you know."[17]

"With his plans for 'Apocalypse' shelved, Francis put his dreams for Zoetrope on hold and went on to direct *The Godfather Part I and II* ... they made Francis a multi-millionaire," said Eleanor.[18]

His original plan was to use the money and profits from that movie to revive American Zoetrope. It would take longer than he thought. He would win an Oscar for *Patton*, and direct not one but two blockbuster *Godfather* classics. He would not be able to return to American Zoetrope, and *Apocalypse Now*, until 1974–75. It would consume him until 1979.

There was some initial confusion regarding ownership of the project. Over the next several years, Lucas made several attempts to revive it, but the Warners deal had a strange effect on its ownership. It did not belong to the estate of Joseph Conrad. Welles never had any proprietary hold beyond his dramatization of it on the radio and a film idea that never went anywhere. It was John Milius's idea and by 1969 he had an early draft written, as contracted by Coppola, probably registered with the Writer's Guild and maybe copyrighted in Washington, D.C., as is the common practice.

He had a verbal agreement with Lucas that may have been formalized as a contract, but when both Lucas and Milius joined American Zoetrope, Coppola, as head of the company, became the de facto owner. Lucas was a bona fide employee. Milius was more of a contract player, a contributor with freelance status. He was already getting steady work in Hollywood and was not reliant on regular income from Zoetrope.

But everybody signed off on the Warners–Seven Arts deal, making the studio the "original" owners of several screenplays, or projects, including "Apocalypse." When that deal collapsed, all ownership reverted back to Coppola ... not Milius or Lucas. At least, it did when Coppola finally paid them back, which did not happen until *The Godfather* hit it big. This leads to several more interesting "what ifs?" If Lucas had obtained ownership, he might have gone off and shot his Vietnam movie like *Medium Cool*, and would probably be as well remembered. Milius, on the other hand, was about to become the star screenwriter for the hated Warner Bros. Who is to say, had he been given ownership, after the box-office success of the right-wing *Dirty Harry* movies he wrote for them, that Warners would not have green-lit *Apocalypse*, allowing him to make it exactly as he originally wrote it, with the U.S. Army exacting *extremely violent* revenge on the Communists? Milius's mid–1970s script was not unlike the *Rambo*, *Delta Force* and *Hanoi Hilton* "revenge" pictures of the Reagan era.

Before ownership of the project could be determined, Lucas had a development deal with Columbia, and sent Gary Kurtz, a USC friend, to scout locations in the Philippines. Lucas was ready to shoot it in a minimalist fashion for a bare bones $2 million or $3 million.

"I sort of had a deal with Columbia to do it," Lucas said. "But we really couldn't reach an agreement with Francis over the participation with Columbia. There was a big disagreement about it. Columbia wouldn't give us enough points, and Francis didn't want to do it with them, so we ended up not doing it at Columbia....

"I couldn't get the same terms Francis had gotten at Warners; it was much less. But he was determined to hang on to the same number of points, his old number, so whatever Columbia took, I had to give up. My points were going to shrink way down, and I wasn't going to do the film for free. He had a right to do it, it's in his nature, but at the same time I was annoyed about it....

"We couldn't get any cooperation from any of the studios or the military, but once I had *American Graffiti* behind me I tried again and pretty much got a deal at Columbia. We scouted locations in the Philippines and we were ready to go." Columbia wanted all of the American Zoetrope rights. Coppola said no. "The deal collapsed," said Lucas. "And when that deal collapsed, I started working on *Star Wars*."[19]

"Everyone was against me," said Coppola of his initial efforts to get *Apocalypse Now* off the ground. "I was doing something on a subject no one dared touch with my own money, and I was getting all this flak. It collapsed."

The political landscape had changed very quickly. When Warners first agreed to finance *Apocalypse* in 1969, the hawkish Richard Nixon was in his first year as president, with a "secret plan" to end the war. Many thought that just meant bombing the Communists into submission, and the war, like all previous American wars, would be won. But, in 1970, the U.S. invaded Cambodia, students were killed at Kent State, and it became obvious it was a quagmire. At that point the administration concentrated on a political tack. Making a movie that ended by stalemate was a lot less attractive than a war won by victory, for which, as General Douglas MacArthur so aptly pointed out, there is no substitute. It was now a toxic subject.

"We then tried to take *Apocalypse* to all the other studios, and nobody wanted to have anything to do with it," recalled Lucas. "They just ... no way.... Because it was during the war, and there was a lot of pressure or just fear, but the studios would not finance a movie about the Vietnam War."[20]

"People were so bitter about the war; we were living in a time when there really were riots," said Milius. "People on the streets were spitting on soldiers, and studio executives are not getting in the way of that, they were the last people who are gonna get in the middle of that thing. Studio executives are not noted for their social courage."[21]

So the movie was shelved. Coppola did two *Godfather* films, Lucas wrote two *Dirty Harry* movies, and directed two, *Dillinger* and *The Wind and the Lion*. Coppola urged Lucas to make a "human" movie. *Apocalypse* did not really fit that bill, but *American Graffiti* did.

"I went to George, I told him we have to do *Apocalypse Now*, I said make it, and at that point he was into *Star Wars*," said Coppola. "If you want to make it, go make it," Lucas told him.[22]

"He was gonna do *Apocalypse*, then *Star Wars*," said Milius of Lucas. "Once he made *American Graffiti*, then he got rich and he didn't want to make *Apocalypse Now* and didn't want to go where they have many different varieties of poisonous insects, go to a place that rained every day and was miserable and had tigers."[23]

Then Coppola asked Milius to direct, but he was already into *The Wind and the Lion*. Francis's insistence it be ready for the Bi-Centennial (1976) did not give him enough time. It was very rare for Milius, the ultimate doer, to turn down something like this, especially since it was so completely "in him," as Arnold Schwarzenegger said of most Milius projects.[24] No challenge was too great for him. He had seamlessly broken in as a screenwriter, getting lucrative work straight off the USC campus with AFI, then with a huge studio, Warners. He was wealthy and in demand, but quickly realized he needed to direct in order to protect the integrity of his vision. This led to his directing *Dillinger* and *The Wind and the Lion*, and, later, *Big Wednesday*.

But this was *Apocalypse Now*, his ultimate fantasy, and the chance to be a set commander of a movie that ultimately would be like the war experience he craved but missed because he washed out with asthma. In retrospect, to consider that he was off on some beach with Gary Busey and Jan-Michael Vincent when he could have been directing Robert Duvall in a helicopter is almost primal injustice.

However, Milius, while respected, was not Francis Ford Coppola. He did not have Coppola's money, access to money, line of credit, or ability to raise more funds. He did not have studios like UA willing to go on a limb with him as they were with Francis. Of course, they had very different views on the war. Coppola later believed had Milius directed it he might have left the project based on politics. That could have left Milius figuratively stranded in the jungle with no way out, like the doomed characters in his screenplay.

"I'm in a real pickle, we need to make a movie that's a big hit so we can make a lot of money so we can make all these little arty films, so I said what if I make *Apocalypse Now* and instead of doing it the way George wants to do it, as a kind of *Battle of Algiers*, what if I do it as an Imax spectacle, as big as I can do it, the opposite direction?" Coppola recalled. "A hit like *The Guns of Navarrone*, make a lot of money, then I can make little movies. I said I'll do it. I liked the script and *Heart of Darkness*, but this was a chance to make a ton of money then be a writer, direct my own scripts instead of being addicted to a writer I have to drag along."

At the time Coppola reasoned, "The script's done, it'll be so easy," contemplating shooting in Hawaii.[25] "You were really worn out after *The Godfather II*," said Milius to Coppola in the 2010 wine country interview, "and when they gave you all the Oscars you said it was worth it but 'I don't ever want to go through that again.'"

"I was on top of the world, but nobody would let me make *Apocalypse Now*," added Coppola.[26]

The same bitter political attitudes that pervaded the country had metastasized into a cancer eating away at the soul of America by the mid–1970s. The greatest director in the industry, perhaps of all time, could not get a film about this subject matter made. That made the decision easy for him. He had always wanted to make his films under the American Zoetrope banner, not under the control of the studios. He would finance it himself, and reap all the benefits and rewards absent Hollywood accountants taking their pound of flesh. At least, that was the plan.

"In 1975 he revived his plans for Zoetrope and chose 'Apocalypse Now' as its first project," said Eleanor Coppola.

"I was in a position, I wanted to always write original work," said Coppola. "Original work really takes six, eight months at the minimum to do, and here was this script of *Apocalypse Now* that we could clean up and send out immediately, so I basically just said, well what if I just did *Apocalypse Now*, and in so doing were able to make our company independent, and further our goals, but nothing really prepared me for the modern telling of *Heart of Darkness* in a Vietnam setting."

"Francis's money was in it, but that was Francis's style," said co-producer Tom Sternberg. "His philosophy was always, and it remains to this date, 'I am gonna go make the movie, and if everybody knows I'm gonna make it, it'll fall into place. If I don't go forward as if I'm making it, nothing will happen.'"

"My attitude towards money has always been, I don't have very much of it, but if I use it in a very audacious way, if you have a thousand dollars but you're willing to use it, really not caring of risk, you can make like $10,000," said Coppola.[27]

"I gave him all the information we had, on filming in the Philippines," said Lucas. "I said, 'Francis, it's one thing to go over there for three weeks, with like five people, and sort of scrounge a lot of footage, using the Philippine Army, but if you go over there as a big American production, they're going to kill you. The longer you'll stay, the more in danger you are of getting sucked into the swamp.'"

Lucas always harbored some form of bitterness that Coppola took on *Apocalypse Now* for himself. He had tried to get it made but the deal fell through. Coppola asked him to direct but he declined in favor of *Star Wars*, yet Lucas felt a certain sense of entitlement, that his "Vietnam movie" was still *his* regardless of the contractual realities, and that it should still be there waiting for him to make it after he wrapped *Star Wars*.

"Whatever Francis does for you always winds up benefiting Francis the most ..." said Lucas. "He finds it incredible that people do things he doesn't wish them to do, since he's controlling it all and they're all here for *him*."

"I was always on Francis's side," said Milius. "George had nothing whatsoever to do with it, other than the fact that he was going to direct it. 'Just go do your Vietnam thing, John.' Francis gave George ample opportunity to make the movie. George never did. He was too good for it. Francis has a lot of terrible qualities; he is a supreme egotist, and he will take everything for himself. He is like what they said of Napoleon, he was great as a man can be without virtue. But if Francis hadn't done it, that movie never would have been made."

Coppola may well have been relieved when Lucas turned down the directing gig. He had learned many a lesson, and the ultimate lesson was to get total control, which he would not have if Lucas directed it. The idea of Lucas doing it in 16mm is ludicrous compared to what it was. Lucas was a great science-fiction, special-effects storyteller but would have been in over his head in the jungle, literally and figuratively. It might have died out there.

Coppola had always urged Lucas to write. Coppola read the *Star Wars* screenplay and thought little of it. When Coppola posed a *fait accompli*, an ultimatum, Lucas was resigned that he would not do it.

"All Francis did was take a project I was working on, put it in a package deal, and suddenly he owned it," Lucas said.

Carroll Ballard also wanted to make a movie out of *Heart of Darkness* but could not get it off the ground. "Many years later, I discovered that Francis and George had sort of taken that idea and run with it," he said. "At one time, I was very bitter about it."[28]

Coppola did not dispute Ballard but just said that he had tried to get it made, could have written a script but never did, never had rights, while "neither he nor I optioned the Conrad material or registered the title.

"There's no question that *Apocalypse Now* was John Milius's idea, with George egging him along. George was going to direct it. Carroll really had nothing to do with it, but he was around, talking about wanting to do *Heart of Darkness*. So John and he just naturally started to borrow the river journey from that, though they didn't think of it as a version of *Heart of Darkness*. They were listening to Carroll's enthusiasm about *Heart of Darkness* and it influenced them.

"The original script was profoundly interesting, and made a really interesting and unusual statement about the war, that was not political in a very short or myopic sense, but in a big sense was really political. It [had] a lot of offensive paramilitary stuff that [was] irrelevant and shouldn't be stressed—Milius's whole mythology of hunting people down, and so on, which I did not particularly want in. Yet aside from that there was an incredible film in *Apocalypse*."[29]

Milius had begun writing, making notes, and creating a treatment of *Apocalypse Now* while at USC. Coppola said that the "Vietnam movie" was not originally an adaptation of *Heart of Darkness*, even suggesting the novel's influence came from Ballard, but it was and had been since Milius first inquired of the novel's film viability in Irwin Blacker's class.

Independence motivated all of Coppola's moves from the beginning. He justified making huge films for Bob Evans and Paramount by saying once he had enough money in the bank, he would return to his roots; re-start Zoetrope, and make "personal films" with his own dough.

Lucas wanted to do the same thing, and held to that vision more so than Coppola. He had agreed to do *American Graffiti* for Universal, hated the experience, but emerged a wealthy man. He gave Coppola his blessing to make it his way. He filmed *Star Wars* while Coppola made *Apocalypse*, so he was unable to be part of it, certainly not as originally envisioned back at USC and in San Francisco.

As for Milius, he never cared about independence. He made his name at Warner Bros., took jobs for big money, had finally directed, and was happy to work for anybody who would pay him. He was just finishing *The Wind and the Lion* when Coppola approached and told him he wanted to make *Apocalypse*. It was a good window for Milius. He would make *Big Wednesday* eventually, but *Apocalypse* seemed relatively easy work. Coppola read *Heart of Darkness*, agreed to adapt its themes, and tasked Milius to rewrite his original draft in 1975. Milius was always a fast worker. Coppola would assemble financing, hire a crew, and film on location. Milius would be available for rewrites as the need arose; he could fly out to the film's location if necessary. It would be like a tropical vacation.

A piece of cake!

10

Hubris

By 1975 rumors were buzzing on *Apocalypse Now*. Marlon Brando and Steve McQueen were up for the lead. Freddie Fields, Dino DeLaurentiss, and even Bob Hope were said to be connected. There were rumors that the story, with certain modern changes, was an homage to Joseph Conrad's *Heart of Darkness*, which along with J. D. Salinger's *Catcher in the Rye*, was being taught to most public high school students by this time. But Coppola was not his usual gregarious self with the press. He held the story and the production close to the vest. Milius had finished the script, financed under the Coppola banner.

But by 1975 the original script was six years old. The U.S. had essentially lost the war in the spring of that year when the North Vietnamese Army overran Saigon and the entire southern part of the country. Red China asserted its Communist influence on the entire region, and Communist forces took control of neighboring countries. Eventually, Vietnam fought a war with China. Pol Pot murdered 1.5 million people in the Cambodian "killing fields" between 1975–79.

President Richard Nixon was elected in 1968, promising a "secret plan" to extract the U.S. from Vietnam "with honor." President Lyndon Johnson had fomented the war by creating a Naval conflict at the Gulf of Tonkin in 1964. Jim Morrison's father, Admiral Steve Morrison, was one of the top commanders of American forces at the time.

In 1965, LBJ escalated U.S. troop involvement, but by 1966 the war was stagnating into a "quagmire," with public support, heavily behind the war at first, beginning to dissipate. By the mid–1960s, Communism was a known evil. Joseph Stalin had already killed most of the 35 million people estimated to have been murdered by the Soviet Union, although the majority of the 70 million Mao Tse-tung would murder in Red China had not died yet, as their deaths came about largely during the Cultural Revolution (1966–76).

However, Senator Joseph McCarthy (R.-Wisconsin) was exposed largely as a charlatan. This combined with sympathy for blacklisted filmmakers, some (but not all) of whom were innocent, created an odd vacuum in America in which, for psychological reasons that cannot be explained, a growing segment of the population identified either with the Communists or with the radical left. Experts have never been able to explain why America, and the world, so thoroughly saw and reacted to the threat of Adolf Hitler and the Nazis, yet failed to act with the same urgency on the threat of Stalinism or Mao, which to date has killed an estimated 120 million human beings, a figure that far exceeds the Nazis.

By 1967–68 students at the University of California, Berkeley, Columbia and the University of Wisconsin were carrying placards of Mao, while waving North Vietnamese flags. LBJ chose not to run for re-election in 1968.

By October of 1969, when the protest movement formed a "moratorium" on the war, it was being called "Nixon's war." Instead of immediately pulling troops out, he escalated the bombings of the north and expanded into Cambodia. Throughout this time, his NSC advisor, Dr. Henry Kissinger, was engaged in secret peace talks with the Communists in Paris. Nixon's provocative actions brought them closer and closer to an agreement.

At the same time, Nixon and Kissinger were involved in "triangulated diplomacy" with the U.S.S.R. and Red China. In 1972, Nixon opened up diplomatic relations with the Chinese for the first time since Chiang Kai-Shek's *Kuomintang* lost a civil war to the Communists in 1949. On the strength of this pressure, the Soviets signed a radical nuclear arms deal greatly easing the potential of an exchange with the West. Finally, in the winter of 1972–73, the North Vietnamese agreed to a peace treaty with the U.S., largely similar to the terms of the 1953 Korean peace agreement signed at Panmunjom. In 1973, the prisoners of war were returned, and the war ended.

Shortly thereafter, Watergate hit. Drip by drip, the Democrats ripped away at Nixon's presidency until he resigned in 1974. Watergate drained his administration from effectively maintaining the position of strength with the Soviets, the Chinese, and the North Vietnamese necessary to hold the agreement together.

After Nixon left office, the key provision of the deal was not upheld when Senator Teddy Kennedy (D.-Massachusetts) refused to allow further funding of the South Vietnamese military defending themselves against growing NVA incursions. Abandoned by Kennedy and the Democrats, the South Vietnamese were unable to hold. In April of 1975 the Communists conquered Saigon, forcing an evacuation from the American Embassy. All Nixon and Kissinger had won had been lost, out of political revenge with Watergate the pretext. An estimated 1 million Vietnamese died.

Milius had written his first draft of *Apocalypse Now* when many, at least on the right, still harbored John Wayne's jingoistic fantasy that the Communists could be "bombed back into the Stone Age." But by 1970, when the war escalated into Cambodia and the campuses went absolutely nuts, it was obvious that a military victory, the kind of all-out conquering of an opponent that required public support, was not in the cards.

This shifted Milius's thinking. Both he and Lucas, despite their differing politics, had originally based their idea on the seemingly inevitable conclusion that the U.S. would prevail because she always did. By 1975 Milius's fully conceived screenplay was based on a new premise: what would have happened if the military were allowed to fight without their "hands tied behind their backs," the expression so many veterans used to describe the frustration of fighting an enemy they rarely saw, were not allowed to pursue, and often were not allowed to kill in any appreciable numbers?

The United States never lost a battle in Vietnam. The Tet Offensive of 1968, which led Walter Cronkite of CBS to declare the war was unwinnable, had in fact been a series of American victories, a fact the American public was practically not *allowed* to know about. As far as the veterans were concerned, they won the war, and when Nixon pulled the troops out, and the POWs came home in 1973, it was a victory. In fact, for that brief, shining moment in time, America stood on the pinnacle of world power like no empire ever had; not the Romans, Alexander's Greece, or the British. Only the period 1945–49, when the U.S. alone had access to the atomic bomb, had the nation ever been more thoroughly in control of global events, yet it slipped away, nothing less than a Shakespearean tragedy involving Nixon, the Kennedy family, a series of historical "what ifs?" involving the 1960 election, the Berlin Wall, the Cuban Missile Crisis, John and Robert Kennedy's assassination, the war, Chappaquiddick, eventually Watergate, Ted Kennedy's political future, the conservative revolution, and the presidency of Ronald Reagan.

In looking at Vietnam with the long view, as tragic as it was, and as hard as it was to admit defeat, at least politically, it can be argued that it was for the Communist world merely a *Pyrrhic* victory in which the sheer cost of fighting it depleted their movement of vital energy, draining them of resources at what otherwise was their historical moment, leading eventually to Reagan overseeing the United States' victory in the Cold War, as British Prime Minister Margaret Thatcher said, "without firing a shot," symbolized by the fall of the Berlin Wall in 1989.

But neither John Milius nor Francis Ford Coppola knew, or probably would have dared predict, the results of just fifteen years later. From the colossal heights of January 1973, the nation had fallen precipitously by 1975 (and would continue to do so until the Iranian hostages were returned in 1981). It seemed a *fait accompli* that a movie about Vietnam would be a liberal diatribe accusing the country of war crimes, but so long as John Milius had any say in the matter, *that* was not going to happen!

In the original script, when Willard finally meets Kurtz, he is swayed to his side and fights with him to defend the compound against an American helicopter attack. Milius did rewrites turned in by the spring of 1975; then Coppola started his rewrites. Coppola, who was equally influenced by Conrad, did more *Heart of Darkness* shading.

In one of the original drafts Kurtz is seen at the beginning "literally rotting from within," wrote Michael Schumacher, but Coppola preferred to keep him until the end so he would be fully mythologized by the suspense-building tension. In some ways it was reminiscent of *Jaws* (1975), although Spielberg's decision to show the shark only at the end was more practical than creative. Milius thought him an ordinary man driven mad by power over Montagnard minions.

"Do you know what it is to be a white man who can summon fire from the sky?" Kurtz says to Captain Willard in the final scenes, after he has turned his would-be assassin into his cohort, and they are defending the compound not just from the Communists but from the *Americans*, as well. "You can live and die for these things—not silly ideals that are always betrayed."[1]

Coppola wanted Kurtz to recognize the madness within himself and view his own death as the only solution. While Coppola found Milius's ending jingoistic, he did not insist on changing it or re-writing it himself as he went into pre-production. He always said the key to a successful film was to have a screenplay as finalized as possible so it could be followed as best as the shoot allowed. However, he was filled with *hubris* at that time. He figured he could rewrite the ending as he went along.

He certainly did not think it would be a huge project. It was the summer of 1974 when he decided to do it, proposing that it could be ready by the Bicentennial on the fourth of July 1976.

"All I had out of this whole catastrophe was *Apocalypse Now*," said Coppola of the American Zoetrope deal. "George wasn't able to do it, John wasn't able to do it, and I thought, *Well, if I direct this movie—it's a great script—as a war film it will make a lot of money and then I'll do personal films*. That's always been the rationale. Begin everything we've ever done. So I jumped into making *Apocalypse Now* and it eventually seduced me."[2]

The film gestated between December of 1974 and March of 1976. The highlight of his career, the power of *The Godfather* films being such huge a hit—many thought the sequel better than the first—made him a "triple threat" writer-director-producer; golden, "bullet proof." *The Godfather II* was Coppola's, where the first was Mario Puzo's, or Bob Evans's or Marlon Brando's.

He had in the minds of most achieved both mainstream financial success while still being independent and personal to his vision. He was at the top as none—not even Orson Welles or later Spielberg—ever had been or would be. He was still only thirty-five.

"The success ... went to my head like a rush of perfume," said Coppola. "I thought I couldn't do anything wrong."

He mortgaged his homes in San Francisco and the Napa Valley to finance it. "One of the great virtues of being young as a filmmaker is that you don't realize what some of the issues really are, and what it really takes to make a good film and put it all together, but that's a benefit, to sort of go fearlessly into areas that a wise person would not," he rationalized.

"It was surreal; and not a normal war," said producer Fred Roos. "Francis, one of his intentions was to capture the craziness of that war."[3]

The first tiny waves of Vietnamese refugees were starting to arrive in America, the "boat people" escaping the Communists. Their harrowing stories were just beginning to seep out. In the days before Fox News, they were telling the stories the networks had not bothered to uncover during the war.

"I always thought throughout my career that everything I did was an experiment, some lofty idea for a future time in which all the things I tried, I'd kind of say well, what I've learned is this wisdom, and the irony is now at the age of sixty-five I should go back and be a student again, and make student films, but with this great wisdom I have," recalled Coppola of his philosophy, which certainly propelled this project.[4]

In the spring of 1975 Coppola sold off the foreign rights to European distributors for $7 million on the condition he have "brand name actors" like Steve McQueen, Al Pacino, Jack Nicholson, or Robert Redford, all of whom turned him down. None of them wanted to be stuck in the jungle with Francis Ford Coppola. Coppola, the control freak, also did not offer any of the potential stars gross points, insisting on keeping them for himself.

Coppola's key in raising money was foreign distribution, based on a bitter taste about the U.S. in Vietnam. He also asked for Defense Department and Army cooperation, but worried about American audience reaction to the violence and the war. The project required his best work both artistically and as a businessman, which he had been forced to become in his many ventures.

In May of 1975 Coppola and Fred Roos flew to Washington for a Pentagon meeting. They provided an early Milius draft and asked for stock footage, but what they really wanted were helicopters. Since Coppola was going to make the picture no matter what, the DoD recommended the Army cooperate to maintain "proper perspective." They did not like the scalping, surfing, dark humor, and pot smoking depicted by Milius.

It was much different from *The Green Berets* (1968), John Wayne's comically jingoistic portrayal of Special Forces winning the "hearts and minds" of the Vietnamese. Wayne secured full cooperation from President Lyndon Johnson and the DoD, who practically funded the picture through locations and equipment. Wayne told LBJ he wanted the picture to help the U.S. win the war and assure his re-election, an odd hope since Wayne was a conservative Republican opposed to Johnson's domestic agenda. He was in 1968 a "Nixon man."

The only real Vietnam movie before *The Deer Hunter* (1978), *Coming Home* (1978) and *Apocalypse Now*, *The Green Berets* was a box-office smash and remains popular to this day, but critics lambasted it as cartoonishly unrealistic, even calling it a "lie." It certainly never had the effect of winning the war or helping Johnson, who, by '68, decided not to even run again.

By the time Coppola and Roos came to them in 1975, the war was over, but was unpopular and could not be revived by a movie or any other spin. The Watergate fall out, resulting in Senator Kennedy de-funding the South Vietnamese, leaving them hung out to dry, resulted in the disastrous, successful invasion of the south by the Communists. This made the war even more unpopular: a total, unnecessary disaster resulting in 1 million dead Vietnamese and 58,000 American casualties.

The left and the right viewed it differently, of course. The left saw the defeat as justification for their protests: it never should have been fought. The right saw the vicious genocide committed by the North Vietnamese and Communists in Cambodia, with millions murdered, and felt this proved their point; it was why they opposed such an ideology and tried to stop them in the first place. The left countered that the Communists were pushed to genocide only by America, a specious argument that history refutes as a practical matter of human nature. The right then said if the left had not protested, the media not given "aid and comfort" to the Communists, they would not have had to fight with their "hands tied behind our backs," and might have prevailed, saving the day.

But none of these arguments *popularized* the Vietnam War. The Pentagon seemed unable to grasp reality, seeing the film as something that could make America's involvement in the 'Nam look bad, as if the general attitude about the war was not already as bad as possible from all perspectives—left, right, and international.

They argued that the Army would never order Kurtz's murder, which may or may not be true. They would not *admit* such things could, or even did, happen. When it comes to "black ops" and the CIA, the public believes almost anything is possible. The Phoenix Program was almost as vicious as what Colonel Kurtz proposes, in the screenplay and on screen. Also in 1975, the Church Committee hearings, headed by Senator Frank Church (D.-Idaho), came on the heals of the Pentagon Papers, revealing CIA tradecraft, opening the door to much speculation that the killing of President John Kennedy was not merely the work of a lone gunman.

But the Pentagon seemed stuck in the 1950s. If they cooperated with Francis Ford Coppola, they said it implied agreement "with the fact of the philosophy of the film." They also added that the screenplay was "garbage." Milius may have been stung by this assessment. He thought he wrote a pro–U.S. story of gung-ho Special Forces warriors adapting to the jungle and beating the Viet Cong at their own game, the way the Americans went into the jungles—which Tokyo Rose told them was where "we live ... and you die"—only to emerge victorious over the Japanese. But Milius had gone too far. His men were dressed in loincloths, with human body parts hanging from their bandoliers like trophies, scalping the enemy, terrorizing the Communists in a way that might be viewed as un-American by the John Wayne crowd.

Finally the Pentagon did admit the movie would "make a bundle." They could not stop its production anyway. "You aren't going to see this picture—this picture is going to happen to you," Coppola told them. The trade unions had helped nix the government deal.

But being rebuffed by the government was a precursor of difficulties to come. It frustrated Coppola, who always had seemingly gotten his way or prevailed, as he had with Robert Evans. When Brando turned him down the first time, it caused a furious Coppola to throw his Oscar statuettes out the window, shattering four of them just like his father Carmine's had when he accidentally dropped it right after winning at the 1975 Oscars. None of his previous success seemed to count at this point.

His foreign distributors required in the contract "big name stars." *Variety* reported that Brando, then later McQueen or Gene Hackman, would headline the film. By November, however, nobody was signed on. Money or other concerns, perhaps in the form of premonitions or dark foreboding, scared most everybody off. McQueen wanted to be paid more than Coppola, who at first was willing to go along with it. Perhaps the chance to work with the man who wrecked the marriage of his nemesis, Robert Evans, motivated Francis.

James Caan wanted a similar amount of money. Jack Nicholson, Robert Redford, and Brando all declined. Al Pacino liked the script but not the idea of four months in the jungle. He had enough health problems on *The Godfather II*, when they filmed in the Dominican Republic. Then Brando said he would reconsider.

Fred Roos and Dean Tavoularis scouted locations in Australia, which would certainly have been much more comfortable than the Philippines. One Philippines location scout had told him, "Don't come here, it's dangerous. Go to Australia, go to Thailand, go to Stockton! You're talking about building a $20 million set. This is November. On May 15, the first typhoons are gonna hit, and it's gonna rain until October 15. The water rises fifty feet. The sets are going to be washed out to sea."[5]

Coppola was like President Franklin Roosevelt when the FBI came to tell him his administration was filled with paid Soviet spies. Coppola, like FDR, did not want to hear it. Roosevelt told the agent, 'Fuck you." Coppola replied, "What're you, a fuckin' weatherman?"

Coppola called his old boss, Roger Corman, and asked his advice about shooting in the Philippines, a place with geographical terrain similar to Southeast Asia.

"Don't go," was Corman's succinct advice. He warned him of the rainy season coming up, from May to November. Coppola, at the apex of his powers, like a king drunk with *hubris*, could not be warned of his mortality. Ironically, in the final scene of his classic screenplay *Patton*, George C. Scott, in voiceover, states that Roman slaves would whisper in the emperor's ear, "All glory is fleeting" (*sic transit gloria*). Bravely he told Corman, "It'll be a rain picture."

It'll be a rain picture!

But the Philippines it would be, once the nation's authoritarian strongman, Ferdinand Marcos, agreed to supply helicopters and air force planes, which had been supplied by the U.S. to provide security in their ongoing conflict with Communist rebels. Roos had worked on films in the Philippines and had important contacts there. The local populace offered cheap labor; the kind of "exploitation" the "bearded Marxist" Coppola opposed until it benefited him.

Coppola budgeted more than $21 million but only had $7 million locked in from foreign distributors. He was already $1 million into his own money. The question at that time was how to get more backing without relinquishing ownership, the conundrum that motivated him from the moment he got into the business.

United Artists agreed to provide $7.5 million for U.S. distribution rights. It did not help that Coppola complained publicly in *Variety* and said the breakup of the old studio system was one of the reasons he was having so much trouble, raising money and getting his film off the ground. He and Lucas were two of the people most responsible for breaking that up.

As Coppola spent more time reading the screenplay, he felt it was one-dimensional Milius jingoism, which it was originally, and in light of the war now seemed more apparent than ever.

"The film continued through comic strip episode and comic strip episode until it came to a comic strip resolution," is how Coppola described it. "Attila the Hun (i.e., Kurtz) with two bands of machine gun bullets around him, taking the hero (Willard) by the hand, saying, 'Yes, yes, here! I have the power in my loins.'"[6]

Francis always saw it as surreal.

"People used to ask me, 'What's this movie gonna be like?'" he continued. "And I would say, 'Like Ken Russell.' The jungle will look psychedelic, florescent blues, yellows, and greens … it means the war is essentially a Los Angeles export, like acid rock…."[7]

Now he needed a cast. Coppola gave some Socialistic dogma to the press, pleading that actors not actually be paid what they commanded in the marketplace, but on some sort of percentage presumably negotiated by a union but given a percentage of the film's profits. Most disagreed with Coppola on general principle. Free agency was just then inflating baseball salaries, suddenly creating million-dollar paydays for top talent.

Brando was still his first choice. They had captured glory together just a few years earlier with *The Godfather*, and Coppola reasonably assumed Marlon would be grateful that he had revived his career. Brando had made *Last Tango in Paris* (1972) and was a sex symbol again. He did interviews in a pony tail, giving suave answers and making sly eye contact with the audience, seducing them. He was the master. He had turned Coppola down, then reconsidered. Coppola was unaware of Brando's physical condition, however. After doing nude scenes with Maria Schneider he was gaining weight. He could play Captain Willard or Colonel Kurtz. He was coy, as was his wont. Coppola finally secured Brando at a cost of $1 million per week for three weeks of work, along with 11 percent of the gross profits, to play the role of Colonel Kurtz.

Coppola went to another old standby, Al Pacino, offering him the Willard role. "I know what this is going to be like," Pacino told him when he turned it down. "You're gonna be up there in a helicopter telling me what do, and I'm gonna be down there in the swamp for five months."[8] It was a lot different than looking beautiful in period costume, doing romantic scenes with Diane Keaton, and going toe to toe with his idol Brando, whom Pacino did not know prior to *The Godfather*. Pacino was a New Yorker who made urban movies in New York settings. This was a whole new kind of movie.

Coppola approached Martin Sheen, a rising young talent who was affordable but was slated to be in *The Cassandra Crossing* in Italy, so he signed Harvey Keitel, an ex-marine and Scorsese regular, for the Captain Willard role. Robert Duvall was signed on to play Colonel Kilgore. Duvall had played the role of Boo Radley in the film adaptation of Harper

Lee's *To Kill a Mockingbird*. He had worked with Coppola on *The Rain People* and Lucas in *THX 1138*, but was a big star having performed the classic role of "Lucky Ned" Pepper opposite John Wayne in *True Grit*, then portraying attorney Tom Hagen in both *Godfather* epics.

Coppola was already $1 million into the project when he told Dean Tavoularis to cast unknown "young Pacinos. The war was fought by children. Redford and McQueen are too old."[9]

Sam Bottoms was picked to play Lance, a surf champion from Southern California; Frederick Forrest (*The Conversation*) as Chef, an uptight professional cook from New Orleans; Laurence (then billed as Larry) Fishburne as Mr. Clean, a seventeen-year-old black kid from the Bronx slums; and Albert Hall, the veteran Navy boat chief. That was the crew of the PBR.

"I knew what there was on a PBR," said Milius. "I took the crew, I knew there'd be a chief in charge, that there'd be a Mr. Clean from the Bronx or someplace, the rock 'n' roller, but Chef was one of my ideas. I thought this absurd a kind of trait, to be a saucier, and he ends up in the Navy, and can't stand it 'cause all the food is ruined."[10]

"Lance was just a surfer, his family were all surfers," said Sam Bottoms, "and he overcame his innocence throughout the whole thing."[11] He liked Coppola's Socialistic notions at first, but over time, like the characters in George Orwell's *Animal Farm*, came to realize some are "more equal than others."

"One of his big dreams was that we'd all work together in harmony for the good of the project, like Communists," said Bottoms. "That's why I was attracted to him in the first place. But like any utopia, the truth is there is one person who gained, and everyone else suffered. He was living like a king—the cigars, the limos, the mansions—and complaining he didn't have any money. When someone's abusing their power to the point where they become inhuman, lashing out at people, criticizing people who were working for nothing, where's the humility there? After *Apocalypse Now*, it was like, 'I only make commercial movies, I don't even write my own scripts anymore.' So because of that illness—not wanting to share—he never was really able to tap into the fledgling artists. I learned that I couldn't wait for someone like Francis to take me by the hand anymore, because guys like him can't even take care of themselves."

Harrison Ford, not yet a star in *Star Wars*, would play a minor role as an aide to a general—a colonel in Milius's screenplay—played by G. D. Spradlin, the corrupt senator from *The Godfather II*.

Scott Glenn, then an unknown, was picked to play the role of Colby, the soldier sent on an assassination mission prior to Willard's. At the time his role was expected to be larger. Dennis Hopper, his career in the toilet—people thought he was dead or out of the business—signed on, trying to make a comeback as a crazed photo-journalist based on the Russian in *Heart of Darkness*.

Coppola signed the young actors to his kind of contract, and negotiated with Keitel for the same. "Coppola felt abandoned by people whose careers he felt he had significantly advanced," *Variety* wrote of Pacino saying no.[12] The incentive-laden back-end deals he negotiated—the Screen Actor's Guild would disallow them today—were his way of getting some "pay back" from an industry he arrogantly felt never gave him his due.

Frederick Forrest felt he was coerced into terms not favorable to him. It tied him to

Coppola for seven years, which he thought would be two or three films' worth, not a long isolation in the jungle. The contract issue was another indication this was a totally groundbreaking film in all ways.

With the requisite stars in tow, he needed to cash in the European deal he had made. He sold the U.S. rights to United Artists for $10 million, going into production with $1.7 million, the control he sought, with a new release date of April 7, 1977, Coppola's thirty-eighth birthday.

Days before leaving, in front of a reporter, Coppola dropped to his knees before the Trans-America Building, recently completed and already an iconic highlight of the San Francisco skyline. It was across the street from his own offices in the Sentinel Building on Montgomery Street. Trans-America was the conglomerate parent of United Artists.

"Someday I won't just own this, but I'll own you too," Coppola said. This was the man who wrote *The Godfather* as a metaphor for corrupt capitalism, whose appearance had been described as Castro-like, and who had originally envisioned American Zoetrope, symbolically and now literally *behind him*, as a "counter-culture M-G-M." Now he was kneeling and worshipping at the very essence of American corporatism like a pagan idol, boasting that he would become so wealthy he would control it on his own terms, presumably not to be run like Fidel Castro ran Cuba.

Coppola told *Playboy* his film was "about war and human soul," not a commentary on America's involvement. Milius's writing was practically a war college manual that could have been titled, "How We Could Have Won in Vietnam."

"But it's dangerous, because I'll be venturing into an area that is so laden with so many implications that if I select some aspects and ignore others, I may be doing something irresponsible," said Coppola. "So I'll be thinking hard about it."[13] Coppola was not really political, but he was anti-war and had written *Patton* that way. Only Franklin Schaffner's direction and George C. Scott's blazing performance had colored it the other way.

11

Ordeal in the Jungle

In February 1976 the crew went to the Philippines. On March 1, Coppola, his wife, Eleanor, their three children, a housekeeper, nephew Matt, and a projectionist arrived. Two of Coppola's kids were on *The Godfather* set during that shoot. "They were not only welcome on all of my shoots, but I took them out of school wherever I went on any location, and I always had them there," Coppola said.[1] He felt the location shoots were unique educational experiences for his children.

They set themselves up in a mansion in Manila with all the creature comforts. This contrasted with scenes of abject poverty amid stifling heat. The idea that the American military could function, let alone defeat an entrenched, heavily outfitted Japanese Army in such conditions, seemed impossible to them, yet they had, and so too could Coppola win his own personal "war." They expected a fourteen-week shoot. Tavoularis had already picked out locations all over the island of Luzon, scene of a famed World War II battle between General MacArthur's forces and the Japanese. They relied on air transportation and assumed the Philippines had a modern air-traffic system.

The production immediately ran into a set of problems, one on top of the other. Conditions were beyond strange; sometimes dangerous, including guerrilla war in the nearby jungles. It was the height of the Cold War. Marcos was in dread fear of Communism; that he could meet the same end as South Vietnamese president Ngo Dinh Diem, assassinated in a 1963 *coup d'état* tacitly allowed to happen by the Kennedy Administration. Marcos desperately needed American support. Henry Kissinger and the U.S. overlooked his colossal corruptions so long as he fought the Communists. Everything was always damp, a major hindrance to equipment (as the Marines had discovered when they fought there). Snakes were everywhere. Brutal insects attacked day and night. The mountains posed a danger for the helicopters, especially in the rain. The rivers were dangerous. Men working on the boats wore markings so their remains could more easily be identified when they drowned.

Shortly after arriving in the Philippines, United Artists told Francis that they wanted to send a documentary team over to get some material. Eleanor recalled,

> At the time, it was customary to run five-minute pieces on television to promote films. Francis was already having difficulties and didn't really want a team coming out and snooping around, plus all the systems of getting people out to the locations were overtaxed and he just thought that having more people to look after would be too much. He told UA that he would do it "in house." He looked around and everyone but me had a job. He said, "Ellie, you do this." I had never made a movie or been to film school, though I had made some very short art films and he knew I had a good eye.
>
> The equipment arrived on the porch of our house in Manila, and I sat down and read the instructions, taught myself how to load magazines, and so on. I was using a small 16-millimeter newsreel camera, but it was still fairly heavy for me. I made every mistake there was to make. The tripod blew over while I was trying

to shoot on the main set. I thought that if I shot everything in sight, surely I would get five minutes of usable film. I wasn't getting paid—just getting raw stock. At home, Francis would start talking about all his problems, and I would just stick the tape recorder on the table and turn it on. He didn't care. He was too overwhelmed with what he was saying. By the end, I had sixty hours of film and about forty hours of sound tape.[2]

Initially, the footage and interviews were for the short promotional film, or for her diary, not a documentary. Eventually, Ellie Coppola's "in house" camera shots became *Hearts of Darkness: A Filmmaker's Apocalypse* (1991).

"The film Francis is making is a metaphor into the journey into self," says Eleanor, early in the documentary. "He is making that journey and still making it. It is difficult to watch someone you love confront his fears: fear of failure, fear of death, fear of going insane. You have to die a little, go insane a little to cross to the other side. This is not over for Francis."

On the first day of shooting, Coppola told them that, for luck, everyone should touch someone and say this word three times: "Kuala."

As Coppola said on Ellie's documentary: "On one level, the film is an adventure story, it's the story of a journey into a strange and unknown area, but it hopefully will also exist on an historical and social and allegorical level, so that ultimately it sheds some light on the events that took place, and why they took place, and what it did to the people involved in them."[3]

"Almost we are persuaded that there is something essential, something waiting for us in the dark areas of the world; aboriginally loathsome, immeasurable, nameless," Orson Welles presciently said on his radio broadcast of *Heart of Darkness*.[4]

On March 20, production started on a salt farm near a river; Keitel being taken by helicopter to the patrol boat, but a mix-up found Keitel and others stranded on a raft. He called on a walkie-talkie, "Hello, this is Harvey Keitel." There was no answer. "You wouldn't do this to Marlon Brando," he said, half-joking.[5]

At the time, Brando was on Tahiti with his family. Keitel was scheduled for another movie shoot in the fall. The quintessential urbanite, with a heavy East Coast accent, he hated the jungle immediately, complaining long and loud.

Muslim separatists inhabited the southern part of the island. Many helicopter scenes were canceled at the last minute as they headed off to skirmishes. All the equipment needed to be constantly guarded by heavy security, since the rebels might want to steal ordnance positioned on the set. Coppola had a full-time bodyguard armed with an M16.

Tavoularis designed a set near Baler, a small town on the northeastern coast of Luzon, a six-hour drive from Manila. There were complaints from everybody; the shoot was completely lacking in modern amenities. The script seemed incomplete to Coppola as he got into filming; the revelation that much of the character development had not been fleshed out.

The crew partied hard and took lots of drugs. Subic Bay hookers and booze were plentiful. Sam Bottoms would go to a massage parlor where "you could go in there and get jerked off for five bucks," he said. Coppola brought in the best wine and Lalique crystal, along with state-of-the-art stereo equipment and top-of-the-line cooking utensils. He had the best food flown in. Money was no object. They drank Champagne from Tiffany glasses.

"The practice on the set was, when in doubt, buy it!" Peter Biskind wrote.[6]

On his thirty-seventh birthday, April 16, Coppola threw a party for three hundred American, Filipino, and Vietnamese extras, who consumed hundreds of pounds of hamburgers and hot dogs flown in from San Francisco. A six-foot cake was decorated with mountains, river, and oceans with waves of icing in the form of palm trees. The shipping and duty tax alone cost $8,000.

Italian cinematographer Vittorio Storaro kept olive oil and canned tomatoes to make pasta sauce. Coppola made espresso. "I like how the Italians came to the Philippines always beautifully dressed," said Eleanor. "The Italian crew was always different from the American crew. The Americans were all in their sloppy T-shirts and scruffy shorts, and the Italians coming with Vittorio Storaro had linen shirts and gold chains and had a different sartorial approach to being on location. They lived their lives on location; they actually brought their coffee and their espresso, which they would have in the afternoons, and they would make their spaghetti on the weekends....

"They lived in the present."[7]

After viewing footage of Harvey Keitel's first week of shooting, Francis decided to replace him. He watched the first week's rushes with Fred Roos and Gray Frederickson. Coppola asked his editors what they thought.

"We bit the bullet, and did a very unpleasant thing, which is replace an actor in mid-shooting; not only unpleasant but expensive," co-producer Fred Roos recalled. "We had to throw out several weeks of work and start over."[8]

"Jesus, Francis, how do you have the guts to do it?" Frederickson asked him.

"Firing my lead actor was so bad," said Coppola. "It's a terrible thing. Sure, it jeopardizes the production, but it can also ruin an actor's career, to be fired like that. It was a very, very hard decision....

"I had searched for someone to be in the film. I had hoped for McQueen for the part. After I realized that that wasn't going to happen, I settled on Martin Sheen, but he wasn't available. Fred Roos pushed hard for Keitel, whom I admired as an actor, but I didn't feel he was right for the role, which was really very much that of an observer—a man gazing out into the jungle, and I didn't think he'd be the kind of passive man—a face, if you like—gazing out into the jungle.

"When we got [to the Philippines], I could see that he was very uncomfortable about conditions in the jungle, and I thought, *Not only do I think he's wrong casting, but what's it going to be like for six months in these difficult conditions in the jungle, for a city guy who's afraid of it?* I just decided to make this tough decision. Harvey's always been gracious about it, so I'd say that this was just one of the most difficult things that happen. But I feel I made the right decision for the picture."

Frederickson said Keitel was almost relieved. "I think Harvey realizes, as well as Francis, that it wasn't his kind of role," he said. "He's a New York street guy, and this was a different role for him; he didn't quite feel right with it. It was a mutual thing."

Keitel had only a verbal agreement per Coppola's contractual arrangement, which they voided. The day after the firing Francis caught a flight to L.A. He needed to quell rumors in town about Keitel's firing along with problems on the set, which were not rumors. He had already lost thirty-five pounds and remained as anonymous as possible, arranging through an agent to meet Martin Sheen in the VIP lounge at the airport.

"I had shaved my beard off when I went back to L.A. when I was involved in the casting of Willard, and I didn't want to have controversy, so I shaved my beard so I could be back in the U.S.A. without being recognized," Coppola said.

"I left Rome on Good Friday," Sheen said of his departure from *The Cassandra Crossing* shoot.[9] There was only a fifteen-minute meeting with Coppola before his flight was due to leave. Coppola gave him the script, telling him he was in the running to replace Keitel. Sheen already wanted the part. Coppola flew back. The next day Sheen got a call from one of Coppola's associates saying they wanted him. The next day he said goodbye to his wife and kids, then flew to the Philippines.

Coppola came back and found problems on top of problems. Marcos was facing more difficulty coping with the rebels than anticipated, meaning he needed his helicopters and airplanes.

Coppola again reached out to the Department of Defense, but they were adamantly against involvement. Coppola hoped Secretary of Defense Donald Rumsfeld would agree to practically "finance" his project the way they did for John Wayne's *The Green Berets*. It was typical liberal thinking: government funding of the arts. The Pentagon remained adamant; they would "cooperate" only if the production would revise the "objectionable" parts of the script. For the most part they were still working on the original Milius version. Milius would have thought that to be a pro–American, pro-military piece of work. Those were certainly his sentiments, and the action was largely based on his sympathetic understanding of what many war veterans he befriended told him about their experiences.

However, the crux of the story still based itself on the military, working with the CIA, ordering the assassination of an officer. They insisted this would not happen. Milius's colorful descriptions of U.S. soldiers, dressed in "native" costumes to adapt to the jungle, not merely killing the enemy but doing so in the manner of hunters slaughtering their prey, a bloodthirsty orgy of death that represented Colonel Kurtz's vision of the only way America could terrorize the opposition into submission, was not acceptable to the brass. It represented a Euro-colonialist understanding of "pacification," as the way the Belgians terrorized natives of the Belgian Congo (largely inspiring the original Conrad novel), or the way the British Empire suppressed the Mau Mau uprising. Rejection of these practices by the United States was then (and is still today) at the heart of a notion of American Exceptionalism: that this country does it better, is more moral and decent than previous empires. (It resonates in the way the U.S. has fought the War on Terror in the Middle East, with profound questions remaining as to how to ultimately quell Al Qaeda and Islamic jihad.)

The Pentagon objections certainly would have grown over the changes to the Milius script, much shot on the fly by Coppola; at first to Milius's consternation. The director veered the story sharply to the left politically, replacing much (if not all) of the jingoism with couched representations of America as pseudo war criminals in the form of frightened boys forced to perform horrible acts in which they would otherwise never engage. But all of that was still in the future; for now Coppola was forced to go it alone, increasingly in every way. Neither the government nor the "Hollywood system" was with him. He had some backing from UA, but was on the hook in an unconventional way never seen before, not by Orson Welles or any other maverick.

Some "suggestions" the Pentagon offered were to have Captain Willard acting as an "investigator," not an assassin, tasked with bringing the guilty back for a court-martial, their crimes based not on military strategy but on a need to administer "medical/psychiatric treatment," not to simply eliminate Kurtz with "extreme prejudice." Coppola offered to have a civilian give the orders to Willard instead of a general, but that was rejected.

It was not surprising. The Republican administration was happy to administer some payback against what they deemed years of liberal bias. In Coppola's mind his film was still a 1950s World War II epic, of bravery and valor, only using the Green Berets. *Patton* had been done without U.S. government cooperation; the battle scenes were shot in Spain using equipment the Spanish government had been given ... by the United States.

But the rejection by the Pentagon at what Coppola deemed a crucial time discouraged him. He told Eleanor his film would fail. She was taping his conversations without his knowledge for the publicity shoot she had been tasked to make with the studio PR department, but was already envisioning as a documentary.

Coppola then paid Marcos a large fee (bribe?) to have his air force made available, but he sent over different pilots every day. Each had to be brought up to speed anew, so rehearsal was a problem. Daily, time-consuming briefings were required. Coppola needed a large Chinook, which the government did not have, to pick up and drop the patrol boat in the river.

"With my helicopters, the boats and the high morale of the well-trained extras we had, there were three or four countries we could have taken easily," recalled Dick White, a Vietnam veteran helicopter pilot in charge of aerial battle sequences.[10]

But there were many problems with the helicopters. Some came in too high, wrecking tens of thousands of dollars of shoots. The rebels were fighting in the hills only ten miles away. In the middle of a complicated shoot they were called away to fight them.

Gray Frederickson was impressed with the footage, but frightened as well.

"I was a wreck for about two weeks, with all these explosions and helicopters and everybody running around," he recalled. "There would be all of this smoke going up in the air, and two or three helicopters coming from different directions would be flying into these smoke clouds. I would just sit there, crossing my fingers: 'Don't let them hit each other up in these clouds. I hope they can see.' They could see, obviously, but it was horrifying when you were looking from down below. Then they'd have these explosions that would blow these fishnets into the sky. I'd think, 'My God, if a helicopter rotor caught one of these fishnets, that would be the end of everybody.' It's lucky we didn't get anybody hurt."[11]

"It took its toll clearly, on everyone involved.... I'm proud there was no loss of life," recalled Coppola.

"The heat and the humidity are overwhelming," said Eleanor on *Hearts of Darkness*. "It is the first time any of us have seen rice paddies, water buffalo, and nipa huts. Sofia [Coppola, Francis and Ellie's then-very-young daughter] said, 'It looks like the Disneyland jungle cruise.'"

"It was six hundred people working on this thing," said Tavoularis. "In Hollywood and New York, with each person it's quite a big deal with their fringes and their salaries, it's thousands of dollars. So for a dollar a day or $3 dollars day, I hope we weren't taking advantage of people, but that's what they were paid. So, you could get not one person but ten or twenty or a hundred."

"Every day the project seems to get bigger," Eleanor Coppola observed after the fifth week of shooting. The special effects had some problems, but, when working, were spectacular. "I hate to say it, but this whole movie is special effects," said special effects coordinator Joe Lombardi. "You got three stars, but the action's gonna keep the audience on the edge of their seats." Despite all the troubles, the rushes were incredible. This was the single thread keeping the filmmaker going, to stay sane and hopeful in the face of enormous trouble. There was an incredible excitement in the helicopter scenes.

Initially there seemed little substance, just explosions, much shot out of sequence. There were times everybody thought Coppola to be lost, but this had been the impression on *The Godfather* set. But he still had no ending. He was dissatisfied with Milius's "cartoon" conclusion, but his own rewrites for a Kurtz/Willard confrontation and ending summing up the entire war, a "big idea," a truly Aristotelian morality tale with an appropriate message, escaped him. This haunted him more than anything. The press came on the set, asking about the delays.

"Well, we're behind, but we haven't stopped shooting," Coppola told them. "The film is enormous. I'd say it's twice the scope or production of any film I've ever done, including the two *Godfathers*. It's such an enormous film with so many aspects to it. We're out here hacking inch by inch, and you're up against a hundred problems every day, it's like a great war itself."

"Francis always reminds, this is not just a documentary about the Vietnam War," said cinematographer Vittorio Storaro. "This is a main show, in the sense that wherever America goes, it makes a big show, on everything. They make a big act, they make a big show about lights, music, even put Wagner on the battle scene, it's part of the operation, is part of the major fantasy that the American people has."[12]

Logistics were impossible. They went through assistant directors "like Kleenex," wrote Biskind. First the Italians, who were part of Vittorio Storaro's crew, "fell by the wayside." Jonathan Reynolds was brought on for a "making of" book.[13] Francis made him the first assistant director. He had hardly been on a set before.

"In the movie, when Martin Sheen walks up to that guy in the trench and says, 'Who's the commanding officer here?' And the guy says, 'Ain't you?'—that was the essence of *Apocalypse Now*," said Frederick Forrest. "We didn't know who was in charge, man."[14]

Meanwhile, laborers were carving out Coppola's swimming pool at his Manila residence with their bare hands. Biskind wrote that it was metaphor for the hole he was digging for himself on set. Fred Willis had argued with Coppola on *The Godfather* set, but he centered the director on the task at hand. Storaro was a laid-back Italian who did not correct Coppola when he went too far. "My reality feels like a foreign movie," Ellie wrote in her diary. "Part of me is waiting for the reels to change and get back to the familiar scene in San Francisco and Napa."[15]

"His personality had changed," said Nancy Tonery, Coppola's script supervisor since *The Godfather*. "Something happened to him either before or during the filming in the Philippines. He was no longer bound by any normal conventions. Francis would tread on anyone he could tread on. Anytime anybody had his belly full or annoyed Francis, he or she would be fired. There was a constant parade of people coming and going. Each time anybody left, the next person wouldn't come for any less than twice as much as his predecessor had been making."[16]

Coppola would never admit it, but he needed somebody like Bob Evans; a boss. Ellie thought Francis was identifying with the demonic Kurtz, becoming him. There was nothing to inhibit him. He cursed and yelled; he broke things. He treated the well-respected Fred Roos badly and threw a two-by-four at the amiable Gray Frederickson.

"Francis didn't pay anyone anything," recalled Al Ruddy. "And he treated these guys—

Gray and Fred Roos—like they were fuckin' slaves. But, hey, if you buy into 'he's the emperor and he can do what the hell he wants,' then you gotta take it."

Muslim rebels battling Marcos in the South closed the Manila airport every night after sundown. No aircraft could fly after dark. "It's your plane, you fly it," one pilot told Coppola. One evening a pilot would not take off after dark in his Mitsubishi. Coppola went ballistic, stomping his brand new state-of-the-art miniature Nagra NSN tape recorder. "I'm sorry, I've killed my little Nagra," he said.

It began to dawn on people, most especially Coppola, that their personal experience was beginning to mirror that of the American combat experience, which had started out as adventure, then became a slog, and, finally, turned into horror. This did not bode well for *Apocalypse Now*.

"The real phenomenon on being in that situation, of being in the middle of that jungle, dealing with all the unfriendly elements, was part of what Vietnam was about," said Coppola. "That was the first directorial decision, to put us all in a circumstance that reflected, you know, what the movie was all about."[17]

"The whole thing's really fun, I mean the war is fun," said Laurence Fishburne, who was fourteen years old when cast. "Heck, you can do anything you want to, that's why Vietnam must have been so much fun for the guys who were out there. I mean, I know this one dude, he came back, shit, and he's nothing but a dope smoker, and all he does is smoke dope. He said, 'Vietnam, was the best thing they could've done for my ass.'"

On April 24, Sheen arrived. "I had some personal concerns over my own physical condition," he said. "I was thirty-six at the time, and I felt old and out of shape, and I was smoking three packs a day; not a healthy guy. I was concerned that I wouldn't be able to handle a strenuous schedule. At the time I hired on, it was only a sixteen-week shoot, which didn't prove to be the case, but who could have known that at the time, you know?"[18]

Adding to their woes, on May 19 Hurricane Olga blew in from the South China Sea, causing heavy rains and floods that washed out roads, creeping into the buildings, even the home in which the Coppola family lived. It rained ten days straight, burying sets in mud. The mud dumped on the speedboat and on the helipad, stranding people with no food, toilet facilities, or drinkable water. Roofs were blown off. Then the vodka ran out. They had six inches of water on their floors. The kids played in it while Francis cooked pasta, loudly playing *La Boheme* until the electricity went out.

The rains caused a $2 million budget overage and delayed the production six weeks. It was precisely what Roger Corman had warned Coppola to avoid. He had blithely told his old boss it would be a "rain picture," but that *hubris* now threatened to be his undoing. Damage from the typhoon practically destroyed the carefully crafted sets.

In retrospect, the rains may have been Coppola's finest hour. He responded by thinking on his feet; improvising and working with the limitations forced upon him. In this respect he was like a great military commander, a role John Milius always equated with being a film director. On May 21, he moved the set and crew to the coastal town of Iba for six weeks of "*Playboy* scenes," the memorable and iconic shots of *Playboy* bunnies entertaining the troops in a USO show, inspired by a 1965 appearance by Playmate of the Year Jo Collins at the ironically named Black Virgin Mountain.

But the rain persisted, blowing tents away. Coppola doggedly filmed through it. There was much destruction of sets and equipment, setting Coppola "on some brittle edge," Ellie recalled.

"I remember sheets of corrugated steel coming off the roofs and flying through the air," said Dean Tavoularis, "the howling winds and bamboo trees bent way over. This yellow light. It was strange. When it was over, the set had been blown away."[19]

"I knew if weather came I would try to incorporate it," said Coppola. "But I didn't realize it was on such a big scale...."

The ships were set up against the shore. "Even after that typhoon hit, we continued to film," said Sheen. "[Coppola] said, 'This is happening. Monsoons hit Vietnam. There was a lot of mud and rain around. Let's film.'"

A scene in Eba got cut. There was mud up to the actors' knees. "It was like pissin,' it was hittin' you so hard it hurt," recalled Fishburne.

"It started out it was raining a lot, then we realized it was knocking out centers of civilization, and rivers were overrunning and people couldn't get to places, the hotels and stuff, and we had to stop, and I realized that certain sets had been destroyed," said Coppola.

The Coppolas were dehydrated and weak, malnourished and salt-deprived. Both were ordered to the hospital for intravenous feedings and medication. Ellie was down to eighty-nine pounds.

Filming shut down for six weeks, during which time new sets were erected, small "cities" were built practically from the ground up, infrastructure created on the fly, in Pagsanjan, north of Manila. It added to the growing sense that the filming mirrored the conduct of the war itself, with enormous operations resulting in huge temporary "civilizations" that would be removed after the people eventually left.[20]

Coppola, trying to make the most of his time, returned to California to work on story elements. Milius had him read up on Genghis Kahn. "Attila was a slob, but Genghis Kahn was a great man," Milius told him. It took two months to rebuild sets. The cast and crew were sent home.

"It was an opportunity for everybody to have a little relief from the pressure," said Eleanor. "It became apparent it was going to go on longer than anybody realized in the beginning."[21]

The Coppolas went to Napa and the family slept on the lawn. Francis had a dream on how to finish the script, but, once awake, realized it wasn't any good.

"He realized he couldn't go on making the John Milius script because it didn't really express his ideas," said Eleanor on the documentary. "He still doesn't know how to make the film into his personal vision. He's been struggling with this for so long. He knows the material backwards and forwards. He is practically chasing his tail."

"I call this 'the idiocy' ... none of my tools, none of my tricks, my ways of doing things, works," said Coppola in *Hearts of Darkness*. "I have tried so many times, that I know I can't do it. There might be a big victory, but I can't do it. I can't right the ending...."

Coppola had always had reservations about the Milius screenplay; the ending was the total opposite of his personal message about the meaning of the Vietnam War. Despite the relative languidness of the California respite, he could not reconcile an ending that matched his perfectionist vision.

"I was on the spit," Coppola said. "I had gotten myself into something big. A lot of people, some people had come through, a lot hadn't. It was my job and also my financial burden to put together all the pieces and finish the movie...."

"I didn't understand all the fluctuations of the financing, so I felt that he'd do it, and if he needed to, we'd borrow the money, but I really supported him as an artist," said Eleanor, "and I feel that whatever the artist needed to do, to make his art work, is okay, I always felt confident and thought, *Well, what's the worst that can happen? We have to move out of a big house and they take away your car. But so what?* He was a very creative person and another film, another job, and he could earn his living and provide for us, so I didn't feel, I wasn't really frightened by it, and in fact at that point in time, we just sort of escalated our lifestyle into this big Victorian house and a staff. Life is kind of complicated for me, and entertaining, and I'd love to have my lifestyle reduced to some smaller scale. So part of me was just fearless in that regard. It didn't matter if it all went down the tubes and financing this project was all okay."

Coppola's return to California fed growing Hollywood rumors that the film was out of control and he was running out of money. There was truth to all of it. Coppola screened footage for his friends, who did not like it. He had already spent $7 million, yet had only fifteen minutes of usable footage.

In Los Angeles Coppola met with the UA brass, securing a $3 million loan on the condition that his movie earn $40 million in rentals. If not, Coppola would have to pay them back. Somehow, despite all his success, he was again on the hook to a studio the way he had been with Warner Bros.-Seven Arts when he started American Zoetrope in 1969. He was courting chaos and disaster; a $20 million production in a rainy jungle. He "stood a reasonable chance of being wiped out," wrote Biskind.

"I didn't know what I was getting into," said Coppola. "I was a big prophet of technocinerama, I would say there's gotta be a better way, I'm sitting here in the mud, I'm in bankruptcy, the thing isn't going to open for two years, the helicopters, every scene you see two helicopters there's another six where the pilots were afraid to get too low in the shot. I went into the filming of a big war film that's gonna make me a lot of money, I'll be a writer the rest of my life, and it was absolutely different, it didn't happen."

Then Coppola's worst fears—at least up until that point—were realized. The press got a hold of it and began a typical feeding frenzy.

"A melodrama is currently playing itself out in Hollywood, and for sheer emotionalism rivals anything put on film," said Hollywood gossip commentator Rona Barrett on her popular TV program. "The embattled figure in this drama is director Francis Coppola, who once again finds himself waging a war to keep his dream financially afloat."

"Now if you read newspapers, at all, or listen to the radio, you know that Mr. Coppola has been involved in the production of this motion picture for more years than even he would care to count," said TV talk host Tom Snyder, who also had a huge audience.

"Coppola Hocks Assets for 'Apocalypse,'" read one newspaper headline.

"The press sort of painted a picture of me as sort of a crazy person, and actually irresponsible, which I don't think is really true," said Coppola. "There was no doubt that it was my money, but the difference with *Apocalypse Now* is it was about Vietnam, that was what made it sound like such a crazy financial bet." Asked if he ever thought about quitting he replied, "How am I gonna quit from myself? Do I say 'Francis, I quit you now,' I was financing the movie, how could I quit?"

"There is a kind of powerful exhilaration in the face of losing everything; like the excitement of war, when a soldier takes the chance of being killed," said Eleanor. "Francis has taken the biggest risk of his life in the way that he's making this film. The film is now $4 million over budget, which the financier, United Artists, has agreed to put up, but Francis has to pay it back if the film doesn't make $40 million or more. That just gets me all the more focused on the present moment, and not allow myself to think about the 'what ifs?' of the future."

"I know that every big building that's built runs into big production overages; every bridge that's built, every NASA project, any large project that involves a lot of people, conditions of a reconstruction nature, go to overages all the time, and a movie is not an exception," said Coppola. "It's true that since it was my own money, and once I felt it was going in a direction I wanted to, I wanted to continue going in that direction. And since it was my own money, I just did it, really."[22]

Coppola, Eleanor, and daughter Sofia returned to the Philippines for phase II, but the Coppolas' marriage was undergoing major pressures; it had been that way since the success of *The Godfather*. It was, in fact, a miracle of sorts that Eleanor was still married to him. Coppola went to a hotel in Olangapo with a porn star. Skylarking actors and stuntmen broke into his room to throw him in the pool.

"I started smoking grass," said Coppola. "The grass affected me a little bit. I was more able to say how I felt. It was like Vietnam—it was there, and everybody was doing it. I also started getting very paranoid."

Stop Hing Koing, the mayor of Pagsanjian, felt the crew was like sin invading paradise as the locals spent windfall money from the Westerners on "women and liquor."[23]

12

"I was going to the worst place in the world"

One of the most famed lines in the film comes in Sheen's voiceover: "I was going to the worst place in the world, and I didn't even know it yet, taking me up a river that snaked through the war like a main circuit cable, plugging me straight into Kurtz."[1] Indeed, Sheen was entering his own personal ordeal; he was in the "worst place in the world" and would be there for a very long time.

"When Marty came home after the typhoon, he was real scared," Sheen's friend Gary Morgan recalled. "He said, 'I don't know if I am going to live through this. Those fuckers are crazy.' At the airport, he kept saying goodbye to everyone."[2]

Sheen is in practically every scene in *Apocalypse Now*, and dominates the early part of the film, which begins with his waiting for a CIA mission in a Saigon hotel room. He was a well-known actor before the film, a movie star after it was released. He would make countless films and be the star of one of the most successful television programs of all time, playing the president of the United States in *The West Wing*. Two of his sons would become major movie stars. Of all the scenes, all the movies, all the lines he ever uttered, the ones he says in *Apocalypse Now* are the most powerful, and no scene was ever more dramatic than the infamous Saigon hotel scene in which he drunkenly cuts his hand karate-chopping a mirror, only to continue filming while giving a heartbreaking rendering of his own personal demons amid blood and tears.

Sheen was a Catholic, but a struggling one. Born in Dayton, Ohio, he was equal parts Irish and Mexican, but his good looks reflected an Anglo quality. Choosing to emphasize his white identity and hide his Mexican heritage, he eschewed his born name of Estevez in favor of Sheen (he made up for it by naming one of his sons Emilio Estevez). He was married with a large family, but moved to Malibu, the ultimate fleshpot. He pursued movie stardom and fell for the Hollywood lifestyle. He was an alcoholic. He believed in God but was wracked with guilt over what he felt was a dishonest life. He was torn apart over the issue of abortion. His Christian beliefs compelled him to abhor it as the ultimate abomination, but he lived and worked in an industry that practically worshipped the practice, legalized nationwide just a few years earlier in the Roe v. Wade case. Sheen also had conflicting views of the Vietnam War. To most in Hollywood, Vietnam was morally relative to the Holocaust. *Bourgeoisie* French children were routinely taught just that.

"I was classified 4F because I had a birth defect, my left arm was crippled, most of my classmates ended up in Vietnam …" said Sheen. "I would have gone. I had two brothers in Vietnam, one who was decorated, a Marine, my brother John was a decorated hero, he survived, he had a very difficult time, and he's one of my heroes. He's still alive, God love him. My feelings for him are of joy ... he became a corpsman in the Navy ... the Marines took all the corpsmen into combat. He found himself in some horrible conflicts and lost all his friends. He became a raging lunatic and ended up in jail and beat people up, and finally had a moment of clarity."[3]

Coppola felt Sheen was tentative. He decided to push him. He thought Willard should be more vain. Coppola had heard that elite military personnel were like that; powerfully-built Adonises who looked like young gods with their uniforms and medals, their hair perfectly coiffed.

"I remember complaining to Francis one day, about my confusion over my character," Sheen recalled, "and I said, 'I don't know who this guy is, who is this Willard?' And Francis just stares me straight in the eye and says, 'He's you. Whoever you are. Whatever we're filming at the time, you are that character.'"

Eleanor described a dream Francis had with Marty and a Green Beret advisor. The Green Beret told him Marty's character would be vain. He would stare at himself in the mirror, so Francis had Marty do that. Then he saw that Marty had "turned into Willard," said Eleanor, who added he wanted to find his primeval side. Coppola said staring in the

"Crazy" Dennis Hopper (left) is a photojournalist who tries to convince Captain Willard (Martin Sheen) of the "greatness" of Colonel Walter E. Kurtz (Marlon Brando, not pictured) (courtesy of Francis Ford Coppola Presents).

mirror was his way of finding "different levels of good and evil in himself," and that he imagined Willard did things that "nobody had ever seen," and therefore had a "Kurtzian other side in him."[4]

He drank and smoked too much, and was not in good physical condition. Nor was he in good "spiritual shape." Sheen had been seduced away from Christ and was filled with guilt over it. He had already fainted from the heat and needed four stitches from cuts after standing too close to an on-set explosion. He hated the poverty of Manila. When he saw a pig chased by kids with no teeth, it further aroused his Catholic guilt and his place in the world. He fought with Coppola over money. The short duration of his on-set time had been extended and he could not commit to other jobs, much less having left his previous job to come on board. He had a "very heavy falling out," said Sheen. "I don't know if I'm going to live through this," he told friends. "Those fuckers are crazy; all those helicopters are really blowing things up."

August 3, 1976, was Sheen's thirty-sixth birthday. He drank heavily all day, and Coppola decided to use his drunkenness in a key scene. Sheen was waiting for his mission. In the film his purpose was not yet explained; only later would it be revealed he was not merely an Airborne captain but a CIA assassin. In voiceover, Sheen's Willard character speaks of the claustrophobia of waiting in his room; he wants to be in the jungle, the only place he feels alive, the place he knows the enemy is waiting for him.

Coppola wanted to use his inner turmoil, Sheen's private feelings of doubt, to show on screen. Apparently urged by the director, Sheen drank until he was almost falling down.

"You're evil; I want all the evil, the violence, the hatred in you to come out," Coppola told him. A crew member said Sheen was a guilt-ridden Irish Catholic and he had "no chance ... it was devastating."[5]

He admired his shirtless body in the mirror with Coppola barking instructions. The music of Jim Morrison reverberates as the room seems to encircle him—master filmmaking. In a series of cuts, Sheen drinks, sobs, wails, emotes, and, in his underwear, does karate. When he hits the mirror, cutting his hand, it is an accident, but the filming went on. Coppola wanted to cut but Sheen insisted on continuing. It was a personal catharsis for him, a moment of truth.

"I begged to continue to let me keep rolling, I said please, I must do this for myself, he allowed me to wrestle with some demons I had been wrestling with for quite a while," he recalled. There are other reports that it was Coppola who decided to keep rolling the cameras without telling Marty. Sheen improvised, insisting—or being directed—to continue with a bloody hand that had been cut by the shards of glass. Sheen's private agony was caught on screen. Weeping, smeared in blood, he started singing "Amazing Grace," asking others to pray for him. Everybody who witnessed it was shaken.

"That opening sequence was shot on my 36th birthday, August 3, and I was so drunk I couldn't stand up, frankly," said Sheen. Coppola's directions were to be vain and admire himself; then he told him to "frighten yourself," so he accidentally broke the mirror.

"I was so intoxicated I didn't realize how close to the mirror I was, so when I struck it, I ended up cutting my thumb in the mirror and split it open a bit...."

"Francis tried to stop it, he called for a doctor and there was a nurse standing by, I said, 'No, let it go,' I said, 'Let's have it out right now.' It had to do with facing my own worst enemy, myself. I was in a chaotic spiritual state inside." His groans heard on camera are real, partly exhorted by Coppola, but mainly from his inner turmoil.

"I fought him like a tiger," said Sheen. "It was real hard for me to reveal myself." Half of what Sheen said in the actual movie was directed personally at Coppola for putting him in this position.

Eleanor said there was a "possibility that Marty might lunge at the camera or attack Francis.... There was an electricity in the room, anything could happen. They were inside somebody, in his personal territory. Man alone in his most private moment."

"My heart is broken," he says in an outtake from *Hearts of Darkness*.

"I was just stunned by it, I'd never seen it ..." he said years after making *Apocalypse*. "That is who I was and not who I am.

"It was a transcendent scene. I am an alcoholic, and the insanity of alcoholics is, you think that's who you are ... that's where I was at that time. It was my thirty-sixth birthday, I'd been drinking all day, I knew I was gonna wrestle one of the demons ... some part of me wanted to see it on film.... *I had to look* at that, and see what family members had seen in me: self-loathing, guilt. All the things that destroy our humanity. I had to live that."

Sheen initially resisted watching the scene. "Francis told me you have to look at that, and I told him I have no interest in seeing it ..." said Sheen. "He kept asking me ... when it premiered at Cannes it was not in the film.... I couldn't go watch it.... I went with a friend in New York who'd been in the Army, and I was shocked to see that ... not until then was I able to crack through something really important....

"I pretended I couldn't remember a lot of the things I'd done that night," said Sheen. "Actually I remembered it all."

Coppola was known for getting the maximum performance out of his actors, and this was an example of the lengths to which he would go to achieve that level of intensity.

"He was tough on me," said Sheen. "I had not planned to do it, but I had done that scene in bars and at home in drunkenness, I am an alcoholic, it looked pretty frightening, it was a dead man ... immature in a lot of ways....

"Francis had a lot of courage in me, bringing me in to play that part. I was too old, frankly. I was [thirty-five] when I came to the Philippines, but we formed a friendship over the years that started with that. He opened a lot of areas to me and allowed me to explore a lot of areas...."[6]

"Willard was my Marlow, a very complex character, a guy who was ahead of his time, written of a lot now, but not then," said Milius. "He was a warrior, but not warlike, but got high on war, it was his drug, and he had no where else to go, he didn't know what else to do. Willard is a poster boy for post-traumatic [stress disorder] syndrome, especially the first scene. I love the idea that he hopes they're gonna come to get him: 'I needed a mission, they brought me one, and after that I'd never want another.'"[7]

(Milius's descriptions of Willard, particularly his earlier vision of who Willard is, how he is a warrior but not warlike, how he is addicted to war like a drug, "written of a lot now, but not then," is virtually identical to the character Sergeant First Class William James, played by Jeremy Renner in Kathryn Bigelow's 2008 Academy Award–winning *The Hurt Locker*, a realistic portrayal of Iraq War bomb demolition experts.)

"Marty's character was coming across as too bland," Coppola said. "I tried to break through it. I always look for other levels, hidden levels in the actor's personality and in the personality of the character he plays. I conceived this all-night drunk; see another side of the guy."[8]

This may have been the director's greatest filmmaking gift. Even the crewmembers who felt he was lost and out of control on *The Godfather* set all raved that he drew astounding performances out of his actors. On-set witnesses, however, thought it dangerous and terrible. Some said it looked like brainwashing.

It *was* ... the *Heart of Darkness*!

Coppola sent for Dennis Jacob, who showed up with books and fresh fruit from Napa. Jacob had attended the UCLA film school and was friends of fellow alumni Coppola and Jim Morrison. He had played an integral role in Morrison's intellectual development, and was thought to be something of a New Age guru type. He was shocked at Coppola's condition.

"By the time I got there, he had run out of emotional gas," said Jacob."[9]

Jacob argued that Kurtz needed to die at the end. He compared it to *The Fisher King* and gave Francis a copy of Sir James Frazer's *The Golden Bough*, plus *From Ritual and Romance*, a 1920 book written by Jessie L. Weston, which was an influence for T. S. Eliot's "The Waste Land."

But Jacob may have played a greater role than merely this one key plot point, important as it was. He and Morrison had been "partners in crime" during their college years. Somewhere along the way—John Milius was also influential in this musical choice—it was decided that the music of The Doors would bookend *Apocalypse Now*, not to mention agitate some of the movie's most powerful motivations.

"Ah, Jim Morrison!" recalled Coppola. "You know, he was a film student at UCLA. He was such a quiet, sweet soul, I mean he was I guess before he became a rock star he was such a gentle, serious person, so intelligent, interested in philosophy, and wrote poetry; he was very, very serious. Whenever I hear his voice I think of this person I remember, I didn't know him very well, but he was a very sympathetic person."[10]

But on stage Morrison transformed, perhaps inhabited by the spirit of a "dead Indian," as he always insisted. While "The End" begins *Apocalypse Now*, it also plays during the key Willard-Saigon hotel scene. While a shirtless Sheen stares in the mirror, flexes his muscles, then goes crazy on the mirror, and finally flails, sobbing, to the floor, Morrison sings "The End," but it is not the studio-produced version. Morrison's "fuck-fuck-fuck" sequence was discovered by David Robinson, buried in master tapes and mixed with "The End" in *Apocalypse Now*. It also overlays Willard's final, ritualistic killing of Walter Kurtz.

The theme music of *The Graduate*, *Patton*, and *The Godfather* notwithstanding, Morrison's "The End," must be the most perfect, fitting music ever on film. Even though the song was written in the mid–1960s, long before *Apocalypse* was even conceived, originally about unrequited love, then a strange ode to sex, death, and Oedipus, it was always *Apocalyptic* in tone. It starts with lyrics about "the end," losing a "beautiful friend," interpreted as life, and with it all that stands in life to be replaced by whatever is on the other side.

Morrison's mournful vision of a "desperate land" is filled with on-point metaphors of the entire failed hope of American's Vietnam mission. It is incredible how perfect each word, each syllable is to the subject, but it does not end there.

The "Roman wilderness" is completely aligned with John Milius's historical view of America as the New Rome. The lyrics reference insanity, which is perfectly realized by the early mission Willard is given to terminate a Green Beret colonel who has gone berserk, and also refers to Kurtz's Montagnard army. The opening stanza fades out as the initial scene—a devastating napalm strike in the jungle, an "Apocalypse"—morphs to Captain Willard's voiceover in his Saigon hotel room: Morrison's voice, the volume now much lower, singing about waiting for rain. This perfectly brings to mind the typhoons the production endured in the Philippines.

From there Morrison refers to a lurking sense of peril which is fulfilled in every scene on the river, the primeval jungle representing Morrison's "ancient lake," the river being the highway, and strange scenes reflecting the *Playboy* show and the LSD-laced Do Lung Bridge vision.

The song infers the dance humanity engages in with Satan, certainly one Willard, who had his "sins" brought up to him as if he were a guest at a hotel, engages in all the way. The arrogance of America's Messianic complex is referenced, followed by a call to adventurous youth to join in the fight against Godless Communism.

13

"Kill ... gore"

After Sheen is brought to Nha Trang and advised of his mission, he meets Colonel Kilgore ("kill ... gore"), based on someone Milius actually knew. The part was played by Robert Duvall. In the early Milius script he was given a similarly metaphorical name (Kharnage). Duvall delivered a brilliant portrayal.

At first, larger than life, Kilgore regally presides over all he surveys; the aftermath of a massive U.S. helicopter attack he spearheaded. But amid the carnage is a scene in which Kilgore saves the life of a little Vietnamese boy.

"To this day I don't know why he cut it," Duvall said, obviously miffed. Duvall was and remains an anomaly in Hollywood; a conservative and a Christian. "Here was a guy who saved the life of a baby ... we had heard from certain technical advisors how these interesting contradictions happened ... maybe it was pressure from his liberal friends in San Francisco, *we have to make this guy all one way*, a guy like that wouldn't save a baby's life, people aren't black and white. Maybe the character was getting too much emphasis on that one guy, that was the implication, it stopped a little bit there, maybe you don't give as much emphasis to Kilgore, but as long as you're emphasizing him I don't know why, it didn't make sense to me. He said, 'I'll put it in when we put it on television,' but I never got any kind of answer as to why he cut it out, there was no reason why it was cut, it was not ugly visually or logically."[1]

In a 2010 Napa Valley symposium, Coppola asked John Milius where he got the idea of using Richard Wagner's "The Ride of the Valkyries" for the helicopter attack.

"I love Wagner," replied Milius. "It lends itself to helicopters.... I knew the Wagner worked, and I knew they had psy-ops [psychological operations] where they placed speakers, they didn't play Wagner, they played rock and roll, but I thought the Wagner worked, and it works so well that you can't do helicopter assaults anywhere in the world without using Wagner today. During Desert Storm, when the 101st landed behind the Iraqi lines, they had the helicopters playing the Wagner, so everybody would run away when they heard 'Ride of the Valkyries,' and the same thing in 2003 when they invaded, every time the Apaches went overhead they played the Wagner."

Of the many iconic scenes in *Apocalypse Now*, the operatic helicopter attack of a VC village remains the highlight of the film. It was also Homeric. Once the helicopters land, Kilgore—a huge surf fanatic—orders Lance and several of his own men, also surfers from Southern California, to ride swells.

"It was a combination of not just *Heart of Darkness*, but *The Odyssey*," said Milius. "Kilgore was like the Cyclops, something that had to be overcome, it had to be tricked, and then the *Playboy* bunnies were the sirens, you know...."

"The war was taking on an interesting turn. It was a psychedelic war, you know, and the culture, the influence was sort of seeping into Southeast Asia. This strange U.S. culture that was going on. Where you really get a tone that it's a rock 'n' roll war, that things are going a little further than anyone realized."[2]

"I guess these air cavalry guys did some pretty crazy stuff," said Robert Duvall. "I've heard from some of the technical advisors some stories about the air cavalry that are real, that would serve my fulfilling fiction, that they would, for instance, a guy would be a pilot flying above the North Vietnamese, and would try to hook a bicycle, try to steal it, with the runner, and they'd shoot at him, and he'd hover for a while, and finally hooked the bicycle and stole it. I mean they'd play these games to break up the boredom. Men play strange games."[3]

"What we had done was string together all of John's friends, those things from his friends who were fighting over there, and it is was really a quest, or trek or something, to take us through the various aspects of the Vietnam War, and see it for the insanity that it was," said Lucas.[4]

After ordering a napalm attack to clear out the last vestiges of resistance, Colonel Kilgore then says, "I love the smell of napalm in the morning." Discussing this oft-quoted line during a TV interview with Bob Costas in 1991, Duvall said:

> People come up to me on the street and say, "I love the smell of napalm in the morning" like I never knew it and forgot it.... I hear it so much.... There was another guy slated to play it, I went to Francis and told him I'd love to play him, I know it's written as a much bigger guy than I am, and then he came to me, and I really liked playing it a lot.

Colonel Kilgore (Robert Duval, gesturing) points out waves in the middle of a combat sequence to the famed surfer Lance Johnson (Sam Bottoms) (courtesy of Francis Ford Coppola Presents).

> People called the guy crazy, which he wasn't. It was like adult day camp in war, breaking up the monotony by doing fun things, like the surfing, it wasn't crazy, it was men doing bizarre things, as children, in a life or death kind of perimeter....
>
> I talked to some air cavalry people, and there were some bizarre things that went on. I heard or read a general of air cavalry used to deer hunt on the Cambodian border, that's how he got killed, he crashed into a tree. One of the technical advisors said he was with the air cavalry, and he would fly into North Vietnam and try to hook a bicycle, they'd shoot at him, then he'd steal it. They'd do crazy things, the air cavalry, they were on dope, they did this and that, and the guy I talked to said in the compound where they worked on the helicopters they didn't allow any marijuana, but in the field it was going on like crazy. These were like a wild bunch of guys, at Ft. Hood there's a museum ... they'd wear spurs and hats that go back to the Indian wars.[5]

Milius and Coppola discussed the script in depth during the 2010 Napa Valley Symposium.

> *Milius*: I don't type, I write. When I was doing those scenes with Kilgore for the AirCav stuff, and I was aware, like most writers know, that this was sort of like the Cyclops in Homer, and their meeting the Cyclops. The *Playboy* bunnies were sirens, and he has to fool the Cyclops and the only way to fool him is with those surfers, and he encourages him by telling him there is really good surf up there.
>
> *Coppola*: I love when he says, "I'm a goofy foot."
>
> *Milius*: It makes perfect sense that he would be interested in surfing, plus going back to the Six Day War, there was an article I read about Ariel Sharon, and Sharon had led this armored incursion on a deep strike all the way to Aqaba, and he got off his tank, and he loved to spear dive, and there were these fish that were only in Aqaba, and he went out with his spear and shot some of these fish and ate them with his command staff, and said, "We're eating their fish." Not only have we gotten here and destroyed everything, but we're eating their fish, so that was the whole thing that, "We're gonna surf their point, we're gonna take their village, we're gonna annihilate them and take their waves," and when somebody says you can't do that, "It's Charlie's place," he says "Charlie don't surf," and that goes back to the idea of the whole thing with Kilgore, I came up with the idea that it was a California war, as opposed to World War II, where the guys, in all the movies about World War II it was always guys from the Bronx, or Brooklyn, maybe from the Midwest, but our culture was centered at this time in California, the hippies and everything, the whole world was California, and you constantly saw pictures of helicopters with flames on the front, you know, flames on the rocket pods, psychedelic signs everywhere, everything had a peace sign, which was ridiculous—"peace through superior fire power"—on their helmets, and they were constantly listening to rock music. So there was this clash between California culture and this ancient place that had resisted even Genghis Khan. Indochina had resisted even the Chinese and had absorbed and resisted everything and now had this veneer of Communism, but underneath there was this deep film of Oriental mysticism, this wonderful, inscrutable Oriental character, was coming up against California, rock and roll, drugs, immense fire power, water skiing....
>
> It makes sense if you're in a PBR you'd want to water ski. I thought that up, surfers did that all the time....
>
> Some of the stuff you think are just great when you first write it you go, "*Oh my God!*" What's interesting are the famous lines like Duvall's "I love the smell of napalm in the morning." I thought this is so over the top it'll be the first thing that comes out.

Copolla: He did it well.

Milius: He did it *so* well…. Duvall came to me and wanted to know what all those surfing terms were. He came to Malibu and walked around and saw what they did. He wanted to know what a cutback was. I love the later version where they come to the conclusion that they steal his board. I love the fact they steal his board and he comes looking for it, then recording, "It's awfully hard to get a good board…."

How would you know that anybody will repeat that? When I write, "I love the smell of napalm in the morning," I thought, *Well, this is the first thing they'll take out.*

Coppola: We cut out the nice opening where Kilgore steps out, we cut out the stealing of the boards, we cut a lot of stuff and later on when people started to go see it, I was saved from the jaws of defeat, I dodged a bullet … years later we just put it all back in.

After breaking free of Colonel Kurtz—"tricking" the Cyclops–Captain Willard disparages him in voiceover, and the crew continues upriver. At this point they engage in drug use and begin to show less discipline. They become more ragtag and less respectful towards the authority figure, Willard.[6]

"At the point we were developing this, nobody knew there were drugs over there, nobody knew all the craziness that was going on," said Lucas. "A lot was being kept back, so there was a chance to make a movie that would reveal a lot of things."

The end of phase II shut down in December of 1976. The crew flew back to the States. Pauline Kael warned Coppola not to use "The Ride of the Valkyries" because Linda Wertmuller used it in *Seven Beauties*.

"She was a real know-it-all," Coppola said of Kael, who famously said after Richard Nixon won forty-nine states and over 60 percent of the popular vote to beat George McGovern in 1972, "I can't believe he won. I don't know anybody who voted for him."

"I always felt that Kael turned on me because I didn't kiss her ass as much as I was supposed to," said Coppola.

He screened some footage and was thrilled.

"He was never, on any of his films, excited and up like he is now," Ellie wrote in her journal. "He was always a real torture-sufferer type…."[7]

The movie had gone on far longer than anybody anticipated and still had major obstacles to overcome, but the trip back to Napa Valley for Christmas revitalized him. He had hope that he could still pull this thing off. The inconsistent availability of helicopters and a monsoon had seemed the worst that could happen, but Coppola hadn't seen nothin' yet.

14

"He's not dead unless I *say* he's dead"

In late January 1977, Coppola returned to the Philippines for what he believed would be the last few weeks of shooting. To those who had seen Coppola work on *The Godfather*, especially the first one, the seeming lack of organization and order was not so startling, but to those who had not, it still seemed there was no real film in the offing.

Eleanor stayed in San Francisco when Coppola returned to the Philippines. She shipped regular supplies of air conditioners, table linens, frozen steaks, wine, utensils; and worried about him from afar. Then she sent a telex and said his supplies reminded her of the American experience in Vietnam. It was "the very situation he went there to expose." She called him an "asshole," making sure Tavoularis, Storaro, and the production manager saw it. Coppola was furious.[1]

Five days later, on March 5, 1977, at 2:00 A.M. Sheen had a heart attack. Sheen was drained by the experience in the Philippines, which played on his sensibilities as a pacificist, a liberal Democrat, and an anti-war activist. He considered himself a patriot, and admired General Dwight Eisenhower, although this was ironic. Kurtz was arguing, as Douglas MacArthur and others said, that there is no substitute for victory, and the only way to achieve it is to go all out and win. Ike had the "freedom" to do that, and the result is a paradox perhaps invented by Satan. In becoming a great man, one of the most heroic in world history, this believing Christian is also responsible for the planning and eventual mass killing of more human beings than any person, other than perhaps only four or five others.

The mosquitoes ate Sheen alive, which was exacerbated by the squalor and depravity of the Philippines. The rain added tension on the set. He ate bad food and smoked all the time; several poignant scenes featured him puffing away.

He was sitting alone in his room reading when he felt sharp pains. His wife, Janet, was in Manila at the time. Sheen was unsure if he was having a heart attack or not. He rested and listened to the wind blow, trying to sleep.

"I kept waking up, feeling like there was a hot poker on my chest," he said.[2] In the morning he sought help, barely making it outside the door, where he boarded a public bus, then got off when it passed near Tavoularis standing next to the wardrobe department. He got off, and when Tavoularis saw him, Tavoularis started to cry. He put him in a van and took him to the production office.

"Get me a priest," Sheen asked. A priest was found, who gave him his last rites. He did not speak English.

"I was at the production compound that morning, and there was a very agitated Filipino waving his arms and saying something I didn't understand," Tavoularis recalled. "He led me to the wardrobe truck full of army shoes, and in the back, lying on the shoes, was Martin Sheen. He was pale and sweaty. I held his hand and said, 'What happened?' Finally, another Filipino said they had been bringing in these shoes when they found Marty on the side of the road. He'd apparently had a heart attack. I felt the main thing to do was to get a helicopter."[3]

Doctors in Manila said he had suffered a major heart attack, plus a nervous breakdown. "I really had a close call and I realized, there is nothing I can put into words, but I just knew that if I wanted to live it was my choice, and if I wanted to die it was my choice too," said Sheen. "There wasn't any fear. The fear really came later when I realized how close I came to the end. Then I got scared."

"I remember the phone ringing, and my secretary said, 'Marty's had a heart attack, and Francis doesn't want to admit it,'" recalled Dave Salvin.

Coppola addressed this in footage captured by Eleanor.

> Dave Salvin told Melissa Hirsch that Marty had a heart attack. What the fuck is that? What the fuck is that? This will be all over Hollywood in half an hour. If Marty is so seriously stricken that he must go back, of course he'll go back and we'll eat it, but I talked to the doctor, they didn't know, Marty's a young man, and probably would be up and about in three weeks. I said, "Could he do non-strenuous work, such as close-ups, sitting and acting?" He said, "Possibly."
>
> That's all I need to hear from the doctor, so what's going on in the fucking trade winds is fucking gossip. Gossip. That gossip could finish me off, because if UA hears that we've lost eight weeks, then UA with a $27 million investment, if they're gonna force me to complete it with what I've got, then I don't have the movie yet....
>
> If Marty dies, I want to hear everything's okay. Until I say Marty is dead, if it's not done, the ship, the whole office ... out of here.
>
> I'm really scared, guys, the first time I've been scared on this movie.

"When Francis gets in trouble on a picture, the first thing he does is to keep going, which I respect and admire," said Doug Claybourne, the special assistant to the producer. "You have to keep moving forward, for Marty to get back.

"Of course he had mortgaged his home and everything else in order to afford to make this movie. We shot master scenes, a lot of that material we shot with doubles over Marty's shoulder, from the back, and when he came back we shot the close-ups. So we had to find work for the shooting unit for as long as it was gonna take."

"What did I accomplish today?" Coppola said in *Hearts of Darkness*.

"Marty was a big smoker, and he also jogged every morning, but he was well muscled, and he was so fit it was ridiculous, but he had this heart problem, and as soon as it happened I went to where the doctors were and very quickly learned how serious it was, but learned he was going to survive," said Coppola.

A part of Francis did "not want to admit" Marty had a heart attack, but Coppola was adamant that both the footage in the documentary and assertions from outside that he refused to face the reality of Sheen's medical condition was "absurd."

> Marty had a heart attack and I was there, and the family was there, and we knew that he was going to survive, and what was happening was that all the crew, everybody was making phone calls to L.A. saying how we don't know what's happening with the film, it's gonna stop, Marty's had a heart attack, but others were saying Marty is dead and I was berserk because I realized that if the rumors were Marty had this heart attack, that was going to preclude us from finishing the film, or that if people believed that Marty was dead, then the

people who were supplying money for the film basically would stop, and the film could be canceled, and they would of course capture the money from me and the movie would have been uncompleted, I would have half a movie, and that would be the end of it. They say "loose lips sink ships," I was furious that people were breaking that trust and were calling home with the news of this heart attack or worse, of Marty having passed away, and of course I was in a very delicate situation because now I was concerned that Marty get the best care possible. I said to his wife, "Please, take Marty and have Marty go with you home or whatever facility or hospital you choose; all I ask is that you don't take him out of the movie," in other words I will continue to shoot with Marty's brother, and we'll keep shooting as long as it takes, four weeks, five weeks, much of the movie in this section was shot not with Marty but with his brother in longer shots because he had very much the kind of physique as Marty.

"And at some point in the future—four weeks, six weeks—whatever you say, if you feel that Marty is well enough, that Marty can come back and shoot the close-ups, then we will," but I was really taking a chance with Marty. His wife, Janet, thought enough of his acting career as being so important that she wouldn't want the word to get out that he was going to have this medical problem and perhaps wouldn't be able to act again, and she had complete authority over what would happen with him, first for his health and survival, and second for his personal love of acting, so I thank her and Martin that much because they gave me that chance, they didn't pull him out.

Sheen also tried to keep it under wraps. If he could not come back the movie was over, and maybe his career with it. Janet told him that, with recovery, he could come back and finish the movie, but word spread into dark Hollywood rumors. UA might remove Sheen from the picture, some said. If Sheen left, Coppola would have to scrap almost all of it. Coppola lied to the press, saying Sheen collapsed jogging in the heat, and was resting. Rumor spread that Sheen was dead but Coppola was keeping it a secret.

"I sort of panicked that rumors would start flying, and of course they did, and I knew that that alone could finish me off," admitted Coppola. "In a crisis like that I'm usually calm, but when everyone stated yapping away I remember becoming outraged, and I think that was misunderstood by a lot of people, the press in particular."

In the documentary *Hearts of Darkness: A Filmmaker's Apocalypse*, Coppola was captured by his wife's camera raving that Sheen could only be dead if *Coppola himself* declared he was, but Francis said that was misleading. "The idea was not to tell anyone that it was more serious than it was," he explained. "Then I heard that people and crew members were calling home and saying that he'd died. So I was furious, which was that whole bit about me saying, 'He's not dead unless I *say* he's dead.' I'd say that again. But if you view that out of context, then it seems I don't care about him." He blamed himself for Sheen's heart attack.

"I completely fell apart," Sheen said. "My spirit was exposed. I cried and cried. I turned gray—eyes, my beard—all gray. I was in intensive care. Janet slept on the floor beside me. She called a therapist in New York and I talked to her every day and these two ladies pulled me through. I knew I would never come back until I accepted full and total responsibility for what had happened to me. No one put a gun to my head and forced me to be there. I had a big ego and wanted to be in a Coppola film."

"Marty is an extremely generous, big-hearted man," said Bottoms. "He's filled with a lot of love, and much unlike Willard, and so when you ask Marty to examine the darker nature of his character, it meant closing himself down a lot, and becoming inward, in order to find that killer, who could carry out the task and terminate Kurtz. I think Willard was definitely responsible for Marty's breakdown."[4]

"I chose to have that heart attack. I needed to have that heart attack, because there was a part of myself that had already died.... I need to start over.... I'm talking metaphysically and spiritually, I was a dishonest man," said Sheen. "There's two kinds of existence, and you cannot live that, and you can't live healthily or whole, you can't live that way.... Francis is a very sensitive man.... He wanted me to fully realize myself in this piece."⁵

Sheen was asked in a 2011 radio interview whether *Apocalypse Now* would get made today. "It would but not in the way we did, there was no blue screen, there was not a single special effect in the picture ..." Sheen said. "We had some very close calls on those choppers, they were terrifying. We were warned even when they were on the ground not to get to close to the tails; they'd all be in position on the beach, the tails spinning, the noise was terrifying, you could not hear a word, a guy with a mambo stick would whack you if you got too close.

"The whole film was dangerous, it was almost a year-and-a half, I was not as nimble as some of the lads, all of them were much younger than I. I felt like an old man ... the storm wiped out whole areas where we were, there were no radios, we had to evacuate, the film went on hiatus, so I went home and learned how to swim. I was on a boat without a life jacket. I took some training to be a soldier, small weapons, and that gave me confidence. I came back more prepared....

"I have a lot of mixed feelings about Francis," Sheen said. "I am very fond of him personally. The thing I love about him most is that he never, like a good general, asked you to do anything he wouldn't do. He was right there with us, lived there in the shit and mud up to his ass, suffered the same diseases, ate the same food. I don't think he realizes how tough he is to work for. God, is he tough. But I will sail with that son of a bitch anytime." Sheen's comments that Coppola lived as his actors and crew lived seems far-fetched; stories of his excess while the crew did without are legendary, but he was there the whole time, was never "sick at sea," and did leave it all on the line.

Sheen made lasting friendships with Forrest, Hall, Fishburne, and Bottoms, but would not talk about *Apocalypse Now* for a decade. "I'll just say that it was a deeply personal, long, and painful memory," he said. "There was a lot of darkness and a lot of despair—and a lot of humanity, too—but if you'd told me, 'This is what you're in for,' I would have passed in a minute. When they were rolling me down that corridor in the hospital, some four or five hours after I'd had a heart attack, my wife appeared alongside me, running with the gurney, and she leaned down and whispered in my ear, 'It's only a movie, babe.' And that saved my life. She saved my life. *It's only a movie.*"

Prior to Sheen's heart attack, Coppola seemed to have finally gathered some momentum. He had dealt with his own personal demons and overcome obstacle after obstacle in the form of financing, firing Harvey Keitel, bad weather, script problems, Marlon Brando's intransigence, but with all of that behind him he thought he might have an ending, to the story and the project, once and for all. Now he faced still another major downswing. He still needed Martin, having spent most of his time doing helicopter scenes, dealing with egos and logistics. He had practically taken Sheen for granted amid all the problems.

Again, Coppola proved at his best in a crisis, improvising with Martin's brother Joe for some scenes. He also took the time to orchestrate the destruction of the Kurtz compound, one of the most spectacular scenes ever filmed. He and the crew maintained their morale, but he was again at a low ebb himself. In addition, he was going through marital difficulties. Divorce was discussed, but Eleanor, who must be credited as one of the more understanding and supportive of wives, felt he was in the throes of a nervous breakdown and did not want to end their marriage under such duress.

He was able to get three or four weeks of shooting done, but after that they were in trouble. "Francis works in very intuitive ways, so he likes to take advantage of things as he moves along through a picture," said Lucas.

Coppola reflected:

> I was there in the middle of the jungle, with everybody looking to me. We were having problems with tremendous storms and difficulties and work relations, and were really at a point where we couldn't finish the film. I was in trouble and I had no one to turn to. I had no producer, I had no big brother, I didn't have a boss, I was the boss, I had total power over this thing, and I would go to bed thinking, "It's over for me, I can't do it," and at one point, the lowest point in the film, I realized it didn't matter, I don't need the new car, I don't need to be a big deal in my career, there are more important and beautiful things in life, so since I'm already washed up I'll make it a personal film that I believe in....
>
> I was the dark horse and I didn't have a lot of help from a lot of establishment aspects, who had no reason to wish me well, and naïvely I thought the film would go very smoothly, we would be a success, and would start the M-G-M of the future....
>
> My intention was that really, I do see *Apocalypse Now* as a film about re-birth. My hope was that if audiences see the film, experience the film, make it sort of personal, make it their own, then they could digest it and rise above it.
>
> We have to let what must die in order to go on, and *Apocalypse* was my small contribution to that way of thinking.

"He likes it to flow, and whenever you do that, you end up with a problem, of having a film that at times is way too long, and a film that doesn't have a really strong narrative line that you can keep the audience hooked in," said Lucas.[6]

15

"I felt like von Rundstedt going to see Hitler"

"I got problems," admitted Coppola to Susan Braudy of *Atlantic Monthly*. "I'm too good at adapting other people's scripts. Better than writing my own. I don't want to be known as an adaptor of other people's work."[1]

Coppola worried that he adapted better than he created. He worried about being pompous, and recalled an event on *The Godfather*, sitting on the toilet when two crewmembers came in, unaware he was there. He lifted up his feet so they would not know he was there. He overheard them say the film was a "load of shit" and the director was an "asshole."

Screenwriter John Milius (left) works with actor Martin Sheen (middle) and director Francis Ford Coppola (courtesy of Francis Ford Coppola Presents).

129

Now he feared everybody thought this again. Ellie felt he was too close to the material. She suggested dictating ideas instead of typing.

Finally, John Milius was brought back. "I was getting divorced when the movie was being made, so I called you and said, 'I need a mission,' and you said, 'I understand,'" Milius said to Coppola in the 2010 symposium at Coppola's Napa Valley winery.

"My contributions were to make it more like *Heart of Darkness*," Milius said, although Coppola, who kept a tattered paperback copy of the novel on the set at all times, referring to it regularly, was also insistent on holding close to its themes. He said that *he* was the one who stayed true to Conrad. "I made the [Dennis] Hopper character out of the Russian in the book. I came up with the opening."

Coppola said he never needed a script, he knew it so well, but carried the Conrad novel and constantly referred to it. "This was my actual Bible," he said. "One of the points I wanted to make was that you created *Apocalypse Now*, I didn't create *Apocalypse Now*," Coppola told Milius, adamantly. Milius's arrival in the Philippines created the temporary belief that somehow he would right the listing ship that was *Apocalypse Now*. Milius, ever the historian, compared the meeting to General Gerd von Rundstedt trying to tell Adolf Hitler that all was lost on the Eastern Front.[2]

"Who knows what Francis had put together, and they brought me back to put the script back together, and everybody said, 'Thank God, he's returned to reason. Thank God, this will be alright, this is a new day. So this thing will finally be released,'" recalled Milius. "So they said, 'Go in and tell him that he's been crazy,' and all this kind of stuff. I felt like von Rundstedt going to see Hitler, you know, in 1944, and I was going to be telling him there was no more gasoline on the Eastern front, and the whole thing was going to fold, you know, and I came out an hour-and-a half later, and he had convinced me that this was the first film that would win the Nobel Prize, you know, and so I came out of the room like von Rundsedt saying, '*Ve can vin,*' and you know, '*Ve don't need gazoline.*' He had completely turned me around, you know. I would have done anything."[3]

March 20, 1977, the one-year anniversary of the shoot, came and went. After an extraordinary two hundred days of filming, they were still thousands of miles from California, with no end in sight. Coppola was under escalating debt himself. On April 15, *New York* magazine reported his movie was "in the running for this year's *Lucky Lady* award as the Hollywood film farther over budget than any other." Where would the additional, needed money come from? It was already $15 million over the $12 million budget.

The *L.A. Times* interpreted the situation as a "fascinating view of an artistic temperament struggling to bring order to the unwieldy business structure that has grown around it." Coppola dictated a sharp memo to all his associates, a regular act on his part that had all the earmarks of an imperialist dictator. It was passed on to *Esquire* magazine by disgruntled Zoetrope employees, depicting him as paranoiad and desperate.

The memo was part *mea culpa*, part manifesto; Coppola claiming he was "cavalier" with money because as an artist "I have to be, in order not to be terrified every time I make an artistic decision," but warning employees not to confuse that with his being "infinitely wealthy."

He re-asserted that he was the boss and made all the decisions, not his wife or anybody else. He took blame for misunderstandings and many of the shoot's problems. He asked for discretion dealing with press or relatives back in L.A., and wanted control of the public's perception of it. The press reacted negatively to the *Esquire* piece revealing contents of the memo. Some employees stole his money and equipment, a real irony since Coppola originally stole equipment from companies he worked for, giving it to Lucas and those guys, like a Tinseltown Robin Hood.

He had the habit of telling people to do what he did not do, despite Sheen advocating that he was willing to do what he asked of his crew. For example, while telling his crew to tighten their belts financially, he threw an extravagant birthday party for Eleanor at an exclusive resort. The press mocked him for that.

But there was good news. On April 19, Sheen returned, less than two months after his heart attack. Coppola announced they would wrap by May 15. If it was incomplete, he could cut and edit it, then finish it later.

"He looks tanned and terrific, just like he came back from Palm Beach," observed Eleanor in her documentary. "Francis put his ear on Marty's heart, and said he looked *too* good."

The film mirrored the story. Inexorably they moved upriver. Eleanor captured Coppola working with his actors. "Francis used to write on these little cards, and I managed to hold on to some of these," recalled Sam Bottoms.

"Some days we'd get pages that said, 'Scenes unknown,' on the call sheet," said Frederick Forrest. "You'd just show up, you know. They didn't know what they were gonna do."

"You want each day to say, 'What will we do today?' " said Fred Roos. "You want a real plan for each day, but Francis is a writer and as the co-writer of the script, he could create things at the moment, and if an idea came up, he'd sit there all night and write it."

Coppola picked Fishburne to play Mr. Clean because he was so very young. At least that is Fishburne's belief: "I think what it was as Clean is I was just a kid, and that's what I think my role was about, it's about the kids that were over there, you know, who didn't know anything about anything, and were kind of just snatched up and used as cannon fodder for this war."

"It was like walking on eggshells, seeing the personal side, and then trying to carry on a professional relationship," Bottoms said. "The key to that was to put on blinders. You just didn't see it...."

"Everyone who has come out here to the Philippines seems to be going through something that is affecting them profoundly, changing their perspective about the world, and themselves," said Eleanor in the documentary. "Well, the same thing is happening to Willard in the course of the film. Something is definitely happening to me and to Francis."

"Filmmaking, at least for me, isn't just about writing this little script and then doing it, as you thought your own life and your own experiences in the making of it as also a very strong element, that somehow the director works with more than just having the script and having a team of people, there's also the condition and the mood of the company, and each individual and what personally the people are going through are also one of the primary elements of the films," said Coppola.

"Most of my character is done under the influence of pot," said Bottoms. "I smoked a lot of that. You know, the film crew just became our guests upriver with us."[4]

Many of the crew were laid low by parasites and tropical diseases, but had to live with the maladies until they could finally get proper medical treatment. Bottoms got hookworm, which damaged his liver and probably shortened his life. A construction worker died of rabies.

When the crew was going to fly to Manila, just to bathe, make calls, get milk products, and take care of health issues, Coppola had a guy stop them, not unlike the Reverend James Jones holding people captive from contact with the outside world.

The megalomania continued. Coppola lavished money on himself and above-the-line talent, but "nickel and dimed" everybody else. The Italian crew had pasta flown in from Italy every week, but when Coppola stopped paying the *per diem* on the rest of the crew, it caused a near mutiny.

"It was a state of siege," Nancy Tonery said. "It was like the people clinging to the landing struts of helicopters trying to get out of Saigon."[5]

By this time, newspaper headlines read, "Apocalypse When?" and "Apocalypse Forever." But Coppola was becoming more paranoid, lost in the jungle, the river journey, and the consuming story elements. He fell for the "siren song," as John Milius referred to the *Playboy* bunnies famously portrayed in the film, referencing Homer's *The Iliad*.

After "tricking" Colonel Kilgore, whom they had to overcome as Ulysses did in *The Iliad* and *The Odyssey*, the crew comes upon the USO show featuring *Playboy* girls. Rock impresario Bill Graham played the host who introduces the three girls, including the "Playmate of the Year, Miss Carrie Foster," played by the actual Playmate of the Year 1974, Cyndi Wood. After they shake their tails, several of the horny soldiers storm the stage in an effort to get to know them a little better.

"*Playboy* bunnies were just logical, these shows," said Milius. "These incredibly sexy girls were brought there, displayed to thousands of men, many of whom died the next day, what's to stop them from taking those girls? Why wouldn't they take those girls? That must have happened many times, although I never heard that it had and most of the people told me they were so happy to see a girl from home, gyrating and sexy, it made them feel good, but there was a desire, 'Why don't we just take these girls?' Because these were the sirens. I like the first version better where they don't touch them, because you can't touch the sirens or you'll end up on the rocks."[6]

Many of these scenes and the Kilgore scenes were cut out, so much of Milius's Homeric message is lost. The stealing of Kilgore's surf board, which is part of Willard's method of confusing the "Cyclops," as Milius saw Duvall's character, was removed. So was the embellishment of the *Playboy* girls, in which Willard, in scenes shot during the tropical rains that pummeled the island, negotiates with Graham's character to get the girls to have sex with several members of the crew in exchange for some gas. (They were restored for the 2001 redux version.)

One night Coppola flew in a Japanese chef to prepare Kobe beef, when he sank to his knees weeping, and had what seemed an epileptic seizure, banging his head against the wall, foaming at the mouth. He had delirious visions of actress Linda Carpenter (the *Playboy* Playmate of the Month for August 1976 under the name Linda Beatty, who was one of the "sirens" in the "bunny scene." He envisioned she was a witch or the devil (she was about to do a tarot card reading scene for the film, one that was later cut, but restored in the redux version).

He began to see himself as a conduit of evil, the movie's title a true depiction of it. He said he saw the "white light." His last request was for Lucas to finish the picture; if not him, then Milius. "I've got to do this picture," Coppola told Milius. "I consider it the most important picture I will ever make. If I die making it, you'll take over. If you die, George Lucas will take over."[7] Two days later he was better and watched a screening of Ernst Lubitsch's *To Be or Not to Be* (1942).

Melissa Mathison, who later married Harrison Ford, was apparently an antidote of some kind to Coppola's depression and set problems.

It was like "the girl who has a crush on her professor," Coppola explained. "Her confidence in me made me feel confident.... Confidence is a very important thing. When everyone is saying, 'You're going to fail....' That's why ... she always made me feel like a million dollars, in terms of 'I was talented, and I could do it.'"

She attended a formal dinner with Francis, screening the movie at the Marcos palace. "The palace was like a fortress, a den of evil," she recalled. "There was a huge dining room table, twenty feet long, that was covered row after row after row of candy bars, a hundred Clark Bars, a hundred Three Musketeers—for us. Imelda came in from one side of this giant room, with all of her ladies-in-waiting dressed to the nines in Chanel, while we were wearing Vietnamese black pajamas. Then Marcos came in from the other side, with all eyes on him. They nodded politely at each other. Obviously they hadn't seen each other in about three years. Vittorio set up this little projector in the back, while Francis was making a speech and Imelda's ladies were giggling and eating candy bars. She was sitting in front of me, and every time a handsome actor appeared on the screen she'd say, 'Is that Marlon Brando?' It was surreal."[8]

"I never felt my wife had any confidence in me," said Coppola. "I felt she was meddling and lining up with people that I—my wife is like a regular person. So she had the same kind of doubts about me as the so-called 'they' at-large." Eleanor sensed he was becoming like Kurtz. She felt nobody else was able to tell him anything.

"There is a kind of franticness.... If I say anything to the contrary, it is taken for negativity, disloyalty, or jealousy," Eleanor said on *Hearts of Darkness*. "I think that Francis is truly a visionary, but part of me is filled with anxiety. I feel as though a certain discrimination is missing, that fine discrimination that draws the line between what is visionary and what is madness. I am terrified."

Eleanor somehow kept their marriage together in what had to be very trying times. Certainly if she and her kids had not experienced it, they might not have taken seriously the descriptions they would otherwise have had to hear secondhand, just as Sheen's children experienced it, at least to an extent. That said, come fall Coppola's sons returned to school, although Eleanor stayed. As the holidays approached, Coppola formulated some scenes, mixing Kurtz's killing with the ritual tribal sacrifice they caught on camera (which was later masterfully overlayed with Morrison's primal screams and intense lyrics from "The End").

He screened five hours of footage, eliciting very positive feedback. Some began to talk of a "masterpiece." Ellie called it "visionary." However, he still appeared half mad. Ellie returned home and Francis moved to Hidden Valley, in a luxury cottage that was part of a spectacular resort inside an active volcano, where he began to indulge in stereo equipment, fine wines, and steaks.

"All those things did contribute to the state of mind that I was a little like Kurtz," Coppola later admitted. He later publicly admitted to an affair, and, in 1991, said the woman "made me feel like a million bucks." But Francis was more like Michael or Don Vito Corelone, loyal family men, than Sonny and Fredo, the philanderers. He was tormented and determined to end the relationship. Whether this was the cause of tensions with Ellie was never known, but she did return to the Philippines in March 1977.

"I was in, like, love triangles, beyond my thing, and I almost—and I was tired, and Marty had just had a heart attack, and it was my own money, and I didn't feel good about my relationship with my wife," Coppola said. "I didn't want to lose my children. A lot of men can do that. But I was just not the kind of person who could go wipe out my family like that and do a second family. I will never do that. I just can't."

Coppola made up with Ellie. "I'll never do it again, I'll never do it again," he pleaded with her.[9]

The weather got better, dryer.

"It was crazy," said Frederick Forrest. "We were slightly mad. The whole thing was mad. I felt after a while like we really went there, like it was a dream or something. We'd say to Francis, 'I'm not here, Francis, I'm in Montana with Jack Nicholson.' So they'd say, 'Where are you today, Freddie?' and I'd say, 'Waco,' 'Des Moines,' wherever I wanted to be. And out of this wildness, you just go through your day, and you weren't in that place....

"That was really crazy, that time in the jungle with me and Marty that time with the tiger, yeah, that was really just insane. We had this guy there with the tiger, a couple, trainers, and he had a slight speech impediment, and he had scar tissue all over his face, where he'd had bouts with the tiger."

The trainer, Monty Cox, explained that the cat usually goes "for the joint" and after that "you can't walk for a year."

"The trainer had this pig on a string," said Forrest. "So, the tiger would see him, then he was gonna pull him back so he'd jump at the right angle. So, the guy'd come around and say, 'Yambi'th very hungry today, Martin. He'th very hungry, Mithter Coppola, I'm sure he will do ecthactly what you want. We haven't fed him in a week.' Oh, shit. We come out there and Francis says, 'Get closer, get closer.' We're saying, '*You* get closer, Francis. *You* get closer.'

"...Man, I never been so frightened in my life, because he comes out so fast, man, guys were running everywhere, climbing trees, and to me that was the essence of the whole film in Vietnam. When you looked in that tiger's eyes, and the madness, like, it didn't matter what you wanted, there was no reality any more. If that tiger wanted you, you were his."

"Francis had us all list a set of things they wanted their characters to do, and I remember we all wanted to do a sort of My Lai massacre," said Sam Bottoms. "We thought an interrogation of the boat, and firefight, and the loss of many lives; we wanted to experience something like that."

David Berrigan talked of "USC war guilt"; privileged rich kids who avoided the horrors of Vietnam and needed to "atone."

"The scene where they come upon the little sampan boat; the fear of the Americans on that boat, triggers the killing that went on, and I think the truth of that scene so portrayed what that war must have been like," said Roos.

Frederick Forrest said there was often just improvised dialogue. "The whole scene where we shoot up the sampan was improvised," Forrest said. "It flowed like music. Francis set it up so the improv really flowed. Before we started, he gave each of us something to do. For instance, I was to search the sampan. And it was an incredible, powerful scene. When we had finished, it was absolutely quiet. Vittorio Storaro was just stunned. He said it was the best scene that he'd ever seen. But none of it was written down."

That was not the kind of depiction John Milius, the American super patriot, wanted to promote, but Vietnam movies—*Apocalypse Now, Platoon, Casualties of War, Born on the Fourth of July*—all had the obligatory "Mai Lai massacre" scenes.

Bottoms also admitted to dropping acid during filming at the Do Lung Bridge, when his *character* is on acid. He said he was also doing speed. "I wanted a sort of speedy sort of edge," he said. "And marijuana and alcohol. We were bad, we were just bad boys, you know."[10]

In re-writing, Coppola began to try for more surrealism. He wanted Kurtz and Willard separated by a thin line. Milius saw the jungle as a character in itself, in that the environment becomes primeval. This was actually one of the first themes of the Milius screenplay, describing an all-encompassing jungle that is the same now as it was a million years ago, although in his version soldiers have adapted all too well to it and are transformed into killing machines by it. Milius wanted the soldiers to be masters of this dangerous environment, whereas Coppola wanted them to be destroyed by its all-consuming evil. Coppola saw this to some extent in the tiger scene, with Chef—a New Orleans Catholic—driven half-mad by the surreal evil, but more so in the river, with water symbolizing baptism, danger, and death, perpetual life amid a timeless place of reality and nightmare.

While previous directors had used symbolism in their films, from Akira Kurosawa to Coppola in *The Godfather* movies, film schools would identify this movie and its river journey as perhaps the most symbol-laden, and significant, ever made.

The crew moved to the Do Long Bridge scene, "the asshole of the world" as a soldier says, which was the most surreal in terms of color, music, and theme, in the film. This scene was meant to demonstrate the futility of the war. Every night the combatants blew each other up with no winners or losers, a metaphor for the way the U.S. fought in Vietnam. There is no discipline, no moral order, and no commanding officer. It took thirteen nights to film and pushed the project way over budget, but is considered a masterpiece. Coppola saw all the hanging lights as like those hanging over Little Italy during religious festivals. Flares, sulfuric smoke, and a hellish fog created both a dangerous and beautiful scene. He wanted the soldiers to look young and scared, even using his twelve-year old son Gio as a uniformed extra. Tavoularis rebuilt the bridge every day, just as the engineers did during the war. He thought the scene reminiscent of *The Bridge on the River Kwai*; whether it should be built or blown up an ambiguity not resolved until the very last scene. There were various difficult shots. Coppola was a perfectionist who insisted on every detail being just so, despite the mud, muck, and quagmire, each day costing between $30,000 and $50,000.

"I had a friend in Special Forces," said Milius, "and he talked about how a Bechtel Corporation construction gang, who were not as public in Afghanistan or Iraq—I'm sure this happened in World War II—this bridge was the last ... they'd say this bridge was open, at night the VC or NVA would mortar it and say the bridge was down, and it would go back and forth; it was the last vestige of real civilization."

Much of the Catholic symbolism of *Taxi Driver* influenced Coppola on *Apocalypse Now*. "Do Lung Bridge was the gate," Coppola said. "After that everything was surreal, you traveled through time, that was the gate."

"There was another gate, too, which was the tail of the B-52 ..." said Milius. "I remember when I wrote that scene, I wrote they went under the tail of the B-52 and I wrote the river widens and there's all these beautiful water falls encircling, and at the end where it widens it goes dark again and the trees go over it and that's of course like hell."[11]

"There was a sequence so called the French plantation, and it involved the PBR coming ashore to this spot that was a rubber plantation still run by these French-speaking people, and they had a whole bunch of cadre, and they'd been fighting the Viet Minh before the Viet Cong and they weren't going to let go," said Sheen.

"The whole scene is gonna be like wisps of fog that's on the ground, and a place that's like a dream," Coppola said of the French plantation set.

He spent a huge amount of money on a fog machine and real machine guns for a scene that was never used. For an elaborate dinner scene Coppola instructed the crew, "I want a French ceremony that is right out of—I want the French to fucking say, 'My God, how did they do that?'..."

"My idea is that as they progressed up the river, they were going back more and more in time. In a funny kind of way we were revisiting the history of Vietnam in reverse, and the first stop was in the '50s almost. We are now with the French. That is what I was looking for in the French plantation scene. It was a kind of ghostly afterview of something that almost is gone. They talk about the light from the stars, but by the time we see it, the star is already dead. It was that kind of thing."

"It was like having dinner with a family of ghosts ..." said Sheen, "still trying to keep themselves convinced that it was still 1950. They weren't French anymore, and they'd never be Vietnamese. They were floating loose in history without a country. They were hanging on by their finger nails, but so were we. We just had more fingernails in it."

"Just the idea of the French still being there," said Milius. "There was some speech that he gives at the end, where he says if they drive us from the house we'll live in a ditch, you know, and if they push us out of the ditch, we'll live in the jungle, and all the time we will clean the blood from our bayonets. I like that."

"You Americans, you are fighting for the biggest nothing in history," the Frenchman exclaims.

"Our budgets were cut way down, and we didn't get the cast we wanted, but of course the art department and other departments didn't cut theirs down, so I was very incensed that I had this very costly set, the decorations and stuff, and I was angry at the French sequence, and I cut it out," said Coppola.

In *Hearts of Darkness* he says, "I was very angry at everything, the light, and just forget that we even shot it. It no longer exists."

Ellie tried to say it was part of the artistic process, to scream to the heavens that he does not know what to do, but he found that insulting.

"What I'm worried about is that I'm getting in a self-indulgent pattern.... I'm sure I've missed all sorts of opportunities, and I'm sure I'll miss others, but I've caught a lot of them too, and in the end it's how many I catch, not how many I lose?" Coppola reasoned.

"Francis is in a place within himself, a place he never intended to reach, a place of conflict, and he can't go back down the river because the journey had changed him," said Eleanor. "I was watching from the point of view of the observer, but realizing I was on the journey too. Now I can't go back to the way it was. Neither can Francis. Neither can Willard."

The French plantation sequence was a total contrast with the other aspects of the film and was quite unrealistic. He did not want the politics of Vietnam to dominate the story, but needed a perspective of the war, so he decided the French would give a brief history of their involvement; their reason for being there fighting. One segment that ended up in neither the original version nor the redux released more than two decades later featured a French woman being raped, and her husband murdered by GIs.

The scene included expensive costume set pieces and an elaborate dinner, with fancy food and exquisite wine served. The French, despite living deep in the jungle, have all the comforts of home. They wear gorgeous, clean clothes, their hair perfectly groomed, totally hygienic and genteel as if in Paris itself. The soldiers on the boat are invited to dinner. Theoretically—although not shown—they have submitted their clothes to a laundry, their muddy boots to a shine, taken refreshing showers, and combed their hair as if ready for church.

The men all argue the French cause, each leaving, one after the other in frustration, having failed to articulate or justify why they are still there, why they fight, until Willard is left alone in the company of a beautiful young blonde woman, conveniently widowed, lonely and horny for male company the Frenchmen apparently cannot or will not provide her, until she and Willard disappear for some lovemaking.

Coppola hated the whole plantation sequence, frustratingly announcing to the chagrined actors that it would, like the French plantations of colonialist Vietnam, disappear as if they were never there in the first place. Captured in *Hearts of Darkness*, the faces of the French actors tell the story; their chance at stardom on the big screen has disappeared at the whim of a temperamental director.

The scene was re-installed for the redux version. It, like scenes eliminated but restored in *The Godfather* director's cut, is interesting and quite telling in many ways, but it is obvious why it was edited out. Aside from time constraints, it did not push the story narrative. Instead, it was a highly unrealistic break from the river journey leading Willard to Kurtz!

Coppola began to see it as a big mistake, expensive yet possibly ephemeral, unneeded, but like a general pushing an attack on a hill with no strategic value, he filmed it in all its time-consuming, expensive glory anyway.

"We were aware that we were going over budget, and I asked everyone to make their best efforts to spend less money," said Coppola. "For example, I didn't cast some of the European actors we were considering for [the scene]. A French actor had agreed to do it, but it was for decent money and I decided to cast lesser actors who'd work for a more modest budget. But then, when I got to the set, I saw that the art and decorating departments had not stinted one little bit; they spent a fortune on the set and furnishings. I was very annoyed and angry at the set, which was basically beautiful, but I would have rather had a cheaper set and the actors I originally was going to have."

Aurore Clement and Christian Marquand were method actors unaccustomed to the American style, which required them to memorize and play out a whole scene. The disagreements they had with Coppola and the American actors they interacted with were a metaphor for the American-French relationship, costing hundreds of thousands while ending up on the cutting-room floor until the redux.

Finally, the boat moves back upriver. Chief Phillips is very upset that Captain Willard insists he continue to ferry him beyond the Do Lung Bridge, but Willard lashes out at him: "*Just get us upriver!*"

Chief's anger wells up inside him and finally bursts out when natives attack the crew, as they get closer to the Kurtz compound. "And when you get to this anger, Albert, don't decide where you're gonna get to," Coppola told Albert Hall before attacking Sheen as Willard. "As long as you get to it, it's okay....

"You're gonna get into this weird speech about, 'Fire, fire, you sons of bitches…. Captain, you made this, this is your hell, your nightmare.'"

"I just thought that he thought a lot of his actors, that they were gems who would bring his ideas to life, and so it took a lot of creative input," Hall said. "Once he set that feel for us, we just started improvising everything that was happening on the boat."[12]

Jaws, Close Encounters of the Third Kind, and now *Star Wars* were all megahits that redefined just how much money could be made by a Hollywood blockbuster. Coppola's friend Dennis Jacob, the eccentric intellectual who worked on *The Rain People*, helped him stitch elements of *Heart of Darkness* with the Vietnam experience, and likely influenced the musical use of Jim Morrison in *Apocalypse*, told Coppola that he needed to make a dramatic masterpiece that would answer the "pop corn" mentality fed by Spielberg and Lucas, ironically two of the young filmmakers influenced and, to differing extents, promoted by him.

"Francis, it's all up to you now, you're the only one," said Jacob. There was not enough pressure on him; now he had to "save Hollywood" for the serious movies. Peter Biskind called him "the last man standing" who had "inherited the historical obligation of the New Hollywood—to make cinematic art the seminal event of their generation."[13]

He was happy to carry this mantel at first. Now, knee deep in the Philippine jungle…?

16

Prima Donna

After turning him down, then reconsidering, Marlon Brando finally agreed to play the role of Colonel Walter E. Kurtz. Coppola sent him a $1 million advance and, amid late summer heat and humidity in 1976, he arrived. He changed his deal from $3.5 million to $3 million against 11.5 percent of the adjusted gross. Brando had done *The Godfather* for far less than his regular salary because he needed to revive his career. Since that film he had not duplicated the power of his Don Vito Corleone role, but he had been on an upswing from where he was in the 1960s with *Last Tango in Paris* and *The Missouri Breaks* (with Jack Nicholson). He would later have a significant role in a hit, *Superman*.

Eleanor Coppola's *Hearts of Darkness: A Filmmaker's Apocalypse* captures her husband in a state of mania, at times seemingly going insane from pressure, overwork, giant problems, heat, exhaustion, primeval conditions, weather, Sheen's heart attack, political issues, and a myriad of other troubles cropping up and dominating his life in the Philippines every single day. For all of that, dealing with Marlon Brando was the single-most difficult issue for Coppola. Brando was the Cyclops of John Milius's Homeric journey, the obstacle to be overcome. Eleanor's camera captured Francis frantically discussing Brando's deal over the phone with his attorney.

"Are they seriously saying that Marlon would take a million dollars, and then not show up?" Coppola says on the phone back to the States. "And imagine here I am with, with fifty things that are just quasi in my control, between the Philippine government and the fucking helicopters which they take away whenever they feel like, they've done it three times already. This will allow him to start a little later, and I know it's all my fault, but what I'm saying is, do I owe and do I have to shoot the last thirty minutes of the movie in the beginning? I assumed there would be some malleability about Marlon, and I also didn't realize the immensity of the construction and stuff, and the picture is bigger than I thought. I personally as an artist would love to be able to just finish the picture up until the end, take four weeks off, work with Marlon, rewrite it, and in just three weeks do it with a new ending. I think I could make the best film. It seems like the right thing to do, and I feel like the people back there feel like postponement is like, 'Uh-oh, the picture's in trouble, it's just an intelligent thing'; major studios used to do things like this all the time. What sort of bugs me is the ludicrousness, that I'm gonna go through all that I'm doing, and after all I've been through in the past, all the pictures I've made, after shooting sixteen weeks I'm not gonna finish a movie in which I've invested all the savings of my life, I mean it's stupid.... Even if Brando drops dead I can still finish the movie, I can get another actor. If I can't get Redford I'll go back to Nicholson, if I can't get Nicholson I'll go back to Pacino, if I don't get Pacino I'll go back to someone else. Sooner or later I can get someone for three weeks. I mean it's just not in the cards that I won't finish the movie."

Brando arrived four months late, at a cost that went from $100,000 a day to $150,000 a day. He insisted on sleeping on a houseboat that had to be carried overland to a nearby lake.

"He wanted to do as little work as possible, and get paid as much as possible," Ellie said. Brando had become "lazy" since *The Godfather*. He was on good behavior to save his career after years in which others refused to work with him, but after that he was back on top again. Brando totally dismissed the idea of a documentary, refusing to grant Ellie's interview request. An appointment was made but he never showed up for it.

"He did it so easily, he just dismissed it as anything of value," Ellie said. Despite that, Brando could captivate other people in a way few possibly can. "Brando was an extraordinarily fascinating person. It was the first time I really realized what charisma was, he just looked at me with this really riveting look, like you were the most fascinating person in the world. It was very seductive. His conversations were the most far-out things … he could talk endlessly about some obscure things … he was immensely intelligent and a fascinating figure when he was behaving himself.… He had this riveting, piercing attention.… I felt this incredible presence of someone who was very intently experiencing everything, and could see through you and into your mind and your heart.…"

Brando had done nude scenes in *Last Tango in Paris*, which were even featured in *Playboy* magazine; Coppola might have hoped the great actor would look good. Milius's script called for an Airborne Ranger, some of the fittest people in the world. He was also modernized, being a fan of The Doors, who listened to "Light My Fire" while smoking pot. Conrad's novel, conversely, described a gaunt, sickly man.

But Brando was now clinically obese, weighing between 250 and 285 pounds. He obviously did not fit the visual of a gaunt Kurtz in the Conrad version, not to mention how unlikely it would be that an Airborne Ranger could be so overweight, especially eating jungle food. He had not read the novel nor T.S. Eliot's poem, "The Waste Land," which he promised Coppola he would do in preparation for the role.

"I lied," he told the director. "I never read it."[1]

Brando's contract called for one month's work. While this was technically in the contract, Francis Ford Coppola might have believed he had a relationship with him; he had helped re-launch his star turn, after all, and Coppola hoped he would be helpful to him. For motivations that have never been fully explained, he was not. Brando would seemingly work against Coppola. Surely he understood, even before he arrived in the Philippines, and then saw upon his arrival, how stressed Coppola was, how difficult the project was. He provided no cooperation, no sense of team work. He was all Hollywood, all ego, all about Marlon Brando.

His arrival forced much of the Martin Sheen work to be delayed, although Sheen's heart attack already created chaos, forcing many scenes to be shot out of sequence. Coppola had to scramble to figure a way to get Brando and Sheen on screen together. It would take all his power as an editor, all the tricks of the trade, to stitch the scenes—many shot at varying different times, when actors looked different, weighed more or less, were more or less tanned, had more or less hair, wore different clothes with different stains and markings, had different cuts and bruises—into a cohesive narrative. But that was all in the future, when Coppola would return to California and his editing bays. For now he was dealing with a prima donna for all times.

Perhaps the most egregious example of Brando's egoism was how he selfishly took all of Coppola's time and attention. Aside from dealing with far more things than could be handled in any given day, Coppola had to divert himself away from all of it to concentrate on this overweight diva. Brando refused to give Francis the time he needed to rewrite the ending or edit anything. The ending of the Milius script was gnawing at the director, keeping him awake at night, causing him to have crazy dreams, but he had to try to set it aside.

They would disappear in Francis's trailer while everybody waited. "Everybody was waiting to shoot, hundreds of people, while Francis and Brando were play-acting, Brando playing Westmoreland, and Francis playing Ho Chi Minh," wrote Peter Biskind, referring to General William Westmoreland, the military commander most responsible for escalation of U.S. forces in Southeast Asia. "Coppola spent days just reading the novel out loud."[2]

For five weeks Brando worked at a snail's pace, always with interminable discussions with Coppola. Coppola was a big fan of his. He had been thrilled to direct the legend in *The Godfather*, and still retained a fan's adulation. He was certainly willing to work with him. He felt he was the finest actor he ever worked with, a belief borne out by *The Godfather*, but Brando thought the screenplay was a mess and felt Kurtz a stereotype not resembling Conrad's characterization; this is odd, since he had not read *Heart of Darkness*. Brando wanted more ominous mystery, but much of that was handled naturally by the length of time the audience had to wait to see him, finally, after the long, tense river trip. This was in line with Conrad's book, but that was a novella, a little over a hundred pages, so while Kurtz's appearance was near the end, it did not take nearly so long for Marlow to travel up the Congo River as Willard had traveled through a river that "snaked through the war like a main circuit cable," as Milius wrote of it.

Coppola and Brando had endless conversations. "I was good at bullshitting Francis and persuading him to think my way, and he bought it, but what I'd really wanted from the beginning was to find a way to make my part smaller so that I wouldn't have to work as hard," Brando later admitted.[3]

Coppola needed to think creatively. Since Brando was overweight, not the gaunt, sickly figure of the literary Kurtz, he had to re-think his character. He saw a wild gauging-like character, now alone in his excess and madness. Brando was more benign. The notion of "excess" could explain his weight. Brando said Kurtz was driven mad by war. Brando wanted him wearing black pajamas like the Vietnamese.

"He was already heavy when I had hired him," Coppola said of Brando, "and he promised me that he would get in shape, and I imagined that he would, if he were heavy I could use that, but he was so fat, and he was very, very shy about it, and I saw him and said, 'I'll write this as a man who really, you know, had indulged every aspect of himself,' and so he was fat and he had two or three tribal girls with him, and was eating mangos, and kind of go the other way, and he was very adamant he didn't want to portray himself that way. So, clearly, he left me in a tough spot."

"The clock was ticking on this deal we had," said Roos. "We had to finish within three weeks or go into a very expensive overage. So the whole company was sitting on the set, the cameras and the crew, waiting to go on shooting, and Francis and Marlon would be sitting, talking about the character, and whole days would go by, and this is at Marlon's urging, and he's getting paid for it."

Brando had only motivational things. Coppola began improvisations beyond the script. This included a question-and-answer session with Brando in the Kurtz character about politics, bloodlust, and American policy.

"He's like a force of his own, and he doesn't give a shit," Coppola said of Brando. "I want a character of a monumental nature who's struggling with the extremities of his soul, and is struggling on such a level that you are in awe of him, and he is destroyed by them."

Brando improvised that his character did not fear "bullets" or "phosphorous napalm," but truly feared the "mind behind all humans," and of our sinful, violent nature, "I accept you. I even love you because you are a part of me, you are an extension of me."

"Why are we in Vietnam?" Coppola asked him in character.

"Because it's our time. This moment in history. It's our time to teach."

Coppola admitted he did not know what he was doing; it was not rational, the script made no sense, yet "no one's listening to me….

"Why can't I have the courage to just say, 'It's no good?'"

He claimed in the documentary that he contemplated suicide, looking for a "graceful way out."

"The film is a $20 million disaster," Coppola moaned. "Why won't anyone believe it?"

It was unlike *The Godfather*, which did not entail his personal fortune, so the stakes were relatively low on that film, at least in the beginning. His success on it, and his desire for independence, upped the stakes of *Apocalypse*. His own money and his family's future, plus his reputation, were on the line.

"I was very much on the spot," Coppola recalled. "I was very, very scared…. Letting the movie get more surrealistic, more heightened, I was painting myself in a corner and I had no way to get out."

He chose self-intoxication, leading to black depression. "He went over the edge," said Mona Skager. "His mental state was a big part of the movie. When you watch the film, you can see how it gets a little crazier as it goes along. Well, that was the state of [his] mind. The whole thing was crazy."[4]

"I think that photo that Mary Ellen Mark took where Francis has the gun to his head, it's just like many, many pranks on a film set … and I think it's been taken out of context to express Francis's desperation," said Eleanor. "It very easily became an iconic photo to use to express what we thought Francis felt, when it was just one of many, many gags that were pulled on set."

"You're ridiculed if you are pretentious but to me in my mind what's worse than being pretentious is to absolutely not try at all anything interesting," Coppola said, speaking of how all movies are "remakes" in one way or another, whereby *Apocalypse Now* was very original.

"He was in just a quandary as to how to conclude the script, and how to really finish it off in a way that was really satisfying to him," said Eleanor. "When he went off to the Philippines to make *Apocalypse Now* he thought he was going to a place where he'd be in the sun and the bright lights and you'd make this kind of Green Beret big Western 'shoot 'em up'; he just wanted contrast from the kind of complicated dark scenes of *The Godfather* and *Godfather II*, and interiors and claustrophobicness of conversations, so this was just a big chance for change, to be out in the sun and in your shorts ... big fun ... and he realized he was doing this story on Vietnam and it began to dawn on him as he did his research that it wasn't just a Hollywood Green Beret 'shoot 'em up,' it was about death, and he kind of matured all of a sudden, and grasped that he was responsible for these themes that were so much more complex than the vision he had when he started, and they were important and he needed to say the right things about them, and it was a great weight on his shoulders."

He fainted at one time, saying he had a vision of himself going down a dark tunnel. "He'd gone to the threshold of his sanity, or something," said Eleanor. "It was scary, but also kind of exhilarating, thrilling that he'd take such risks with himself."

"Nothing is so terrible as a pretentious movie," Coppola famously stated in *Hearts of Darkness*. "I mean, a movie that aspires to be something terrific, and doesn't pull it off, is shit, it's scum, and everyone will walk on it as scum. And that's why poor filmmakers in a way, that's their greatest horror, to be pretentious. So here you are on one hand even aspiring to really do something, and on the other hand you're not allowed to be pretentious, and finally you say, *fuck it, I don't care if I'm pretentious or not pretentious, or if I've done it or not done it, but all I know is I am going to go see this movie*, and for me it has to have some answers, and by that I don't mean just a punch line but I mean on about forty-seven different levels, and it's very hard to talk about these things without being very corny. You use a word, self prerogation or epiphany, they think you're either a religious weirdo or an asshole college professor. Those are the swords for the process, this maturation, this renaissance, this rebirth, which is the basis of all life. The one rule that all men, from the time they first walked around looking at the sun scratching around for food and an animal to kill, the first concept that I feel got into their head was the idea of life and death. The sun went down and the sun went up, they learned how to make crops and in the winter everything died. To the first man it must have been, 'My god, it's the end of the world,' then all of a sudden it was spring, and everything came alive, and it was better. I mean, after all, look at Vietnam, look at my movie and you'll see what I'm talking [about]....

"My greatest fear is to make a really shitty, embarrassing, pompous film on an important subject, and I'm doing it. I confront it, I will tell you, I acknowledge right straight from the most sincere depth of my heart, the film will not be good," said Coppola.

"It's like going to school," Eleanor told him. "Maybe you finish your term paper, and maybe you get a B on it. You want to get an A+ but you get a B."

"But I'm gonna get an F.... This film is a $20 million disaster, and why won't anyone believe me, and I'm thinking of shooting myself."

"When it got difficult Francis just didn't give up. No one up to that time had been on the set shooting relentlessly day after day. I think that's what created why this film had such unique appeal, in that it hadn't been seen before, the nitty-gritty of what goes on on a daily basis. On a set," she said of the documentary she eventually produced.

"I didn't know the production would extend to over two hundred days, nor did I know it would test the family finances ..." said Coppola. "I was to be put in the multiple position of both the producer and the financier....

"This movie I'm making is not in the tradition of the great Max Ophuls. Or David Lean. This movie was made in the tradition of Irwin Allen. I made the most vulgar, entertaining, exciting action-filled sensoramic, give me a new thrill every five minutes, I have everything—violence, humor—because I want people to come and see it, but, the questions I kept facing or running into with this stupid script, about this guy going up to kill a guy, that was the story, but this didn't fit that story, it kept putting me where I couldn't get an answer, yet I knew I had constructed the film in such a way that to not answer would be to fail."

Coppola's bright idea of a burly, overweight Kurtz, surrounded by excess food and native women, maddened by the pagan idolatry the natives bestow upon him, backfired because the vain Brando wanted to hide his size. He had been a major sex symbol in the 1950s, and followed *The Godfather* with his shocking near-pornographic performance in *Last Tango in Paris* with the voluptuous French actress Maria Schneider. A guy who lets the world see him like that is not going to let the world see his giant beer belly.

"He wasn't what everyone expected to see because he had gained so much weight," said Gray Frederickson. "We had drawings of what we thought he was going to look like, in these boots and fatigues, looking the way you remember him to look. We had to shoot it differently."[5]

So Coppola decided on a world of darkness and mystery. The audience would wait a few hours to see him; he would remain a strange, unexplainable figure. His world of darkness could be used to add to the mystery. Coppola still wanted some shots of his girth to emphasize his excess. They settled on a gigantic, hulking presence, and hired Pete Cooper, a six-foot-five Vietnam veteran and military advisor to stand in for Brando during long shots. Brando used five-inch lifts but twisted his ankle, setting the schedule back for days.

Coppola had nightmares during the rare times he actually did sleep. The crew members were using many drugs. It was the heyday of drug use, mostly pot, easily grown and found in that part of the world. Many got in fights at local bars. Pete Cooper, still mired in a jungle from which he seemed unable to escape, screamed in his sleep, so real to this was it to his own war experiences.

"Francis Ford Coppola never intended *Apocalypse Now* to be a *magnum opus*, a cornerstone to his career as a filmmaker, and he certainly never dreamed that it would give him the grief that it did," wrote Michael Schumacher. "He intended it as a good movie to make money he could use to make the *Tucker* bio pic. Instead he was questioning his own sanity."[6] It was "His personal Vietnam," battling the crew, the cast, the jungle, the politics of the Philippines, back home the powers that be in opinion and Hollywood; seemingly the whole world, while his peers heard only the worst rumors thousands of miles away.

His big problem now was writing good scenes for Brando that met with the actor's approval, leading to an ending. In the end, much of the Brando/Kurtz dialogue/monologue was improvised.

"There'd be long discussions with Brando," Coppola said, "and I would take these ideas and go back and write them up as dialogue or sequences. We'd record the longer speeches on a tape recorder, which Marlon would use to refresh himself. He would go off whenever he wanted to, but there was always a written script."

As if Marlon Brando, Sheen's health, Marcos's helicopters, and typhoons were not enough, Coppola still had to deal with a force of nature called Dennis Hopper. Hopper first met Coppola when he was writing *Patton*. Hopper arrived, drunk and stoned, in September 1976. He had been in and out of rehabilitation. A reading of Peter Biskind's descriptions of his out-of-control behavior while filming, and then after the success of *Easy Rider*, leaves one marveling at just how remarkable it was that he had even survived the drugs. He could be violent and schizophrenic. He would arrive at Narcotics Anonymous meetings unaware of his surroundings. He wore a cowboy hat and boots. He was stoned at his daughter's graduation from prim and proper Wooster Academy, near Ridgefield, Connecticut, according to his ex-wife Brooke Hayward. Hopper tried to seduce his daughter's best friend, age seventeen. "Dennis always had that thing about young girls," said Hayward.[7]

Hopper got loaded at the Albuquerque, New Mexico, airport bar. On his way back to Taos he stopped to get a gun. An argument ensued and he fired a shot over the heads of his girlfriend and daughter, then drove off, leaving them stranded by the road. His daughter, Marin, became catatonic when his name came up. Hopper denied all of this, but wild events surrounded his stay at the Pagsanjan Rapids Hotel on location filming *Apocalypse Now*.

"I didn't know until two weeks before I even came here that I was gonna be in the picture," Hopper said in the documentary, "much less play a photo-journalist, in tatters and rags, taking photographs and trying to explain what this was all about, and how it's blown his mind....

"And I really appreciate Francis's writing, even though he does drop it in on you sometimes, and does take you like me a whole day to learn it."

Hopper's appearance in the 1991 documentary was the ultimate in contrast. By that time he had kicked drugs, looked fabulous, and had completely revived his career, having made several star turns.

"I was not in the greatest, you know, as far as like my career was going," he said. "I was delighted to hear I was going to go do anything."

"I have Dennis Hopper playing a spaced out photo-journalist with ten cameras who's here to get the *truth!* ..." said Coppola in *Hearts of Darkness*. "And he's a wonderful apparition."

Coppola made significant script changes to accommodate the Hopper character, who had a strange, maybe drug-induced energy. Hopper always forgot his lines. He—or his clothes—smelled terrible.

"You can't forget your lines," Coppola told Hopper, who appeared every bit as spaced out on set as his onscreen character. Coppola argued that once he learned his lines, he could forget them, and improvise.

"Fred Roos wanted me to be in it," said Hopper. "I was out of work. I went one line with Brando, he said okay.... Francis is on Brando because he hasn't read *Heart of Darkness*.... I say to Brando sitting across at dinner, 'I bet you haven't read the book.' He screams, 'I don't have to listen to this, I don't have to take this from this punk.' I started taking this personally, getting into my cups and some other things that we have....

"Brando refused to be on set at the same time I was.... He was doing me a favor."

After that Brando and Francis conferred for two weeks. Brando said he would not be on the same set with Hopper. "I'm afraid to put Dennis Hopper and Marlon together, I haven't even figured out what Marty's gonna do," lamented Coppola. "What happens if I get crazy Dennis Hopper in there?"

Hopper provided one of the great juxtapositions in movie history. Milius said that the movie showed how American culture—surfing, rock music, sexy girls, drugs—imposes itself on an ancient Oriental civilization. Hopper's crazy character, based on the Russian in *Heart of Darkness*, was a perfect example. The tattered PBR pulls slowly up to the compound. Tribesmen in white skin camouflage representing 1,000 years of tradition, part ways like the Red Sea as the boat moves through them. The ancient compound, resembling ruins from a past long lost to history, surrounded by corpses and severed heads, is suddenly brought alive by Dennis Hopper in full manic psychosis.

Dean Tavoularis was always spreading gore, blood, skulls, and the detritus of death around the Kurtz compound, which did not improve his personality. "I was living in the house of death I was making," he said. "It became such a low level in my life that somehow putting blood on staircases and rolling heads down steps seemed natural to me."[8]

"For the Kurtz compound, which was supposed to be the ultimate madness—Joseph Conrad's vision of the depths of human depravity," his brother Alex recalled, "Dean wanted us to create these piles of human skulls. Of course, many were plastic skulls from Hollywood, but we created these heaps, and there were rats crawling around everywhere. When Martin Sheen came to the set, he was astounded. He had two young sons—Emilio and Charlie—with him, and he was very concerned. To that point, he had not been involved in this kind of madness, and he asked Francis to dismantle these piles of squalor. In our hearts we knew he was right, but we were on a road, hell-bent on creating this world of madness. But Martin Sheen shook us up a little bit."[9]

Not to mention his son Charlie, who later descended into periods of his own madness. Whether Charlie Sheen's long history of bizarre behavior traces itself to this influence is only speculation.

Robert Evans wanted the "smell of spaghetti" on *The Godfather*. In *Apocalypse Now*, Coppola achieved the macabre "smell of death" that envelops the Kurtz scenes, one of his greatest accomplishments, dark as it is. Gray Frederickson worked to have "corpses" all around the Kurtz compound. The extras playing the severed heads had to remain buried to their necks under the broiling sun from 8:00 A.M. to 6:00 P.M., under umbrellas in between takes.

"It turned out the guy procuring the dead bodies who said he was getting them from a media research lab, had actually been robbing graves," recalled Frederickson.

The Kurtz compound was modeled on the Cambodian ruins of Angkor Wat. It was an amazing work of art built by seven hundred laborers carrying handmade adobe blocks weighing 330 pounds each, using bamboo poles lifted into place on bamboo hoists. It seemed to be similar to the way the actual temples were built. Human labor, like those who built the pyramids of ancient Egypt, came cheap here. Coppola, and the good liberals who no doubt made up a fair number of his crew, willingly overlooked the exploitation as a means to an end.

"The original idea was that the compound was going to be blown up, and if you're going to do that, you have to build in a different way than if you're not going to blow it up," said Coppola. "You can't just put up a wall or scaffolding and attach the stone or skin. I remember looking at this *National Geographic* with a centerfold of the building of Angkor Wat. They had used sleds and caribou and bamboo poles, and had created a miniature crane to lift the blocks off these barges or sleds. We were building the same way."

Hopper tells the crew "it's all been approved" and warns the natives not to attack because "these are Americans. *Americans!*"

"It's nice because this is the moment Chef does, that he looks up, and sees this harlequin figure waving all the people away," said Coppola, while typing. "He sees like, essentially,

Dennis Hopper. You know what I mean?" Hopper tells Forrest's Chef to scatter them with his siren, which looks like cockroaches running for cover after a light is turned on them.

"What I have to deal with is Willard's state of mind when he arrives at the compound," Coppola said. "He can arrive either incredibly angry or like a newborn baby. I think what he should find at the end is death. That, at the end of this whole thing, is a frightening place, that smells of death."

Sheen meeting Brando was almost as climactic as Willard meeting Kurtz on screen, since Sheen's heart attack had occurred shortly before Brando's arrival, forcing Coppola to scramble to cut together coherent scenes that emphasized their confrontation. It was a tremendous challenge for the director. Brando fought him every step of the way. There were thirty-eight takes of Willard and Kurtz in the hole. It was never the way Francis wanted it.

"I adored him," Sheen said of Brando. He was intimidated by Marlon, the image, but the last thing he talked about was acting. "He wanted to know what you were like. He was one of my heroes." As Eleanor Coppola said, even though he was narcissistic and difficult, it did not take away from his charisma. He was essentially a friendly person, just extremely eccentric. He was the ultimate difficult artist.

"All my life I'd wanted to be a movie star, here I am, the part of a lifetime, working with the biggest talent in the world on the biggest feature, with one of my idols, Marlon Brando, and I felt terribly insecure," recalled Sheen. "Why me, why now? ... who is this character ... always Francis was clear: 'Willard is you.'"

The scene in which Hopper's photo-journalist speaks to Willard about "fractions" was apparently all improvised by Hopper. Slowly but surely, the scenes were shot and eventually would be cut together. Inch by agonizing inch, Coppola dredged brilliant performances out of Brando and Hopper. They were unconventional, unrepresentative of both of their artistic reputations, but magnificent nevertheless. Brando's Kurtz throws a book—probably T.S. Eliot's poetry—at Hopper, which probably was real antagonism on the part of Brando towards the spaced-out Dennis, who splits the scene. This sets up the climax.

Brando eventually gave Coppola a gamut of improvised scenes that completely drained him. "Francis, I've gone as far as I can go," he told him. "If you need more, you can get another actor."[10] Brando finished filming on October 8, 1976. After that Coppola worked on polishing the scenes in the compound. The rushes were visually beautiful. Storaro's work was astonishing.

Finally, towards the end of Brando's tenure in the Philippines, the great *artiste* threw a party at a resort hotel for the natives and crew. Four hundred people attended. Many point to this evening of camaraderie as the turning point in the production.

17

"He took a face from the ancient gallery"

By now the movie had a life of its own. It engendered full commitment. The idea of dropping it, which haunted Coppola early on, was now gone.

Finally, a confrontation is allowed to take place between Kurtz and Willard, but Willard is so broken down by now, by the beheading of Chef by Kurtz, by the smell of death, by the very essence of *sin*, that he is unable to carry out his assassination. The end is finally nigh. But before that, a scene that was not in the screenplay, one that occurred by pure happenstance yet made its way into the film, set up the final climax. Neither John Milius nor Francis Ford Coppola could have envisioned the strange, beautiful, brutal nature of this scene, which so perfectly fit into this wild, surreal movie.

The local Ifugao tribe held a feast on the last two days. Wearing loincloths and using ceremonial blankets, the tribal elders assembled at the priests' house for fifteen hours, singing and chanting a long tribal legend about a couple and their life together. Ellie filmed it with permission, capturing the hypnotic dancing as they chanted. At one point they chanted Coppola's name. The ceremony lasted all night and into the morning, at such time as they began the ritual slaughter of a chicken, pulling out the chicken's bile to read omens for signs.

Five pigs were butchered and boiled in a cauldron. A caribou was slaughtered, one of the most shocking scenes in the entire history of film. Eleanor told Francis he needed to film this for the movie, so he assembled cameras and captured images of giant knives violently slicing through the bodies of these massive animals, exposing huge flanks of ribs and meat and bone and blood while the animal, in excruciating pain, not yet dead, collapsed. They hacked it with bolo knives; four blows to the back of the neck, beautiful yet horrendous. Coppola posed with two priests. The Indians, from a tribe in the north, were rumored until recently to be headhunters. They had a feast.

"I was interested in photographing and documenting the actual ritual they performed," said Eleanor. This was viewed in Eleanor's documentary *Hearts of Darkness*, which revealed pigs not just killed or slaughtered, but speared, squealing, still alive but in terrible agony, with blood spurting out of them.

The rules have been changed since then. Today, movies with animals carry the disclaimer, approved by the Society for the Prevention of Cruelty to Animals (SPCA), "No animals were harmed in the making of this film." No such claim could be made on *Apocalypse*. The dark truth of animal cruelty fit the narrative of human suffering and depravity within the story itself. Every possible rule about animals not being hurt on the set of a film was broken on this shoot. They killed caribou, chickens, and pigs in a very cruel manner. Eleanor called it "profound and beautiful." Despite the brutality of the slaughter many felt the natives offered a natural calm, which blessed the set in strange ways.

Again, the good pacifist and anti-war peacenik Francis Ford Coppola and his humanitarian wife, who was always concerned they lived too lavishly anyway, were spared the kind of wrath animal rights activists would have reigned down upon any "Republican" or "conservative" who dared produce *anything from anywhere* showing such carnage. If John Milius had directed such scenes—they were not in his screenplay—he might have been run out of the business then and there.

If such a scene depicting the slaughter of real animals happened on U.S. soil, the actual perpetrators of the act would be subject to serious hard prison time. Any filmmaker passively capturing the images, then profiting off them in a movie, would be jailed at least as long the football player Michael Vick was for betting on dog fights.

But according to the moral relativism of liberals, natives are given a pass, just as Mayans cutting the hearts out of live humans and sacrificing virgins are excused by some historians who only blame Christopher Columbus for bringing Christianity to their shores. All of that said, the animal-sacrifice ceremony Eleanor and Francis Coppola captured on film was going to happen whether they were there with cameras or not. "I was getting deeper in debt and no longer recognized the kind of movie I was making," said Coppola, who had no idea how perfectly suited the sacrifice, as seen on camera, would set up the ending for which he was still searching.[1]

Coppola was at wits' end one day. He lay down, apparently unable to continue, and let the rain pound on him. Storaro suggested a scene using smoke and odd lights that Brando might like. Some useful footage was shot from it.

"God! I'd go to see that movie, wouldn't you?" Francis said while looking at it. Storaro had been reluctant and felt he was infringing on Gordon Willis's toes, but was given artistic freedom nonetheless.

"The original idea was to depict the impact of our culture, which had been superimposed over another culture," stated Storaro. "I was trying to show the conflict between natural energy and artificial energy. For example, the dark, shadowy jungle where natural energy reigns, in contrast to the American military base where big, powerful generators and huge, probing lights provided the energy." Vietnam was "a conflict between technology and nature as well as between different cultures. I tried to use the mouths and camera to suggest this."

This influence is seen in many subsequent films, some masterpieces, such as Terence Malick's *The Thin Red Line* (1998). Based on a James Jones novel, the film features a scene in which actor Nick Nolte, playing an ambitious officer, describes how nature is "cruel," demonstrating vines wrapping themselves around a tree, suffocating it, and uses this as justification for the carnage of warfare.

Oddly, the rain sometimes was so intense it prevented Storaro from capturing scenes. On other nights they had to create rain artificially, a true irony. "I don't believe anyone anticipated that [the shoot] would be that long and difficult," said Storaro. Perhaps his greatest contribution was using the natural beauty of the jungle, making it a character, and giving it so much context that it propelled the story even when the script did not satisfy Coppola's vision.

When Coppola got a good day's work he would be ebullient, but when it went bad he soured and was very hard to deal with. But Storaro's magnificent camera work—Eleanor Coppola must be credited, too, for her work capturing the slaughter—made it possible for Francis to find his inspired ending.

"In the original script that John Milius did," said George Lucas, "Willard reaches the end of his journey and the Viet Cong surround Colonel Kurtz's compound. But whenever helicopters are sent in to rescue these guys, Kurtz shoots them down. Kurtz tells Willard: 'My friends died on this land. I have fought for this land. Our community has suffered to own this land, to be on this land, to have this be our land. We have an emotional investment in this. The Viet Cong don't. And the United States doesn't. But we do.'

"There are air strikes, and there is a huge battle with the Viet Cong. Kurtz gets killed, and only Willard and three or four other soldiers are left. The movie ends as headquarters sends a helicopter to get them out of there—and Willard shoots it down. He takes Kurtz's place and continues, because he fought for the land."

"The ending changed many times," said Milius. "I wrote ten different drafts of the script. There was the Steve McQueen draft. That was quite a summer. I had separated from my wife, and I lived out at the beach, and I'd go to Steve McQueen's and hang out with him, it was fun, but he decided he was gonna make Spielberg and me into men, and he'd take us to biker bars, and he was into full-contact karate, ridiculous, he'd get dressed up in these padded suits with these other guys and they'd flail all over the floor."

Milius disliked being rewritten and had his disagreements. He did not like liberal messages. "He sees himself as a great humanitarian, an enlightened soul who will tell you such wonderful things as he does at the end of *Godfather II*—that crime doesn't pay," Milius said sarcastically of Coppola. "We may come up with some great statement at the end of *Apocalypse*, to the effect that war is hell....

"Basically, he wanted to ruin it, liberalize it, and turn it into *Hair*....

"To make an anti-war movie as Francis is trying to do," Milius said at the time, "is about as foolish as trying to make an anti-rain movie. It's gonna rain. It was not an anti-war movie when it started out; it was apolitical. It deals with the nature of war in man altogether, and man's inherent bestiality. It went right into war. It said, 'Here you're going to see it all: you're going to see the exhilaration of it all, you're going to see the horror of it all; you're going right into the war with no hold's barred.'"[2]

Milius viewed war as natural to the human condition. Coppola was horrified by it and intellectually felt humans can stop it. Dennis Jacob, probably the ideological opposite of Milius (and much closer to Francis's worldview) gave the director intellectual inspiration. He was looking for some kind of "truth" and the new books Jacob gave him, plus the Ifugao sacrifice, began to formulate in his mind an ending, with good and evil competing with each other, both being part of the experience.

"When I wrote the script two things I thought about were Wagner and The Doors," said Milius. In this respect he, Jacob—and Coppola—were in sync. "I took that first Doors album, and must have played it until I used it up. The Doors, to me, were always the music of war. I remember telling that to The Doors, and they were just horrified and said, 'It was the exact opposite of that, how can you get this?' Worse yet, this was what was played during war."

"The Doors were all UCLA film students," said Coppola to Milius at the 2010 Napa

Valley symposium. "Ray Manzarek, and Jim Morrison, who was the son of a very important admiral, they were all UCLA film students. I knew them at film school. Morrison was an extremely, quite introspective guy, he was very well read, he was a big Nietzsche fan, he knew all about Nietzsche, he was a poet."

"He had to be," said Milius. "Just listen to the stuff, still, it's just remarkable how good it is...."

Thus they had their setup for the climax. The unbelievable camera work captures Sheen's Willard emerging like primeval man from the swamp, the Dolby Surround Sound beginning the first haunting strains of "The End." Willard, feline-like, at one with the jungle, springs into action. Then it intercuts with Kurtz speaking into a tape recorder. Kurtz says the U.S. pilots are allowed to "drop fire on people, but can't write *fuck* on their aero planes ... because, it's *obscene*."

"When I went to Desert Storm years later," Milius said, "I went to this Marine air group, it was based in Bahrain, all the air planes had won their battles and everything, and all the airplanes were like, 'Air superiority' sprayed with numbers on them and the only thing that distinguished them by persona were the names of the pilots, Bud so-and-so or Moon something, but when you went over to the British, they had naked women on the sides of their warplanes, and all sorts of 'immoral' things, and the British are so straight-laced and everything, but somehow we have accepted the idea that we can't do this."

"While at the same time we were burning people alive," added Coppola.[3]

While only parts of "The End" are played in *Apocalypse Now*, both at the beginning and at ... the end ... the entirety of this, one of the all-time classic rock songs, resonates with many aspects of the film. The operatic Milius and Coppola seemingly drove the story like sheet music.

The lyrics perfectly describe Willard girding for his final confrontation with Kurtz, the death mask an assassin must wear to emotionally detach himself from his task, and the last steps taken before the ancient deed is done, satisfying living sin.

The killer first pays a visit to his brother and sister, perhaps to remind him he is still human. Then, of course, Morrison infamously sings about patricide and matricide, but Morrison's live performances reflected a change in that, to the Oedipal desire to have intercourse with his mother. Early in the film, Coppola used some rare audio of Morrison repeating the word "fuck" in rapid-fire manner, making it hard to tell if he is really saying it, but he is. These scenes reflect the turmoil in Willard's psyche regarding his relationship with his wife and agreeing to an inevitable divorce, and then he returns, like an animal drawn by the scent, back to the primeval jungle, the only place he understands. But no place in the film are Morrison's lyrics more profoundly perfect and disturbing than the scene in which Willard emerges, like a creature, blackened and soaking wet, from the swamp, set to kill Kurtz.

Milius and Coppola both called Vietnam a "rock 'n' roll war," with heavy emphasis on California culture as opposed to the stereotype of New Yorkers discussing the Brooklyn Dodgers as a password in World War II. Here was the ultimate Los Angeles, California, rock act intoning lyrics that could have been a call to love, or adventure, or romance, using the word "baby," a colloquialism with sexual overtones, only now layered over the darkest, eeriest scene possible. The "chance" Morrison urges Captain Willard to take is to physically kill the god-like Walter Kurtz, symbol of all that has gone wrong in this horrible war.

Sheen's Willard emerges, looks around, eyes darting like a cat's, his bare athletic body coiled like a Greek Olympian, gracefully moving like Orson Welles had once read "towards Kurtz," the object of enmity ... and admiration.

As Willard moves toward the final great confrontation, Morrison sings of a "blue bus" which is beckoning them. The blue bus is a commonly used reference to an acid trip, which plays a major role in the surrealism of the journey as they get closer to Kurtz and farther from reality

Lyrics referencing the questioning of authorities' direction correlate with Chief Phillips angrily confronting Willard about his mission; that he is lost, does not know where they are going or what he is doing, and is leading a bunch of innocent American boys to oblivion.

Willard has been given permission by Kurtz to kill him and, as first suggested by the Hopper character, to then tell the world who he was, what kind of man he was, what he represented. This was not Milius's ending.

"I never cared for the ending much," said Coppola of Milius's firefight between Willard and Kurtz, standing like Duke Wayne, Richard Widmark, and Laurence Harvey fighting off Santa Anna's forces to the death in *The Alamo* (1960).

> *Kurtz*: We fight for the land that's under our feet, gold that's in our hands, women that worship the power in our loins.... I summon fire from the sky. Do you know what it means to be a white man who can summon fire from the sky? What it means? You can live or die for these things. Not silly ideals that are always betrayed.... What do you fight for, Captain?
> *Willard*: Because it feels good....

"That wasn't a good ending," Milius finally admitted. "I think my version was much too obvious. Some people liked it, but I prefer the ending that's there now." It took Milius a long time to come around. When he first contemplated and started writing *Apocalypse Now*, he and many others still thought the United States would win the Vietnam War. Then it became a sort of "revenge manual," like the *Rambo* movies of the Reagan '80s, in which America "wins" the war courtesy of Sly Stallone and Chuck Norris. Milius, like any great screenwriter—but especially on this script—looked upon his work like it was his child, and at first was horrified that the "bearded Marxist" Francis Ford Coppola had liberalized *him*. But when he finally saw the movie he realized Coppola, the visionary, was right.

"I always thought the ending was weak," said Coppola. "The ending didn't top what had happened with the helicopters, and it didn't answer any of the moral issues. Instead it got into a real gung-ho, macho kind of comic-book ending....

"And my choice was to make it much more back to *Heart of Darkness* than really George and John were intending. I think very early on I knew that I was going to take John's script and kind of mate it with *Heart of Darkness*, and I knew whatever happened to me in the jungle, I knew that was my concept."[4]

But Coppola still had enough of Milius in his head to keep from creating a peace activist. "Hey, Marlon, I may not know everything about this movie, but one thing I know it's not about *our guilt*," he told his star when he suggested that be the final message.[5] If any of Milius's view were to prevail, and it had to in order to be a great, albeit controversial piece of art, this needed to be made clear onscreen.

Milius was Jewish but a conservative who found much appeal in the Christian right. Coppola was liberal and worldly, but his Catholicism was always a part of his background, making its way into his movies. He made no overt attempt to convert the final climactic death throes of Kurtz at Willard's hands into a religious message, but it was so powerful, spoke to the fears of all humanity so totally, that it simply did that whether he meant to or not.

Even though Milius said he wrote the screenplay with Wagner and The Doors in his head, it was Coppola, perhaps urged by Jacob, who made maximum use of Jim Morrison's power in the ultimate climax. The moment of truth for Milius, the point where he gave up on his ending and realized Coppola had done him one better, was when he heard The Doors bringing the curtain down like German opera. Coppola struggled with the ending. After Willard kills Kurtz, then what? Milius's battle scene was not right, especially if Kurtz is dead. But the music of The Doors is what gave resonance to the climax, and perhaps even saved *Apocalypse Now* from the disaster many thought at the time it would be.

Then, of course, as Sheen attacks Kurtz, using various methods, including a rifle butt to bash his brains in, Morrison urges him to, "Kill, kill, kill …" Morrison's tone becomes increasingly savage, timed to Willard's blows, finally uttering "*Kiiiill*" the way the devil likes people to say it.

The rest of "The End" is an acceptance of death, the hope that there is peace in its embrace, but there is no surety to this Christian notion in *Apocalypse Now*. Kurtz dies on film as he died in Joseph Conrad's masterpiece, uttering "The horror! The horror!" This vision of hatred is not comforting; it portends hell. Jim Morrison, raised in a Southern Pentecostal environment, rejected Christ. He and his band even visited a famed Satanologist, apparently seeking "answers." There is no evidence he found Jesus Christ when he met his Maker in a Parisian bath tub in 1971, and his uncomforted common-law wife drugged herself into the grave in short order after that, again absent the confessions God seeks as the path to salvation.

Coppola always said the core of the movie was Milius. Coppola brought it closer to Conrad. Milius's "mercurial moods," wrote Michael Schumacher, resulted in several versions of its origin. "All the great scenes and lines are Milius's," Coppola asserted. He was very generous artistically, since Milius's screenplay is decidedly different. A lot of very great lines in the film are not in it. Perhaps Milius "wrote" them extemporaneously on location, as much of the film was done that way, and he was called to the Philippines for that purpose. Coppola's gracious crediting of Milius lends credence to his case with Robert Evans. He was egotistical, but generous to a fault. The "weird ending," however, was Coppola's. "The overall opaqueness of the style came from me," he said.[6]

Coppola insisted on the famed death throes of Kurtz—"The horror, the horror"—be kept in the film as it was in *Heart of Darkness*. Eleanor Coppola shot 238 days of principal photography. Of course, when they were filming Kurtz's death scene, they had not edited it, had not scored it with The Doors, and were still unaware of what they had.

Brando's role is generally thought one of the greatest ever, although there are many detractors. It is by no means universally viewed as brilliant in the way his Don Vito Corleone was, but for so little preparation and effort, it was comparable to Babe Ruth eating hot dogs, drinking beer, and having sex with women until four in the morning, then hitting two monster home runs in an afternoon game at Yankee Stadium.

Many still do not connect with that character … but that was part of the character, as Sheen's Willard said, referring to the ambiguity of Kurtz's voice he hears on tape, which like Brando's role over time, eventually sunk into Willard's consciousness.

The movie was still a hodgepodge, a mess. The perfect symbol of how difficult it all had been in the Philippines came on Brando's last day. Coppola turned it all over to his assistant director as a way of saying, "fuck you" to Marlon Brando.[7]

18

"Apocalypse When?"

The rumors were that *Apocalypse Now* was unreleasable.

In early May of 1977, Coppola wrapped principal photography at a cost of $27 million. The crew was totally ready to finish the work. On June 8, he dismissed them, returning to San Francisco in a BAC-111, a sizable airplane, with ninety hours of rushes, and eight minutes of usable film. He watched footage on the jet, and knew it needed tremendous work. He did not yet have an ending he deemed appropriate.

The 238-day shoot was double that of *Jaws*, at the time thought to be the gold standard of overtime movies. Coppola had 250 hours—1 million feet—of raw footage. Previous supposed "boondoggles," like Joseph L. Mankiewicz's 1963 behemoth, *Cleopatra*, were thought now the good old days. Due to his burdensome workload, Coppola missed the *Star Wars* premiere of his good friend George Lucas.

The $13 million budget had now reached $30 million and was still climbing. UA had sunk $25 million into it. They took out a $15 million life insurance policy on Coppola. He joked he was worth more dead than alive, and still needed another $10 million for postproduction.

Coppola put up his Napa house for the future profits of *The Black Stallion*. Carpenters came in to set up editing rooms with laminated maple plywood mahogany brought back from the Philippines. Coppola learned his phone had been turned off for lack of payment. After more than a year in the Philippines, Coppola was still only one-third finished.

At the time, *Star Wars* and *Close Encounters of the Third Kind* were blowing up, on the heels of *Jaws*. There was considerable belief in the movie industry that these were the kind of "pop corn movies" that made money; that the old days of epics, dramatic tension, great acting, and characterization (*Lawrence of Arabia*, *Dr. Zhivago*), were if not over, not blockbuster material. These three films had helped lift the industry out of its 1960s doldrums. Show biz had changed since Coppola entered the jungle. That said, while *Apocalypse Now* contained within those 1 million feet of raw footage all those qualities, it also contained epic aerial battle scenes, stunning visual imagery, and the kind of on-the-seat, rock 'em, sock 'em action of both *Jaws* and *Star Wars*. In fact, it had far more, and in Coppola's case it was absolutely *real*, not computer-animated, not an electric shark, not a cartoon. Real people had flown real helicopters on what was very close to real missions, and, in truth, it was extremely lucky nobody was killed or even injured beyond Sheen's heart attack.

Coppola called Dennis Jacob to help edit this monstrosity. He was already six weeks behind schedule and $3 million over budget. He still needed to rewrite the script, and accommodate the editing to his shifting vision. Jacob, considered an eccentric genius, was an extension of his college friend Jim Morrison. He worked with a skull in his office.

They had a disagreement and he walked off with the last third of *Apocalypse Now*. One day Coppola received a bag of ashes, but it was a fake. Jacob had not burned it, but agreed to return the film.

Coppola divided the editing between several teams of editors. He hired a team of "worker bees." "The cutting was turned over to Francis's groupies," one veteran editor grumbled.[1] But he gave work to aspiring local filmmakers who had a once-in-a-lifetime chance to work on *Apocalypse Now*.

"I owe everything I have to his wonderful madness," sound editor Jerry Ross said.

"We'd come to work every morning and for three months there was literally nothing to do," editorial assistant Richard Candib recalled.[2] A number of people were let go. Coppola battled depression. At times, in the beginning, the monumental task seemed impossible. Coppola jetted off to Europe on his BAC-111. By October he was again having an affair.

"The emotion rose up from my feet like a tide," Ellie wrote. "It hit me in the chest and knocked me backward. I have been comfortable believing the lies. Just like Kay in the last scene of *The Godfather*. All of the evidence tells her that her husband has had people killed, and when she asks him, he says no, and she believed his words. All the evidence through the years, the little presents, notes, things I would find in Francis's pockets after a trip, the pin sent to him in the Philippines that he wore on his hat as a good luck charm. And when I would ask, I would hear, 'Ellie, she is a friend, she had been a big help to me—she is no threat to you.' I believed the words, I denied the evidence. I didn't want to see the truth."

Eleanor began to think of how Jackie Kennedy found her own life, and thought so could she. Then she threw expensive china against the kitchen walls. Coppola kept Mathison in a Sausalito home with sweeping views of the bay. He would bring her to screenings. Coppola's mother, Italia, was bothered when Francis had his affair.

"You're a good Catholic boy," she told her son. "What do you mean carrying on with that girl?"[3] Their argument carried over a speaker that had been set up. Ellie cried a lot.

On November 26, 1977, Coppola flew, along with Spielberg and Lucas, to Washington, D.C., for an event with President Jimmy Carter. Spielberg called themselves the "Billion Dollar Boys." They stayed at the Watergate. *Close Encounters of the Third Kind* and *Star Wars* were blockbusters. The pressure mounted on Francis.

But he could not put off his movie forever. Eventually he needed to wade into the work. "For months, Francis would just sit in the screening room at night, look at cuts of the film, get stoned, and trip on music," recalled a member of the editing crew.[4]

"We'd be working for months without feedback," recalled another, "and then we'd get an insane note from his office in the penthouse: 'Francis would like to recut the scene to The Doors' 'L.A. Woman.' He was in another world."[5]

"I'd ask Francis, 'Whaddaya want me to do with this scene?'" said another editor. "He would go into this exegesis of *The Golden Bough*, the father killing the son, and I'd be sitting there mesmerized by his wonderful eloquence, and then he'd leave, and I'd think, 'Yeah, but what am I supposed to do with this scene?'"[6]

The malaise of the Northern California editing process was telling. There was both good news and bad news. Post-production of *The Godfather* had not been a good experience, and he faced a far greater challenge this time. On the bright side, he did not have to answer to Robert Evans, but whether Coppola ever was willing to admit it, there were times he needed Evans.

Evans had wanted to take *The Godfather* to Los Angeles for editing; Coppola insisted on keeping it in San Francisco. But Evans understood that Los Angeles is an industry town. Editors get up every day and edit. It is a refined, factory-like, industrial process honed over decades of experience. It is not an environment—unlike Coppola's wine country "Shangri La"—where *artistes* can sit around for months on end getting stoned while millions of dollars hang in the balance.

Because of Coppola's lethargy in Napa, *Apocalypse* had to cancel its hoped-for Christmas 1977 release. It was pushed back to April 1978, Coppola's thirty-ninth birthday. People began to drop out of the project, leaving him isolated in his private editing bay, no producer or boss telling him to pull things together.

"Part of the dynamic of the place which I found difficult to be around, was an elitism, the sense that we're all really special," recalled Mathison. "Maybe they were, maybe they weren't. They were not just making movies, and there isn't anything that special about that. I'm sure a lot of people who were part of the 'team' felt like they suddenly became a 'you' or a 'them,' and that was hard to take."[7]

Coppola faced a challenge in controlling the public's perception of his movie. All the talk and interest could, if handled properly, be channeled into positive energy, but it could just as easily—as it had so far—result in self-fulfilling failure.

TV reduced movie grosses from 1946 to 1962. An increase in the cost of movies meant the industry was still in trouble. *The French Connection* and *Love Story* had helped revive Hollywood, but had not returned it to full profitability. But M-G-M stopped making movies. Warner Bros., Paramount, Universal, and UA (once the independent distributor of Chaplin and Pickford's finest films) were all bought by large corporations. The business model was now different.

A helicopter and the crew's Navy PBR were literally parked out front. The Kurtz compound was erected on his property. Costumes and props were stocked in the cook's quarters. He restructured his finances in order to fund the ending. On top of that, Coppola had to oversee pre-production of his UCLA friend Carroll Ballard's Zoetrope film, *The Black Stallion*. Coppola took great pride in his work. He did not just "phone it in," but worked very hard on script rewrites, rejecting major changes Ballard proposed. The film eventually was released to strong box office, good reviews, and even an eventual sequel. It was a nice payoff.

He sold 72,000 common shares of Cinema 5 back to Donald Rugoff at the same price he bought it for in 1974, providing some of his assets as collateral to UA in order to finance the loan for the completion of *Apocalypse Now*.

As he toiled in the editing room, the pressure was on; it needed to be a huge hit for him to break even. He suffered grave worries. After going over the footage with Murch, Coppola felt he had a 20 percent chance of success. Eleanor had an odd desire for him to fail, as fame had disrupted their marriage, threatening the happiness of their children. She yearned to return to a normal life. She felt if he lost his fortune he was talented enough to make it back, and did not place emphasis on material things.

It was around this time that Coppola, no longer seduced like Kurtz by the wild jungle, ended an affair with a young screenwriter he was "deeply in love" with, biographer Michael Schumacher wrote. He later said it was, "The most destructive thing I've ever been through." But his wife rationalized the affair arose out of the pressures of *Apocalypse Now*. If they could get past that the marriage might be saved. Despite being children of the '60s, they were traditional about marriage and relationships. Coppola was an Italian man who believed in the lifelong sanctity of the institution.

But the editing was a massive undertaking, probably the most difficult post-production in movie annals. The July 4, 1976, release date had been given up on almost as soon as the crew arrived in the Philippines and got a look at the weather. The April 7, 1977, date, Coppola's thirty-eighth birthday, came and went; no chance. They were shooting for Christmas, which was a major stretch, but the financiers were getting worried. Murch and Coppola looked at the footage and realized this was impossible, as well, so they decided to shoot for October of 1978. Each announcement was met with howls of gossip and innuendo, complete with headlines like "Apocalypse When?"

Coppola, normally ebullient, remained silent, adding to the press tension. But his experience with Evans girded him. He had not known until the end whether *The Godfather* would work, and even the masterful sequel had questions in post. He understood through the great value of experience, perhaps the best attribute in any endeavor, what the Charlie Bluhdorns and the suits at Paramount and United Artists, did not. A great film is a set of moving parts that must be masterfully pieced together. If one of those parts fails, the entire movie fails, but if the director fails to match up the strengths of each moving part in a final act of synchronization, even if all those parts are great, the film will suffer. Coppola knew he had a great screenplay, the first essential. He knew he had captured on film great acting performances. Without that, unless a movie is a cartoon or cartoonish, it will suffer. He had great cinematography; it was all there in his San Francisco editing bays. *Now* he needed to do a great editing job, and to his great good luck had the magnificent Walter Murch to help him pull it off.

Because of the many problems with the weather, Sheen's heart attack, Marcos's government making the helicopters unreliable, among numerous other factors, the scenes in *Apocalypse Now* were not shot in continuity, the style of artistry that most actors, whose training comes from the stage, prefer. There was a sense of mystery to the random shots, with Murch and Coppola trying to piece together what should be placed before it and after it; what should be cut out altogether. In later years screenwriters have tried to achieve a kind of formula in which scenes have an "up/down" quality to them, with the mood light or happy, followed by dark or sad, always keeping the audience on their toes, propelling the tension of the movie. Early on, such an artistic luxury was completely unavailable to Murch and Coppola. They just wanted to make sense of it first; then they could return to artistry.

In January of 1978 Coppola decided he wanted voiceover work with Martin Sheen. It was not in Milius's original screenplay, and while Coppola has generously said everything good in the film came from Milius, this was a brilliant decision that belonged to him. Michael Herr, a famed Vietnam historian, helped shape Willard's lines.

Meanwhile, outside observers felt the film was a form of madness, an apt observation. To them it seemed out of control. Post-production droned on and on, a depressing, daily grind that got to everybody. One employee even obsessed over it, like a babysitter who decides the child in her charge his really hers; changing, stealing and even burning some footage. Milius was brought in to work with Sheen on his voiceover dialogue.

Sheen had a passive quality that has transcended most of his acting work over the years, but Milius wanted more than that. Fred Rexer, a key Milius advisor, arrived and frightened everybody with stories of torture (probably part of the infamous Phoenix Program), of the Viet Cong pulling skulls apart with their bare hands. He brought a gun to the voiceover session and gave it to Sheen.

"You could shoot anyone in this room," Milius said to him. "You have the power of life and death in your hands." This made Sheen nervous but motivated him to provide some of the most intense movie lines of all time ("I was going to the worst place in the world; weeks away and hundreds of miles up a river that snaked through the war like a main circuit cable, plugging me straight into Kurtz.")

The editing team also discovered the power of changing technology. It was more expensive, but Dolby Stereo was breathtaking. They began to *imagine* what it would sound like in a large, crowded movie theatre, a rapt audience sitting quietly on the edge of their seats, every sound and nuance surrounding and filling their senses.

"First, he wanted it to be quantiphonic, he wanted the sound to fill the room, to seem to come from all sections of the room," Murch recalled of Coppola's desire. Ken Russell had done this on *Tommy* (1975), but no other movie had really used the technology. It was like a brand-new jet aircraft that is so complicated and new that even experienced pilots are afraid to put it to full-throttle use.

The biggest challenge with Dolby Sound came during the "Ride of the Valkyries" helicopter attack scene. The filmmakers did not want to overwhelm the audience with noise. Coppola wanted the authentic sounds of weaponry, reminding Vietnam veterans what it felt like to be there. (Considering how powerful the final product turned out to be, it is a miracle there were not a series of "flashbacks" and post-traumatic stress incidents in theatres.) Despite not having DoD cooperation, Murch managed to get the authentic weapons he needed. He fired them off in the hills outside San Francisco, recording the sounds of ordnance.

"The final thing he wanted," said Murch, who would win an Oscar for his work, "was the film soundtrack to partake the psychedelic haze in which the war had been fought, not only in terms of the music for the soundtrack—The Doors and what kids listened to on the radio—but in general, kind of far-out juxtaposition of imagery and sound; for the soundtrack not to be just a literal imitation of what you saw on the screen but at times to depart from it…. We were moving into unchartered waters. I thought I was doing a job similar to that of a production designer, so I called what I did sound design."[8]

UA had a considerable amount invested and heard it was an "unreleasable mess," wrote Michael Schumacher. If they shut it down in post-production they would be out $30 million, even with certain guarantees they had made with Coppola. Plus, how would they ever collect money from Francis? They were afraid he would ask for more completion money, but they also knew the only chance the maverick genius from Napa Valley had of earning their money was to finish this mad science experiment. UA, like Coppola in the Philippines and the United States in Vietnam, was committed beyond the point of no return.

TransAmerica had bought the studio Pickford, Chaplin, Fairbanks, and Griffith started in 1919, in 1967. At first it seemed a lark, like Charlie Bluhdorn hiring Bob Evans so there would always be a lot of pretty girls with whom to fool around. But the money quickly made it a business for Gulf+Western, and TransAmerica had consistently lost dough, even in the 1970s when Hollywood rebounded. To their bean counters, it was a losing arrangement.

Around 1974–75, TransAmerica had rebounded to some extent, which spurred them to get in business with Coppola, but they became more activist, too. Arthur Krim resigned as UA's president in January of 1978, but his replacements were not artistic types. They were all scared of *Apocalypse Now*, but Coppola knew how to schmooze. Krim took Mike Medavoy, who had played such a big role in the New Hollywood, including representing the young John Milius, with him to form Orion. TransAmerica replaced him with Andy Albeck, a lifer with no vision. Many likened it to the Paramount hiring of Evans a decade earlier, setting him up for the company's fall, only this time Albeck was no Evans and would not produce a string of masterpieces. Production was now headed by two young men with little experience, Steven Bach and David Field.

On April 23, 1978, Coppola screened it for the TransAmerica executives and a select audience at the Northpoint Theatre in San Francisco. It was probably not an accident that this was the same theatre where he saved *American Graffiti* from possible obscurity by arguing its merits to Universal's Ned Tanen, one of the least visionary of all studio executives. It was not close to being ready, and this terrified the suits. The April 1978 release quickly came and went, so at UA's urging they aimed at an August 1979 release, but they still had different versions of different endings.

Lucas wanted to use the helicopter footage for *More America Graffiti* but was refused. UA was collapsing under the weight of the project. In the summer of 1978, everyone talked about *The Deer Hunter*. It cost $15 million, and was way over budget. Michael Cimino insisted on over three hours, and got in a huge fight with Universal. After the film was a big hit, Cimino had leverage. So did his agent, Stan Kasten, who approached UA with a pay to play offer for *The Johnson County Wars*, a sweeping Western, set for $7.5 million. After screening *The Deer Hunter*, United Artists felt they had a poet on their hands, and agreed.

Coppola had to watch *The Deer Hunter* beat his film to the "Vietnam movie" punch, becoming an instant masterpiece. The media dubbed it "Apocalypse First." He met Cimino at a New York screening, and, later, Cimino insulted him in the press.

Still a hodgepodge of beautiful yet unconnected scenes, the 1978 screening engendered no confidence. Coppola begged people not to leak its poor reception to critics. Even the one good reaction bothered him. They all loved the "Ride of the Valkyries" attack scene on the Vietnamese village.

"The film reaches its highest level during the fucking helicopter battle," Coppola said after reading the notes "My nerves are shot—my heart is broken—my imagination is dead. I have no self-reliance. But, like a child, I just want someone to rescue me."[9]

Meanwhile, two of his protégés, Steven Spielberg and George Lucas, were the toasts of Hollywood; their movies surpassing Coppola's *The Godfather* in box office.

In 1978, *Superman* made a star out of Margot Kidder, for her role as Lois Lane. She had finally achieved the goals she set out for herself when she made her house available to any rising filmmaker who showed up, in the hopes of riding their coattails to fame and fortune.

The Deer Hunter won five Oscars. Many on the right liked it, thinking it patriotic whether Cimino agreed with that assessment or not. Cimino won an Academy Award for Best Director, with Coppola handing him his award. It was John Wayne's last public appearance. He handed out the Best Picture Oscar.

Cimino was anointed the "next big thing," further adding to the increasing belief that Francis Ford Coppola was a has-been. *The Deer Hunter* broke numerous rules of supposed film convention. Like *The Godfathers* it was very long, and practically imitated Coppola with a very drawn-out wedding sequence near the beginning. Whereas Coppola's wedding scene contained key plot and character elements, Cimino's movie contained some of that, including a long confluence of music, dancing, Russian Christian pageantry, and drunkenness.

But it was a stunning, wildly beautiful, and powerful story containing astonishing performances. It can be argued that Robert De Niro and Christopher Walken have never been better. The same can be said of a young, pretty Meryl Streep, a cast of awesome character actors, including the amazing John Cazale, Fredo in *The Godfather*. Sadly, his talent was lost to the world when he died of lung cancer after shooting *The Deer Hunter*.

Cimino was a stereotype, a young bull fighter challenging the aging champion, a hot-shot quarterback out of Notre Dame nipping at the heels of a former Super Bowl champ. Cimino made nasty comments about Coppola, arguing that his film was realistic, not Coppola's surrealistic vision, which was becoming a joke among movie insiders.

"Vietnam was not the Apocalypse," Cimino smirked, taking a shot at a generation he said thought the world rose and set with them, while also reflecting the Christianity that was a major theme of his film. Not everybody agreed *The Deer Hunter* was "conservative," but it can be argued that it was. It reflected small-town values; young men who never question their duty, who go off to proudly serve their nation. Even when they return—broken, dead—the final scene shows all of them singing "God Bless America." At Cannes, Coppola felt it was "politically naïve."

Then came *Heroes* and *Coming Home*. However, the films reflected a domestic reflection of Vietnam. *The Deer Hunter* had considerable Vietnam scenes, including a controversial Russian roulette sequence, then hospital and Saigon sequences, but was largely about the effect on the citizens of a Pennsylvania steel town. *Apocalypse Now*'s original screenplay called for Captain Willard to reflect from the splendor of a yacht in Marina Del Rey, but none of that made it onto the screen. It was 100 percent Vietnam War.

Fred Roos, looking for a silver lining, felt hopefully that *The Deer Hunter*'s success was "good for us," proving a Vietnam movie could succeed at the box office.[10] But Cimino's great success did spotlight one thing Coppola did not want spotlighted: his film seemed to be going nowhere, and the media had gone from dubbing it "Apocalypse When?" to "Apocalypse Never."

"It was a very intense, and complicated post-production period, one of the longest in history, for two-and-a-half years to not have a film readied to be released is probably a record," said Eleanor.[11]

Coppola started talking about a new digital technology studio. He had a health episode and was hospitalized, placed on Lithium for manic depression for four years. One day he literally held a group of editors hostage while he regaled them with ideas and concepts. He was convinced everyone was out to get him. He turned forty in April of 1979. Robert De Niro, George Lucas, and Dennis Hopper all chanted, "We will rule Hollywood!" Cheerleaders were brought in to chant, "Francis has the power!" It was textbook megalomania. He decided to stay with Eleanor. He innately understood she was his only link back to sanity. He realized, "It's better to just have one wife."

UA was also not happy, but Coppola took chances. He was forty, unsure of his future. All was riding on this movie. First, he arranged a series of screenings, each very risky in its own right. He arranged a White House showing for President Jimmy Carter and fifty guests. It received a "very, very mixed" reaction. Carter, an Annapolis graduate and former officer in Hyman Rickover's nuclear Navy, perhaps out of politeness, applauded. CIA director Stansfield Turner, furious that a greasy spook could order an Army captain to kill a colonel using "extreme prejudice," sat in silent anger. If Coppola thought an anti-war Democrat administration might enjoy his depictions of Vietnam he was wrong.[12]

What he did, on May 11 at the Mann Theatre in Westwood, looked desperate. He amassed 2,500 people, inviting every big name in Hollywood. Interest, some bordering on the macabre, was at a fever pitch. People scrambled for tickets. Many were expecting, if not hoping, for a train wreck in which the egotistical, bearded Francis Ford Coppola could be embarrassed as he long deserved to be. He had stepped on a lot of toes: studio execs, producers, the media. Robert Evans was a legend, beloved by many, and his rivalry with Coppola was the talk of the town.

Coppola asked the audience members to fill out a detailed questionnaire "to help me finish the film." He had *still* not really figured out his ending, or even a cohesive structure. The movie was still a mess. People looked at one another and shook their heads. Was Coppola going for the sympathy vote?

The movie played in all of its 70mm magnificence, but the incredible Dolby Surround Sound people associate with the final Murch-edited version was not yet laid in. There were no credits. At one showing the audience remained silent. At another they applauded at the end, but Coppola was unsure if they clapped because it was finally over.

Audiences seemed confused. It was very difficult to contemplate at first showing, making Coppola and others extremely nervous. Unlike the best-selling *The Godfather* by Mario Puzo, many were unfamiliar with Joseph Conrad's *Heart of Darkness*. Lacking this literary reference, Kurtz and what he symbolizes went over their heads. At the beginning of the film, Willard says in voiceover, "All I wanted was a mission, and for my sins they gave me one. Brought it up to me like room service."

The term "mission" sounded like a Christian missionary, especially when he makes reference to his "sins." *Heart of Darkness* was set in the Belgian Congo; was this about a missionary in deepest, darkest Africa? Then the "missionary" is found and brought to an Army base wearing a uniform, where he is revealed as not a missionary but an Army captain … working for whom? The CIA? More confusion. A substantial chunk of the movie has played up to this point and suddenly much of the audience, thrown for a loop, has to readjust their understanding of who Sheen's character is, what he is there to do, and what is likely to come next.

The next sequences are visually incredible, and include, first, the aftermath of an Arc Light strike, sensory overload in the form of Robert Duvall's Colonel Kilgore, then an insane helicopter attack that causes Army recruits to jump to their feet, cheering … except Murch's sound design was not yet installed, so all of this is not as magnificent as it later would be.

There is blood, death, and gore … galore. The *Playboy* bunnies are smoking hot, but there is no sex. Then it gets moody and atmospheric, and the long-awaited Marlon Brando is mired in shadows.

Whaaaa?

"It's like watching your mother being killed and asking what you think of it," one viewer wrote. Other reports were generally unfavorable. The press heard of bad-to-mixed reviews and began reporting it. Rona Barrett on ABC's *Good Morning America* called it "a disappointing failure."

Gene Siskel of the *Chicago Tribune* wrote that the first two hours were "mostly stunning," but the last twenty minutes were a mess. "*Apocalypse Now*, in the version I saw, is not easy to comprehend," Siskel continued. "It does not have the broadly drawn, good-and-evil characters of *Coming Home* and *The Deer Hunter*. It's a much more subtle film, which appeared to hold the audience's attention until the ending, when many people seemed confused."

Coppola was mocked for asking people to fill out questionnaires so he could use suggestions to finish the movie. While the practice of showing to a test audience is very common, it is usually done with ordinary citizens in a suburban theatre, not mainstream Hollywood *glitterati*, much less critics such as Siskel. It seemed the act of a man with no answers, not likely to find any in time.

"The film is about moral ambiguity," Coppola told Siskel, as if he could talk his way into making the world like his movie ... and him. "What the film says is that we are all straddled between good and evil, that we each make decisions as we go along and always will, and there is no such thing as absolute good and evil—there never is and never will be."

Conservatives and Christians thought such statements claptrap. America is good. Communism, by this time in history responsible for the murders of an estimated 100 million of their fellow human beings, is evil. Every soldier worth his salt knew to a moral certainty the war should have been won. How? Easy. Bomb the dykes in North Vietnam, flood the country, lay waste to the Communist infrastructure, and, after a bombing campaign like those the U.S. and British laid on Germany and Japan, invade, conquer, and hold Hanoi, then the rest of Southeast Asia, as we invaded, conquered and held Berlin, Tokyo, Prague, Rome, Seoul....

Christians recoiled at the idea that this bearded Marxist—did Coppola dodge the draft?—said there was "no such thing as absolute good and evil—there never is and never will be." It certainly sounded like a rejection of his own Catholic catechisms. God is perfect, Satan is "the enemy," and people who say there is no good or evil are obviously making the devil smile in so doing.

So Francis could not seem to please anybody.

It was obvious UA was in free fall. Coppola tried to get some independent money he still needed for more post-production, not to mention promotions. He offered to bring Warren Beatty in if he would provide some much-needed capital, but the actor-producer said no. Coppola was naïve to believe the press would resist reviewing his movie. He seemed to expect that his past record would guarantee soft treatment.

Russell Baker jumped on the band wagon early, although his lavish praise had the effect of sounding "tongue in cheek."

> *Apocalypse Now* is finally here. It is incredible. It is breath-taking and awe-inspiring. Sensitive, moving and inspired, it is beautiful, acute, brooding, magnificent, spectacular, and stupendous, also wise, witty, a monument to human dignity, and eternal testament to man's inhumanity to man. I look forward to seeing it someday.

"The version you saw," Coppola told *Variety*'s Dale Pollock after the Westwood showing, "*is* Vietnam. It's my version. That's it. There are no other versions, just things people would like to see me do. But this is my version, my ending and my film."[13]

19

"It's not about Vietnam—it *is* Vietnam"

Finally, in May of 1979, Coppola took another risky move, but, then, that had always been his style. He entered *Apocalypse Now* at the Cannes International Film Festival's competition as a "work in progress," which was essentially an unheard of practice. He took Kirk Kerkorian's plane to Cannes. His competition was strong: *Manhattan, Norma Rae, Days of Heaven, The China Syndrome*, and *Hair*.

UA said they were in "harmony" with him, but it was spin. Others sniped that he actually had "momentary insanity" brought on from the jungle. His competition called his entry the "dumbest idea" ever. Negative reaction at Cannes could doom his movie. Coppola called it an "out of town tryout." It was a huge risk. He held the note at the bank and it was his film like few others ever belonged to any *artiste*. He said he was not interested in winning the Palme d'Or. The audience's response was polite but mixed. The ending confused them.

Apocalypse had little or no advertising campaign timed to its Cannes release. While its backers were unique, a combination big studio, independent financing, loans, Coppola's own money, American Zoetrope, and other interests, it was big enough and certainly big-budget enough to be thought of the way Hollywood thinks of a blockbuster release, timed for summer or, if deemed Oscar potential, in December. When *The Godfather* was pushed from Christmas 1971 to March 1972, Gulf+Western went ballistic because it broke from these very conventions.

Apocalyse Now was not finished; it was not the movie countless fans have come to know. It was like inviting the world into his private screening room to judge his movie and air their criticisms for all to hear. Many fantastic films do premiere at Cannes, but as a general rule they are smaller, or semi-independent films, usually with a low budget, at least in those days. Big studio projects, projected as summer or Christmas blockbusters, are reserved for major worldwide marketing campaigns timed at releasing them when interest has been built to a fever pitch.

A thousand reporters were at the press conference when Coppola put on one of his all-time bravura performances, full of bluster and bravado. "My film is not a movie," he stated. "It's not about Vietnam—it *is* Vietnam. It's what it was really like. It was crazy....

"And the way we made it was very much like the way the Americans fought the war in Vietnam. We were in the jungle, there were too many of us, we had access to too much money, too much equipment, and little by little we went insane....

"I think you can see [all this] in the film. As it goes up the river, you can see the photography going a little crazy and the director and the actors going a little crazy. After a while, I realized I was a little frightened."[1]

The film was still a "work in progress" but won the Palme d'Or (Golden Palm), his second Palme d'Or, before an audience of two thousand. Some booed the election results, but it was a huge win. That night he finally relaxed and let it all hang out. He blamed journalists for the picture's problems. Then Ellie threw wine at Francis for flirting with a woman. Milius was so upset at the first showing of *Apocalypse Now* he put his fist through the door. Lucas also disliked it. He had invested six years of his life into the project, only to "see [my] original concept distorted by Coppola's fervid imagination."[2]

It had none of the advance buzz of *The Godfather*. Early reviews were mixed. Nobody understood it. The film's hallucinatory imagery stunned critics. The ending left much to be desired. Brando's scenes were excoriated. People hated all the skulls. The consensus was that Coppola had lost his way. It was sensational in the beginning, but could not sustain that level of power. It was "'*Apocalypse Now* and then,'" joked Robert Towne.[3]

Peter Biskind compared the Brando-Kurtz relationship to a generational father-son divide, with Brando holding court over a kind of Mansonesque "Spahn Ranch." Also, Kurtz was the self-indulgent picture of Brando's rancid self. The ending was still not settled. "To kill him would be to indict himself, commit suicide, metaphorically speaking," wrote Biskind. "To let him live would be to capitulate to the dark side." Originally budgeted at $12 million, it was over $30 million, maybe $40 million. Coppola now looked like damaged goods.

"Filmmaking is like winemaking," said Coppola. "You get all these grapes, some of them are burnt, some of them are not quite ripe, some of them the sugar isn't right, and with the winemaker's sway, you make great wine."

"Even if Coppola isn't haunted by the specter of financial fiascos like *Cleopatra*, there's no assured future for *Apocalypse*," wrote Dale Pollock. "It's a complex, demanding, highly intelligent piece of work, coming into a marketplace that does not always embrace those qualities."

Amid this, other reports were unfavorable, but all felt the film had "brilliance," just not as a complete package. "*Apocalypse Now* feels like one of those awesome pieces by The Rolling Stones or The Grateful Dead that seem to go on forever in a spreading luxuriousness of panic and dread, leaving a residue of anxiety in your stomach while making you high at the same time," wrote David Denby of *New York* magazine.

Coppola accused "American journalism" of being a pack of "decadent … unethical" liars. Coppola admitted he and the crew slowly went insane. The movie, he said, made itself. It was totally "surrealistic." He raved on that he had put his own money on the line and was criticized about pointing out the immorality of war. He sneered at critics who criticized the killing of the water buffalo, comparing it to the horse's head scene in *The Godfather*, complaining that people cared more about animals than people. All of this made United Artists more and more nervous, as it generated bad publicity. Coppola insisted his film was "authentic." He criticized popular fare—basically the paying audience—which had flocked to see *King Kong* and Marlon Brando, of all people, in *Superman*.

However, Coppola's genius for public relations cannot be underestimated. His personal magnetism worked with Robert Evans, with Charlie Bluhdorn, with the suits at Paramount and the brass at Gulf+Western. It had allowed him to raise enormous sums of cash from

UA and other sources. He was Francis Ford Coppola, after all. Through his sheer PR offensive, the press began to write more favorable stories about the movie.

He flew back to San Francisco, trying for an August release. Being the Cannes winner never meant box-office success in the United States, but he seemed to sense he would make his money back. Whether it would be a huge blockbuster, or a critical success, or even a classic for the ages; none of that really mattered so long as he could at least count on making his money back, paying off all the investors, and therefore living to fight another day.

Then Eleanor published *Notes*, her diary from the Philippines, with some embarrassing details of their marriage. Coppola was not happy but he respected his wife as an artist. It was not his nature to censor anybody. In the end, *Notes* helped spur more interest, and today is considered invaluable to research of the film's making.

Back in the U.S., Coppola continued to work with Walter Murch and Richard Marks. It was the Carter years. Interest rates were through the roof. Nobody could get a loan or buy a house. The economy tanked. Summer box office was down and Hollywood was sliding after rebounding from the 1960s in the first half of the 1970s. Gene Siskel felt the public wanted light fare and would reject the heavy message of the film. Coppola wanted it both ways: a classy cultural event, yet with mass appeal.

A reported $9 million was committed to marketing, a key decision. The movie had so much visual stimulation that trailers and TV ads made it look irresistible. While still tinkering with editing and the ending with Murch, Coppola decided to show it in Los Angeles, New York, and Toronto for twelve weeks at a high cost, since audiences were given programs before each showing. The focus was on Brando. The program included credits but no explanations at the end. "We had to put titles in, and we had no choice of putting on at the back at the end or over some footage, and I had tons of this gorgeous infrared stuff so I put it under the titles," explained Coppola.[4]

Art had become "entertainment products," according to James Monaco in *American Film Now*. It was what Coppola feared; in truth, he knew it was and would continue to be, when he went to work for Roger Corman out of UCLA in the early 1960s. It offended his Old World sentiments, but he had been seduced by it just as Michael Corleone had been seduced by power in *The Godfather*. He said he wanted to make "little movies," but he kept returning to the great epics of not just his generation, but of all time.

In 1972, *The Godfather* made $43 million. The Top 10 films that year grossed $123 million. Five years later the Top 10 made $424 million, but fewer movies were being made. *Moonraker, Star Trek, Flash Gordon, King Kong, 1941; Heaven's Gate* following *The Deer Hunter* all were thought of as big models, like *Apocalypse Now*. The big budgets, which had been frowned upon after *Cleopatra* and subsequent corporate takeovers, were not viewed as unique by 1978–79 as they were in 1975.

The merchandizing of *Star Wars* alone took in $500 million, more than its $467 million at the box office. But the artist in Coppola was still not sure if he even wanted his movie to ever even be shown on TV, although one of his favorite excuses to actors complaining their scenes were cut out or shortened was that it would be restored in the television version.

20

Triumph

Apocalypse Now debuted at New York City's Ziegfeld Theatre on August 15, 1979, then at the Hollywood Cinerama Dome, and the Toronto University theatre. A whopping 311,000 tickets were bought the first week, at a cost of $5 each. UA announced it would recoup all costs. It was a giant sense of relief for everybody involved in the project.

Critics lauded the first two-thirds, but many, at first, condemned the ending. They felt the close parallel with *Heart of Darkness* was a stretch. One of the first critiques said it was "emotionally obtuse and intellectually empty."

"For two-thirds of the way," wrote Arthur Schlesinger in *Saturday Review*, "*Apocalypse Now* is really an extraordinary movie. Like the Vietnam War itself, it gets out of control at the end."

"I assume that Mr. Coppola's intention was to create in the finale a sense of Captain Willard's disconnection from reality," wrote Vincent Canby, "but what we get is a disconnection from the rest of the film. When we arrive at the heart of darkness, we find not the embodiment of evil, of civilization junked, but an eccentric actor who has been given lines that are unthinkable but not, unfortunately, unspeakable...."

"In dozens of scenes, Francis Ford Coppola's *Apocalypse Now* lives up to its grand title ... disclosing not only the various faces of war but also the contradictions between excitement and boredom, terror and pity, brutality and beauty. Its epiphanies would do credit to Federico Fellini, who is indirectly quoted at one point."

"When we showed the movie it was really dicey which way the movie was gonna go, and I had financed it and it was starting to get a negative buzz, and it got some bad reviews," recalled Coppola. "Frank Rich said it was the greatest disaster in all of his Hollywood years, and I thought *aren't they the worst?* My feelings were so hurt ... we wanted it to be a conventional war film."

Stanley Kaufman, of the *New Republic*, compared Brando to the arch villain in *Superman* or James Bond scripts. He was called "obese and photographed in shadows" and a "burlesque clown" by Gene Siskel of the *Chicago Tribune*. His words were either inaudible or senseless, he added, creating a "powerful letdown when you've been traveling upriver for two hours to meet the guy."

But there was plenty of praise to go around. It was not the immediate hit *The Godfather* had been, but it was undoubtedly a Coppola epic, which one critic called "a stunning and unforgettable film." Duvall received lavish praise.

"The movie peaks early, both pictorially and metaphorically, when Willard and the crew of a patrol boat assigned to ferry him up the river encounter Colonel Kilgore, a cheerfully brutal, gung-ho air cavalry officer, played by Robert Duvall," wrote Gary Arnold of the *Washington Post*. He then soured on the film, stating the air strike summed up the whole movie's depiction of "wanton American violence." After that it trailed off.

David Denby of *New York* magazine wrote of Kilgore that he was a "vaunting, strutting caricature of military prowess," and that his scenes effectively conveyed the "electric fantasy" that does draw men to war. This was "Coppola's greatest achievement."

Many veterans took exception to the view of unhinged soldiers. One such veteran said films should not portray them as unstable; they were not trigger happy. An infantry sergeant named Al Santoli called it "a cartoon" and a "kind of cocaine fantasy." Most felt the movie was Hollywood predictably serving up soldiers as a national picture of guilt and shame.

"Half the people thought it was a masterpiece, and half the people thought it was a piece of shit," Coppola said of the early round of critiques. "I know I'm losing years of my life."[1]

What audiences saw, beginning in August of 1979, was still not the version mass viewers have come to know. By that time Murch's sound design with Dolby Stereo was in place, which was an enormous plus, but audiences were still confused with the ending, which had long been Coppola's bugaboo. He decided to have Kurtz instruct Willard to return to the United States after killing him, with Kurtz's tacit permission, in order to tell Kurtz's son "everything ... because there is nothing I detest more than the stench of lies," a metaphor of the whole Vietnam experience, captured in Neal Sheehan's *A Bright Shining Lie: John Paul Vann and America in Vietnam*. The notion that U.S. involvement in Southeast Asia was "a lie" was the accepted understanding by 1979. A Democratic president and Democratic congresses had routinely asserted as much. Ronald Reagan, gearing up for his 1980 presidential campaign, called Vietnam a "noble" undertaking, in that it consisted of the forces of democracy taking on the forces of Communism, the greatest mass murderers in human history. But even Republicans admitted it was everything from a mistake to a conflict fraught with strategic errors to a false premise—easy for them to say since the Democrat Lyndon Johnson had orchestrated the Gulf of Tonkin event in order to give himself an excuse to go in full force.

After Willard kills Kurtz, he leaves the compound. The natives give him leeway; he has killed their "god" and so must be one himself. The PBR is seen slowly drifting away from the compound, back down the river towards civilization ... and sanity? As the credits run, heavy musical effects play and the compound is destroyed, presumably in a napalm attack, ordered either by Chef before he was killed or by Willard once back on the boat. Why the attack after Kurtz is dead? Possibly to wipe out the evidence, or more symbolically to depict the "eradication" of evil that was the whole war aim of the United States, no matter how futile. Evil cannot be eradicated.

But the ending, a 90-degree turn from the original Milius version, was now—*finally*—satisfying. This was what most Americans and others began seeing when *Apocalypse Now* eventually saw its finalized version over the Christmas holidays in 1979. Despite its limited August twelve-week run, this made it a holiday marketing movie, timed for maximum box office plus Oscar consideration. Even with the final ending in place, it still confused many. There were plenty of people who walked out of theatres marveling at much of what they saw, but still scratching their heads. But as it became water-cooler conversation, as reviews explained more of it, as people went back to see it a second time, slowly but surely it began to dawn on people that it was a masterpiece.

The suits were not "thrilled about *Apocalypse*, let's face it, 'cause it cost a fortune," remarked Peter Bogdonavich. "It made its money back, but that wasn't what they wanted."[2]

It was not a box-office blockbuster in its first weekend. It took time, but *Apocalypse Now* built and built and built. It eventually became a roaring success. UA, the investors, everybody profited immensely from it. In the end, Coppola made between $10 million and $15 million for himself. By the time *Hearts of Darkness* was produced in 1991, it grossed more than $150 million, won three Golden Globes, two Academy Awards, and the Palme d'Or. Since then, in 2001, *Apocalypse Now* would be re-released in a redux version with scenes originally cut or restored (namely some Kilgore scenes, sex with the *Playboy* girls, and the French plantation). It would become a staple on television, shown in film schools, at festival retrospectives, and honored as one of the greatest movies of all time.

Coppola had hoped *Apocalypse Now* would vault American Zoetrope over the hump. He saw the coming technical revolution, then underway in what was just coming to be called the Silicon Valley, and had hoped his film would jumpstart it. He bought Hollywood General Studios, where Howard Hughes had filmed *Hell's Angels* (1930) and seemed ready to become a mogul. *The Black Stallion* was a success. He began to plan to make *One From the Heart*, his next movie, for $2 million plus points. He was in the money.

But Coppola's profit would lead him to real disaster. His original plan to separate himself from Hollywood had not worked. He had expanded Hollywood to San Francisco and beyond, into the wine country. The lessons of Vietnam, and of *Apocalypse Now*, were lost in that Coppola emerged victorious, but, ironically, had not learned his lessons. He now viewed himself as impregnable. UA would similarly feel that since they had "dodged a bullet" by seeing huge profits from this film, similar big projects in the future would hold similar results. But all of that was still in the future.

The ending, despite some ambiguities, satisfied the core need of the movie to explain itself, and the war. Many saw the war as pointless, so a semi-pointless conclusion to *Apocalypse* made sense. But the ending did allow Captain Willard to complete his CIA mission and assassinate Kurtz. He had already said, in voiceover, of the mission "when it was over, I'd never want another one," so the immorality of what he had been forced to experience and do was established, an allegory of the whole war. Blowing up the compound was uniquely American, as we like to "blow it up big" and make a spectacular show, an overstatement, of everything we do. We have plenty of napalm so we might as well use it all!

Two-and-a-half years after filming the last scene, *Apocalypse Now* was finally released to mass audiences in the form so many now know it to be. Successfully dragging after so many years an ending out of the muck and mire of the entire process probably was Francis Ford's Coppola's greatest filmmaking accomplishment. It saved his movie, making it not just a success but also a blockbuster, at least over time, and not just a well-reviewed film, but a classic. Many, many people rank it the greatest film in history. Such an opinion is subjective: *Gone With the Wind, Citizen Kane, Spartacus, Lawrence of Arabia, Dr. Strangelove, The Graduate, Patton, The Godfather, Chinatown*; these movies often make the various lists, and to make such a ranking is like saying Willie Mays is better than Babe Ruth, Abraham Lincoln better than George Washington, or America is better than ... every other country.

That said, to state that *Apocalypse Now* is the finest movie ever produced is *not* an absurdity, regardless of whether others agree or disagree. But of all the success this controversial film eventually had, all the accolades that were—over time—finally heaped upon it, none spoke more loudly than the words of its original creator.

"When I saw the movie I said, 'I'm glad that's gone,'" Milius said of the changes Coppola made from his screenplay, in particular his first draft. After thinking it liberal, after punching his fist through a wall when Coppola re-wrote him, the final version satisfied him. "I loved *Apocalypse Now*," he said. "That one movie justified my career. I feel I really did something worthwhile by writing it. Even though I share a credit and I didn't direct it, it's a real piece of me."[3]

* * *

The movie begins with helicopters moving languidly across the screen. We hear their blades reverberate wistfully, which morphs into the beginning of Jim Morrison of The Doors singing "The End." Then, suddenly and violently, lush green trees explode in bright orange napalm fireballs, like a bad acid trip (later we are to believe this is the final ending of the film; the air strike destroying the village). The primordial swamp is the god here. All previous visions of mortality and morality are lost in the jungle.

Morrison sings until he reaches the lines that deal with insanity, and then fades away, singing about the "summer rain." From there, the reverberating blades of the helicopters become choppers flying outside the Saigon hotel room occupied by Martin Sheen's Captain Willard. The blades continue to whirl until morphing into the overhead fan in the muggy room. Close-up on Willard's eyes, his face, eventually revealing him. We hear him lament that he is still only in Saigon. Imprisoned by four walls, various shots—a photo of his wife, described in the Milius script as "a classical American beauty," cigarettes, whiskey, military *accoutrements*—we learn by voiceover of his past failed marriage, in which he states that when he was in the jungle all he could think about was going home, but when he was there all he could think about was getting back into the jungle. After his second tour, Willard continues, it was worse, and he barely spoke to his wife "until I said yes to our divorce." It is established that he has little to live for other than whatever beckons in the jungle. Willard philosophizes and gives some insight into his mind as well as the enemy "Charlie" (the North Vietnamese regular army as well as the Viet Cong). The walls "move in a little closer," making him claustrophobic, needful of the jungle's freedoms. The jungle is where Charlie, who "squats in the bush," gets stronger, while each moment in the room makes Willard weaker.

Next is a powerful scene, again making use of "The End," particularly some live audio of Morrison breaking from the original and studio-produced version of the song, this time rapid-firing the word, "fuck" in rat-tat-tat manner, while Willard drinks (Sheen is extremely drunk for real), admires his hair and physique in the mirror, and begins to karate-chop until his hand breaks the glass, opening a nasty, bleeding gash. Sobbing, broken, spiritually empty, Willard collapses, nude, takes a swig from the bottle, and rubs the blood over his teary face while Morrison's voice rages on.

The music ends and we see two soldiers walking up the hotel's stairs. In voiceover, we hear Willard state, "Everyone gets everything he wants. I wanted a mission, and for my sins, they gave me one. Brought it up to me like room service. It was a real choice mission, and when it was over, I'd never want another one."

This is telling, especially as the film moves on and more is revealed. Unless it is Willard speaking from the grave (an occasional movie trick), we believe he has survived at least the end of the mission, and that here is a gung-ho guy champing at the bit to get into the jungle, yet what he is about to embark on will rob him of his enthusiasm. He will never want to do it again.

But, first, the two soldiers, who are experienced with this kind of scenario, must roust him from his drunken stupor/hangover. They knock on the door, then identify Willard's name, rank and affiliation. Willard sits, haggard, unshaven and naked, in bed until he yells, "Hey, buddy, you gonna shut the door?" Told he is to be escorted to the air field and flown to a headquarters for ComSec intelligence, Willard assumes he is being arrested and asks what the charges are. He is told there are no charges, he is being given orders, the mission he covets, but he is still too hungover and collapses back onto the sheets. One of the soldiers says, "We got a dead one," which they deal with regularly, and they drag Willard into a cold shower, which wakes him up with a jolt.

The helicopters approach Nha Trang, the base camp for military intelligence. The name of the village alone evokes the mission to those in the know: covert, special ops, black ops, CIA. In voiceover, Willard says he is going to a terrible place up a river that "snaked through the war like a main circuit cable," connecting him with Kurtz. The audience now gets their first literary reference to the central character in Joseph Conrad's *Heart of Darkness*. Again, a foreshadowing of Willard's eventual survival is allowed when he states that it was "no accident" that he was being made "caretaker" of Colonel Walter Kurtz's memory, any more than being back in Saigon had been accidental. Then follows a Catholic reference, that if Kurtz's story was really "a confession, then so is mine."

Willard is escorted into the makeshift HQ office of a general played by G. D. Spradlin, the corrupt senator in *The Godfather II*. His aide de camp is played by a young Harrison Ford, who filmed the scene prior to the release of *Star Wars*, when he was still unknown outside of a small role in *American Graffiti*. His appearance onscreen, especially in a small role, was startling to audiences, since by the time *Apocalypse* was released he was a superstar for his role as Han Solo.

The scene with Willard, the general, his aide, and a sweaty civilian (a CIA officer named Jerry) is fraught with nuance, unstated direction, eye contact, and requires tremendous performances, which every actor delivers to perfection. Willard enters with a bandaged hand from his drunken karate chop, and stands at attention, nervous, unsure exactly what is in store. He has been given orders, but he has obviously done things serious enough that he thinks charges might be leveled against him. Is *this* what is about to happen?

Told to stand at ease by the Ford character (identified in the credits as Colonel Lucas), Willard is asked if he has ever seen him or the general (whose last name is Corman in the credits). Not personally, Willard replies. Tension builds when he is asked if he has worked for the CIA. He denies it. Details are given, among them a description of his assassination of a government tax collector in Quang Tri province, on June 19, 1968. This provides some exposition through dialogue: Willard, while an Army captain, is also a CIA contract killer, and the war has reached its epic point, the chaotic period following the Tet Offensive of January 1968. Is he about to be charged?

Willard says he has no knowledge of the events described, nor would he be "disposed" to speak of them if in fact they did exist, "sir." It is complete B.S. He knows it and the others know it, too. It is a charade, a game that has to be played, a standard denial taught at Langley to every "spook."

The general rolls his eyes, then breaks the ice. He notices his injury, which Willard says came from "fishing on R-and-R," which, judging by the general's reaction, sounds bogus; perhaps they have been watching him and know he has not been fishing? But he is ready for action, so this is not an issue.

Next, the general advises that he hopes Willard has "brought a good appetite" as it is lunch time. Either he needs some food to fight his hangover … or he is too hungover to eat much. He is ambivalent about the shrimp being passed around. It looks like something wild and nasty. He is told how he feels about them is not known, but if he eats them he will "never have to prove your courage in any other way." The buildup is already tense enough that the audience senses the comedy in this; he is going on a dangerous assignment somewhere and eating shrimp, no matter where they come from, is no comparison.

The general, drinking a Budweiser with lunch, directs the diners to "pass both ways"—in addition to the shrimp they have roast beef "and usually it's not bad." He is a Southerner, as so many military officers were then and still are. He directs Willard to listen to a tape that has been identified as Colonel Kurtz's voice. Lucas gives Willard a dossier, and in an interesting variance, spills its contents on the floor, revealing some photos of Kurtz while Lucas swears.

The tape is of Colonel Kurtz, but the viewer easily recognizes the voice of Marlon Brando. It is a key moment in which Coppola wants the audience to believe from what Kurtz says, and how he says it, that he is dangerously insane enough to justify the mission on which Willard is about to embark. Kurtz discusses a snail crawling, slithering on the edge of a straight razor "and surviving," a reference to the Viet Cong who live every day with the most horrendous danger, yet have mastered the art of staying alive.

Kurtz also talks in genocidal terms about "incinerating" whole armies, calling them pigs and cows, which he hates. They are "nabobs," a semi-racist term. It is a powerful statement, riveting each man with its words. When it is over, the general explains that he knew Colonel Walter E. Kurtz, who was a "good man," a humanitarian with a good sense of humor, and a great officer.

Some years prior, however, Kurtz joined Special Forces (the Green Berets). This was a veiled slap at John Wayne's *The Green Berets* (1968), which painted them as super heroes. Now, this move is viewed as the catalyst for Kurtz's fall from grace, because after this his "ideas … methods" became "unsound … unsound."

The general and the colonel explain that he has crossed over the Cambodian border, an illegal act in and of itself (later, President Nixon ordered bombing of Communist hideouts in Cambodia). He has set himself up deep in the jungle, up the river, in a native village the colonel describes as a "Montagnard army" who have been seduced by his intelligence and ruthlessness into following all his orders, regardless of reason, and worship the man "like a god."

The general then painfully explains that every man has a "breaking point," including both he and Willard, and that Kurtz has reached his. Good, he says, does not always triumph. Sometimes "the dark side" does, "overtaking what Lincoln described as the better angels of our nature." It is a telling statement about the Vietnam War itself, and how Coppola sees the good intentions of America, which resulted in glory, liberty, and democracy in the Revolutionary War, the Civil War, and two world wars, yet has finally gone awry. The mental image of "Honest Abe" is replaced by an insane Green Beret colonel, improbably voiced by Marlon Brando.

It is further explained to Willard that Kurtz is about to be "officially arrested for murder," which sounds quaint by Vietnam standards. Kurtz has rounded up men he believed to be double-agents and gone on a killing spree, committing acts of atrocity and savagery with his native worshippers doing his bidding. Then the general explains that out in the jungle with these natives, the "old morality" does not apply; it must be a temptation to "be god," that Kurtz is not carrying out American military policy, but rather is engaging in acts beyond "practical military necessity"; he has gone, it is reiterated, insane.

Sheen then does great work, his face reflecting confusion. Killing the enemy, is this not what we are here for, his eyes seem to be asking? But he wants the mission and knows how to play the game in order to get it. He agrees wholeheartedly with the general's assessment, even though he is not convinced Kurtz is mad.

"Obviously insane," he says in kiss-ass manner. The general takes a sip of his drink and looks around the room, not terribly impressed. This scene, viewed many times over the years, reveals through later activity that this conversation is one he has had before, probably more than once, and he has not gotten a satisfactory conclusion out of it; he is not convinced this man Willard will provide one, either. He is resigned to hope for the best.

The colonel, played by Harrison Ford, then gives him the details of his mission. In a straightforward manner, interrupted by pregnant pauses and throat clearing, he tells Willard his mission is to take a Navy PBR upriver, where he will link up with an air cavalry unit that will escort him to a particular spot. He will gather whatever information he can along the way, then, on his own, infiltrate the colonel's team "by whatever means necessary," and "terminate the colonel's command." This is not going to be an arrest for murder.

Willard stares and says, "Terminate ... *the colonel*!?"

Kurtz, says the general, is engaging in activity that is "totally beyond the pale of any acceptable *human* conduct, and he is still out in the field commanding troops."

Jerry, the CIA man, then tells him to terminate with "extreme prejudice." Today this term is well known as the Central Intelligence Agency's code words for assassination, but it was not then. This film introduced the phrase into the lexicon. Jerry offers Willard a cigarette, which he had reluctantly turned down before, and now accepts. It is, to quote from *All About Eve*, "going to be a bumpy night."

Incredible aerial photography and sound accompany a view of the boat navigating the Vietnamese delta waters, with Willard, in voiceover, delivering zingers. "How many men had I already killed?" he asks himself. "There were those six that I knew about for sure, close enough to blow their last breath in my face." But this time it was an American officer, which was not supposed to matter to him, except that it did.

"Charging a man with murder around this place was like handing out speeding tickets at the Indy 500," he philosophizes, then reasons with himself, saying, "I took the mission. What the hell else was I gonna do?" Divorced, claustrophobic in normal society, this was the only life a war junkie like Captain Willard now knows or understands. While Kurtz's voice "really sunk the hook in me," he really does not know what he is going to do when he confronts him.

Willard wakes up in the morning on a Navy PBR, "a kind of plastic patrol boat, a pretty common sight along the rivers." A young black sailor who goes by the name Mr. Clean (Laurence Fishburne) practically stands on top of him. "Mornin' Cap'n," he says.

"The only problem was I wouldn't be alone," Willard's voiceover continues. "The crew were mostly just kids, rock 'n' rollers with one foot in the grave.

"Clean, Mr. Clean, was from south Bronx shit hole and I think the light and the space of Vietnam really put the zap on his head.

"The machinist, the one they called Chef, was from New Orleans. He was wound too tight for Vietnam. Probably wound too tight for New Orleans.

"Lance on the forward '50s was a famous surfer from the beaches south of L.A. To take one look at him, you'd figure he'd never fired a weapon in his life. [The Lance/surfer character was a particular creature of John Milius, who saw Vietnam as a "rock 'n' roll/L.A., California/surf culture" experience.][4]

"Then there was Phillips, the chief. It might have been my mission, but it sure as shit was the chief's boat."

The camera then captures Willard and Chief in a two-shot as the boat ferries through the waters. Phillips provides some important backstory by informing the captain that, some six months prior, he took a man who was "regular Army too" far up river, but later "heard he shot himself in the head."

The crew members are just grunts, an average cross-section of American boys who could not afford college and have been caught up in a savage conflict (two blacks, two whites; from New York, California, Louisiana; Phillips has some kind of accent and could be from a protectorate). If they thought that joining the Navy, as opposed to being drafted by the Army, or signing up with the Marines, would spare them, they are sadly mistaken. They have not been assigned cushy duty aboard an aircraft carrier, but rather a plastic boat moving perilously through dangerous waters. We learn that Chef is a saucier from New Orleans, who was "raised to be a saucier," a cook who thought the Navy had better food but quickly learned it was not a place to get trained in the culinary arts. Lance goes water-skiing behind the boat to the tunes of The Rolling Stones' "Satisfaction," a rock sound emanating from the Armed Forces Radio Network, pumping rhythm and rock to the boys "in country." (Fishburne, who was only fifteen at the time, claimed to be seventeen; Coppola wanted a mere boy to represent the tragedy of the black underclass caught up in the conflict.) Chief Phillips is authoritative; his men look to him to lead them in a pinch, and there is tension immediately. Will he someday have to make a decision that spares them from being collateral damage to Captain Willard's mission?

The boat moves through a wide delta until they hear an enormous explosion. It is an Arc Light strike, delivered courtesy of U.S. air power, upon a small peninsula. Willard orders the chief to approach, and discovers it is "the AirCav, First of the Ninth, our escort into the mouth of the Nung River."

There, in the completed 1979 version, the boat lands and the crew warily proceeds onto the beach amid a scene of great carnage and confusion. First, they are stunned to see a camera crew filming them. They stop and stare. The director is played by none other than the bearded Coppola himself, who insists that they not "look at the camera … like you're fighting … like you're fighting." (This is a telling picture of America's first televised war, shown nightly on the news via Walter Cronkite and the other networks. They are not really "fighting," but the camera wants to capture them doing so, whether the action is true or not.)

In voiceover, Willard can barely contain his sense of rivalry with the air cavalry. He is an Airborne Ranger; the two branches of the Army jealously compete with each other for prestige, each elite fighting units. Willard tells the viewer this is an "old cavalry unit," one that has "turned in its choppers" for helicopters and "gone tear-assin' around 'Nam, lookin' for the shit." They had "given Charlie a few surprises," but this action is now a mop-up operation; the attack took place a few hours earlier. A chaplain leads soldiers in the Lord's Prayer. A cow is airlifted by a helicopter (for steaks later on?). Villagers, scared out of their wits, run around, unsure of what is happening to them, many herded onto boats to be ferried to some place, presumably out of harm's way. A loudspeaker and an interpreter inform them that the United States is here to help them. It is very allegorical; the place is in disarray, yet this is "help."

Captain Willard, the crew warily crouched behind him, approaches some soldiers and asks where he can find the commanding officer. He is told the location of the CO, that he "can't miss him." There we see Colonel Bill Kilgore, played by Robert Duvall. He is a helicopter attack commander in sunglasses, straight up-and-down, an authoritative presence with a powerful voice, charismatic to the point of god-like status.

Willard approaches him and tells him he has orders from Nha Trang and that Kilgore should have already heard about the "requirements of my mission." Kilgore, however, dismisses him, saying he has not heard about this, then tells Willard to wait until he is done. Then he begins to place cards on the bodies of the dead, presumably VC. A close-up reveals the cards to have the insignia of Kilgore's unit with a death's head symbol, and Willard explains they are "death cards," meant to let "Charlie know who did this." It is pure psychological operations, aimed at infuriating and terrorizing the enemy into submission before this awesome display of American ordnance, "death from above." Kilgore gleefully tosses the cards upon the bodies, clearly happy with himself. He dispenses confidence and bravado, a martinet walking in pince-steps, his entourage trailing him, a figure in total control of the situation. He tells one despondent G.I. to "cheer up, son." A female photojournalist warily snaps images, practically an act of blasphemy as the Bible tells us nobody is actually supposed to know what God Himself looks like. Kilgore helps a woman with a baby onto a boat.

(Duvall himself later told interviewer Bob Costas he was irritated that the essence of the scene—Kilgore's humanitarianism towards the refugee and infant—was cut out, although it was restored in the 2001 redux version. Duvall truly identified with Kilgore. He was and is a conservative who respects the military ethos and insists Kilgore was not crazy or even bloodthirsty, but that war makes men play "strange games" to pass the time, to prove themselves. This was a heavy theme of John Milius, reflected in his life and work over the years. To Milius, almost all of life was a Homeric journey testing one's manhood.)

Kilgore comes upon an American and a South Vietnamese regular hovering over the badly injured body of a man begging for water. "What's this?" Kilgore demands. The soldier tells him the man is hurt badly and the only thing holding his guts—his entrails—into his body is a "pot lid." Kilgore asks the South Vietnamese soldier to explain the situation, and is told the man is a "dirty VC" who deserves only "paddy water." Kilgore is infuriated, pushes the South Vietnamese soldier away, threatens to kick his ass, bends over and gives water to the dying VC, claiming any man "brave enough to fight in this war can drink out of my canteen any day."

(This is one of the most telling exchanges of the film. It demonstrates the personal nature of the war to the Vietnamese, who hate the Viet Cong and wish to exact revenge against them, but the Americans, symbolized by Kilgore, are above the fray. It is almost a game to them, warfare for warriors like Kilgore, who respect the bravery and tenacity of the enemy because he has not been much affected by them. He dispenses American power on them and has not felt their sting in return. Kilgore is arrogance personified; the U.S. will win this war because we are the U.S., the nation of George S. Patton and Douglas MacArthur. We are favored by God, who has given men like Kilgore superhuman powers to exact His will upon Godless Communism, who get Christian charity from those who have power over them. Once killed or rendered a non-threat, the VC are shown benevolence, as the Japanese and Germans were.)

Then one of Kilgore's guys tells him that one of the sailors with Willard is "Lance Johnson, the surfer." Kilgore now couldn't care less about the dying man, his water carelessly splatters, not given to the dying VC. He sees Lance and Mr. Clean approaching and asks Lance his name. Lance tells him he is a sailor named Johnson, and Clean begins to do the same, but Kilgore waves him away.

"Are you Lance Johnson, the surfer?" he asks him. He says he is. Kilgore then breaks into a huge smile, shakes his hand, and tells him he is honored to meet him. His name is Bill, he need not be addressed as sir, and he is a "goofy foot," a surf expression. He thinks Lance has the "best cutback in the business." His men do a lot of surfing, and like to finish up their operations early in order to catch waves. Kilgore introduces Lance to Mike and Johnny, two handsome California beach-boy types he says are from San Diego and Malibu, respectively. They are both good surfers, but "not in your class," to which Mike and Johnny admiringly admit, "No way, man."

"Is this guy with you?" Kilgore asks Lance of Willard, curiously watching this strange exchange, but Willard realizes he can use it to his advantage somehow. Rank means nothing to Kilgore. Mike and Johnny are enlisted men, as is Lance; Willard is an Airborne captain, but the surfers get his respect.

(The above scene is pure John Milius [see page 16 of his screenplay], the surf guru who is infusing the story with California culture, and was an enormous hook in the film's appeal beyond pure war action or literary shadowing. It says much about America; the powerhouse that can win wars while its citizens play football and baseball and make movies and maintain the economy back home during World War II, and can still win wars now while surfing and jiving like they are hanging out on the beach outside Margot Kidder's party pad in Malibu, California. Much of it is fantasy and propaganda, but it is part of the American myth.)

Next we see the men in repose. It is nighttime, and huge chunks of steak—the cow from the village?—are being barbequed. The soldiers drink beer, bare-toed in the sand. Kilgore makes fun of Willard's Airborne status, eliciting laughter. Willard, in voiceover, informs us that they choppered in the T-bones and the beer, making the "LZ into a beach party. The more they tried to make it just like home, the more they made everybody miss it." Kilgore, Willard surmises, is not a "bad officer, I guess." His men loved and trusted him; they "felt safe with him." Coppola sheds a Godly light on Kilgore while Willard explains he had a "weird light on him," and somehow it was obvious that he would not be injured in any way in this crazy war.

Willard laughs about Willard's mission, asking if Nha Trang "forgot all about you?" His swagger and confidence is palpable, Duvall's greatest work. His is the laughter of the victor, the conqueror. But Willard has an ace up his sleeve: Lance the surfer. Kilgore will want to impress Lance in some way. Willard approaches Kilgore and points to an area on the map where he thinks Kilgore's unit can escort his boat into the mouth of the Nung River.

Willard tells him the village at which he is pointing is "hairy," that he has lost a few re-con ships there every now and then. He asks Mike, the California surf boy, about the point at "Vin Drin Dop or Lop? Damn gook names all sound the same." This symbolizes the racism and contempt for the Vietnamese, the "gooks" whose villages, which have stood for a thousand years, are just strange-sounding places to American soldiers.

Mike does not say anything about the ordnance the enemy has there, or the military importance of the point, only that it has some unusual surfing characteristics, such as a "six-foot swell," that the waves break away from each other, a "bull section" that Mike says is "just tube city." Kilgore, taken aback, is affronted that nobody has told him about any "six-foot swell" before, that Vietnam offers only "goddamned beach break." Mike then says Charlie holds the point; this is where "we lost McDonald."

Willard sees his opening and says they can go in at dawn in order to take advantage of the off-shore breeze he knows might increase the waves. Chief Phillips is cautious, saying the mouth of the river's opening might not be deep enough to get the boat in, but Kilgore is fired up, grabbing his crotch as if the whole idea of surfing the point excites him sexually. With full swagger he says he can drop the "young captain's" boat anywhere he likes and hold it is as long as he pleases, making it possible to go anywhere upriver that Willard wishes. The plan is set in motion.

Kilgore instructs an underling to get his "Yater Spoon—the eight-six," his personal surf board, and to have Lance pick out his board. Excitement ripples through the campsite, but a major objects that the point is too "hairy" for R-and-R.

"What do you know about surfing, Major, you're from goddamn New Jersey," Kilgore tells him. He replies that the point belongs to Charlie.

"*Charlie don't surf!*" Kilgore replies, a line reverberating throughout movie history. It says it all.

The next morning a bugler gives an old-fashioned cavalry charge reminiscent of General Custer on the march, and amid spectacular scenery, imagery, and musical accompaniment, the helicopters take to the skies and proceed toward "Charlie's point." (It all seems beautifully choreographed and organized; there is absolutely no evidence of the chaos Coppola went through to get these scenes shot, the aircraft that had to be diverted by the Marcos government to fight insurgents, or any other factor.)

Inside his helicopter, Colonel Kilgore discusses inside-surfing techniques with Lance, until word comes down that the target has been spotted. Kilgore tells Lance "about a mile out we'll turn on the music." Lance inquires skeptically, and Kilgore says he likes Wagner—German composer Richard Wagner—because "my boys love it, and it scares the shit out of the slopes." ("Slopes" is another racist slang for the Vietnamese. The choice of Wagner's "Ride of the Valkyries" is quite telling. Wagner was said to be anti–Semitic, his music an unofficial anthem of Nazi Germany favored by Adolf Hitler, and this particular piece considered an affront to Jews. Perhaps Coppola wanted to convey the idea that Kilgore's militarism was just an American version of the Nazis, although Wagner was undoubtedly the brainchild of the Jewish John Milius.)

Lance excitedly informs everybody that music is about to be played. Kilgore's men are battle-hardened, confident but cautious. The Navy men assigned to Willard are scared but impressed by Kilgore's bravado. "Ride of the Valkyries" begins on loudspeakers, and the quiet village is shown hearing its ominous approach. A group of children wearing Catholic school-style clothes are gathered up and herded away. (Coppola was perfectly happy showing the Americans dropping fire on children, oddly a "fantasy" John Milius actually said he harbored. It would seem unlikely the kids were Catholic; the Communists were atheists after all, but perhaps the clothes were a remnant of French colonialism.)

With German opera music pounding—Dolby Surround Sound enhancing the experience in theatres—the choppers come in hot, in attack formation, and fire a series of deadly rocket strikes with pinpoint accuracy, blowing fleeing Viet Cong and NVA regulars to bits, knocking out weapons, and eliciting an incredible, emotional surge of bloodlust and even patriotism in much of the audience who witnessed it in theatres. (For this one scene, Milius achieved his goal of demonstrating just how the U.S. could have won this war. It is total jingoism and the audience feels the brief fantasy, which they almost are allowed to believe, that America is not only re-fighting but this time *winning* the Vietnam War. This scene would spur a slew of 1980s war-action flicks based on this very theme. Coppola himself would say that this scene seduced audiences into "loving" war; a perfect setup for the letdown the film would eventually give them, for it cannot be maintained indefinitely.)

The glory of war is quickly turned into confusion. Kilgore, code-named Big Duke Six, admires the efficiency of the attack, radioing one pilot he has performed "outstanding" work and will earn his men a case of beer. He gives Lance a play-by-play, then points out some waves breaking both ways.

One of the choppers lands in the main square. A black soldier—audiences thought it Mr. Clean at first—screams in agony while medics attend to him. Kilgore radios he wants his men in a hospital in fifteen minutes. It sounds antiseptic, and exceptionally American. His men matter; everybody else is war dead.

A flare lands in the chopper and there is panic, but Kilgore calmly assures all it is just a flare, asking especially if his prize surfer, Lance, is okay. Kilgore calls the VC "fucking savages." When a heavy weapon is spotted, he says, "Don't these people ever give up?" It symbolizes North Vietnamese resistance, but Kilgore does not understand it. Why would they not want to be on the winning side? He radios that he is going to take care of the weapon himself, aims, fires, and perfectly destroys a vehicle carrying a large-caliber weapon.

"Nice shot, Bill," Lance says.

But a Vietnamese woman hurls a grenade into the helicopter in the square and everybody dies in a fiery explosion. Kilgore swoops in and identifies the "dink bitch," using a machine gun to tear her to shreds.

The choppers then land on the beach. The camera closes on a fresh-faced young soldier. As audiences might have thought the injured black soldier was Mr. Clean, many might have been mistaken that this was Lance. It is not.

"I'm not going," the soldier repeatedly yells, until somebody grabs him and throws him into the breach.

Kilgore's chopper lands. The LZ is still hot. Incoming fire explodes around them. Kilgore struts about with more swagger than ever, oblivious to explosions around him while everybody takes cover. He tells Mike and Johnny to surf the break. Warily, they suggest it is still too hairy, but Kilgore gives them the option to either "surf or fight," so they change into shorts and go ride the waves, which are disappointingly low. He urges Lance to get out there, too. Lance says they should wait for the tide to come in. Kilgore stands like the Colossus of Rhodes, the camera looking up at him, and announces that the tide will not be in for another six hours.

"Do you wanna wait here for six hours?" he states in his most baritone voice.

Willard admonishes him that it is still too hairy for R-and-R. Frustrated, Kilgore rips off his shirt. He is muscled and bare-chested, wearing an old-fashioned cavalry officer's cowboy-style hat, a colorful scarf gallantly hung around his neck. He looks like a total stud and announces to Willard and all within earshot that if he says it is safe to surf this beach, by God, it is safe to surf it. He says he is not afraid to surf it. Then he gets on the horn and screams at the pilots, waiting on standby, that he wants the tree-line where the line of fire is incoming to be "butt-holed" with napalm.

Fighter jets swoop toward the point. Voices come over the radio directing Kilgore to move his ships back, "It's gonna be a big one." Kilgore tells Lance he will have this beach cleaned up "in a jiffy." The planes descend and suddenly the jungle is literally turned into fire. It is a monumental display of air power.

Finally, Kilgore stares at the blast and asks, to Lance as much as anyone, if he smells that, and does he know what it is?

"That's napalm, son," he explains. "Nothing else in the world smells like that." He relates that once after a napalm drop he "walked up" and examined the remains, and could not find so much as "one stinkin' dink body," but that the whole hill had been obliterated.

With everybody staring at him, in awe, in horror, in amazement, he announces, "I love the smell of napalm in the morning. It smells like … *victory!*"

After a pause he sadly admits, "Some day this war's gonna end." (This guy is the ultimate war lover and he does *not* want the war to end. He is addicted to it. While Kilgore is a product of John Milius, he is also a Coppola creation. If Coppola wanted to portray George S. Patton as a crazed war lover, and that portrait was tempered by George C. Scott's charismatic portrayal of him, he has succeeded in fully developing this syndrome in the form of Colonel Bill Kilgore. It should be said that Duvall did not share Coppola's politics and identified with Kilgore as necessary in war; a year later he practically copied what Kilgore would be like absent war in his magnificent performance as *The Great Santini*.)

Drumbeats emphasize the change in tone as the patrol boat finally departs, leaving Kilgore. In voiceover, Willard now changes his mind about the colonel, who he first said was "not a bad officer, I guess," because his boys "loved" him and "felt safe with him." Now he states that if they let guys like Kilgore fight the war, what did they have against Colonel Kurtz? How much crazier or immoral did he have to get, beyond dropping napalm on a few snipers just to catch some waves?

"Some day this war's gonna end?" Willard repeats Kilgore's line. That would be just fine with the crew. (This is a reflection of a conversation in *Patton* between Scott's Patton and Karl Malden's Omar Bradley, in which Bradley tells the general the soldiers do not share his dreams of glory, they are stuck day by day with death dogging them, and that there is one big difference between the two of them. Bradley says he does this work because he is trained for it, but Patton *loves* it! But the crew on Chief Phillip's little plastic patrol boat, like the G.I.'s of World War II, are just looking for a way home. This juxtaposes not merely with Kilgore, who it could be presumed uses scared soldiers as props for his own Valhallic vision, but of Kurtz, who has been equally seduced by war—its power, its gore, and even its beauty—until he becomes mad. Some of Milius's screenplay, which did not make it into the 1979 cut but was restored in the redux version, allows Willard to partially explain this dynamic. Willard tells the crew the excitement and adventure of Vietnam is better than working in a factory back in Ohio. This is telling. Officers may be college-educated, but that does not mean they hold high positions in society. Their status as officers gives them a far greater status in the military than most people ever achieve in civilian life. Willard sees himself in a factory. What would Kilgore be? A chopper pilot for the movies? In *The Great Santini* Duvall is a frustrated fighter jock adjusting to family life, and not doing very well at it. But the surreal visual beauty of *Apocalypse Now*, which throughout the Kilgore sequences is nothing less than sensory overload, is far from over. At this point audiences were enamored of it and thought they might be seeing the greatest movie ever made. Even anti-war activists were mollified, that the gory attack on a poor agrarian hamlet, cheered by the patriots, was then brought down a notch when Kilgore's surf safari does not go off without a hitch.)

The little boat continues on. Willard keeps reading the dossier on Kurtz. He cannot figure this guy out. His voice on the tape back at Nha Trang sounded like a guy who *might* be insane, but that is by no means set in stone. He might very well just be a political liability the CIA, in its wisdom, deems expendable. There might be something well beyond Willard's understanding or even pay grade.

But a man like Walt Kurtz? He is the *scion* of several generations of West Pointers. The camera glimpses his résumé, which includes a graduate degree from Harvard. The photo is one of a younger, handsome, noble Brando. He was being "groomed for one of the top slots in the corporation. General, chief of staff, anything." He had "about a thousand decorations." He did an early tour of Vietnam and was asked to write a report for President Lyndon Johnson and the Joint Chiefs of Staff. This reflects Daniel Ellsberg's "Pentagon papers." Had Kurtz wished to be politically viable, to protect his own career and ensure advancement, he would have written what Johnson and the generals in Washington wanted to hear; a confident prediction of ultimate victory.

It is inferred he did not, since the report was classified. "It seems they didn't dig what he had to tell them," says Willard. Like the "Pentagon papers," Kurtz's report was leaked to the press. They lauded him and he was promoted.

"Ah, the bullshit piled up so high in Vietnam you need wings to stay above it," Willard says.

Then Kurtz applied for the Airborne, which was crazy. It assured his limited rise in the military. He was thirty-eight years old, "humping" his way through one of the toughest courses in the military, one Willard took when he was only nineteen, "and it damn near wasted me." Kurtz's superiors tried to talk him out of it but when he threatened to resign his commission, he was allowed to do it, and made it through training.

Now a Green Beret colonel, he was re-assigned to another tour in Vietnam, but this time on the front lines. From there he fought the war *his* way: aggressively, using terror as a tool, beating the VC at their own game. He wrote his wife and son suggesting a dark conspiracy of sorts, justifying his methods.

As Willard learns more about Kurtz, the boat arrives at an outpost along the river. It is nighttime, the music portends strange jungle rhythms, odd drug-laced lighting shines, and Clean, still "zapped out" by Vietnam, exclaims, "Sure is a bizarre sight in da middle a dis shit."

The boat pulls up amid ominous surroundings until the scene reveals they are safe; it is an American military camp. The crew get off the boat and walk around. Hot motorcycles are parked for no apparent reason. It is typical American excess. Clean is instructed to get some fuel from the supply depot. Chef asks the supply sergeant if he can get some "Panama red," which is strong marijuana. Sure, he is told, it can be had … for a price, no doubt. Willard tries to talk sense to the supply man, telling him his mission is classified and he only wants some fuel, but when the sergeant shouts out a heavy black-market price for Camel cigarettes, Willard loses his temper, grabs him and pulls him one-handed over the counter before recovering his cool, telling him he just wants fuel.

The supply sergeant, cowed by Willard, offers him a bottle of booze "on the house" and front-row seats to see the bunnies. They have happened upon a USO show featuring *Playboy* Playmates. (Jo Collins, a 1964 Playmate who later married baseball player Bo Belinsky, was one of the most popular Playmates ever, and appeared at a 1965 show. Raquel Welch would appear with Bob Hope, dressed in a delectable mini-skirt and go-go boots. According to *The Making of a Hero: The Story of William Calley, Jr.* (1971) by Wayne Greenhaw, the military even brought in pseudo-prostitutes, disguised as "nurses," hospital staff, or just civilian support staff, to provide sexual release for the men.)

The show begins, with Willard and his crew given excellent seats, with a helicopter complete with bunny insignia landing on the stage. A band plays thumping, grinding music. A USO host, played by rock impresario Bill Graham, comes out and warms up the crowd. Then three exquisite *Playboy* chicks, dressed for sex, depart the helicopter amid wild applause, and Creedence Clearwater Revival's version of "Suzie Q." The third is the actual Playmate of the Year 1974, Cindy Wood.

The girls are suggestive and flirtatious. Graham's character, who has seen what can happen when sex-deprived men see beautiful women, watches nervously. One of the girls lustily depicts intercourse with an M-16 rifle. Lance calls one of the girls "you bitch," while Chef pleads for another, his favorite Playmate, to let him be with her. It all gets out of control, and eventually soldiers cross the moat between the stands and the stage and begin pawing the girls. Graham's character ushers the girls back into the helicopter and they begin to depart, with soldiers hanging on for dear life until they fall into the water. The whole show is a disaster.

(The bunny show was largely part of John Milius's sexual fantasy, which, if explored to its fullest extent, most probably involved hot *Playboy* girls satisfying the entire group of ravenous men. Milius was a particular fan of the Greek and Roman empires, which were notorious for orgies and the pillaging of conquered villages, in which victorious soldiers considered the wholesale rape of local girls to be their right. But in the Coppola-directed version, the girls all escape on the helicopter and all that is left on the stage was a giant "clusterfuck," to use popular Army slang. According to film historians, the riotous events of the *Playboy* debacle were supposed to be reminiscent of the disastrous Rolling Stones concert at Altamont, near San Francisco, in 1969 [filmed for a documentary by George Lucas]. The Hells Angels—of all people—provided "security," and ended up stabbing a black man to death amid much drug-taking and rowdiness. The show had to be canceled before it ended. It was considered the end of the peaceful '60s, and the *Playboy* show symbolized the last look at civilization before the crew moves upriver into truly dangerous waters.)

Apparently, Chef *did* score some "Panama red," and Lance, at some point, got hold of some LSD. The crew begins to get high and surly, less respectful of Willard and his mission. Murch and Tavoularis combined to create some darker images. Chef, high on drugs, begins to fantasize about Raquel Welch. His proximity to his favorite Playmate has aroused in him deep sexual frustration. He begins to describe how he would like to turn mangoes into a cream pudding that he and Raquel could spread all over themselves. Then he declares he wants to go and find some mangoes.

Willard, sensing that he is losing the respect of the crew, decides to go with Chef into the jungle to look for mangoes, an act of conciliation. At first, Chef is surly and reticent in conversation with Captain Willard, until Willard asks him why he is called Chef; is it "because you like mangoes and stuff?"

Chef then pipes up and tells him, "No sir, I'm a real chef," in fact a saucier from New Orleans, trained to make French sauces. When he got drafted he decided to join the Navy because he heard they had better food; this was dashed when he encountered cook school, where he observed a long row of beautifully marbled prime rib placed in cauldrons and boiled, ruining the flavor. After that he applied to radioman's school, which is why he is now on the boat running the radio for Chief Phillips.

In the middle of this, Willard hears a sound and the two grow deathly silent, afraid Charlie might be hiding behind a tree. The tension is unbearably thick when a tiger springs out and jumps past them. Willard and Chef race back to the boat. There are wild shouts and shooting. They board the boat and depart while the crew fires wildly into the jungle, until Chef, who was "wrapped too tight for Vietnam … probably wrapped too tight for New Orleans," has a fit and blurts out that they came across a tiger. The shooting stops, and Chef mumbles over and over, "Never get off the boat."

It is literary reference to Conrad's novel: the boat is the last tie to civilization, to depart it is to become one with the jungle in all its beauty and blind terrors. "Never get off the boat," Willard repeats in voiceover. "Absolutely goddamned right." Not unless you're prepared to go "all the way." Kurtz, he adds, got off the boat. "He split with the whole fuckin' program."

(This event very effectively switches the film's mood. Up until then it was almost a traditional war picture, albeit with quirkier characters than those played by Audie Murphy or Duke Wayne. The attack on the village was an old-fashioned American ass-whippin'. The *Playboy* girls reminded the boys, as pin-up girls had in the past, why they fight; what waits for them back home. But now the movie becomes dark, eerie, which is emphasized by its reflective, haunting music. The forthcoming confrontation with Kurtz has been in the background; now, it is an irresistible challenge for Willard that the audience desperately wants to see, no matter what happens. This is master filmmaking, first in the setup Milius creates in the original screenplay, but, truly, in Coppola's art. It is the most intriguing drama, whether it is Quint and his crew meeting the shark, or Luke Skywalker confronting Darth Vader; it is the buildup leading to a major battle of rivals. It is why bowl games, playoff games, the World Series, excite a nation. It is George S. Patton vs. Erwin Rommel. But Coppola and Murch did not have this when they first arrived from the Philippines to San Francisco more than two years earlier with miles of raw footage. There was no way to be sure all that photography would yield such a coherent, compelling journey leading the crew, and the audience, inch by perilous inch, up a river that "snaked through the war like a main circuit cable ..." until Captain Willard finally was face-to-face with Colonel Kurtz.)

As the boat moves up the dangerous river, there are visual metaphors, such as a huge phallic symbol in the form of a crashed jet, its back wings sticking to the sky. A burned-out helicopter is perched awkwardly in a tree, like a giant insect. The enemy is never seen. Lance begins to lose his mind after taking acid. Willard concentrates on the dossier.

(It was inevitable, certainly considering Coppola's politics, that the film would have a "My Lai massacre" scene. Lieutenant James Calley had come across villagers he believed to be VC, or NVA collaborators, running supplies to the enemy. Hoping to send a message to the Communists, he ordered men, women and children rounded up. Events quickly spun out of control, and the soldiers opened fire, killing most of the unarmed people.)

The boat comes across a sampan. Chief Phillips draws nearer for a closer look. Captain Willard argues that routine procedures be thrown out, that his mission's requirement had priority and Phillips would not even be in this part of the river if not for him. Phillips shoots back (Willard: "It might have been my mission, but it sure as shit was the Chief's boat") that these sampans run supplies to the enemy and, until they get there, Willard is "just along for the ride."

He then orders Chef to board and inspect it. Chef, however, wants nothing to do with this: It just *smells* wrong. Arguing with the Chief, Chef finally jumps onto the sampan, haphazardly ransacking baskets filled with fruit and foodstuffs, but Phillips is on him to keep looking, including inside a rusty can. A woman on board lunges, and Mr. Clean opens fire with his machine gun. Lance and Chef then fire like maniacs, tearing up everybody on the boat. Chef, distraught and crying, gives in to the worst, most sinful side of his nature, babbling they should just kill 'em all: "Why not?"

Clean is still zapped by Vietnam, and when asked of his status, puts his machine gun on safety and dazedly says, "I'm good." Then Chef sees that the woman was lunging to grab not weapons but a little puppy. Lance grabs the dog from Chef.

Then Chef sees the woman is still barely alive. Phillips insists they take her to a hospital, which would totally disrupt Willard's mission. Willard is an assassin; this is known about him, but heretofore the audience has not seen this side of him. They have mostly seen Martin Sheen, a fairly well known, pleasant-looking actor, playing a role. But Sheen transforms from passive observer into Willard, the cold-blooded killer, pointing his gun at the woman and blowing her brains out as easily as he might eat a banana.

He tells Phillips he told him not to stop; now get him up the river. Everybody is shocked and they leave the scene of carnage. In voiceover, Willard philosophizes over the war. "It was a way we had of living with ourselves," he says. "We tear 'em to pieces, then offer them a Band-Aid. It was a lie." The more he sees of lies—the whole Vietnam *leitmotif*—the more he hates them, and in this regard, as we find out eventually, he becomes more like Kurtz, who has had his own Vietnam conversion, has seen his own horrors. The crew, Willard reasons, will never look at him the same way again.

(The film is now totally dark and gets even darker until they arrive at the Do Lung Bridge. Coppola wanted the audience to feel like they were on an acid trip when viewing these extraordinary sequences, which took so long to shoot and took so much film to accomplish that nobody had any idea what it would look like after post-production.)

It is a night scene, with strange hanging lights swaying above a bridge, the last outpost on the Nung River before Kurtz. Bombs explode, people shout, soldiers with suitcases are in the water begging for a place on the boat to take them home; it is complete chaos. A young officer asks if Captain Willard is on board. He gives him some communications from Nha Trang, and has mail for the occupants of the boat. He tells Willard he is happy, he can now leave this horrible place … "If I can find a way. You're in the asshole of the world, Captain."

Willard goes looking for fuel and the CO, Phillips, tells somebody to go with him. Wacked out on LSD, Lance eagerly follows the captain like a puppy dog. Willard inquires as to the whereabouts of the CO and is told, "Beverly Hills … where the hell else is he supposed to be?" (Again, Milius and his theme of "California war.") Lance steps on a soldier's face, who complains. "I thought you were dead," Lance tells him.

"You thought wrong, dammit."

Then they come across a black G.I. firing wildly at some "gooks beyond the wire." Asked where the CO is, the soldiers replies, "Ain't you?" Then a wired black soldier called Roach is called upon. He is the picture of the wild-eyed, jungle-soldier in the opening scenes of Milius's screenplay, complete with body paint, half flower child, half killer, trinkets hanging from his person that could be fingers or other assorted body parts. He turns off a wild Jimi Hendrix guitar solo and senses that Charlie is "close. He's *real close*." He loads up a LAWS rocket, aims it into the night, his sense of distance his only guide, and blows a sniper off the wire.

Victory at last … for about five seconds. Willard asks him if he knows who is in charge.

"Yeah," he says. That is all he says. Apparently, *he* is in charge. Then there is return fire, the bridge is hit, and they are back at it, war without end or reason. Willard leads Lance, who is so stoned he does not duck despite the danger, back to the boat. He has some fuel but there is no CO here. He orders Phillips upriver. Phillips has seen enough and says every day the Army rebuilds the bridge, every night the enemy blows it back up, and it is rebuilt just to please the generals. "Who cares?" he says.

"Just get us upriver," Willard admonishes him.

Tediously, grudgingly, they keep moving. (Coppola wanted an intermission around the Do Lung Bridge sequence. From here it will be all about the approach to Kurtz and Willard's confrontation with him.)

The crew gets mail, which is like oxygen for them. Lance reads a letter from a pal back in Orange County, asking if Vietnam is like Disneyland. Lance agrees that it is. Chef gets a letter, apparently from a love interest back home, that pictures him sitting at home drinking a beer, watching TV. Instead, he is thousands of miles away "trying to have a relationship with my ass," meaning to stay alive and connected to it.

Sheen receives more communication from ComSec Intelligence. A soldier sent on an identical mission to his, many months earlier, has now been identified as being alive and with Kurtz. His name is Richard Colby. This is the "regular Army" soldier Phillips ferried upriver and later "heard he shot himself in the head."

Willard learns more about Kurtz and the actions he took and tries to justify them, as much for his son's sake as any other reason. War requires ruthless as well as tender action, Kurtz has written. Sometimes those actions are intertwined, confused with one another. Kurtz claims a certain moral clarity, apparently gleaned only out of the pure crucible of war absent politics or even feelings. He acted swiftly, like a soldier.

Willard begins to admire something in Kurtz: his naked honesty. His desire to confront him transforms Willard, who is girding himself for the event like a boxer heading into a championship match. Willard finally tells the skeptical Phillips he is close to his destination; just get him close and "I'll cut you and the crew loose."

"Alright, Cap'n," Phillips says.

Clean has received a package, his mother's voice on an audio tape back in the Bronx. She speaks of mundane family matters, urging that he get home in one piece. Then Clean is shot, instantly killed. Tracer bullets fill the air. The boat careens madly. But the gunfire has been replaced by the firing of sticks, straight out of a scene in *Heart of Darkness*. The crew is hysterical, firing wildly at an unseen enemy.

Phillips screams at Willard that he does not know where he is going and now he cannot get the crew out of there, a picture of the incremental mission-creep of Vietnam. Finally Phillips grabs a weapon, and, just as suddenly, he is speared.

"A spear," he whispers. He collapses, but grabs Willard in a death grip, trying to pull him onto the tip end of the spear, to bring him down with him. Willard must suffocate Phillips just to save himself.

The boat escapes further conflict and floats down a hostile river filled with mangled bodies. A traumatized Lance, stoned on acid, covers his face in "war paint." The dog has been lost. Phillips and Clean are "buried" in the waters. Finally, Captain Willard tells Chef he has been sent on a classified mission to kill a Green Beret colonel who has gone insane.

Chef is disgusted. "Vietnam mission," he blurts out. He thought Willard was going to "blow up some railroad tracks or something," although there are no railroad tracks near this part of the jungle. Willard is ready to depart the boat, making his way by foot to the Kurtz compound he knows is very close, but Chef insists they go together, although on the boat.

Amid thick fog and sounds emanating from the shores—much of the imagery derived from the Conrad novel—the boat moves slowly towards the end of the river. Slowly, but surely, the compound comes into focus: it is an ancient shrine, surrounded by Montagnard soldiers, natives coated by a white substance, possibly war paint of some kind. They have spears and are capable of doing damage to the boat, but they part as the craft moves cautiously through them. Then, suddenly, a voice calls out from shore.

"It's all been approved," a man shouts. He is a whacked-out photo-journalist played by Dennis Hopper, (the Russian in *Heart of Darkness*). Chef says he does not want to come in, the "bastards attacked us." Hopper says not to worry; "Stop 'em with you're siren, man."

Chef employs the boat's siren and the natives scramble like cockroaches. They land and the photo-journalist comes onto the boat, ebulliently shouting that they are Americans, and so is he. He gets a cigarette, which he has been craving, and tells Willard these "are all his people, as far as the eye can see."

The photo-journalist expresses some concern with Willard's intentions, but Willard tells him he only wishes to speak to Colonel Kurtz. They begin to walk and the crew members all notice grotesque, severed heads all over the place, some on sticks. The place smells of death and evil. Chef is freaked out.

The photo-journalist becomes defensive about the heads, and begins to justify Colonel Kurtz, whom he calls a great man who sometimes "goes too far; he's the first to admit it." When Chef calls him evil, the photo-journalist replies, "*Wrong*," desperately trying to convince the crew of Kurtz's "greatness." The photo-journalist tries to give an example of Kurtz's wisdom, saying Kurtz said if he took his photo again he would kill him, "And he meant it." But Kurtz can "get friendly," so Willard should just "dig it."

Willard sees Colby, a non-speaking role played by a bearded, unrecognizable Scott Glenn, with native women draped around him, holding a weapon at the ready. Willard identifies him by name but does not proceed further. Finally, the photo-journalist tells them Kurtz has "gone away" to be "with his people," whom he feels "comfortable with."

Finally, with extreme caution, Willard directs Chef—and the dazed Lance—back to the boat. There, Chef tells him he now sees why Willard was sent on this mission. It can be assumed Chef is a Catholic, being from New Orleans. He tells Willard that Kurtz is evil, that "this is pagan idolatry, that's what the guy's got set up here." It is an accurate assessment. Chef offers to kill Kurtz himself. He tells Willard he always feared if he dies in an evil place, his soul could not make it to Heaven, but now … "I don't care where it goes, so long as it's not here."

Willard instructs him to stay on board while he returns to the compound. If Willard is not back by a certain time, Chef is to call in an air strike. He gives Chef the coordinates. Willard then returns to the compound. Lance more or less runs free, mixing with the natives. The natives slowly envelop Willard in a creepy scene, pawing him, and turning him upside down while Willard cries out for Lance, who seems to find it amusing. He is dragged through mud as the rains pour down.

Willard is placed in a bamboo cage, hardly able to move. The photo-journalist admonishes him, "Why would a nice guy like you want to kill a genius?"

Willard stares at this man, remaining silent. He is filthy. He puts a cigarette in Willard's mouth. He goes on and on about Kurtz's greatness and genius, lamenting that "when he dies, when it dies, who's gonna tell 'em, man? *Me*? Look at me." He stares right at Willard and intimates that *he* is going to be the one who kills Kurtz, to put him out of his misery because "he hates all this" and he "is dying." Then Willard will return to the United States to "set 'em straight." (The freaked-out photo-journalist lacks credibility; his account would not be believed. But Willard is an officer on a mission. If he goes back and tells the generals, the CIA … the press (?) who Colonel Kurtz really was, what he tried to accomplish, then his memory will live on, and not be tarnished as an insane renegade. This is the literary Marlow character, who returns to give comfort to Kurtz's grieving fiancée. Will Willard give honor to Kurtz's memory by telling his wife and son he was a man who meant to do good? He had said earlier, in voiceover, that he had been put in charge of "Colonel Walter E. Kurtz's memory," and that it was not an accident. That is about to be fulfilled. Kurtz's story is really a confession, but so too is Willard's.)

Finally, Willard is brought to Kurtz. The camera catches Marlon Brando's face and his girth, but he is kept in shadows, half-hidden. He wears black "pajamas" like the Viet Cong.

"Are you an assassin?" he asks Willard.

"I'm a soldier," he replies.

"You're neither. You're an errand boy, sent by grocery clerks, to collect the bill."

Asked what his commanders told him, Willard says it is classified, but Kurtz rudely informs him it is obviously not classified anymore: he knows all about him. Kurtz asks where Willard is from. Ohio, he says (Sheen is from Ohio). Kurtz says that, as a kid, he took a boat ride on the Ohio River, where he came across a flower plantation that was overgrown with gardenias, and that it seemed, "Heaven had fallen on the Earth in the form of gardenias."

The conversation veers between semi-pleasant and hostile. Several sequences demonstrate the two together in a cave-like dwelling that Willard describes as "slow death ... malaria," which might be what is killing Kurtz. Kurtz reads from T.S. Eliot's "The Hollow Men," and the photo-journalist goes off on a strange tangent about traveling through space on fractions, until Kurtz calls him a "mutt," throwing his book at him. The photo-journalist gets up and says he is splitting the scene, and off he goes.

Back at the boat, Chef has not heard from Willard and gets on the radio to call in the air strike. He begins to deliver coordinates. From here, in a picture of hell, Kurtz appears from the shadows, ominous music playing. His face is grotesquely painted, his bald head framing fierce eyes. He slowly moves towards Willard, tied up and sitting in squalor. Rain pounds, and Brando takes a huge breath, girding himself for what he is about to do. Each sound is acutely heard in the theatre on the Dolby Surround Sound.

Kurtz drops something on Willard's lap. It is revealed to be Chef's head. Willard cries, utterly broken, beaten, his soul in agony. Kurtz has defeated him; Willard will only do what Kurtz wants him to do after this ultimate act of "warfare." The extremity of Kurtz's action symbolizes his approach to combat. He takes the gloves off and terrorizes the enemy into submission. This is the only way to win against as enemy as implacable as the Vietnamese.

Time passes, day after day, and Willard is nursed to health by a native girl, presumably Kurtz's mistress. In voiceover, he says he is unguarded, free to move around, but Kurtz seems to know what he is going to do before he does. Willard senses that he is not "allowed" to kill Kurtz, but a final climax is inevitable.

Kurtz discusses the "horrors that I've seen," which he knows Willard has also seen, and therefore he will understand him. Kurtz, "riddled with malaria, comes across as part Buddha, part Jim Jones," wrote Coppola's biographer Michael Schumacher. For brief moments, light frames his bald head.

Kurtz discusses a terrible event he witnessed when he was with Special Forces. His unit came to a village and inoculated the children for polio, part of America's campaign to win "hearts and minds." After they departed, an old man tracked them down, crying, and led them back. The enemy had come to the village and hacked off every inoculated arm, and they were all lying in a pile of "little arms." Kurtz said he cried "like some grandmother."

It occurred to him the men who had done this were not purely evil, that they were "trained cadres" with wives and children who were normal humans "filled with love." Yet they had "the *will*" to do this thing, which Kurtz called "genius."

(This was the message Milius wanted to send, not just how America could have won the Vietnam War, but the nature—and horror—of all war ["war is hell"], and offers an important understanding of Islamic jihad today. It is the essence of Nietzsche's "will to power.")

Kurtz tells Willard if he had ten divisions of such men America would quickly win in the 'Nam. The genius of their action was the necessity of it. It was an act of terror, the victims of it were innocent, but it was something the Communists felt they had to do in order to win the war. The war could not be won by victory on the battlefield, but by convincing the other side they would do anything; they would do what the Americans would refuse to do. The final calculus of the act, in their view, was that while sacrifices were made, it would save lives by making the Americans leave.

There may be a certain genius to this way of thinking. If the U.S. had employed such tactics, and used all their power, they would have defeated the North Vietnamese in no time, just as there is not an Islamic military power capable of stopping the United States today. But in performing atrocities, the perpetrator risks his soul.

"For what doth it profit a man, to gain the whole world, and suffer the loss of his own soul?" [Matthew 16:26–28]. Christ Himself allowed himself to be tormented on the cross rather than lead His people in a military victory over the Romans, because the soul is more important than the world. History also does not lend credence to Kurtz's theories in *Apocalypse Now* [and therefore Milius's]. The logic behind committing atrocities is that it is necessary to win, and once victory is achieved, peace will prevail, but when the NVA finally conquered South Vietnam, they murdered 1 million innocents. Those people did not need to be cowed by acts of terror in order to be pacified—they were defeated after the Americans bugged out in 1975.

In the case of Islam, the same can be said. The jihadists would like to "justify" beheadings and torture in the name of their religion, but in 2014 it was revealed that since the creation of Israel, more Muslims had died at the hands of other Muslims [11 million] than all the people killed by the Nazis in the Holocaust. The logic of war can therefore only be attributed to the devil, who made Abraham Lincoln order the deaths of massive numbers of his fellow citizens in order to achieve a "great" thing. It is the ultimate conundrum of man, who faces no good worldly choices and therefore has only one non-worldly choice, that being God.

Willard is obscenely attracted to Kurtz. In absorbing his logic and "wisdom," he formulates in his mind the plan, what he must inevitably do. Kurtz finally gives him permission. He tells Willard he wishes for him to go back and tell his son all he saw here, leaving nothing out, because he despises the "stench of lies." He makes sure Willard understands his request. The plot is now hatched, the climax is nigh. Willard must finally assassinate Kurtz.

A series of sequences are intercut. The strains of "The End" begin. Kurtz records a message, which is commentary on the odd commandment from military brass that pilots, who "drop fire on people," are not allowed to write "*fuck* on their aero planes, because … it's *obscene!*"

Willard ignores a radio communication to confirm the earlier air strike that had been called in, but not completed by Chef, because Kurtz beheaded him before he could complete the task. Then Willard emerges, shirtless, from the primordial swamp. He looks different. He now has a face from an "ancient gallery," as Jim Morrison sang, and is ready to walk on down the hall.

Kurtz waits for him, waiting for Willard to take the pain away. In voiceover, Willard asks what the generals back in Nha Trang would do if they could see Kurtz now? They would want him dead more than ever, of course. They could not understand his genius. Willard voices that he is not killing Kurtz to fulfill orders from the general; he was "not even in their fuckin' Army any more."

Willard moves, machete in hand, through the compound, while the ritual slaughter of the water buffalo is graphically shown. Huge chunks of the animal are sliced, practically cutting the beast in half. The animal's face is unable to show the pain it suffers, as it slowly sinks to the ground in death throes, the natives dancing and chanting. Lance, face painted, still high, is half-naked and enjoys the "party."

Kurtz reads *Heart of Darkness*, glancing up to see the approaching Willard. Morrison sings "The End," the music reaching its apex. Kurtz does not defend himself; this is his will being done. To music by The Doors, Willard uses his knife and a rifle butt to kill Walter Kurtz. The song begins to reach its soft conclusion, and Kurtz lies, dying, on the floor repeating Conrad's words: "The horror! The horror!"

(No movie audience had ever seen anything like this. It was not just the horror, the brutality, but the visual imagery, utterly beautiful and yet savage, like the jungle itself. The surround sound captured every scrape, every step, every breath, reverberating through theatres, the audience shocked and stilled, transfixed.)

Willard, his face painted, unrecognizable—only his piercing, beady eyes seem to penetrate the screen—moves into the crowd. The natives are silent, their king is dead; long live the king. Willard could easily become their next god, if he so chooses. All kneel before him, dropping machetes, all form of weaponry, in symbolic obeisance to him as he moves through them, the people parting for him like the Red Sea opening for the Israelites. Eerie, mysterious music lends the perfect accompaniment to the magisterial power of the scene.

Then Willard spots Lance, staring like a lost child. The music changes and becomes religious and hopeful, a light shining on Lance, the last vestige of innocence left in this evil place, a place of war, of man's worst ancient sins. Willard takes him by the hand and leads him away.

Finally, the boat drifts silently away, back to civilization. The credits run. This was probably the first film that did not run credits until the end. Even the title did not run at the beginning. Forbidding, climactic music plays while the compound is destroyed silently in the 35mm theatrical release. Apparently, Willard has called in the air strike after leaving and all evidence of what happened there is destroyed in a fireball of napalm. There will be only Willard to tell Kurtz's son "everything." The credits end, and then the music stops, the sound of silence and rain over a dark screen, and *Apocalypse Now* is finally over.

21

The Milius Screenplay

John Milius is considered the "author" of *Apocalypse Now*, although IMDB.com lists Francis Ford Coppola as a co-writer, the name of Michael Herr for the narration, and, of course, *Heart of Darkness* by Joseph Conrad as the book from which it was adapted.[1]

Some directors take undue credit for their "writing." The acclaimed Dalton Trumbo wrote *Spartacus* (1960), but he was one of the blacklisted Hollywood Ten, so producer Kirk Douglas was unsure whether he should credit him.[2] Director Stanley Kubrick cheerfully offered to take the "credit," but Douglas courageously credited Trumbo, effectively ending the Blacklist altogether.[3]

But Coppola was a screenwriter at heart, an acclaimed one for *Patton*. His co-writing credits for both *Godfathers* were not cheap. He adapted the Mario Puzo novel and added unmistakable cinematic quality to it. He took out key passages from the book, which made the movie better.[4] The sequel was really his work, going beyond the novel's reach, and Coppola was its major author.

Unquestionably, it was Milius who first thought of adapting *Heart of Darkness*, asking Irwin Blacker at USC about it, and after being told how difficult an undertaking such an endeavor would be, decided to defy the odds and do it anyway.[5] Caroll Ballard later claimed he was "working" on a screenplay adaptation of the Conrad novel at UCLA, but it was never a tangible work, either in terms of rights, or a written work registered with the Writer's Guild or the Library of Congress.[6]

Milius, on the other hand, had written a tangible "first draft," or, at the very least, substantive notes describing scenes, dialogue, and theme, which was called *Psychedlic Soldier*. It was also Milius and George Lucas who envisioned it as a "Vietnam movie," thus giving birth to the 1960s-themed title, as opposed to Ballard's plans to make a more straightforward adaptation of the Conrad novel set in the 1890s.[7] Milius never argued over the odd way Coppola obtained ownership over the property, and was happy when Francis decided to direct it. To the extent that a screenplay existed, Milius's *Psychedelic Soldier* existed at least in the form of notes at USC, then he created either a rough draft, treatment or outline around 1969. When Coppola decided to green light the project, Milius completed the screenplay in earnest. It has many adaptations. The final movie version is significantly different from what Milius wrote.[8] Milius was brought on set and contributed much of the dialogue and scenes in the "on the fly" method Coppola used, so much of Milius's work is not officially captured in completed versions of the script.[9] So, too, are many of Coppola's changes. They are co-authors, each due equal credit for a masterpiece. Neither has begrudged the other. Milius had early reservations about political changes, but inevitably came to love the film, his role in it, and the abiding notion that what Coppola did to finalize it was make the best version it could have been.

While there were many rewrites of *Apocalypse Now* along the way, many committed to paper the morning the scenes were shot, the screenplay considered the version, the one the cast and crew read for and went into production using, was dated December 3, 1975, originally written by Milius, this draft also by Coppola. Having seen the 1979 original (first the release for Cannes and early theatre release; then the version generally seen over Christmas), then the 2001 redux, it is very interesting to read *Apocalypse Now* in its "DNA," before it was cast, shot, fought over, and eventually birthed. That screenplay opens in a primeval swamp of "a million years ago."[10] Soldiers are colorfully garbed in elaborate jungle camouflage, like Indians of the Old West. They are completely in sync with their swamp surroundings. They are hunting Vietnamese. The Vietnamese move through the swamp until the Americans rise up and ambush them, blowing them all away.

The Americans take pleasure in violently, savagely killing them all in a very artistic and visual manner; like jungle poetry. They scalp the dead and blast the Vietnamese with a flamethrower, all in a highly psychedelic manner.

Titles run. They seem to be from outer space, conveying the sense that we are seeing some alternate universe, in which this time all the wrongs will be made right. This moves back to the Earth, finally settling on Los Angeles.

The scene is now Marina Del Rey, a beautiful swinger's enclave near the Pacific Ocean. On a luxury cabin cruiser corporate hustlers enjoy the day. The main corporate titan, Charlie, employs a bodyguard named Willard. In voiceover, Willard begins to tell his story after the fact. He is cynical of Charlie and his fat cat friends, none "of whom would understand," which is why he tells them everything is "classified" instead of telling them what really happened over there.[11]

The script then flashes back to Saigon, 1968. Willard is an Army officer in uniform. He starts drinking with a captain in a bar, but avoids his nosy questions. Willard notices a civilian tracking him. Willard then tells the soldier he knows he is being trailed, so the civilian approaches him. He is a CIA agent, and takes Willard to a helicopter.

Outside Nha Trang, at intelligence headquarters, Willard reports to a colonel. Next to him is a major and a "seedy-looking civilian." This is page 11, and really the first time the original script intersects with a scene in the actual movie.[12]

Willard is asked about his past assignments, which he is not "presently disposed to discuss." The conversation is similar but not the same as the film. The colonel talks about not favoring "elite units." The major says in Korea all they needed were "an Ohio farm boy and an M-1 Garand."[13] The "Ohio farm boy" could be the genesis of Willard being from Ohio, although Martin Sheen was an Ohioan as well.

The colonel is directed back to the task at hand by the civilian. He then describes Special Forces troops along the Cambodian border, training Montagnard natives. He says a detachment at Nu Mung Ba, an old Cambodian fortress, concerns them. VC activity around there is down to almost nothing, and six months prior communications stopped.

M'Nong tribesmen are being driven out. They are not afraid of the VC. They have fought there for centuries, but now something is truly frightening them.

Willard asks who is causing this. The major says, "You see, no one has really gone into this area and come back alive."

"Why me?" Willard asks.[14]

Then he is told about Walter Kurtz. A radio transmission is played, different from the movie. It sounds like an air strike or heavy ordnance being called in, a lot of static, insane laughter, then Kurtz calling in a napalm strike.

In script, Willard has met Kurtz once before. Willard thought he was "a lame." They had argued over the general philosophy of the war, Kurtz using big words to describe "why we kill."

Willard tells them he does not think Kurtz is capable of the wholesale killing of civilians, but is told Kurtz "or somebody attacked a South Vietnamese Ranger Platoon three days ago." Also, a reconnaissance helicopter was lost in the area. This is very different. In the movie there is no indication of Kurtz attacking U.S. forces, only VC "civilians." Willard is then given his orders, which are to go upriver in a Navy PBR and "find out what happened—and why. Then terminate his command."

From there he is told to "terminate with extreme prejudice."

The boat scene on the Delta resembles the movie, with some variations. There is a "famous surfer from the beaches south of L.A." Nobody is "wound up too tight for Vietnam …" The boat "sure as shit was the chief's boat." Mr. Clean is not from "some south Bronx shit hole."

Phillips indicates he used to "drive a taxi," and is more amiable and pliable than Albert Hall's film character.[15] Chief describes taking "a man up to Lo Ming Bridge. He was regular Army too. Shot himself in the head." When asked why, Chief offers no real theory. From here they run into the First of the Ninth, along with the black silhouette of four B-52 bombers.

While approaching this scene Willard reads from his dossier and finds out all the men assigned to the Kurtz operation before Willard had to maintain silence due to the "nature of their work," and none had been heard from in half a year.

He also reads some information on Kurtz not revealed in the movie; mainly his "broad background in the Humanities, the Arts and Sciences…. He views his military career as the dedication of his talents to bringing our values and way of life to those darker, less fortunate areas of the world."[16] This is inferred in the film but not broadly expounded on. The film allows a quick view of his résumé, indicating post-graduate work at Harvard, but little beyond that.

It adds that his request to attend jump school was especially unusual considering his "somewhat liberal politics," as most of the Airborne were gung-ho right-wingers. This would seem to be a message from Milius, that liberalism is a theory, but when people are faced with reality they are forced by circumstance to respond with conservative principles.

The reports further advance the notion that Kurtz can "bring a sense of Western culture to the backward peoples of these areas" in accordance with "Vietnamization." It is here where Lance sees a Chris-craft pulling a water skier, a scene earlier in the movie in which Lance is the skier.

As they land they come across new recruits. This is not the Kilgore scene, it is the bunny scene, coming earlier than the film version. Willard has his confrontation with the supply sergeant. In this screenplay the sergeant gives in and signs Willard's orders for some supplies. This is a scene that was shot and shown in the redux, with Chef admiring Miss December's centerfold.

Mr. Clean tells a story of a guy in the Delta who went crazy when they took his *Playboy* magazine away. He blew away a "gook" lieutenant for mutilating his magazine. The actual *Playboy* scene in the screenplay reads virtually the same as it was shot in the movie, although it was cut, restored in the redux.

Then they run into the First of the Ninth. These sequences read the way the redux version plays out, giving greater detail to Kilgore, especially his care in saving a baby and making sure she stays with her refugee mother, who his placed upon a transport carrier. Kilgore reflects a certain sadness—and humanity—that the original movie did not reflect. Duvall later complained in interviews that this was removed because of Coppola's "liberal San Francisco friends" who wanted to depict the soldiers not as decent people, but rather as "baby killers."[17]

Milius's screenplay does not contain Willard's voiceover, such as his saying he was "going to the worst place in the world …" and his observation that the First of the Ninth was "an old cavalry unit that had turned in their horses for choppers and gone tear-assin' around 'Nam lookin' for the shit."

The voiceover dialogue is credited to Michael Herr, but Martin Sheen's film voiceovers grew organically out of Coppola's desire to incorporate it in order to move the story along; then bringing Milius in to work on it, in person, with Sheen. Milius even arranged to give Sheen a loaded weapon in order to increase the tension in his voice.[18]

Some of the dialogue in the screenplay is not used in the film. Some that is not in there ends up in the movie. This is reflective of Coppola, who was heard typing away, changing the screenplay almost daily in the Philippines.[19]

The script contains a conversation between Kilgore and Willard about where Willard has been. Kilgore also talks about Kurtz. The whole scene about the "T-bones and the beer" is not in the script. From there is the scene discussing the size of the swells at "Charlie's Point."

Then the scene plays out like the movie, with the helicopter attack. At dawn they take off, as in the film. There are some variations on the attack and the battle. Kilgore does not say, "Don't these people ever give up?" but does call them "fucking savages." Willard asks who. Kilgore replies, "The enemy. Who else?" There is never the scene with the girl throwing the grenade into the helicopter.

From here the surf scene plays out the way the film depicts it. Kilgore refers to people a lot as "boy," whereas in the film he generally calls them "son." Then the famed "do you smell that?" scene is in the screenplay, but it also contains somewhat elaborate sequences on the beach after they land and the napalm strike is called in. This, too, appears in the redux.

Most notably, Milius writes of Willard stealing Kilgore's surfboard. After escaping with the board, Willard reveals that he has a marijuana joint, and shares it with the crew. These sequences, in the script and the redux, humanize Willard, making him almost comical, but in studying why they were taken out of the 1979 production, like many deleted scenes from the director's cut of *The Godfather*, it makes sense that they were not shown. They do not particularly move the narrative along. They seem forced. Willard's persona, as a cold assassin, needs to be maintained rather than indicating he is a prankster who has chosen this life because his alternative was a factory job in Ohio.[20]

On the boat, Willard gives Chief a lesson on the inside game of tracking people in the jungle, Indian-style. Soldiers in 'Nam often referred to enemy territory as "Indian country."[21] Milius wanted to show that in order to defeat this kind of enemy, he had to think, and fight, like one.

Then Milius writes of the chopper circling above the boat, which is hidden under cover, with the recording from Kilgore asking Lance to return his surf board because it was a "good board" and Lance would understand how hard it is to find a board that is to one's liking. This is all in the redux, not the original.

The tiger scene was almost exactly as written. Right after that, on page 65, the script flashes forward to Marina Del Rey, with Willard, in voiceover, reflecting on his time in the jungle, his pursuit of Kurtz, and "all his liberal bullshit about the end of savagery—and the role of our culture, our way of life…."[22]

Back to the waters. Here is written the "Satisfaction" scene that in the film comes much earlier, with Lance water skiing, as did the other man he had observed earlier. Willard then reads a letter from Kurtz's wife expressing how terrible it is not knowing where he is. Kurtz's kids are getting in fights at school.

Kurtz writes back:

> Sell the house.
> Sell the car.
> Sell the kids.
> Find someone else.
> Forget it.
> I'm never coming back.
> Forget it—.[23]

In the film Colby wrote this intercepted letter. Coppola makes a major change in not attributing it to Kurtz; his later conversations with Willard, and eventual request of Willard to go back and tell his son "everything" are largely affected by this dramatic choice, propelling the ending Coppola sought and finally chose.

In the rain, which was in the screenplay and certainly was in the early shooting in the Philippines, they come across the Playmates. In the script the girls take on all the men, apparently including Willard, in orgy, or "sloppy seconds" fashion. In the redux Clean is denied and has a huge fit, probably racially motivated. Phillips declines and there is no indication Willard does it as well. In the script at the end Willard "thanks" the Playmates, one of whom throws a shoe at him apparently, having been ridden hard and put away wet by the crew.

All of this was in an exchange for fuel, followed by the approach to the Do Lung Bridge. The 1979 movie depicts Mr. Clean in a major argument with Chef, but the reasons behind the argument are not fleshed out. The redux explains that the motivation behind the argument was that Clean was forced to stand outside the tent while the white men, Chef and Lance, make love to the Playmates. Clean is never allowed to get any, and he is pissed. This was used by Coppola to change the mood on the boat, and the film, towards a much darker turn as they get closer to Kurtz, and danger.

Then there is a little political commentary. In the film Chief Phillips speaks of the stupidity of keeping the bridge "open" just to be blown back up again.[24] The script is more psychedelic, more viewed from Lance's vantage point on acid.

A soldier approaches Clean with mail for all his acquaintances and describes how they are surrounded, abandoned, and all will die. When he finds out the boat is going upriver and not back to the base camps, he takes the letters back.

From there, Milius writes in the elaborate French rubber plantation sequences, which were not in the original film, but were fleshed out in the redux.[25] Again, viewing these scenes is extremely interesting, and educational, but it is understandable why they were not included in the '79 edit.

Milius's version contains the conversation with the French woman Roxanne. We learn Willard was discharged from the Army four years earlier, quickly grew bored, and re-upped. They also find that the French have heard of Kurtz.

Willard has sex with her. Willard then kills two Vietnamese who are guarding the boat, then goes back to Roxanne's room in a scene that at first makes no sense. The next day the French take half of the boat's ammunition and assume the Vietnamese have deserted. It turns out Willard was transferring rocks and sand into the ammo bags. Willard has figured out the French would take his ammunition, so he did this so they would think they are getting ammo, but the boat keeps the ammo after all. This is why he had to kill the Vietnamese guards.

The approach to Kurtz's compound is very Homeresque, in keeping with Milius's classic love of *The Iliad* and *The Odyssey*.[26]

The wailing, groaning sounds in the fog are reminiscent of Homer's depiction of the siren songs.

The Chief does not tell Willard, "You don't know what you're doing" and "You don't know how to get us out of here." He is felled by the spear, but does not draw Willard to him, forcing Willard to suffocate him as he does in the film. The screenplay does contain some Willard voiceovers that are not used in the film.

Then it flashes forward to the Marina Del Rey scene, where Willard provides some quick philosophizing on life before it returns to the river. There is no scene in which Willard explains to Chef, now in charge of the boat, of his mission or Chef responding that he thought he was going to blow up some railroad tracks.

The men now seem more like the killers Milius describes at the beginning of the movie. They are part of the jungle. The boat finally reaches the end of the river. The hippie character (played by Dennis Hopper) is a black Australian, probably an aborigine. The encampment is pockmarked by shells, signs of recent battles. They come across Colby among other "ex-Americans."

A man identifies himself as formerly being with the Fourth Battalion, Royal Australian regimental task force. He is an ex-corporal who has deserted. He explains it is Tet, and the NVA plan to attack them that night. This puts the screenplay in early 1968, whereas the film was at least set in 1969–70, because Chef received an article from an American newspaper describing the Manson family killings. Manson and his followers were not arrested and identified as suspects until the fall of 1969, even though the killings had taken place in early-to-mid-August.

Then they meet Kurtz. The exchange, more closely, parallels the Conrad novel.[27] The scene where Chef is sent back to the boat is not there. They have a sit and Kurtz smokes dope. Kurtz asks Willard if he is "the final justice." Kurtz then randomly shoots and kills a man as a display of some kind; obviously his power over life and death has elevated him to his god-like status in this strange place.

Only here does Willard explain that his mission is to kill Kurtz, which Chef has already figured out. "This don't look good for America," Chef tells Willard.[28] Kurtz is surrounded by the sayings of the German philosopher Friederick Nietzsche. Much of the screenplay dialogue is not in the movie; not surprising since Marlon Brando did not read *Heart of*

Darkness, could not memorize screenplays, and spoke mostly in an extemporaneous manner, always after long conversations with Coppola. Most of Brando's dialogue came in answer to questions the director posed to him such as, "Why are we in Vietnam?"[29]

Kurtz is a big fan of Jim Morrison and The Doors. Willard says he has gone crazy and Kurtz replies, "No. My thinking is clear. But my soul has gone mad."[30] This line came from Hopper's character in the film. Kurtz has some kind of gut injury, which is likely killing him slowly, and could very well be making him slightly insane. Kurtz explains that it would be "stupid" to carry out the assassination mission, since he's dying from the gut injury anyway. Then they drink water laced with LSD.

Lance is completely stoned. Willard is the one who utters the paradox of dropping fire on people, but can't write "fuck" on the planes. The whole time Chef is off to the side urging Willard to kill Kurtz, but he seems to have no interest in doing that. Chef tries to do it and Willard guns him down. Lance is too stoned to care and thinks it is exciting.

Music begins, in this case "Light My Fire" by The Doors.[31] The men await the attack they know is coming. Willard has transformed his appearance. He now looks like Genghis Khan. Everybody now worships Willard. Kurtz is dancing and singing to The Doors while calling orders and ordering napalm.

The North Vietnamese attack but are blown up by Claymore mines. The Montagnards and Americans counter-attack with savage fury. Lance is apparently killed. Willard calls in an air strike. The enemy surround Kurtz but he has booby-trapped the perimeter, which turns them into fire in sync with Morrison's song.

Finally it looks hopeless, with Kurtz fighting them hand-to-hand like Davy Crockett at the Alamo, when the air strike begins. Willard hauls the wounded, dying Kurtz to the near-wrecked boat to escape and save him. The scene then fades into morning. Vultures fly overhead. Lance is dead. The Kurtz command has survived.

The PBR moves downriver, Colby at the helm. The Montagnards pay their respect by the riverbeds as the boat moves along. We hear Kurtz say, "My river … my people … my jungle." Willard tells Kurtz he is taking him back. Kurtz sees into the distance and whispers, "The horror, the horror."

A medevac helicopter descends. They think Kurtz is dead and fire at the medevacs. Then the Milius screenplay flashes forward to Marina Del Rey. Willard says he brought a few papers to Kurtz's wife, as Marlow brought some inconsequential documents to the novelistic Kurtz's fiancée.

Willard visits Kurtz's wife in a California neighborhood. "He was a remarkable man," says Willard. "It was impossible not to—."[32]

"Love him…" his wife finishes the sentence.

Willard tells her his last words were of her, not "The horror! The horror!"

This is a significantly different theme, not to mention a scene not filmed by Coppola, in that while Willard does as Kurtz requested, which is return home, he has not assassinated the colonel; he visits his wife, not his son; and he lies to her, instead of telling the son "everything" because Kurtz despises the "stench of lies."[33]

From Marina Del Rey Milius's version closes on the boat; the half-dead Colby and the dead Kurtz. "The End" plays over the final credits. It is worth noting that in the December 1975 draft credited both to Milius and Coppola, there is not a scene that Milius in interviews often lamented was cut out. That scene described Willard and Kurtz shooting at American helicopters while Kurtz rambles on about how god-like and powerful a thing it is "to be a white man who draws fire from the sky."[34]

In reading at least this version of what appears mostly to be John Milius's work, then comparing it to the 1979 general public release of *Apocalypse Now* (and later the 2001 redux), it is obvious that Francis Ford Coppola is a filmmaking genius. Milius is among the greatest of all screenwriters, but he is also over the top. This is seen in his *Jeremiah Johnson* screenplay, which director Sidney Pollack described as essentially a "piece of violence," in which Milius said only about 60 percent of his script made it onscreen.[35] Milius is not a writer who holds jealously onto every word. He is a director himself, a filmmaker, a historian, and a collaborator who knows the process of filmmaking. His politics allow him to understand the business end of movies as well as the art, and this appears to make him relatively easy to work with, at least as long as he respects the director.

At first Milius was unhappy that so much of what he wrote was changed, but like *Jeremiah Johnson* he was very happy with the end result.[36] A read of the 1975 Milius-Coppola screenplay reveals a brilliant piece of story telling. It is easy to see why it was made into a movie. Despite the warnings that *Heart of Darkness* would break any filmmaker who tried to do it, the fact is the story, and presumably a treatment if not an early draft, was enough to get Warner Bros.-Seven Arts to agree to make it as part of the original American Zoetrope deal. This did not happen only because *THX 1138* was such a disaster, and Hollywood's subsequent refusal to back the project being shopped around from 1969 to 1975 by Coppola and Lucas (Milius was busy directing two other films) was in response not to the screenplay, but to America's failures in Vietnam.[37]

Had the movie been shot exactly as Milius wrote it, it would have been an extremely good film, maybe even a masterpiece. Think of *Red Dawn*, for instance. But it would not have been nearly as good as what Coppola eventually produced. Almost every major and minor change Coppola instituted made it better. Coppola had a vision for the piece beyond the confines of the Milius screenplay. Milius's jingoism would have been too much. Liberal critics would have excoriated him as they did for *Red Dawn*. It may well have played regularly on TNT's "Movies for Guys Who Like Movies" along with *The Dirty Dozen*, *Dirty Harry*, and *Die Hard*, but it would not be studied in every film school in the world as one of the greatest examples of the American art form ever made.[38] It took courage and confidence—Coppola had enough ego—to make the directorial changes that were made. These choices are likely the greatest accomplishment in his fabled career; it is what separates him from almost every other director who ever lived. Coppola is a genius.

22

"I've been blacklisted as surely as anybody in the '50s"

Perhaps no explanation for Hollywood's mediocre turn is better explained than the fact that John Milius was practically run out of the business. Why? He was too conservative. Probably the greatest of all the film school talents of the 1960s, the one who, along with Coppola, first broke through and succeeded in the game, he is probably the greatest screenwriter who ever lived. He is certainly the most prolific. The movies he directed were well reviewed and made a lot of money. Several are staples of cable television, shown constantly, and maintain a huge, enthusiastic audience. If any truthful poll were taken, perhaps more filmmakers would cite Milius as their greatest influence, the most brilliant of all the poets and artists in this crazy business; yet that business literally chose to phase him out as a director because he voted Republican and had the temerity not to hide it.

"I'm not a reactionary—I'm just a right-wing extremist so far beyond the Christian Identity people like that and stuff, that they can't even imagine," he said. "I'm so far beyond that I'm a Maoist. I'm an anarchist. I've always been an anarchist. Any true, real right-winger if he goes far enough hates all form of government, because government should be done to cattle and not human beings."[1]

For years Milius was a member of the board of directors of the National Rifle Association, where he was a leader (with Charlton Heston) in resisting a takeover attempt by advocates of the so-called Militia Movement.

"Hollywood was always left-wing, and I was always a pariah," said Milius. "Culturally I am uncool, cutting edge. The codes of behavior I live by, the institutions I admire, were probably dead before I was born. I thought I was a more traditional American conservative, more in the line of rugged individualism. I was more in the line of resisting the power, the idea of revolution is very, very romantic...."

There are those who dispute the assertion that conservative political views are hurtful to a filmmaker's career. "If a white or a grey list exists, I feel like I would know about it, but I can tell you there is not a single client of mine who is hired or not hired for their political views," said Sam Haskell, a conservative Hollywood talent agent. "I can tell you that in my twenty-five years in this business I have never personally experienced any evidence of any exclusion because I'm a conservative."[2]

"I think the dark days of the blacklist are ugly, disgusting, often misguided and misdirected, and when Casey Kasem was targeted, his award for his contributions to the film industry, I don't think he should have been booed," said game show host Pat Sajak, a conservative. "We are a very forgiving people. We have forgiven the Germans, we have forgiven the Japanese for bombing Pearl Harbor, but it's a generational thing and I think we're getting closer and closer to the point where the Blacklist will be truly ancient history, but it's difficult for people to get excited about, but that comes up so often, as if McCarthy is prowling the hallways here and is gonna go *boo* one of these days. It's amazing how much the left-right divide still relates, even though its been forty years, or more, ago."[3]

"I know John Milius but I don't know that he was denied work because he's conservative," said Lionel Chetwynd. "John was a wild, independent spirit."[4]

After *Big Wednesday*, which disappointed at the time but became a cult classic, followed by *Apocalypse Now*, Milius was the executive producer of *1941*, directed by Spielberg and co-written by two USC protégés, Bob Gale and Robert Zemeckis.

He followed that up with *Conan the Barbarian*, the film that turned Arnold Schwarzenegger into a big star. It did huge business and established Milius as one of the elite's in the industry. "I was born to do this movie," he said of *Conan the Barbarian*.[5]

Then came *Red Dawn*. When it comes to the divide between the left and the right in Hollywood, since the Blacklist nothing else has so polarized the industry. TV viewers and theatregoers first saw a trailer that said U.S. soil had never been invaded … "until now." After establishing that the Communists had taken over America, the trailer demonstrates that a few freedom fighters were kicking back. While a young girl is chased by evil Russians, suddenly gun-toting kids emerge from holes dug in the ground to shoot them down. Hearing audiences go crazy over that, there was no doubt *Red Dawn* would be a hit. It was.

Released during the presidential campaign year of 1984, when Ronald Reagan was successfully starting to tear down the Soviet Union, it starred an all-star cast of young Hollywood, headlined by Patrick Swayze and Charlie Sheen. Their characters live in a small Colorado town, mirroring Milius's experience when his dad sent him to high school there to get him away from the beach. Like Milius, they are taught to become mountain men. They can shoot, hunt, fish, trap, and survive in the woods.

An airborne assault, combined of Soviet and Cuban paratroopers, lands in their town, shoots the place to smithereens, and establishes dominance. They round up all the NRA members, boy scouts, and patriots, putting them in a re-education camp. The brothers, played by Swayze and Sheen, and a few others, escape to the mountains. Over time they discover that World War III has started; Europe is "sitting this one out"; the Soviets have nuked Red China into submission; and they live in a part of the United States occupied by the enemy. Somewhere is a place called "Free America," which sends coded radio messages every night to the resistance. They are the resistance.

They engage in increasingly well-coordinated attacks on Russian columns and supply depots, slowly building the resistance to the invaders, until they are killed, but are remembered by history for having helped the United States prevail.

Soviet diplomats formally protested *Red Dawn*. Liberals lambasted it. It was said to be "Fascist" and "Red-baiting" at a time when nuclear war was a real threat and everybody hoped if we would be nice to the Communists, they might stop murdering people, which up until then they had done to the tune of 80–90 million since 1917. Even BBC commentators got in on the act, criticizing it roundly.

"The critics always hated me," Milius said. "They said, 'This guy is dangerous. He's subversive.' *Red Dawn* really rang their bell. I didn't think it would cause such a cheap shot reaction from the left. It was not their political view and it was to be made fun of and suppressed. I've been blacklisted as surely as anybody in the '50s. I should have made twenty more films."[6]

But President Reagan, Secretary of Defense Caspar Weinberger, and that crowd loved *Red Dawn*. It made a huge sum of money and continues to make money drawing big TV ratings, but whatever list or edict or memo or secret handshake exists orchestrating such things, John Milius, vibrant, young, energetic and in his prime, was stopped dead in his tracks. He was not offered another directing job for five years, and when his movies failed to generate the same kind of business, he was out.

Screenwriting gigs still came his way. He wrote for TV (*The New Twilight Zone*, *Miami Vice*), wrote all of Sean Connery's "big speeches" in *The Hunt For Red October* (1990), penned an incredibly intelligent and great script for *Geronimo: An American Legend* (1993), then *Clear and Present Danger* (1994), punched up *Saving Private Ryan* for Spielberg ("Did I live a good life?"), *Texas Rangers* (2001), before co-creating and executive producing the HBO show *Rome* (2005). But he did not direct again until *Rough Riders* (1997), about his hero Teddy Roosevelt leading the charge up San Juan Hill.

He gave up surfing at age fifty and suffered financial reversals when a good friend absconded with his money. He also had a stroke that left him unable to speak or walk. However, he recovered.

"The great American tradition of larger-than-life narrative filmmaking best embodied by John Ford, Howard Hawks, and John Huston lives on in the screenplays and films of John Milius," wrote John Andrew Gallagher in *Film Directors on Directing*.

"John is our scoutmaster," said Steven Spielberg. "He's the one who will tell you to go on a trip and only take enough food, enough water for one day, and make you stay out longer than that. He's the one who says, 'Be a man. I don't want to see any tears.' He's a terrific raconteur, a wonderful story teller. John has more life than all the rest of us put together."[7]

Just as George Lucas's creation John Milner from *American Graffiti* was inspired by Milius, so was Walter Sobchak (played by John Goodman) in the 1998 film *The Big Lebowski*. Milius was also instrumental during the startup of the Ultimate Fighting Championship organization: it was his idea to use the octagon-shaped cage, and his association with UFC helped provide interest and investors to it.

In 2007, Milius was the recipient of the Austin Film Festival's Distinguished Screenwriter Award. Mickey Rourke has been in talks with Milius to star in a biopic of Genghis Khan. In 2013 he was the subject of a fabulous documentary, *Milius*, that rates with *Hearts of Darkness* among the greatest Hollywood documentaries ever.

"I've always been considered a nut," he said. "They kind of tolerate me. It's certainly affected me. I've been blacklisted for a large part of my career because of my politics—as surely as any writer was blacklisted back in the 1950s. It's just that my politics are from the other side, and Hollywood always veers left."[8]

Milius is the "best writer of the co-called USC Mafia, a tight-knit group that resuscitated—some say homogenized American cinema in the 1970s ..." wrote Nat Segaloff. "Raised on Ford, Hawks, Lean and Kurosawa, shaped by filmmakers as disparate as Fellini and Delmer Daves, Milius favors history books over comic books, character over special effects, and heroes with roots in reality, time, place and customs. Milius's stories reflect his own deeply held ethic, which embraces the values of tradition, adventure, spiritualism, honor and an intense loyalty to friends…. Although he privately chafes at his public image as a gun-toting, liberal baiting provocateur, he allows himself to be painted as such, at times even holding the brush. He plays the Hollywood game like a pro, yet sticks to his own rules; he is a romantic filmmaker who avoids love scenes; his movies contain violence, yet no death in them is without meaning."

"George and I went to school together, so I hardly think of it in terms that it's all become," Milius said of his film school associations. "It's hard to imagine the whole thing becoming so big. I can believe that Francis is a big director. I still can't believe Steven and George are big directors. It's hard to believe. I think Francis is the best of the 'New Wave,' so to speak."

Milius compared dealing with studios to "the rip at Sunset Beach. If you wipe out you get caught in the rip. If you don't want to swim in the rip you don't go swimming in there….

"Whatever I say sounds okay when I say it, but when it's printed it's awful. I end up being this terrible guy that has guns and likes to shoot hippies. They always take the humor out of what I say."

"Milius favors full-blooded characterizations, vigorous action, and a moralistic code of honor, rooted in his love of history and traditional story telling," wrote Gallagher. Milius's overall philosophy: "Pull out all the stops."[9]

He has also been consultant to a military think tank, and is enthusiastically received at military bases. *Apocalypse Now* (particularly the helicopter assault) and *Red Dawn*, among other Milius films (*Dirty Harry, Jeremiah Johnson, The Wind and the Lion, Conan the Barbarian, The Hunt For Red October, Saving Private Ryan, Rough Riders*), are constantly shown to basic training recruits, OCS classes, war colleges, at West Point, the Naval Academy, to officers and enlisted personnel alike, formally and informally. Among members of the U.S. Armed Forces, John Milius is easily and without question the favorite and most well-known Hollywood filmmaker. Only *The Sands of Iwo Jima, Patton*, and Clint Eastwood rival Milius's war films among them.

"He writes for men because John's a man," said Sam Elliott, who starred in *Rough Riders* (1997).[10]

Soldiers routinely seek him out for thanks. Medal of Honor recipients tell him he is the single artist who understands what they have to do, and why. But perhaps his greatest legacy, at least the one Milius himself would appreciate beyond Oscars or money or fame, is the fact that U.S. military actions regularly name themselves from his movies. In 2003, when the Army captured Iraqi dictator Saddam Hussein, it was called Operation Red Dawn, the subsequent capture given the sobriquet Wolverine I and Wolverine II, the name used by the high school kids-turned-guerrilla fighters in *Red Dawn*.

23

Postscript

Jim Morrison lived off and on in a seedy dive called the Alta Cienega Motel, which to this day exists and celebrates the "Morrison room" as a strange tourist spot, complete with a photocopy of Morrison's biography, *No One Here Gets Out Alive*. This line, from "Five to One," fits perfectly with the Philippines narrative of Coppola's struggle to make *Apocalypse Now*, although it is an odd message to give people checking into a motel.

Of all the fall-out from *Apocalypse Now*, the ups and downs of both Francis Ford Coppola and John Milius; the demise of American Zoetrope and United Artists; the mediocrity of Hollywood after *Heaven's Gate*; the rise of the USC and UCLA film schools; perhaps nobody benefited more from the movie than the man who died eight years before it was released. For the rest of The Doors—Ray Manzarek, John Densmore, Robby Krieger—the film revitalized their music and made it possible for them to achieve the riches they thought had been lost when Jim Morrison left this mortal coil in Paris, France, in 1971.

Apocalypse Now turned Morrison into an icon on par with James Dean, Marilyn Monroe, and John F. Kennedy. It pushed him beyond the other two American rockers who also died within a year of his demise, Jimi Hendrix and Janis Joplin. It probably gave impetus to Oliver Stone's 1991 movie, *The Doors*.

No One Here Gets Out Alive was one of the most well-timed books ever written. Published in 1980, it was the story of the meteoric rise of The Doors, written by Jerry Hopkins and a man named Danny Sugarman. Coming on the heels of *Apocalypse Now*, it generated enormous interest and sales. It eventually became the template for Stone's movie, starring Val Kilmer as Morrison. Stone's movie was a major hit, released for the twentieth anniversary of Morrison's death.

Sugarman had been The Doors' assistant since wandering into their Hollywood offices as a teenager, where he answered fan mail and befriended Morrison. He followed that up with *Wonderland Avenue*, perhaps an even better book; maybe the best ever written about American rock music. Stone optioned that, too, but it has never been made.

No One Here Gets Out Alive spurred wild rumors, lasting years, that Morrison was not really dead. It described how there was no French death certificate, and much mystery regarding circumstances of the singer's last hours. In 1982, a Los Angeles FM rock radio station did a fake "news conference" featuring an actor playing Morrison announcing his return from Africa, where he supposedly lived since staging his death in 1971. People throughout Los Angeles called one another, repeating the information. It was almost like Orson Welles's *War of the Worlds*.

Elektra Records put out *The Doors: Greatest Hits* with the movie's release. It sold a shocking 2 million copies in 1980. People still flock to Morrison's grave at the Pere Lachaise

Cemetery to pay homage, listening to "The End," watching *Apocalypse Now* on handheld devices.

With the fall of the Berlin Wall, Eastern Europeans came to the West already huge Doors fans. By 2000 The Doors had sold 20 million records, were elected to the Rock Hall of Fame, and most movies that were either set in Vietnam or used the war as a backdrop normally used music by The Doors. Prominent among those were Coppola's own *Gardens of Stone* (1987), and *Forrest Gump* (1994) by an acolyte of John Milius from USC, Robert Zemeckis.

Francis Ford Coppola's success with *Apocalypse Now* led indirectly to Michael Cimino's disastrous conclusion he could pull off a similar feat. The result was *Heaven's Gate* (1980). That film's failure, and Coppola's own subsequent failures, demonstrated that *Apocalypse Now* was in many ways a "one-off," a unique blend of great story (John Milius) and talent that cannot be replicated, certainly not without luck.

But Cimino was equally seduced by his own success with *The Deer Hunter* (1978), his ability to break major filmmaking rules and get away with it; also influenced by Coppola. The wedding scene at the beginning of *The Deer Hunter*, similar in some ways to the wedding scene that opens *The Godfather II*, was incredibly long. Like the wedding in Coppola's classic, however, it succeeded in telling key aspects of the story, pushing character and narrative. Cimino tried to duplicate it with an elaborate formal dance scene at the beginning of *Heaven's Gate*, which had the effect of making people get up and walk out.

Heaven's Gate was budgeted at $10 million. It had enormous problems, the kind only a genius like Francis Ford Coppola could have overcome, but Cimino, who thought he was a true genius, was *not* the genius Coppola was. It was a disaster. *Time* called it "Apocalypse Next."

UA was so desperate with *Heaven's Gate* they ignored it, failing to market it, but again a certain amount of "blame" can be accorded Coppola and *Apocalypse Now*. That film also broke many rules and conventions, but UA backed Coppola, whose vision saw it through to a successful conclusion, even if it did take forever. UA seduced themselves into thinking that this could be duplicated, and that Cimino could recapture the brilliance of *The Deer Hunter*.

People walked out in droves, the after party was canceled, the L.A. premiere was canceled, and it goes down among the worst cinematic disasters of all time. It led to UA's sale to Kirk Kerkorian, and eventually the destruction of a venerable old Hollywood movie studio, started by Chaplin, Pickford, Fairbanks, and Griffith as a place where the talent could have some say in the process. Oddly, it was the inspiration of Coppola and Lucas for American Zoetrope (eventually LucasFilm), and at a time in which those two stood like Colossuses of Rhodes astride the movie business, this studio was now gone from the face of the Earth. Many projects were canceled while a new gloom fell over Hollywood.

"*Heaven's Gate* undercut all of us," said Coppola, whose place in the pantheon was not nearly as secure as Lucas's. "I knew at the time it was the end of something, that something had died. There was a kind of *coup d'état* that happened after *Heaven's Gate*, started by Paramount. It was a time when the studios were outraged that the cost of movies was going up so rapidly, that directors were making such incredible amounts of money, and had all the control. So they took the control back."[1]

This form of corporate conspiracy also played itself out in professional sports. In 1981, the Major League baseball players struck from June to August, gutting what was on pace to be a marvelous season. The owners, behind closed doors, eventually reacted by collectively deciding—for several seasons—to stop paying huge free agent salaries.

In Hollywood it was, at least for awhile, the end of the *auteur* era. "Now, here we are, twenty years after *Heaven's Gate*," said Coppola in the late 1990s. "Directors don't have much power anymore, the executives make unheard of amounts of money, and budgets are more out of control than they ever were. And there hasn't been a classic in ten years."[2]

William Goldman's *Adventures in the Screen Trade* states, "This book was begun at the greatest time of panic and despair in modern Hollywood history—late January of '82. Future film historians may well term it 'the *Heaven's Gate* era.'" That is exactly what happened.

While Cimino was the victim of his own *hubris*, so was Coppola. All the bad luck and disaster he flirted with on *Apocalypse Now*, but averted and from which he emerged victorious, sunk his 1982 production of *One From the Heart*. Something called American Zoetrope would still exist and even produce some good work (*Hearts of Darkness*, *The Good Shepherd*), but the hope revived by *Apocalypse* that Zoetrope become a powerful force independent of Hollywood, Coppola's original vision, ended once and for all with *One From the Heart*.

Like Cimino, Coppola believed he was "bullet proof." He had proved all his critics wrong, and was like a military commander who thought he had rewritten the rules of warfare. His idea of making little films was lost amid a $27 million budget-buster. Coppola directed it like he was a football coach in a tower, using a loudspeaker. It was a total disaster. Critics called it "One Through the Heart," and it made less than $2.5 million. All the *gravitas*, not to mention the hard-earned money from *Apocalypse Now*, was wasted.

Matthew Robbins said at first he thought this new version of Zoetrope would fulfill its vision of 1969 until he realized it was "a Trojan horse"; in fact was "just us guys." It certainly did not produce great cinema.

"With the collapse of my studio, everything fell into a black hole," said Coppola. "I have no present at all. I live like a flea, in between two blocks of granite. There's no space. It's horrible."[3]

Francis Ford Coppola has been marginalized ever since. Incredibly, he *did* return to business with Robert Evans. There is a symbolic break in Hollywood's golden age, often thought to have reached its conclusion after Marty Scorsese's *Raging Bull* (1980). Michael Cimino's disaster, *Heaven's Gate*, is most often blamed, as it led to United Artists' bankruptcy. But there is something cosmically justified about two of the most ballyhooed of the New Age maverick geniuses, Francis Ford Coppola and Robert Evans, patching up their differences, thinking they were so great they could recapture the past and make it better, only to fail miserably, ushering in a period of mediocrity that still exists.

The movie was *The Cotton Club* (1984). It was set during the Harlem renaissance, the Jazz Age. It was dubbed the "black *Godfather*," and it was written by Mario Puzo. This trio was irresistible, audiences' mouths watering to see Evans, Coppola, and Puzo, the masterminds of cinema, back together again. Trailers looked awesome. It starred Richard Gere, one of the handsomest of all leading men, and on top of the world after *American Gigolo* and *An Officer and a Gentleman*. How could it go wrong?

After the fall of UA, studios were tighter than a drum. They wanted explosions and comic-book framing, not cost overruns from period pieces. It was just bad timing. Evans had dealt with the Arabs on *Black Sunday*, the beginning of his downfall after a long run of success. He claimed the Arabs offered him what he called "fuck you money" for his points on the Super Bowl disaster flick. Convinced *Black Sunday* would perform like *Jaws*, he turned it down. The movie failed to deliver.

It was Arab money that originally funded *The Cotton Club*, but he eventually went to other foreign investors to fund it outside the studios. Nefarious go-betweens and brokers were involved, and at one point an investor was murdered. A woman associated with Evans was found guilty, ostensibly because she believed he had stiffed her on money he owed her for brokering the connection. Evans was only a tangential witness, but his name was huge and splattered all over "*The Cotton Club* murder" headlines. On top of that he was caught with cocaine. His reputation was in shatters. But what killed *The Cotton Club* ultimately was its lack of great drama.

"Starting a flick minus a script is tantamount to waiting for an accident to happen," Evans said. "When it happens in a major studio, they send in the troops. The only troops here were the three investors, and Coppola got them to think they were Selznick, Thalberg, and Zanuck combined. For me, I was quarantined to what was commonly called the 'crisis center,' a town house originally rented to be my home and office during production."

Threats followed along with mob money and Arab money. Robert Osborne of LA/11 news reported $1 million wasted on extras in a single nightclub sequence due to "insufficient preparations." He also charged that drugs led to a set in which all was anarchy. All of this led to infamous telegrams exchanged between Coppola and Evans encapsulating their long, checkered history together. This led to legal action, in which Coppola and the investment group tried to sue and get him off the picture. After Evans prevailed he said to the media, "Francis's work is brilliant. And I hope we'll be working together many times," adding he hoped for "the same luck as we had in *The Godfather*."

It was not to be. *The Cotton Club* was a terrible disappointment. It does not hold up over time, either. TV viewers, trying to watch it and find entertainment value in Gere's performance, the lavish set designs and the ambience of Jazz Age Harlem, do so in vain, and usually ending up switching stations.

For Evans, it was a disaster with a capital "D." He lost his Beverly Hills home, Woodland, was sent packing by Paramount, and was left for dead professionally. He almost did die, contemplating suicide. With the help of Jack Nicholson he bought the house back and returned to producing. His book and subsequent documentary, *The Kid Stays in the Picture*, cemented his position as a "comeback kid" and legend of which few approach a similar level of color and drama. His films since coming back have been mixed; some successes, a few failures, none approaching *The Godfather* or *Chinatown*, but he is the ultimate survivor. His story is intimately intertwined with Francis Ford Coppola, who said his middle name was "second guesser."[4]

* * *

"I didn't expect more than two or three minutes of it to ever be shown," said Eleanor Coppola of the footage she shot for what United Artists said would be a five-minute promotional of *Apocalypse Now*.

Eleanor's footage faded into obscurity until *Hearts of Darkness: A Filmmaker's Apocalypse* was released in 1991, but Ellie felt that despite the embarrassment and unflattering way it portrayed her husband, it was fair to shed light on such an important piece of film history as the monumental making of *Apocalypse Now*. Glossy documentaries do not show that kind of honesty. But Francis was so aware of how the producers always edited him on his films, that he did not want to do that to the filmmakers of the documentary. "He allowed them their freedom, but in the end he resented some of the portrayals," said Eleanor.

> Francis was so engrossed in his work, my own personal process is a kind of looking, and talking and observing, an interacting with different artists and friends, so I began writing letters to people I had dialogue with.
> All these short notes I was writing became a manuscript, and Francis read the manuscript and said, "This ought to be published ..." and it came out as a book called *Notes* in 1979....
> After the book came out, because it included personal aspects of our marriage relationship, at the time, for that time, for 1979, it was kind of revolutionary to speak truthfully about your marriage relationship in that way, and it embarrassed Francis, it made him uncomfortable, so it wasn't a happy publication, and he always, after the fact, resented it, and felt uncomfortable.
> In 1990 these young men who had been just teenagers when *Apocalypse Now* came out had heard these rumors there was documentary footage somewhere in storage and were so intrigued and interested ... and they came to Francis and said they wanted to see that footage and make something out of it, and they developed enough to get a deal with Showtime, and Showtime approached Francis and his company, and they had some money to pay for it, and Francis wouldn't have to pay for it, the development of the documentary, and he said yes, and these young men started to develop the documentary.

"I look at this *Hearts of Darkness* film and I see those shots of the skinny me, so amped up and talking about how I'm gonna make this as a super-audience action picture and what have you, you know the only interpretation I can have is that I indeed was really on the spot, and scared, and didn't have many people to talk to about this, or gain some sort of solace," recalled Coppola. "I would come home at night to my wife and I would say, 'Oh, Eleanor, this is gonna be the worst movie in history, it's gonna be terrible, I'm gonna get an F, it's a failure,' and she would say 'Oh, would you wait just one second until I get the camera and then say it again.' Of course what I was hoping for was she was gonna say, 'Oh, Francis no, it's not gonna be a failure, it's gonna be a wonderful film, it's all right, I have faith in you.' I guess that's one of the consequences of having your wife be the filming documentarian working on your film, but I was scared, and clearly had more on my plate than I ever imagined I would."

"I felt his creative process was so out front, was so prevalent, it placed every moment of our lives out there in the Philippines so that when he started off about his problems I felt it was totally appropriate to bring out the tape recorder, turn on the camera, and whatever was available to record the process, because it just went on day and night during his experience here," said Eleanor.

"I was so sure I was gonna lose it," Coppola said on *Hearts of Darkness* of his fear of losing his Napa home.

"His process was sort of front and center in his mind and he could go forward with his dialogue in his mind," said Eleanor. She said the "understanding" with Francis was he would have "final control" over it. If he did not feel comfortable about something that was "ultimately embarrassing to him" he could edit it out. Therefore he felt he could say what he wanted and could control what ended up in the documentary onscreen.

"I reacted with a degree of embarrassment because the film is essentially of me, in which I'm trying to work and struggle with whatever your struggles are, and you're being eavesdropped on," said Coppola. "When we had the film *Hearts of Darkness*, it was made for Showtime, and the idea was it would be shown on television twice, and that was the end of it, and although there were parts of it I found very embarrassing, just like anybody you can look at photographs taken of you and say, 'Oh, I don't like that photograph, it makes me look funny' or 'I don't like the way I look,' but on *Hearts of Darkness* I thought it would be shown twice on television and that's the end of it, and I saw that the filmmakers, George Hickenlooper and Fax Bahr, and Ellie's work, and what your editor Jay Miracle had done, they'd done such a terrific job on the film, I thought who was I to let my ego stand in the way?"

The filmmakers added new material, interviews or reflections with key people, done in 1990. "The documentary was clearly taking a new turn, aided by Fax Bahr and his associates," said Eleanor.

"My behavior at Cannes that begins the Cannes Film Festival is really embarrassing to me, I'm speaking in such a clearly exaggerated way," said Coppola. "I'm embarrassed by that. I'm a person easily embarrassed, I think it comes from the kind of youth I had being the new kid in school all the time, being the kid named Francis, so I'm easily embarrassed, and *Hearts of Darkness* embarrasses me."

"We were in the jungle, there were too many of us, we had access to too much money, too much equipment—and little by little we went insane," said Coppola of *Apocalypse Now* in *Hearts of Darkness*.

"The section concerning Martin Sheen's heart attack particularly embarrassed me," said Coppola. "I hold Martin Sheen in very high regard, his family and his wife, and the last thing I felt or wanted depicted as was being callous as to something so serious as his heart attack, and that was one of the sections of *Hearts of Darkness* that used to upset me, because I didn't feel the documentary made clear what the circumstances were and what was going on at the time, and if I'm doing this commentary at all it's mainly for that reason, it was to explain what was really going on at that moment...."

"It was the first time people in the film industry could see me beyond being just Francis Coppola's wife, they could see me as a thinking, real person, and that helped a lot, because in the film business, the entertainment world, the spouse is this kind of invisible person who's shifted to the side, and the wives and husbands of the person who is with this famous person is always in this awkward position," said Eleanor of *Hearts of Darkness*. "The responses I got from people in the industry and beyond the industry gave me a sense that they could see me as a person instead of just the wife of.... Gene Siskel put it on his lists of the best films of that year ... that was really touching."

In recent years, Coppola said *Hearts of Darkness* should have been called "Watch Francis Suffer." For him it was an embarrassment that the documentary, originally filmed "in house," had been given wide distribution.

On his wife's documentary, Coppola expressed the hope that technology would make it so "for once this whole professionalism about movies will be destroyed forever," and it will "really become an art form. That's my opinion." *Hearts of Darkness: A Filmmaker's Apocalypse* is one of the great filmmaking documentaries of all time.[5]

Francis Ford Coppola was the ultimate survivor. He always tried to maintain independence from Hollywood. Ultimately he failed to truly achieve this, certainly not in the wholesale way his protégé George Lucas most assuredly did.

Coppola tried to buy UA but did not succeed. He bought Hollywood General Studios, a mid-size company on a corner lot at Santa Monica Boulevard and Las Palmas, in 1980 for $6.7 million. Spielberg refused to join in. Lucas said he was still in trouble with *The Empire Strikes Back* and said no. "It's like your brother wouldn't help you out," said Mona Skager, Coppola's producer.

"Some people have that kind of generosity in their nature, it's easy for them," Coppola said. "For other people, it's just not. I don't think George is wired that way."

"Francis helped me and gave me a chance, but at the same time he made a lot of money off me," reasoned Lucas. "Francis has a tendency to see the parade marching down the street and to run in front of it with a flag and become the leader." He also was not impressed that Coppola bought a studio in L.A., in "enemy territory." That was "betraying all of us in San Francisco."[6]

Coppola thought he was the master of the new techniques Lucas was indeed bringing into the business, although in truth it was his people at Industrial Light & Magic, some of whom were underpaid and left because of it, who were the real masters and innovators. In some ways Lucas was like Steve Jobs, who was a great salesman while Steve Wozniak and others were the real wizards of Apple. Coppola bragged to *Newsweek* that he would control the business through his new technology. Coppola actually had been the man with the early technological vision, and in fact was the guy who personally learned how to use all the equipment on a set. But Lucas was the better businessman. Coppola brought in a lot of Europeans and signed long-term contracts, spending money he did not have. The venture failed.

"*Apocalypse Now* was totally financed outside of the establishment," said Coppola. "People felt that if directors started to realize that all they needed to do was that, there would be no place for the traditional hierarchy of agents and studios. Zoetrope was considered a threat. With my interest in technology, my studio was a dangerous precedent. And someone who (a) made the kind of megalomaniac comments that I did, and (b) actually was doing it, I think you have to brand a person like that a little bit of a nut."[7] He said the man who made *The Godfather* died in the jungle.

After that, Coppola worked as a director for hire. He produced and directed some good films, but the promise of greatness found in the heady days of *Patton*, two *Godfathers*, then *Apocalypse Now*, was gone along with the Hollywood that never returned, either. In many ways Coppola's career arc resembled Orson Welles, the man who first wanted to make *Heart of Darkness*.

"Before *The Godfather*, he was a nobody," said Al Ruddy. "After, he was one of the most important directors in the world. Nobody is prepared for a trip that heavy. He got very caught up in being the kind of man that Charlie Bluhdorn was. He lost some of his focus, was another example of a director destroyed by living the movie."[8]

After *The Cotton Club*, Coppola wanted Marlon Brando for the lead role in *Tucker: The Man and His Dream*. The actor originally agreed to play him, but it did not work out. He made *The Godfather III* in 1990. Unfortunately, Robert Duvall could not reach a financial agreement to again play the role of the Corleone family *consigliore*, Tom Hagen. The idea was that the power of the family would now go to him, with some very interesting possibilities inherent. Without him, it was a creditable film and decent tale of Vatican corruption, but anybody looking to recapture the magic of the first two was disappointed.

Coppola cast his daughter, Sofia, in a key role opposite Andy Garcia. She was roundly criticized for her performance. While nobody was going to confuse her with Diane Keaton, she was not nearly as bad as many claimed. The criticism seemed more personal and aimed at Coppola by his many detractors, not a few of whom had been jilted by him over the years. He helped produce several films Sofia directed, and she turned out to be a respected filmmaker in her own right. Coppola's well-known nepotism paid dividends in the long run—his father's Oscar for *The Godfather II*, Talia Shire's stardom, and Nicolas Cage (who had changed his last name to avoid the nepotism charge), who certainly earned his stripes. Eleanor's documentary proved she was an artist, as well.

After the publication of Norman Mailer's *Harlot's Ghost*, in the early 1990s Coppola announced he was going to make a sweeping saga of the Central Intelligence Agency. He did not direct *The Good Shepherd* (2006) starring Matt Damon, but it was a Zoetrope project. Probably too complicated for most filmgoers, it nevertheless holds up as one of the greatest CIA movies.

"The stuff that brought it all to an end came from within," said John Milius. "[Jeff] Diller, [Michael] Eisner, and [Jeffrey] Katzenberg—they ruined the movies." A story pitch all became "twenty-five words or less," as depicted in *The Player* (1992).[9]

The best barometer of this statement, and the determination that the 1970s built on the 1960s as the two greatest of all Hollywood decades, and that all that followed was mediocre in comparison, is to walk around a video store (if one can be found) or scroll just-released movies on-demand. *Nada*. Today, the real talent is in cable television, mainly at Home Box Office (HBO), Showtime, FX, and American Movie Classics (AMC). To a lesser extent it can be found in the sports documentaries made by ESPN, plus the online content found at Netflix, Amazon Instant Video, and even YouTube. Hollywood is lucky to make one or two fairly good Christmas movies. Summertime, the old standby when some of the best films hit the screen, comes and goes with nothing worth the price of admission. Academy Award winners are a joke, as is the entire Oscar ceremony, which strikes the religious as little more than pagan worship of idols, as in the golden calf of the Old Testament. The political favoritism of liberal Hollywood is so obvious, so ill advised, and results in such bad choices on- and offscreen, as to render the industry a parody of itself.

Outside of the young, who find their entertainment on the Internet and through social media, and do not know much better, real movie buffs revert most often to the classics that the New Hollywood gifted the world, which all stand up as just as good today as when they were released, and as if a spigot were turned off, simply stopped making for a variety of reasons. Capitalism is not its downfall, since as so many have always said, "Show biz is not a business."

Even black-and-white classics like *The Longest Day*, *The Manchurian Candidate*, *Seven Days in May*, and *Dr. Strangelove*, like other great movies that followed—*Patton*, *Chinatown*, *Apocalypse Now*—do not just hold up as drama, but offer production value and sound quality that, no matter the technological innovations George Lucas ushered in, are as excellent as anything the industry currently produces. There have been few sequels and no remakes that can be mentioned in the same breath.

"None of us were prepared for the '80s," said Margot Kidder. "Our heads were still in the '70s, and we were at sea in a business run by young agents with blow-dried hairdos." Terence Malick disappeared for twenty years until *The Thin Red Line*. Coppola's *One From the Heart*, and *The Cotton Club*, produced by Evans, were flops. *The Two Jakes*, which actually featured Evans *acting* in a sequel to *Chinatown*, was a disaster. John Belushi died on March 5, 1982.

Art houses still exist in large-population communities. Art films do get shown at Cineplexes. Companies like Miramax and Fine Line grew out of the 1970s blockbusters. Independent film probably reached its heyday with Quentin Tarantino's *Reservoir Dogs* and *Pulp Fiction* in the early 1990s.

Peter Biskind's *Easy Riders, Raging Bulls* generally backs this premise, but both Robert Altman and Martin Scorsese disagreed. Altman went to see movies in 1997–98, complaining, "There wasn't one picture an intelligent person could say, 'Oh, I want to see this.' It's just become an amusement park. It's the death of film."

Altman's conclusion ignored the best work of Spielberg: *Schindler's List* (1993) and *Saving Private Ryan* (1998), but in the 1960s and 1970s movies of that breadth and scope came out every year, sometimes more than once a year. Those two films were five years apart, and in the succeeding eighteen years since *Saving Private Ryan* and *The Thin Red Line*, arguably nothing like it has hit the screen. Instead, movies designed for busy mothers to sit through and keep four eight-year-olds amused for an hour and a half get the budgets and the marketing.

"Right now, I'm just disgusted by the American film industry," Marcia Lucas remarked. "There are so few good films, and part of me thinks *Star Wars* is partly responsible for the direction the industry has gone in, and I feel badly about that."[10]

Today, when film connoisseurs check new movies on Comcast on-demand, weeks often pass and nothing worth seeing appears. Desperate, these film buffs do searches and see *The Graduate*, or *Patton* ... or *Apocalypse Now*. Somehow, the education system and social media have created a world in which the more information people have at their disposal, the more people go to college, the dumber they are. The old days, when John Milius grew up reading Greek mythology, the classics, poetry, rugged novels describing individual heroism; those kinds of men do not exist anymore, and Hollywood is a near-joke as a result of it.

There are some talents. David Fincher is one. He grew up as George Lucas's neighbor in San Anselmo, delivering newspapers to his house. But his talents have yet to produce anything close to a classic movie.

"Today we have the news that Ingmar Bergman died, and I believe tomorrow they'll have the news that Michelangelo Antonioni died," Coppola lamented on *Hearts of Darkness*. "Bergman, Kurosawa, are now gone, and now Antonioni is gone. What is the hope of the cinema? 'The horror, the horror.'"

According to *The Cinema of George Lucas* by Marcus Hearn, foreword written by Ron Howard, as of 2005, since 1965 when Lucas completed his first year at USC, only two years had passed in which at least one USC graduate had not been nominated for an Oscar.

Caleb Deschanel had four Academy Award nominations for cinematography. Walter Murch coined the term sound designer. Robert Dalva was nominated for cinematography for his work on *The Black Stallion* and *Jurassic Park*. Howard Kazanjian and Charles Lippincott both became producers with Lucas and outside LucasFilm. Donald Glut and Christopher Lewis featured exploitation cinema. Basil Poledouris worked as a composer of film music, scoring *Conan the Barbarian*. Randal Kleiser made *Grease* (1978) and *The Blue Lagoon* (1980). Taylor Hackford directed *An Officer and a Gentleman* (1982), *The Devil's*

Advocate (1997), and many others. Producer Kerry McCluggage oversaw numerous TV hits and is developing *One Night, Two Teams: Alabama vs. USC and the Game That Changed a Nation*, the story of the 1970 USC-Alabama football game, credited with ending segregation in the Southeastern Conference once and for all. A Milius protégé, Bryan Singer, directed *The Usual Suspects*.

Marlo Thomas, John Ritter, Ally Sheedy, Forrest Whittaker, Will Ferrell, John Singleton, David L. Wolper, Darren Cole, Marilyn Horne, Herb Alpert, Lionel Hampton, Jerry Goldsmith, producer Barney Rosenzweig, *Mad Men* impresario Mathew Weiner, and *The OC* creator Josh Schwartz are all Trojans. Many credit famed cinema instructor Andrew Casper. Producer Ron Schwary, a USC classmate of Lucas and Milius, won an Oscar for *Ordinary People*, beating out *Raging Bull* for Best Picture of 1980. In 1982, Schwary won a second Oscar for producing *Tootsie*.

Aside from Francis Ford Coppola, Jim Morrison, and Paul Schrader, UCLA alumni include director Rob Reiner; producers Harve Bennett and Frank Marshall; actors James Dean, Carol Burnett, Beau Bridges, Lloyd Bridges, Tim Robbins, Corbin Bernson, Michael Warren, Steve Martin, and George Takei; Academy Award-winning cinematographer Dean Cundey; Grammy Award-winning singer Marilyn McCoo; singer/composer Randy Newman; Tony Award-winning composer John Rubinstein; and Emmy Award-winning producer Gene Reynolds. John Williams, who scored so many of Steven Spielberg's films, attended UCLA but taught at USC. According to rumor, Tom Cruise was set to enroll at USC until *Risky Business* (1983) made him a movie star.

USC has leaped far ahead of UCLA in recent years. Many credit this with the decision to offer a producer's discipline, which has mated so many writers and directors with producers and agents, all with Trojan connections. While USC dominates the industry, Hollywood has never come close to replicating the glory years of George Lucas, John Milius, Francis Ford Coppola, Jim Morrison, Paul Schrader, Steven Spielberg, and the film school "brats" who make up the New Hollywood emerging in the 1960s, continuing into the 1970s, but abruptly changing direction in the 1980s, never to make films with the same kind of character and dramatic narrative again.

"There's this dangerous extreme with some film school kids," Trea Troving, of Miramax, explained. "They are so pumped up with craft and camera technique that they forget the basics of good story telling."

"Guys who worked in video stores have seen a lot more films than us, especially Quentin with that Hong Kong stuff," Rory Kelly of the USC archives said, referring to Quentin Tarantino. "But there is a big difference between watching a clean print on a big screen and watching a video."[11]

In 1981, after some spiritual moments with Terence Malick, Martin Sheen re-joined Catholicism. "I surrendered to my own humanity and found a way to live an honest life," he said. After that he became very involved in what he called "social justice."[12] His career took off. He is still active today, considered one of the finest actors of his generation. Despite a magnificent body of work, nothing comes close to his performance in *Apocalypse Now*.

Laurence Fishburne has gone on to enjoy a long, productive career. G. D. Spradlin and Albert Hall remained working actors. Sam Bottoms had health troubles, possibly caused by the conditions he lived in on the *Apocalypse* set, and died in 2008. His brother Timothy has enjoyed success. R. Lee Ermey, the Eagle Thrust helicopter pilot, is now synonymous with playing tough-guy military characters. Charlie Sheen, an uncredited extra, starred in *Red Dawn*, *Platoon*, and *Wall Street*. Hollywood tried to make Frederick Forrest into a star based on his role in *Apocalypse Now*, but it did not materialize.

Harrison Ford became one of the biggest movie stars in the world. Robert Duvall practically re-invented his Colonel Kilgore role, essentially playing Kilgore in peace time in *The Great Santini*. Dennis Hopper got clean, starred in *Hoosiers*, and had a long, successful career after 1979. Scott Glenn became a big-time star, known especially for his role as a Naval officer in *The Hunt For Red October*, largely written by John Milius. Marlon Brando made questionable choices, but reprised his role as a Mafia Don, with a comedic turn, in *The Freshman* (1990).

"Who else would have done, *could* have done *Apocalypse Now*; the passion in *Apocalypse is* so incredible, it's a film of passion on every level?" said Irvin Kershner, George Lucas's professor at USC whom he hired to direct *The Empire Strikes Back*.

"*Apocalypse Now* was like no other war movie that ever came out of Hollywood," remarked Caleb Deschanel. "The Vittorio Storaro photography is so extraordinary, and you know visually it's so stunning, it's a very seductive movie because of its beauty. The scene when the napalm explodes, it's almost like candy, the idea that Francis takes into almost seducing you into loving war, then dragging you along until you suddenly realize you've been seduced into loving something that's really horrible."

"The sound format for *Apocalypse Now*, which was a one-off—there was nothing like it before—is now the standard for motion pictures and for home video; the 5.1 sound," said Walter Murch. "It had to be carefully designed in order to take advantage of this new environment. I still have some of the charts that indicate the three-dimension parameters of the sound placed in the film."

"I remember vividly coming out of that movie thinking, the sound in that movie, who did the sound?" recalled writer Anthony Minghella. "It's unbelievable how that movie sounds, it was unlike anything I've ever experienced."

"In a way I could really relate when Francis made *Apocalypse Now*," Steven Spielberg said. "When Hollywood was calling Francis self-indulgent, I was just looking at Francis saying, *Well, he's just a human being going through what we went through on* Jaws."[13]

Apocalypse Now is a movie that cannot be replicated. The kinds of computer graphics and tricks utilized by Steven Spielberg in making *Saving Private Ryan* (many invented by George Lucas's ILM) have changed filmmaking. Today, a movie depicting a large stadium full of fans does not need an actual large stadium filled with fans; computers will do the trick. But the kind of realism depicted by Francis Ford Coppola's amazing direction of helicopter attack scenes, river battles, and a journey through a real jungle, using actors living that very existence, while so difficult nobody would of sane mind try to duplicate it, are great beyond measure, making his masterpiece something that stands far above all other consideration.

The classic education of John Milius, who brilliantly envisioned setting *Heart of Darkness* in Vietnam, is likely not to return in a world dominated by smart phones and apps that have made his kind of romantic mind a thing of the past.

On April 8, 2010, John Milius visited Francis Ford Coppola at his Napa Valley winery. Cameras were set up, and Coppola interviewed the great screenwriter about the classic film they made together.

Milius: You re-defined the whole image of the director, this guy strutting around the set … that was the original image of the director. Then it became the French New Wave director, now to be a real director you have to be able to put all your money on the line, go off to some horrible place, where there was a strong possibility you would not come back, and it had to be malarial, this horrible situation, and you have to be knee deep in a swamp.

Coppola: And you had to put your sanity at stake.

Milius: You had at some point in it be convinced you had lost your sanity.

Coppola: That's all John Milius [all the great lines]. I was not involved in the original writing of the script *Apocalypse Now*; it was you and George Lucas.

Milius: People should go back and read the original reviews of *Apocalypse Now*, because there are no good ones.

Coppola: Read *Variety*'s review of *The Godfather*. Young filmmakers, remember, these movies come out that might be considered a failure, but real success is later, when people go see it.

Milius: You cannot ever give up. Realize that is the top quality of people, I say the greatest quality of a director is the tendency, to be able to overcome sleep depression. You have to be like Geronimo, keep going, [making] great movies, every one can tell a story, they'll bury you, there's times you'll want to kill yourself; don't worry until the seventh time.[14]

"This is … the end."

Chapter Notes

Chapter 1

1. Peter Biskind, *Easy Riders, Raging Bulls: How the Sex-Drugs-and-Rock 'n' Roll Generation Saved Hollywood* (New York: Simon & Schuster, 1998), p. 375.
2. Joseph Conrad, *Heart of Darkness* (New York: Alfred A. Knopf, Inc., 1902), p. 1.
3. *Ibid.*, p. 2.
4. en.wikipedia.org/wiki/Heart_of_Darkness.
5. Harold Bloom, *Joseph Conrad's Heart of Darkness* (Infobase Publishing. ISBN 1438117108., ed., 2009), p. 15.
6. Chunua Achebe, Lecture (University of Massachusetts, Amherst, 1975).
7. *Hearts of Darkness: A Filmmaker's Apocalypse.*
8. Bret Wood, *Orson Welles: A Bio-Bibliography* (Westport, CT: Greenwood Press, 1990), p. 137.
9. *Milius.* Epix Original, directed by Joey Figueroa and Zak Knutson, Amazon Instant Video (http://www.amazon.com/Milius-Steven-Spielberg/dp/B00JM7IVFS/ref=sr_1_1?s=instant-video&ie=UTF8&qid=1426809901&sr=1-1&keywords=milius, 2013).
10. *Apocalypse Now—John Milius interviewed by Francis Ford Coppola,* YouTube (https://www.youtube.com/watch?v=JZswrVALi2M, 2010).
11. *Ibid.*
12. *Ibid.*

Chapter 2

1. Michael Schumacher, *Francis Ford Coppola: A Filmmaker's Life* (New York: Crown, 1999), p. 5.
2. *Ibid.*
3. *Ibid.*, p. 6.
4. *Ibid.*, p. 8.
5. Jim Murray, *Jim Murray: The Autobiography of the Pulitzer Prize Winning Sports Columnist* (New York: Macmillan Publishing Co., 1993), p. 3.
6. Schumacher, *Francis Ford Coppola: A Filmmaker's Life*, p. 13.
7. *Ibid.*, p. 17.
8. *Ibid.*
9. *Ibid.*
10. *Ibid.*
11. Ladislas Farago, *Patton: Ordeal and Triumph* (Yardley, PA: Westholme Publishing, 2005), p. 10.
12. John Matthew Smith, *The Sons of Westwood: John Wooden, UCLA, and the Dynasty That Changed College Basketball* (Urbana: University of Illinois Press, 2013), p. 17.
13. Bob Woodward and Carl Bernstein, *All the President's Men: The Greatest Reporting Story of All Time* (New York: Simon & Schuster, 2014), p. 116.
14. Bruce Jenkins, *A Good Man: The Pete Newell Story* (Lincoln, NE: University of Nebraska Board of Regents, 1999), p. 150.
15. Leo Verswijver, *"Movies Were Always Magical": Interviews With 19 Actors, Directors and Producers From the Hollywood of the 1930s Through the 1950s* (Jefferson, NC: McFarland, 2003), p. 68
16. *Milius.* Epix Original, directed by Joey Figueroa and Zak Knutson, Amazon Instant Video (http://www.amazon.com/Milius-Steven-Spielberg/dp/B00JM7IVFS/ref=sr_1_1?s=instant-video&ie=UTF8&qid=1426809901&sr=1-1&keywords=milius, 2013).
17. Schumacher, *Francis Ford Coppola: A Filmmaker's Life*, p. 18.
18. Dale Pollock, *Skywalking: The Life and Films of George Lucas* (New York: Harmony Books, 1983), p. 120.
19. Norman F. Cantor and Mindy Cantor, *The American Century: Varieties of Culture in Modern Times* (New York: HarperPerennial, 1998), p. 367.
20. Peter Biskind, Easy, *Easy Riders, Raging Bulls: How the Sex-Drugs-and-Rock 'n' Roll Generation Saved Hollywood* (New York: Simon & Schuster, 1998), p. 13.
21. Schumacher, *Francis Ford Coppola: A Filmmaker's Life*, p. 19.
22. *Ibid.*
23. *Ibid.*
24. *Ibid.*, p. 20.
25. *Ibid.*
26. *Fog City Mavericks.* Directed by Gary Leva. Burbank, Calif: Alpha Dog Productions, 2007.
27. Schumacher, *Francis Ford Coppola: A Filmmaker's Life*, p. 20.
28. Biskind, *Easy Riders, Raging Bulls*, p. 16.
29. Schumacher, *Francis Ford Coppola: A Filmmaker's Life*, p. 20.
30. *Fog City Mavericks.*
31. Schumacher, *Francis Ford Coppola: A Filmmaker's Life*, p. 20.
32. *Ibid.*
33. *Ibid.*
34. *Ibid.*
35. *Seven Minutes Film, The,* https://en.wikipedia.org/wiki/The_Seven_Minutes_(film).
36. Schumacher, *Francis Ford Coppola: A Filmmaker's Life*, p. 24.
37. *Ibid.*
38. *Ibid.*

39. *Ibid.*, p. 25.
40. *Ibid.*, p. 27.
41. *Ibid.*
42. *Ibid.*, p. 30.
43. *Ibid.*, p. 31.
44. *Ibid.*
45. Robert K. Johnson, *Francis Ford Coppola* (Boston: Twayne Publishers, 1977), p. 33.
46. *Ibid.*
47. Schumacher, *Francis Ford Coppola: A Filmmaker's Life*, p. 36.
48. *Ibid.*, p. 37.
49. *Apocalypse Now—John Milius interviewed by Francis Ford Coppola*, YouTube (https://www.youtube.com/watch?v=JZswrVALi2M, 2010).
50. Schumacher, *Francis Ford Coppola: A Filmmaker's Life*, p. 38.
51. *Ibid.*
52. *Ibid.*, p. 39.
53. *Ibid.*
54. *Ibid.*, p. 40.
55. *Ibid.*
56. Biskind, *Easy Riders, Raging Bulls*, p. 36.
57. *Ibid.*
58. *Ibid.*, p. 37.
59. *Ibid.*, p. 36.
60. Marcus Hearn, *The Cinema of George Lucas* (New York: Harry N. Abrams, 2005), p. 35.
61. Biskind, *Easy Riders, Raging Bulls*, p. 38
62. *Ibid.*
63. Schumacher, *Francis Ford Coppola: A Filmmaker's Life*, p. 41.

Chapter 3

1. Marcus Hearn, *The Cinema of George Lucas* (New York: Harry N. Abrams, 2005), p. 10.
2. *Ibid.*, p. 11.
3. *San Francisco Chronicle*, May 23, 1971.
4. Judy Stone, *Eye on the World: Conversations with International Filmmakers* (Los Angeles: Silman-James Press, 1997), p. 715.
5. Sally Kline, ed., *George Lucas: Interviews* (Oxford, MS: University of Mississippi Press, 1999), p. 5.
6. Kline, *George Lucas: Interviews*, p. 5.
7. D. L. Mabery, *George Lucas* (Minneapolis, MN: Lerner, 1987), p. 10.
8. Dana White, *George Lucas* (Minneapolis, MN: Lerner Hardcover, 1999), p. 19.
9. *Los Angeles* magazine, May 1999, p. 51.
10. Randy Roberts and James S. Olson, *John Wayne: American* (Lincoln, NE: Bison Books, 1997), p. 55.
11. White, *George Lucas*, p. 10.
12. Bill Lee and Richard Lally, *The Wrong Stuff* (New York: Three Rivers Press, 2006), p. 22.
13. Steven Travers, *What It Means to Be a Trojan: Southern Cal's Greatest Players Talk About Trojans Football.* (Chicago: Triumph Books, 2009), p. 116.
14. Hearn, *The Cinema of George Lucas*, p. 18.
15. Chris Salewicz, *George Lucas: The Making of His Movies* (New York: Thunder's Mouth Press, 1999), p. 14.
16. Hearn, *The Cinema of George Lucas*, p. 13.
17. *Fog City Mavericks*, directed by Gary Leva (Burbank, CA: Alpha Dog Productions, 2007).
18. Charles Champlin, *George Lucas: The Creative Impulse* (New York: Harry N. Abrams, 1992), p. 18.
19. Hearn, *The Cinema of George Lucas*, p. 13.
20. Hearn, *The Cinema of George Lucas*, p. 104.
21. *Fog City Mavericks*.
22. Salewicz, *George Lucas: The Making of His Movies*, p. 15.
23. Hearn, *The Cinema of George Lucas*, p. 14.
24. Champlin, *George Lucas: The Creative Impulse*, p. 23.
25. Steven Travers, *One Night, Two Teams: Alabama vs. USC and the Game That Changed a Nation* (Lanham, MD: Taylor Trade, 2007), p. 227.
26. *Fog City Mavericks*.
27. White, *George Lucas*, p. 23.
28. *Ibid.*, p. 25.
29. Richard Schickel, *Steven Spielberg: A Retrospective* (New York: Sterling, 2012), p. 17.
30. Joseph McBride, *Spielberg: A Biography* (New York: Simon & Schuster, 1997), p. 146.
31. 19. Hearn, *The Cinema of George Lucas*, p. 15.
32. 19. Hearn, *The Cinema of George Lucas*, p. 105.
33. White, *George Lucas*, p. 30.
34. 19. Hearn, *The Cinema of George Lucas*, p. 106.
35. Michael Schumacher, *Francis Ford Coppola: A Filmmaker's Life* (New York: Crown, 1999), p. 58, 72.
36. *Fog City Mavericks*.
37. Hearn, *The Cinema of George Lucas*, p. 107.
38. *Ibid.*

Chapter 4

1. Jerry Hopkins and Danny Sugarman, *No One Here Gets Out Alive* (New York: Warner Books, 1995), p. 90.
2. *Ibid.*, p. 90.
3. *Ibid.*, p. 9.
4. *Ibid.*, p. 15.
5. *Ibid.*, p. 95.
6. *Ibid.*, p. 19.
7. *Ibid.*, p. 96.
8. Dylan Jones, *Jim Morrison, Dark Star* (New York: Viking, 1992), p. 194.
9. Hopkins and Sugarman, *No One Here Gets Out Alive*, p. 22.
10. Jones, *Jim Morrison*, p. 194.
11. Hopkins and Sugarman, *No One Here Gets Out Alive*, p. 96.
12. *Ibid.*, p. 96.
13. *Ibid.*, p. 97.
14. *Ibid.*, p. 100.
15. *Ibid.*, p. 23.
16. *Ibid.*, p. 25.
17. *Ibid.*, p. 100.
18. *Ibid.*, p. 101.
19. *Ibid.*, p. 28.

Chapter 5

1. John Andrew Gallagher: *Film Directors on Directing* (Westport, CT: Praeger, 1989), p. 169.
2. *Milius*. Epix Original, directed by Joey Figueroa and Zak Knutson, Amazon Instant Video (http://www.amazon.com/Milius-Steven-Spielberg/dp/B00JM7IVFS/

ref=sr_1_1?s=instant-video&ie=UTF8&qid=1426809901&sr=1-1&keywords=milius, 2013).
3. Gallagher, *Film Directors on Directing*, p. 169.
4. *Ibid.*, p. 170.
5. *Apocalypse Now—John Milius interviewed by Francis Ford Coppola*, YouTube (https://www.youtube.com/watch?v=JZswrVALi2M, 2010).
6. *Milius*. Epix Original.
7. Gallagher: *Film Directors on Directing*, p. 170.
8. *Milius*. Epix Original.
9. *Ibid.*
10. *Milius*. Epix Original.
11. Joseph McBride, *Spielberg: A Biography* (New York: Simon & Schuster, 1997), p. 136.
12. *John Milius on How Hollywood Liberals are Blacklisting Conservatives*—YouTube (https://www.youtube.com/watch?v=yQljnlWW9j4, 2011).
13. *Milius*. Epix Original.
14. *Ibid.*
15. *Ibid.*
16. *Ibid.*
17. *Milius*. Epix Original.
18. McBride, *Spielberg: A Biography*, p. 136.
19. *Milius*. Epix Original.
20. *Apocalypse Now—John Milius interviewed by Francis Ford Coppola*, You Tube (https://www.youtube.com/watch?v=JZswrVALi2M, 2010).
21. *Milius*. Epix Original.
22. Peter Biskind, *Easy Riders, Raging Bulls: How the Sex-Drugs-and-Rock 'n' Roll Generation Saved Hollywood* (New York: Simon & Schuster, 1998), p. 22.
23. *Milius*. Epix Original.
24. *Screenwriter John Milius on Apocalypse Now*—YouTube (https://www.youtube.com/watch?v=5v-G_c4f9RM, 2006).
25. *Milius*. Epix Original.
26. *Ibid.*
27. *Ibid.*
28. *Ibid.*

Chapter 6

1. *Screenwriter John Milius on Apocalypse Now*—YouTube (https://www.youtube.com/watch?v=5v-G_c4f9RM, 2006).
2. Peter Biskind, *Easy Riders, Raging Bulls: How the Sex-Drugs-and-Rock 'n' Roll Generation Saved Hollywood* (New York: Simon & Schuster, 1998), p. 96.
3. *Ibid.*, p. 81.
4. *Fog City Mavericks*. Directed by Gary Leva (Burbank, CA: Alpha Dog Productions, 2007).
5. Marcus Hearn, *The Cinema of George Lucas* (New York: Harry N. Abrams, 2005), p. 31.
6. Michael Schumacher, *Francis Ford Coppola: A Filmmaker's Life* (New York: Crown, 1999), p. 67.
7. *Fog City Mavericks*.
8. Biskind, *Easy Riders, Raging Bulls*, p. 96.
9. *Ibid.*, p. 97.
10. *Ibid.*
11. *Ibid.*, pp. 90–93.
12. *Ibid.*, p. 97.
13. Schumacher, *Francis Ford Coppola: A Filmmaker's Life*, p. 85.
14. D. L. Mabery, *George Lucas* (Minneapolis, MN: Lerner, 1987), p. 12.
15. Sally Kline, ed., *George Lucas: Interviews* (Oxford, MS: University of Mississippi Press, 1999), p. 9.
16. Janet Riehecky, *George Lucas: An Unauthorized Biography* (Chicago: Heinemann Library, 2001), p. 22.
17. *Fog City Mavericks*.
18. Biskind, *Easy Riders, Raging Bulls*, p. 98.
19. Schumacher, *Francis Ford Coppola: A Filmmaker's Life*, p. 45.
20. *Ibid.*, p. 99.
21. *Fog City Mavericks*.
22. Schumacher, *Francis Ford Coppola: A Filmmaker's Life*, p. 45.
23. Biskind, *Easy Riders, Raging Bulls*, p. 52.
24. Biskind, *Easy Riders, Raging Bulls*, p. 53.
25. Biskind, *Easy Riders, Raging Bulls*, pp. 100–101.
26. Schumacher, *Francis Ford Coppola: A Filmmaker's Life*, p. 85.
27. *Fog City Mavericks*.
28. Biskind, *Easy Riders, Raging Bulls*, p. 102.

Chapter 7

1. Jerry Hopkins and Danny Sugarman, *No One Here Gets Out Alive* (New York: Warner Books, 1995), p. 22.
2. *Ibid.*, p. 143.

Chapter 8

1. Robert K. Johnson, *Francis Ford Coppola* (Boston: Twayne, 1977), p. 33.
2. Nicholas Evan Sarantakes, *Making* Patton: *A Classic War Film's Epic Journey to the Silver Screen* (Lawrence: University of Kansas Press, 2012), p. 50.
3. Michael Schumacher, *Francis Ford Coppola: A Filmmaker's Life* (New York: Crown, 1999), p. 43.
4. Sarantakes, *Making* Patton, p. 59.
5. *Ibid.*, p. 57.
6. *Ibid.*, p. 84.
7. *Ibid.*, p. 51.
8. *Ibid.*, p. 143–144.
9. Steven Travers, *The Duke, the Longhorns, and Chairman Mao: John Wayne's Political Odyssey* (Lanham, MD: Taylor Trade, 2001), pp. 204–205.
10. Michael Munn, *John Wayne: The Man Behind the Myth* (New York: Penguin, 2005), p. 190.

Chapter 9

1. Joseph Conrad, *Heart of Darkness* (New York: Penguin Books, 1999), pp. 7–8.
2. *Apocalypse Now—John Milius interviewed by Francis Ford Coppola*, YouTube (https://www.youtube.com/watch?v=JZswrVALi2M, 2010).
3. John Andrew Gallagher, *Film Directors on Directing* (Westport, CT: Praeger, 1989), pp. 174–175.
4. *Apocalypse Now—John Milius interviewed by Francis Ford Coppola*, YouTube.
5. Eleanor Coppola, *Notes* (New York: Simon & Schuster, 1979), p. 17.
6. Michael Schumacher, *Francis Ford Coppola: A Filmmaker's Life* (New York: Crown, 1999), p. 57.

7. *Hearts of Darkness: A Filmmaker's Apocalypse* (San Francisco: Zoetrope Studios, 1991).
8. *Ibid.*
9. *Apocalypse Now—John Milius interviewed by Francis Ford Coppola*, YouTube.
10. Peter Cowie, *The Apocalypse Now Book* (New York: De Capo Press, 2000), p. 1.
11. *Apocalypse Now—John Milius interviewed by Francis Ford Coppola*, YouTube
12. Peter Biskind, *Easy Riders, Raging Bulls: How the Sex-Drugs-and-Rock 'n' Roll Generation Saved Hollywood*. (New York: Simon & Schuster, 1998), p. 93.
13. *Apocalypse Now—John Milius interviewed by Francis Ford Coppola*, YouTube
14. *Ibid.*
15. *Milius*. Epix Original, directed by Joey Figueroa and Zak Knutson, Amazon Instant Video.
16. Michael Schumacher, *Francis Ford Coppola: A Filmmaker's Life* (New York: Crown, 1999), p. 197.
17. *Apocalypse Now—Interview with John Milius*, YouTube (https://www.youtube.com/watch?v=i4nY2J1gRzg, 2015).
18. *Hearts of Darkness: A Filmmaker's Apocalypse*.
19. Schumacher, *Francis Ford Coppola: A Filmmaker's Life*, pp. 197–199.
20. *Fog City Mavericks*. Directed by Gary Leva (Burbank, CA: Alpha Dog Productions, 2007).
21. *Hearts of Darkness: A Filmmaker's Apocalypse*.
22. Schumacher, *Francis Ford Coppola: A Filmmaker's Life*, p. 199.
23. *Apocalypse Now—John Milius interviewed by Francis Ford Coppola*, YouTube.
24. *Ibid.*
25. *Hearts of Darkness: A Filmmaker's Apocalypse*.
26. *Apocalypse Now—John Milius interviewed by Francis Ford Coppola*, YouTube.
27. *Hearts of Darkness: A Filmmaker's Apocalypse*.
28. Schumacher, *Francis Ford Coppola: A Filmmaker's Life*, p. 56.
29. Schumacher, *Francis Ford Coppola: A Filmmaker's Life*, pp. 192–196.

Chapter 10

1. John Milius, *Apocalypse Now* screenplay (1975), p. 130.
2. *Hearts of Darkness: A Filmmaker's Apocalypse* (San Francisco: Zoetrope Studios, 1991).
3. Schumacher, *Francis Ford Coppola: A Filmmaker's Life*, p. 56.
4. *Hearts of Darkness: A Filmmaker's Apocalypse*.
5. Peter Biskind, *Easy Riders, Raging Bulls: How the Sex-Drugs-and-Rock 'n' Roll Generation Saved Hollywood* (New York: Simon & Schuster, 1998), p. 40.
6. Schumacher, *Francis Ford Coppola: A Filmmaker's Life*, pp. 189–193.
7. *Ibid.*, p. 243.
8. *Ibid.*, p. 48.
9. *Ibid.*, pp. 200–201.
10. *Apocalypse Now—John Milius interviewed by Francis Ford Coppola*, YouTube (https://www.youtube.com/watch?v=JZswrVALi2M, 2010).
11. Schumacher, *Francis Ford Coppola: A Filmmaker's Life*, p. 48.

12. Schumacher, *Francis Ford Coppola: A Filmmaker's Life*, pp. 200–201.
13. *Ibid.*, pp. 202–203.

Chapter 11

1. *Hearts of Darkness* (San Francisco: Zoetrope Studios, 1991).
2. Eleanor Coppola, *Notes* (New York: Simon & Schuster, 1979), p. 175.
3. *Hearts of Darkness* (San Francisco: Zoetrope Studios, 1991).
4. Joseph Conrad, *Heart of Darkness* (New York: Penguin Books, 1999), p. 4.
5. *Hearts of Darkness* (San Francisco: Zoetrope Studios, 1991).
6. Peter Biskind, *Easy Riders, Raging Bulls: How the Sex-Drugs-and-Rock 'n' Roll Generation Saved Hollywood*. (New York: Simon & Schuster, 1998), p. 347.
7. *Hearts of Darkness: A Filmmaker's Apocalypse*.
8. *Ibid.*
9. Michael Schumacher, *Francis Ford Coppola: A Filmmaker's Life* (New York: Crown, 1999), pp. 203–205.
10. *Ibid.*, p. 207.
11. *Hearts of Darkness: A Filmmaker's Apocalypse*.
12. *Ibid.*
13. Biskind, *Easy Riders, Raging Bulls*, p. 351.
14. *Hearts of Darkness: A Filmmaker's Apocalypse*.
15. Eleanor Coppola, *Notes* (New York: Simon & Schustrer, 1979), p. 49.
16. Schumacher, *Francis Ford Coppola: A Filmmaker's Life*, p. 221.
17. Biskind, *Easy Riders, Raging Bulls*, pp. 350–351.
18. *Hearts of Darkness: A Filmmaker's Apocalypse*.
19. *Ibid.*
20. *Hearts of Darkness: A Filmmaker's Apocalypse*.
21. Schumacher, *Francis Ford Coppola: A Filmmaker's Life*, p. 210.
22. *Hearts of Darkness: A Filmmaker's Apocalypse*.
23. Schumacher, *Francis Ford Coppola: A Filmmaker's Life*, p. 211.

Chapter 12

1. John Milius, *Apocalypse Now* screenplay (1975), p. 10.
2. Jean Valley, Rolling Stone (http://www.rollingstone.com/movies/features/martin-sheen-heart-of-darkness-heart-of-gold-19791101, 1979).
3. *Martin Sheen (Apocalypse Now)*, YouTube (https://www.youtube.com/watch?v=AFiFQZeYeTU, 2010).
4. *Hearts of Darkness: A Filmmaker's Apocalypse* (San Francisco: Zoetrope Studios, 1991).
5. Michael Schumacher, *Francis Ford Coppola: A Filmmaker's Life* (New York: Crown, 1999), pp. 210–213.
6. *Hearts of Darkness: A Filmmaker's Apocalypse*.
7. *Apocalypse Now—John Milius interviewed by Francis Ford Coppola*, YouTube (https://www.youtube.com/watch?v=JZswrVALi2M, 2010).
8. Schumacher, *Francis Ford Coppola: A Filmmaker's Life*, p. 221.
9. *Ibid.*, p. 221.
10. *Apocalypse Now—John Milius interviewed by Francis Ford Coppola*, YouTube.

Chapter 13

1. *Robert Duvall (Apocalypse Now)*, "Bob Costas Interview" (https://www.youtube.com/watch?v=ZWAkTFoKcpE, 1991).
2. *Apocalypse Now—John Milius interviewed by Francis Ford Coppola*, YouTube (https://www.youtube.com/watch?v=JZswrVALi2M, 2010).
3. *Robert Duvall (Apocalypse Now)*, "Bob Costas Interview."
4. *Hearts of Darkness: A Filmmaker's Apocalypse* (San Francisco: Zoetrope Studios, 1991).
5. *Robert Duvall (Apocalypse Now)*, "Bob Costas Interview."
6. *Apocalypse Now—John Milius interviewed by Francis Ford Coppola*, YouTube.
7. *Hearts of Darkness: A Filmmaker's Apocalypse.*

Chapter 14

1. Eleanor Coppola, *Notes* (New York: Simon & Schuster, 1979), p. 175.
2. *Martin Sheen (Apocalypse Now)*, You Tube (https://www.youtube.com/watch?v=AFiFQZeYeTU, 2010).
3. *Ibid.*
4. *Hearts of Darkness: A Filmmaker's Apocalypse* (San Francisco: Zoetrope Studios, 1991).
5. *Hearts of Darkness: A Filmmaker's Apocalypse* (San Francisco: Zoetrope Studios, 1991).
6. *Ibid.*

Chapter 15

1. Michael Schumacher, *Francis Ford Coppola: A Filmmaker's Life* (New York: Crown, 1999), p. 211.
2. *Apocalypse Now—John Milius interviewed by Francis Ford Coppola*, YouTube (https://www.youtube.com/watch?v=JZswrVALi2M, 2010).
3. *Hearts of Darkness: A Filmmaker's Apocalypse* (San Francisco: Zoetrope Studios, 1991).
4. *Ibid.*
5. Schumacher, *Francis Ford Coppola: A Filmmaker's Life*, p. 215.
6. *Apocalypse Now—John Milius interviewed by Francis Ford Coppola*, YouTube.
7. *Hearts of Darkness: A Filmmaker's Apocalypse.*
8. Michael Schumacher, *Francis Ford Coppola: A Filmmaker's Life* (New York: Crown, 1999), p. 210–213.
9. Peter Biskind, *Easy Riders, Raging Bulls: How the Sex-Drugs-and-Rock 'n' Roll Generation Saved Hollywood.* (New York: Simon & Schuster, 1998), pp. 356–358.
10. *Hearts of Darkness: A Filmmaker's Apocalypse.*
11. *Apocalypse Now—John Milius interviewed by Francis Ford Coppola*, YouTube.
12. *Hearts of Darkness: A Filmmaker's Apocalypse.*
13. Biskind, *Easy Riders, Raging Bulls*, p. 346.

Chapter 16

1. *Hearts of Darkness: A Filmmaker's Apocalypse* (San Francisco: Zoetrope Studios, 1991).
2. *Ibid.*
3. *Ibid.*
4. *Ibid.*
5. *Ibid.*
6. Michael Schumacher, *Francis Ford Coppola: A Filmmaker's Life* (New York: Crown, 1999), p. 87.
7. Peter Biskind, *Easy Riders, Raging Bulls: How the Sex-Drugs-and-Rock 'n' Roll Generation Saved Hollywood.* (New York: Simon & Schuster, 1998), p. 356.
8. Michael Schumacher, *Francis Ford Coppola: A Filmmaker's Life* (New York: Crown, 1999), p. 85.
9. Michael Schumacher, *Francis Ford Coppola: A Filmmaker's Life*, p. 122.
10. *Hearts of Darkness: A Filmmaker's Apocalypse.*

Chapter 17

1. *Hearts of Darkness: A Filmmaker's Apocalypse* (San Francisco: Zoetrope Studios, 1991).
2. *Ibid.*
3. *Apocalypse Now—John Milius interviewed by Francis Ford Coppola*, You Tube (https://www.youtube.com/watch?v=JZswrVALi2M, 2010).
4. *Hearts of Darkness: A Filmmaker's Apocalypse.*
5. Michael Schumacher, *Francis Ford Coppola: A Filmmaker's Life* (New York: Crown, 1999), p. 366.
6. *Apocalypse Now—John Milius interviewed by Francis Ford Coppola*, YouTube.
7. Schumacher, *Francis Ford Coppola: A Filmmaker's Life*, p. 235.

Chapter 18

1. Michael Schumacher, *Francis Ford Coppola: A Filmmaker's Life* (New York: Crown, 1999), p. 129.
2. *Ibid.*
3. *Ibid.*, p. 125.
4. *Ibid.*, p. 122.
5. *Ibid.*, p. 123.
6. *Ibid.*
7. Michael Schumacher, *Francis Ford Coppola: A Filmmaker's Life*, pp. 237–246.
8. *Ibid.*, pp. 244–245.
9. *Ibid.*, p. 246.
10. *Ibid.*, p. 247.
11. *Hearts of Darkness: A Filmmaker's Apocalypse* (San Francisco: Zoetrope Studios, 1991).
12. Schumacher, *Francis Ford Coppola: A Filmmaker's Life*, p. 248.
13. *Ibid.*, p. 248.

Chapter 19

1. *Hearts of Darkness: A Filmmaker's Apocalypse* (San Francisco: Zoetrope Studios, 1991).
2. Michael Schumacher, *Francis Ford Coppola: A Filmmaker's Life* (New York: Crown, 1999), p. 247.
3. Peter Biskind, *Easy Riders, Raging Bulls: How the Sex-Drugs-and-Rock 'n' Roll Generation Saved Hollywood.* (New York: Simon & Schuster, 1998), p. 375.
4. *Ibid.*

Chapter 20

1. Michael Schumacher, *Francis Ford Coppola: A Filmmaker's Life* (New York: Crown, 1999), pp. 256–259.

2. *Ibid.*, p. 259.
3. *Milius.* Epix Original, directed by Joey Figueroa and Zak Knutson, Amazon Instant Video (http://www.amazon.com/Milius-Steven-Spielberg/dp/B00JM7IVFS/ref=sr_1_1?s=instant-video&ie=UTF8&qid=1426809901&sr=1-1&keywords=milius, 2013).
4. *Apocalypse Now—John Milius interviewed by Francis Ford Coppola*, You Tube (https://www.youtube.com/watch?v=JZswrVALi2M, 2010).

Chapter 21

1. John Milius, *Apocalypse Now* screenplay (1975).
2. *Ibid.*
3. *Ibid.*
4. *Ibid.*
5. *Ibid.*
6. *Ibid.*
7. *Ibid.*
8. *Ibid.*
9. *Ibid.*
10. *Ibid.*
11. *Ibid.*
12. *Ibid.*
13. *Ibid.*
14. *Ibid.*
15. *Ibid.*
16. *Ibid.*
17. *Ibid.*
18. *Ibid.*
19. *Ibid.*
20. *Ibid.*
21. Randy Roberts and James S. Olson, *John Wayne: American* (Lincoln, NE: Bison Books, 1995), p. 520.
22. John Milius, *Apocalypse Now* screenplay (1975).
23. *Ibid.*
24. *Ibid.*
25. *Ibid.*
26. *Ibid.*
27. Ibid
28. *Ibid.*
29. *Ibid.*
30. *Ibid.*
31. *Ibid.*
32. *Ibid.*
33. *Ibid.*
34. *Ibid.*
35. *Ibid.*
36. *Ibid.*
37. *Ibid.*
38. *Ibid.*

Chapter 22

1. John Andrew Gallagher, *Film Directors on Directing* (Westport, CT: Praeger, 1989), p. 180.
2. Michael, Schumacher, *Francis Ford Coppola: A Filmmaker's Life* (New York: Crown, 1999), p. 124.
3. *John Milius on how Hollywood Liberals are Blacklisting Conservatives*, YouTube (https://www.youtube.com/watch?v=yQljnlWW9j4, 2011).
4. Steven Travers, *What is Truth? Powers That Were, Powers That Are* (unpublished manuscript).
5. Gallagher, *Film Directors on Directing*, p. 178.
6. *John Milius on how Hollywood Liberals are Blacklisting Conservatives*, YouTube.
7. *Ibid.*
8. *John Milius*. Wikipedia (https://en.wikipedia.org/wiki/John_Milius).
9. Gallagher, *Film Directors on Directing*, pp. 180–181.
10. *Milius.* Epix Original, directed by Joey Figueroa and Zak Knutson, Amazon Instant Video (http://www.amazon.com/Milius-Steven-Spielberg/dp/B00JM7IVFS/ref=sr_1_1?s=instant-video&ie=UTF8&qid=1426809901&sr=1-1&keywords=milius 2013).

Chapter 23

1. Peter Biskind, Easy, *Easy Riders, Raging Bulls: How the Sex-Drugs-and-Rock 'n' Roll Generation Saved Hollywood* (New York: Simon & Schuster, 1998), p. 383.
2. *Ibid.*, p. 21.
3. *Fog City Mavericks.* Directed by Gary Leva (Burbank, CA: Alpha Dog Productions, 2007).
4. Robert Evans, *The Kid Stays in the Picture* (Beverly Hills, CA: Dove Books, 1994), pp. 349–353.
5. *Hearts of Darkness: A Filmmaker's Apocalypse* (San Francisco: Zoetrope Studios, 1991).
6. Michael, Schumacher, *Francis Ford Coppola: A Filmmaker's Life* (New York: Crown, 1999), p. 442.
7. *Hearts of Darkness: A Filmmaker's Apocalypse.*
8. *Fog City Fog City Mavericks.*
9. Biskind, *Easy Riders, Raging Bulls*, p. 23.
10. *Ibid.*, pp. 20–24.
11. *Ibid.*, p. 25.
12. *Martin Sheen (Apocalypse Now)*, You Tube (https://www.youtube.com/watch?v=AFiFQZeYeTU, 2010).
13. *Fog City Fog City Mavericks.*
14. *Apocalypse Now—John Milius interviewed by Francis Ford Coppola*, YouTube (https://www.youtube.com/watch?v=JZswrVALi2M, 2010).

Bibliography

Books and Articles

Biskind, Peter. *Easy Riders, Raging Bulls: How the Sex-Drugs-and-Rock 'n' Roll Generation Saved Hollywood*. New York: Simon & Schuster, 1998.

Cantor, Norman F., and Mindy Cantor. *The American Century: Varieties of Culture in Modern Times*. New York: HarperPerennial, 1998.

Champlin, Charles. *George Lucas: The Creative Impulse*. New York: Harry N. Abrams, 1992.

Conrad, Joseph. *Heart of Darkness*. New York: Alfred A. Knopf, Inc., 1902.

Coppola, Eleanor. *Notes*. New York: Simon & Schuster, 1979.

Cowie, Peter. *The Apocalypse Now Book*. New York: Da Capo Press, 2000.

Evans, Robert. *The Kid Stays in the Picture*. Beverly Hills, CA: Dove Books, 1994.

Farago, Ladislas. *Patton: Ordeal and Triumph*. Yardley, PA: Westholme, 2005.

Gallagher, John Andrew: *Film Directors on Directing*. Westport, CT: Praeger, 1989.

Hearn, Marcus. *The Cinema of George Lucas*. New York: Harry N. Abrams, 2005.

Hopkins, Jerry, and Danny Sugarman. *No One Here Gets Out Alive*. New York: Warner Books, 1995.

Jenkins, Bruce. *A Good Man: The Pete Newell Story*. Lincoln: University of Nebraska Board of Regents, 1999.

Johnson, Robert K. *Francis Ford Coppola*. Boston: Twayne, 1977.

Jones, Dylan. *Jim Morrison, Dark Star*. New York: Viking, 1992.

Kline, Sally, ed. *George Lucas: Interviews*. Oxford: University of Mississippi Press, 1999.

Lee, Bill, and Richard Lally. *The Wrong Stuff*. New York: Three Rivers Press, 2006.

Mabery, D. L. *George Lucas*. Minneapolis: Lerner, 1987.

McBride, Joseph. *Spielberg: A Biography*. New York: Simon & Schuster, 1997.

Milius, John. *Apocalypse Now* screenplay, 1975.

Murray, Jim. *Jim Murray: The Autobiography of the Pulitzer Prize Winning Sports Columnist*. New York: Macmillan, 1993.

Pollock, Dale. *Skywalking: The Life and Films of George Lucas*. New York: Harmony Books, 1983.

Puzo, Mario. *The Godfather*. New York: Signet, 1983.

Roberts, Randy, and James S. Olson. *John Wayne: American*. Lincoln, NE: Bison Books, 1997.

Ross, Steven. *Hollywood Left and Right: How Movie Stars Shaped American Politics*. Oxford, England: Oxford University Press, USA, 2011.

Salewicz, Chris. *George Lucas: The Making of His Movies*. New York: Thunder's Mouth Press, 1999.

Schickel, Richard. *Steven Spielberg: A Retrospective*. New York: Sterling, 2012.

Schumacher, Michael. *Francis Ford Coppola: A Filmmaker's Life*. New York: Crown, 1999.

Smith, John Matthew. *The Sons of Westwood: John Wooden, UCLA, and the Dynasty That Changed College Basketball*. Urbana: University of Illinois Press, 2013.

Stone, Judy. *Eye on the World: Conversations with International Filmmakers*. Los Angeles: Silman-James Press, 1997.

Travers, Steven. *What It Means to Be a Trojan: Southern Cal's Greatest Players Talk About Trojans Football*. Chicago: Triumph Books, 2009.

_____. *One Night, Two Teams: Alabama vs. USC and the Game That Changed a Nation*. Lanham, MD: Taylor Trade, 2007.

_____. "What Is Truth? Powers That Were, Powers That Are." Unpublished manuscript.

Verswijver, Leo. *"Movies Were Always Magical": Interviews with 19 Actors, Directors, and Producers from the Hollywood of the 1930s through the 1950s*. Jefferson, NC: McFarland, 2003.

White, Dana. *George Lucas*. Minneapolis: Lerner Hardcover, 1999.

Wood, Bret. *Orson Welles: A Bio-Bibliography*. Westport, CN: Greenwood Press, 1990.

Woodward, Bob, and Carl Bernstein. *All the President's Men: The Greatest Reporting Story of All Time*. New York: Simon & Schuster, 2014.

Secondary Sources and Suggested Reference Material

ABC Evening News, Reporters: Harry Reasoner, Bob Clark, Barbara Walters, and John Scali. "Nixon-Frost Interviews." Wednesday, May 4, 1977.

Abels, Jules. *The Truman Scandals*. Chicago: Henry Regnery Company, 1956.

Acuña, Rodolfo. *A Community under Siege: a Chronicle of Chicanos East of the Los Angeles River, 1945–1975*. Los Angeles: Chicano Studies Research Center, Publications, University of California at Los Angeles, 1984.

_____. *Occupied America: a History of Chicanos*. New York: Harper & Row, 1981.

Alinsky, Saul D. *Reveille for Radicals*. New York: Random House, 1946.

_____. *Rules for Radicals*. New York: Vintage, 1972 edition.

_____. *John L. Lewis. An unauthorized biography*. New York: G. P. Putnam's Sons, 2010.

Alterman, Eric, and Kevin Mattson. *The Cause: The Fight for American Liberalism From Franklin Roosevelt to Barack Obama*. New York: The Penguin Group, 2012.

Anderson, Jack, and Les Whitten. "Frost: Tough Questions for Nixon." *Washington Post*, November 22, 1976.

Anderson, Jack, with James Boyd. *Confessions of a Muckracker: The Inside Story of Life in Washington During the Truman, Eisenhower, Kennedy and Johnson Years*. New York: Random House, 1979.

Andrew, Christopher, and Vasili Mitrokhin. *The World Was Going Our Way*. New York: Basic Books, 2005.

Avila, Eric. *Popular Culture in the Age of White Flight: Fear and Fantasy in Suburban Los Angeles*. Berkeley: University of California, 2004.

Axelrod, Alan. *Patton: A Biography*. Palgrave Macmillan Trade, 2006.

Baker, Carlos. *Ernest Hemingway: A Life Story*. New York: Collier Books, 1969.

Baldaev, Danchik Sergeyevich. *Gulag Zeichnungen*. Frankfurt am Main: Zweitausendeins, 1993.

Baritz, Loren. *The American Left: Radical Political Thought in the Twentieth Century*. New York: Basic Books, 1971.

Barsam, Richard M. *Filmguide to* Triumph of the Will. Bloomington: Indiana University Press, 1975.

Baxter, John. *Hollywood in the Sixties*. London: C. Tinting, 1979.

BBC News (Vincent Dowd). "Historic Nixon Interviews On Stage," August 21, 2006.

Beat Generation in New York: A Walking Tour of Jack Kerouac's City, The. Google Books, 2011.

"Becoming Tennessee Williams." Exhibit at the University of Texas, 2011.

Benson, Jackson J. *The True Adventures of John Steinbeck, Writer*. New York: The Viking Press, 1984.

_____. *John Steinbeck, Writer: A Biography*. Penguin, 1990.

Berenbaum, Michael. *The World Must Know: The History of the Holocaust as Told in the United States Holocaust Memorial Museum*. Washington, D.C.: United States Holocaust Memorial Museum, 2007.

Bezold, C., ed. *Anticipatory Democracy*. New York: Vintage, 1978.

Billington, Michael. "Frost/Nixon." *The Guardian* (London), August 22, 2006.

Blair, Gwenda. *Almost Golden: Jessica Savitch and the Selling of Television News*. New York: Avon Books, 1988.

Block, Ben. *George Lucas's Blockbusting: A Decade-by-Decade Survey of Timeless Movies Including Untold Secrets of Their Financial and Cultural Success*. New York: HarperCollins, 2010.

Blumenson, Martin. *Patton: The Man Behind the Legend*. New York: William Morrow Paperbacks, 1994.

Bly, Nellie. *The Kennedy Men: Three Generations of Sex, Scandal and Secrets*. e-reads.com, 1999.

Boman, Steve. *Film School: The True Story of a Midwestern Family Man Who Went to the World's Most Famous Film School, Fell Flat on His Face, Had a Stroke, and Sold a Television Series to CBS*. BenBella Books, 2011.

Bond, Paul. "Our Viewing Tastes Are 'Polls' Apart." *Newsmax*, February 2012.

"Books: Uppie's Goddess." *Time*, November 18, 1957.

Bottles, Scott L. *Los Angeles and the Automobile: the Making of the Modern City*. Berkeley: University of California, 1987.

Bradlee, Ben. *A Good Life: Newspapering and Other Adventures*. New York: Simon & Schuster, 1995.

Broder, David S. *Behind the Front Page: A Candid Look at How the News is Made*. New York: Touchstone Books, 1987.

Brodie, Fawn M. *Richard Nixon: The Shaping of His Character*. New York: W. W. Norton, 1981.

Brown, Dee. *Bury My Heart at Wounded Knee: An Indian History of the American West*. New York: Henry Holt, 1970.

Brown, Les. "NBC News Seeks Nixon Interview; Watergate Would Be Part; Fee Put at Under $1-Million." *New York Times*, July 29, 1975.

_____. "Advertising Spots for Nixon TV Interview Sell Slowly." *New York Times*, February 14, 1977.

_____. "Last-Minute Publicity Drive for Nixon TV Series Helps Swell Ad Revenues and Network of Stations; ... Hinted $2 Million in Gross Revenues." *New York Times*, Sunday, May 1, 1977.

_____. "Nixon's TV Audience Placed at 45 Million; Surveys Rank Program With Leading Series." *New York Times*, May 6, 1977.

_____. "Frost Plans 5th in Nixon Series." *New York Times*, August 2, 1977.

Bruccoli, Matthew J., ed. *The Sons of Maxwell Perkins: The Letters of F. Scott Fitzgerald, Ernest Hemingway, Thomas Wolfe, and Their Editor*. Columbia: University of South Carolina Press, 2004.

Buchanan, Patrick J. *The Death of the West: How Dying Populations and Immigrant Invasions Imperil Our Country and Civilization*. New York: Thomas Dunne Books, 2002.

Butenko, I. A., and K. E. Razlogov. *Recent Social Trends in Russia, 1960–1995*. Kingston, Ontario: McGill-Queen's Press, 1997.

Cannon, Lou. "Haldeman Disputes Nixon on Tapes." *Washington Post*, September 12, 1977.

Capra, Frank. *The Name Above the Title: An Autobiography*. New York: Da Capo Press, 1977.

Carynnyk, Marco. "The *New York Times* and the Great Famine." *Ukrainian Weekly*, September 11, 1983.

Chambers, Whittaker. "Problem of the Century." *Time*, 1946.

Chase, A. *The Legacy of Malthus: The Social Costs of the New Scientific Racism.* New York: Alfred Knopf, 1980.

Cheshire, Ellen. "Leni Riefenstahl: Documentary Film-Maker or Propagandist?," *Kamera*, 2000.

Constitution of the United States. Washington, D.C.: United States Government Printing Office, 1952.

Coulter, Ann. *Treason: Liberal Treachery from the Cold War to the War on Terrorism.* New York: Crown Forum, 2003.

———. *How to Talk to a Liberal (If You Must): The World According to Ann Coulter.* New York: Crown Forum, 2004.

———. *Guilty: Liberal "Victims" and Their Assault on America.* New York: Crown Forum, 2008.

———. *Demonic: How the Liberal Mob Is Endangering America.* New York: Crown, 2011.

Courtois, Stéphane, et al. *The Black Book of Communism: Crimes, Terror, Repression.* London: Harvard University Press, 1999.

Cross, Nigel. *Man Made Futures: Readings in Society, Technology, and Design.* London: Hutchinson, 1974.

Crowl, James W. *Angels in Stalin's Paradise: Western Reporters in Soviet Russia, 1917-1937; A Case Study of Louis Fischer and Walter Duranty.* Washington, D.C.: The University of America Press, 1981.

———. *Witness.* New York: Random House, Inc., 1952.

Dalton, Dennis. *Power Over People: Classical and Modern Political Theory.* Recorded course from Barnard College at Columbia University, New York. Available at www.teach12.com.

Dargis, Manohla. "Mr. Frost, Meet Mr. Nixon." *New York Times*, December 5, 2008.

Darwin, Charles. *The Descent of Man and Selection in Relation to Sex, 2nd Ed.* London: John Murray, 1882.

"David Can Be a Goliath." *Time*, Monday, May 9, 1977.

"David Frost Signs to Interview Nixon; Sum Is Undisclosed." *New York Times*, August 11, 1975.

Davis, Stephen. *Jim Morrison: Life, Death, Legend.* New York: Gotham, 2005.

Dawson, Jeff. *Quentin Tarantino: The Cinema of Cool.* New York: Applause, 1995.

Dean, John. *Blind Ambition: The White House Years.* New York: Simon & Schuster, 1976.

Dearborn, Mary V. *Mailer: A Biography.* Boston: Houghton-Mifflin, 1999.

Diaz, David R. *Barrio Urbanism: Chicanos, Planning, and American Cities.* New York: Routledge, 2005.

Donald, David Herbert. *Look Homeward: A Life of Thomas Wolfe.* Boston: Little, Brown, 1987.

Drew, Elizabeth. "Frost/Nixon: A Dishonorable Distortion of History." HuffingtonPost.com, December 14, 2008.

D'Souza, Dinesh. *Obama's America: Unmaking the American Dream.* New York: Threshold Editions, 2014.

Duranty, Walter. *I Write as I Please.* New York: Simon & Schuster, 1935.

Ebert, Roger. "The Wonderful Horrible Life of Leni Riefenstahl." *Chicago Sun-Times*, June 24, 1994.

Eco, Umberto. *Travels in Hyperreality.* London: Picador, 1987.

———. "Triumph of the Will." *Chicago Sun-Times*, May 4, 2011.

Eisenstein, Elizabeth. *The Printing Press as an Agent of Change.* Cambridge, UK: Cambridge University Press, 1979.

Ellis, Joseph J. *His Excellency George Washington.* New York: Alfred A. Knopf, 2004.

Emery, Fred. *Watergate: The Corruption of American Politics and the Fall of Richard Nixon.* New York: Times Books, 1994.

———. "Making a Drama Out of a Crisis: Nixon's Last Stand." *The Independent* (UK), Sunday, July 23, 2006.

"'The Ends of Power': It's Haldeman's Turn to Talk." *Washington Post*, February 3, 1978.

"Excerpts from Interview With Nixon About Watergate Tapes and Other Issues." *New York Times*, Sunday, September 4, 1977.

Front Page: A Collection of Historical Headlines from the Los Angeles Times 1881-1987. New York: Harry N. Abrams, 1987.

"Frost and a Researcher Disagree on Nixon Respite." *Washington Post*, May 6, 1977.

Frost, David. *I Gave Them a Sword: Behind the Scenes of the Nixon Interviews.* New York: Morrow, 1978.

"Frost Quotes Nixon: Wallace's Reticence Cinched Resigning." *Washington Post*, January 27, 1978.

"Frost Reaffirms Control over Nixon Interviews." *New York Times*, April 8, 1977.

"Frost's Big Deal." *Time*, Monday, August 25, 1975.

Gallagher, John Andrew: *Film Directors on Directing.* Westport, CT: Praeger, 1989.

Gallup, George. "Intense Dislike of Nixon Eases After TV Show." *Washington Post*, May 29, 1977.

Gerd, Albrecht. *Nationalsozialistische Filmpolitik.* Munich: Hanser, 1969.

Gold, Sylviane. "The Interview That Was a Play Becomes a Film." *New York Times*, November 2, 2008.

Goldberg, Bernard. *Bias: A CBS Insider Exposes How the Media Distort the News.* Washington, D.C.: Regnery, 2002.

Goldman, William. *Adventures in the Screen Trade.* New York: Warner Books, 1984.

Gottlieb, Robert, and Irene Wolf. *Thinking Big: The Story of* the Los Angeles Times, *Its Publishers, and Their Influence on Southern California.* New York: G. P. Putnam's Son, 1977.

Gottlieb, Robert, Mark Vallianatos, Regina M. Freer, and Peter Dreier. *The Next Los Angeles: The Struggle for a Livable City* (2d ed.). Berkeley: University of California Press, 2005.

Green, Stephanie. "Bradlee Slams 'Frost/Nixon': 'Nixon Never Was Sorry.'" *Washington Times*, Tuesday, December 2, 2008.

Grosswiler, Paul. *The Method Is the Message.* London: Black Rose Books, 1998.

Halberstam, David. *The Fifties.* New York: Villard Books, 1993.

_____. *The Powers That Be*. New York: Alfred Knopf, Inc., 1979.

_____, ed. *The Best American Sports Writing of the Century*. Boston: Houghton Mifflin Co., 1999.

"Haldeman Accuses Nixon." *Washington Post*, February 16, 1978.

Halliwell, Leslie. *The Filmgoer's Companion*. New York: Avon Books, 1978.

Harding, Luke. "Leni Riefenstahl, Hitler's Favourite Film Propagandist, Dies at 101," *The Guardian* (UK), September 10, 2003.

Harris, Leon. *Upton Sinclair, American Rebel*. New York: Thomas Y. Crowell, 1975.

Hauptfuhrer, Fred. "Frost's Frontiers." *People*, May 23, 1977.

Hicks, D., and R. Slaughter, eds. *Futures Education. World Yearbook of Education*, London: Kogan Page, 1920.

Hines, Thomas S. "Housing, Baseball, and Creeping Socialism: The Battle of Chavez Ravine, Los Angeles 1949–1959." *Journal of Urban History*, 1982.

Hinton, David B. "*Triumph of the Will*: Document or Artifice?" *Cinema Journal*, University of Texas Press, 1975.

Hodgson, Godfrey. *America in Our Time: What Happened and Why*. Garden City, NY: Doubleday, 1976.

Horwitt, Sanford D. *Let Them Call Me Rebel: Saul Alinsky, His Life and Legacy*. New York: Knopf, 1989.

Humane Society of the United States, "The Jungle: Upton Sinclair's Roar Is Even Louder to Animal Advocates Today." March 10, 2006.

Images of Our Times: Sixty Years of Photography from the Los Angeles Times. New York: Harry N. Abrams, 1987.

"Interview with Saul Alinsky." *Playboy*, March 1972.

Johnson, Haynes. "Nixon Stirs All the Old Memories." *Washington Post*, May 5, 1977.

_____. "Nixon, Haldeman, Frost and ... Hype." *Washington Post*, February 15, 1978.

_____. *The Age of Anxiety: McCarthyism to Terrorism*. New York: Harcourt, 2005.

Jürgen, Spiker, *Film und Kapital. Der Weg der deutschen Filmwirtschaft zum nationalsozialistischen Einheitskonzern*. Berlin: Volker Spiess, 1975.

Kagan, Robert. "Why the World Needs America." *Wall Street Journal*, February 11, 2012.

Kamm, Henry. "Illegal Refugee Exodus Increasing, but Hanoi Denies Encouraging It." *New York Times*, May 3, 1979.

Karnow, Stanley. *Vietnam: A History*. New York: Viking, 1983.

Kennicott, Philip. "Meant for Each Other: 'Frost/Nixon' Is a Good Fight with Two Winners." *Washington Post*, Friday, December 12, 2008.

Kershaw, Ian. *The Hitler Myth*. Oxford, NY: Oxford University Press, 1987.

Kessler, Ronald. *The Sins of the Father: Joseph P. Kennedy and the Dynasty He Founded*. New York: Warner Books, 1996.

Kissinger, Henry. *White House Years*. Boston: Little, Brown, 1979.

Kolin, Philip. *Something Cloudy, Something Clear: Tennessee Williams's Postmodern Memory Play* (PDF), 1998.

Lawlor, William. *Beat Culture: Lifestyles, Icons, and Impact*. ABC-CLIO, 2005.

Lelyveld, Joseph. "The Enduring Legacy." *New York Times Magazine*, March 31, 1985.

"Leni Riefenstahl: Hand-held History." *The Economist*, September 11, 2003.

Lennon, Michael J. *Critical Essays on Norman Mailer*. Boston: G. K. Hall, 1986.

Leverich, Lyle. *Tom: The Unknown Tennessee Williams*. New York: W. W. Norton, 1997.

Liddy, G. Gordon. *Will: The Autobiography of G. Gordon Liddy*. New York: Dell, 1981.

Limbaugh, Rush. *The Way Things Ought to Be*. New York: Pocket Books, 1992.

_____. *See, I Told You So*. New York: Pocket Books, 1993.

Linenthal, Edward T., and Tom Engelhardt. *History Wars: The Enola Gay and Other Battles for the American Past*. New York: Metropolitan Books, 1996.

López, Ronald William. "The Battle for Chavez Ravine: Public Policy and Chicano Community Resistance in Post-war Los Angeles, 1945–1962." Diss. University of California, Berkeley, 1999.

Lucid, Robert F., ed. *Norman Mailer: The Man and His Work*. Boston: Little, Brown, 1971.

Macdonald, Dwight. *McLuhan Hot & Cool*. Middlesex, UK: Penguin Books, 1968.

Maher, Paul, and Davis Amram. *Kerouac: His Life and Work*. Boulder, CO: Taylor Trade, 2007.

Mailer, Norman. *The White Negro*. San Francisco: City Lights, 1957.

_____. "Portrait of Picasso as a Young Man: An Interpretive Biography." *Atlantic Monthly Press*, 1995.

_____. *Oswald's Tale: An American Mystery*. New York: Random House, 1996.

_____. *The Prisoner of Sex*. New York: Little, Brown, 1971.

Malcolm, Muggeridge. *Winter in Moscow*. Grand Rapids, MI: William B. Eerdmans, 1987.

Mamet, David. *On Directing Film*. New York: Penguin Book Group, 1991.

Manchester, William. *American Caesar: Douglas MacArthur 1880–1964*. New York: Dell, 1978.

Marchand, Philip. *The Medium and the Messenger*. Cambridge, MA: MIT Press, 1989.

Martinez, Manuel Luis. *Countering the Counterculture: Rereading Postwar American Dissent from Jack Kerouac to Tomás Rivera*. Madison, WI: University of Wisconsin Press, 2003.

Marx, Karl, and Friedrich Engels. *The Communist Manifesto*. CreateSpace, 2011.

Mattson, Kevin. *Upton Sinclair and the Other American Century*. Hoboken, NJ: John Wiley & Sons, 2006.

McCluggage, Matt. *The Construction of Dodger Stadium and the Battle for Chavez Ravine*. Diss. Chapman University, 2010.

McConnachie, Alistair. "The Morality of Means and Ends." *Sovereignty*, 1949.

McDougal, Dennis. *Privileged Son: Otis Chandler and the Rise and Fall of the L.A. Times Dynasty*. Cambridge, MA: Perseus, 2001.

McLean, Gareth. "When The Playboy Met the Liar." *The Guardian* (UK), Tuesday, August 1, 2006.

McLuhan, Eric, and Frank Zingrone, eds. *Essential McLuan*. New York: Basic Books, 1995.

McLuhan, Marshall. *Understanding Media*. New York: Signet Books, 1964.

McLuhan, Marshall, and Quentin Fiore. *The Medium is the Massage*. Berkeley, CA: Gingko Press, 2001.

"Memoirs of Nixon Rejected by CBS." *New York Times*, July 20, 1975.

Miller, Jonathan. *McLuhan*. London: Fontana/Collins, 1971.

Miller, Peter. "A Dickens of a Celebration," *Newsmax*, February 2012.

Mitchell, Ted. *Thomas Wolfe: An Illustrated Biography*. Cambridge (UK): Pegasus Brooks, 2006.

Minzesheimer, Bob. "Frost Rewinds Nixon Tape to 1977 and Hits Play." *USA Today*, October 22, 2006.

Michaels, Daniel W. *The Gulag: Communism's Penal Colonies Revisited*, The Journal for Historical Review (http://www.ihr.org), January/February 2002.

Mitchell, Greg Mitchell. "The Campaign of the Century: Upton Sinclair and the EPIC Campaign in California." *Atlantic Monthly Press*, 1991.

Morgan, Peter. "Morgan Savors Howard's On-Set Vibe; Duo's 'Frost/Nixon' Confab Produces a Winner." Variety.com, December 18, 2008.

Morgan, Ted. *Reds: McCarthyism in Twentieth-Century America*. New York: Random House Trade Paperbacks, 2004.

Mueller, Carol Lea. *The Quotable John Wayne*. Lanham, MD: Taylor Trade, 2007.

Munn, Michael. *John Wayne: The Man Behind the Myth*. New York: Penguin, 2005.

Murray, Jim. *The Best of Jim Murray*. Garden City, NY: Doubleday, 1965.

_____. *The Sporting World of Jim Murray*. Garden City, NY: Doubleday, 1968.

_____. "Hatred shut out as Alabama finally joins the Union." *Los Angeles Times*, September 13, 1970.

_____. "If You're Expecting One-Liners." *Los Angeles Times*, 1979.

_____. *The Jim Murray Collection*. Dallas: Taylor Trade, 1988.

_____. *Jim Murray: An Autobiography*. New York: Macmillan, 1993.

_____. *The Last of the Best*. Los Angeles: *Los Angeles Times*, 1998.

_____. *The Great Ones*. Los Angeles: *Los Angeles Times*, 1999.

Nasaw, David. *The Chief: The Life of William Randolph Hearst*. Mariner Books, 2001.

Naughton, James M. "Nixon, Conceding He Lied, Says 'I Let the American People ... Down,' Denies Any Crime on Watergate." *New York Times*, May 5, 1977.

_____. "Watergate Evidence Cited in Frost Talk; Nixon Says He Told Aide to Ruin Tapes." *New York Times*, Sunday, September 4, 1977.

"NBC Terminates Talks for Memoirs of Nixon." *New York Times*, August 8, 1975.

Negrete, White, and Charlotte Rebecca. "Power vs. the People of Chávez Ravine: a Study of Their Determination and Fortitude." Diss. Claremont Graduate University, 2008.

"New Nixon Tapes Are Just Another Deal for Media Showman David Frost." *People*, September 1, 1975.

Nichols, Peter M. "Home Video; Promoting the Famous." *New York Times*, November 12, 1992.

Nicosia, Gerald. *One and Only: The Untold Story of On the Road*. Berkeley, CA: Viva Editions, 2011.

Nightingale, Benedict. "Frost/Nixon." *The Times* (UK), August 22, 2006.

"Nixon Admits Plan To Use Hughes Cash." *Washington Post*, May 25, 1977.

"Nixon and Frost in May." *Washington Post*, February 12, 1977.

Nixon, Richard. *Memoirs of Richard Nixon*. New York: Warner Books, 1979.

"Nixon Says Watergate Cover-Up Sought to Protect the Innocent." *Washington Post*, May 2, 1977.

"Nixon Sells Hard-Cover Rights to Memoirs." *New York Times*, Saturday, September 28, 1974.

"Nixon Talks," *Time*, Monday, May 9, 1977.

"Nixon Tells Frost Kissinger Differed on Cambodia." *New York Times*, May 9, 1977.

"Norman Mailer Arrested in Stabbing of Wife at a Party." *New York Times*, November 22, 1960.

Norwich, Grace. *I am George Lucas*. New York: Scholastic Paperbacks, 2013.

O'Reilly, Bill. *The O'Reilly Factor: The Good, the Bad, and the Completely Ridiculous in American Life*. New York: Broadway Books, 2000.

_____. *Culture Warrior*. New York: Broadway Books, 2006.

_____. *A Bold Fresh Piece of Humanity*. New York: Broadway Books, 2008.

Pace, Eric. "Nixon Is Said to Be Open to $2-Million for Memoirs." *New York Times*, Thursday, August 29, 1974.

Paine, Thomas. *Common Sense, Rights of Man, and Other Essential Writings of Thomas Paine*. New York: Signet Classics, 2003.

Paglia, Camille. *Glittering Images: A Journey Through Art from Egypt to Star Wars*. New York: Pantheon, 2012.

Parini, Jay. *John Steinbeck: A Biography*. New York: Holt, 1996.

Parson, Donald Craig. *Making a Better World: Public Housing, the Red Scare, and the Direction of Modern Los Angeles*. Minneapolis: University of Minnesota, 2005.

Pearson, Drew. *The President: The blistering novel of Washington in the 1970s*. New York: Avon Books, 1970.

Pendergast, Christopher. *The Order of Mimesis*. Cambridge, (UK): Cambridge University Press, 1986.

Petropolous, Jonathan. "Leni Riefenstahl, Coy Propagandist of the Nazi Era." *Wall Street Journal*, September 11, 2003.

Pippert, Wes. "Celebrating 125 years." *San Francisco Chronicle*, March 4, 2012.

Poe, Edgar Allan. "A Descent into the Maelström." In *The Portable Poe*. Middlesex (UK): Penguin Books, 1977.

Pollack, Sam, and Meg Belviso. *Who is George Lucas?* New York: Grosset & Dunlap, 2014.

Preston, Andrew. *Sword of the Spirit, Shield of Faith*. New York: Alfred A. Knopf, 2012.

Prugh, Jeff. "George Wallace was America's merchant of venom." *Marin Independent Journal*, September 15, 1998.

Pynchon, Thomas. *Slow Learner: Early Stories*. Boston: Little, Brown, 1985.

Rand, Ayn. *Atlas Shrugged*. New York: Random House, 1957.

Rand, Susan. "Photo Gallery: Tennessee Williams inducted into Poets' Corner—Wicked Local Wellfleet." Wickedlocal.com, 2011.

Rau, Dana Meachen. *George Lucas: Creator of Star Wars*. Danbury, CT: Children's Press, 1999.

Reed, John. *Ten Days That Shook the World*. CreateSpace, 2011.

Reston, James, Jr. "Trial by Television." Book Review: *The Conviction of Richard Nixon: the Untold Story of the Frost/Nixon Interviews*. *Washington Post Book World*, Sunday, July 15, 2007.

_____. "Frost, Nixon and Me." *Smithsonian*, January 2009.

Richards, Clay F. "Watergate Legacy After Five Years: Fame, Disgrace." *Washington Post*, June 17, 1977.

Riding, Alan. "Leni Riefenstahl, Filmmaker and Nazi Propagandist, Dies at 101." *New York Times*, September 9, 2003.

Riehecky, Janet. *George Lucas: An Unauthorized Biography*. London (UK): Heinemann Library, 2001.

Rising, David. "Hitler's filmmaker Leni Riefenstahl, Revered and Reviled for Her Work, Dies at 101." Associated Press, September 9, 2003.

Robertson, Priscilla. *Revolutions of 1848: A Social History*. Princeton, NJ: Princeton University Press, 1952.

Robison, Bruce. "Mavericks on Cannery Row." *American Scientist*, vol. 92, no. 6, (November–December 2004).

Rogers, Mary Beth. *Cold Anger: A Story of Faith and Power Politics*. Denton: University of North Texas Press, 1990.

Rollyson, Carl. "Leni Riefenstahl on Trial." *New York Sun*, 2008.

Romerstein, Herbert, and Eric Breindel. *The Venona Secrets, Exposing Soviet Espionage and America's Traitors*. Washington, D.C.: Regnery, 2001.

Rose, Frank. *The Agency: William Morris and the Hidden History of Show Business*. New York: HarperBusiness, 1995.

Rossi, Jacques. *The Gulag Handbook*. New York: Paragon House, 1989.

Russell, Bertrand. "ICARUS or the Future of Science," 1924.

Sánchez, George J. *Becoming Mexican American: Ethnicity, Culture, and Identity in Chicano Los Angeles, 1900–1945*. New York: Oxford University Press, 1995.

Sanders, Marion K. *The Professional Radical: Conversations with Saul Alinsky*. New York: Harper & Row, 1970

Sanger, Margaret. *The Pilot of Civilization*, 1922.

Santow, Mark E. "Saul Alinsky and the dilemmas of race in the post-war city," ScholarlyCommon@Penn (University of Pennsylvania).

Sarantakes, Nicholas Evan. *Making Patton: A Classic War Film's Epic Journey to the Silver Screen*. Lawrence: University of Kansas Press, 2012.

Savage, Michael. *The Enemy Within: Saving America from the Liberal Assault on Our Schools, Faith, and Military*. Nashville, TN: Nelson Current, 2003.

Schweizer, Peter. *Reagan's War: The Epic Story of His Forty-Year Struggle and Final Triumph Over Communism*. New York: Anchor, 2011.

Seib, Charles B. "The Richard Nixon Show." *Washington Post*, August 18, 1975.

Shaw, George Bernard. Lecture to the Eugenics Education Society, Reported in the *Daily Express*, March 4, 1910.

_____. "On the Rocks," 1933.

_____. *Prefaces*. London (UK): Constable and Co., 1934.

Shifrin, Avraham. *The First Guidebook to Prisons and Concentration Camps of the Soviet Union*. New York: Bantam Books, 1982.

Shillinglaw, Susan. *A Journey into Steinbeck's California*. Berkeley, CA: Roaring Forties Press, 2006.

Shirer, William L. *Berlin Diary: The Journal of a Foreign Correspondent 1934–1941*. New York: Alfred A. Knopf, 1941.

_____. *The Rise and Fall of the Third Reich: A History of Nazi Germany*. Greenwich, CT: Crest Books, 1959.

Silberman, C. E. *Crisis in Black and White*. New York: Random House, 1964.

Sinclair's 'The Jungle' Turns 100. PBS, May 10, 2006, Sinclair, Upton. "What Life Means to Me." *The Cosmopolitan*, 1906.

_____. *The Jungle*. London: Penguin Classics, 1906.

_____. *The Autobiography of Upton Sinclair*. New York: Harcourt, Brace & World, 1962.

Slaughter, Richard A. *Futures Studies: From Individual to Social Capacity*. Queensland, Australia: Foresight, 1996.

Smirnov, M.B. et al. *Sistema ispravitel'no-trudovykh lagerey v SSSR. 1923–1960*. Moscow: Zven'ya, 1998.

Smith, David Calvert. *Triumph of the Will: A Film by Leni Riefenstahl*. Richardson, TX: Celluloid Chronicles Press, 1990.

Smith, John Chabot. *Alger Hiss: The True Story*. New York: Holt, Rinehart & Winston, 1976.

Snoddy, Raymond. "Frosty the Showman." *The Independent* (London, UK), Monday, May 30, 2005.

Solomon, Deborah. "Talking Head: Questions for Ron Howard." *New York Times Magazine*, Sunday, November 9, 2008.

Solomon, Norman. *The Power of Babble: The Politician's Dictionary of Buzzwords and Double-Talk for Every Occasion*. New York: Laurel, 1992.

Sontag, Susan. "Fascinating Fascism." *The New York Review of Books*, February 6, 1975.

Spoto, Donald. *The Kindness of Strangers: The Life of Tennessee Williams*. Cambridge, MA: Da Capo Press, 1997.

Steele, Jonathan. "Frost's Standing Rises in the U.S." *The Guardian* (Washington correspondent), Friday May 27, 1977.

Steinbeck, Thom. "Steinbeck Knew He Was Dying." Audio interview, September 13, 2006.

Stettner, Ralf. *Archipel Gulag: Stalins Zwangslager: Terrorinstrument und Wirtschaftsgigant* [*The Gulag Archipelago: Instrument of Terror and Economic Giant*]. Munich: Ferdinand Schöningh, 1996.

Stevens, George, Jr. *Conversations at the American Film Institute with the Great Moviemakers*. New York: Alfred A. Knopf, 2012.

Stewart, James B. *Blood Sport: The President and His Adversaries*. New York: Simon & Schuster, 1996.

Sugarman, Danny. *Wonderland Avenue*. New York: Little, Brown, 1993.

Sviridova, Aleksandra. *In V novom sverte* (*In the New World*), May 18–24, 2001.

Swanberg, W. A. *Citizen Hearst: The Monumental and Controversial Biography of One of the Most Fabulous Characters in American History*. New York: Bantam Books, 1961.

Tanenhaus, Sam. *Whittaker Chambers: A Biography*. New York: Random House, 1997.

Taylor, Sally J. *Stalin's Apologist: Walter Duranty: The New York Times' Man in Moscow*. London: Oxford University Press, 1990.

"10 Questions for Ron Howard." *Time*, Thursday, December 4, 2008.

"Thomas Wolfe's Final Journey." *Virginia Quarterly Review*, 2009.

Thomson, David. *The New Biographical Dictionary of Film, Fifth Edition*. New York: Alfred A. Knopf, 2010.

Thornton, Margaret Bradham. *Williams, Tennessee. Notebooks*. New Haven, CT: Yale University Press, 2006.

"Times Co. Buys Serial Rights to Nixon Memoirs; Work Will Be Offered Prior to Warner's Publication of Book in Fall of '77." *New York Times*, Wednesday, June 16, 1976.

Thubron, Colin. *In Siberia*. New York: HarperCollins, 1999.

Toffler, Alvin. *Future Shock*. New York: Random House, Inc., 1970.

_____, ed. *Learning for Tomorrow*. New York: Vintage, 1974.

Toffler, Alvin, and H. Toffler. *Creating a New Civilisation*. Atlanta: Turner, 1994.

Tomalin, Claire. *Charles Dickens: A Life*. New York: Penguin Press, 2007.

Torrey, Jack. "Nixon Said No to Recount in '60." *Toledo Blade*, November 10, 2000.

Travers, Steven. *God's Country: A Conservative, Christian Worldview of How History Formed the United States Empire and America's Manifest Destiny for the Twenty-first Century*. Unpublished manuscript, 2003.

_____. "The Dominant Media Culture." Redroom.com, 2009.

_____. "Orange Countification: The True Story of How the GOP Helped the South Rise Again." Redroom.com, 2009.

_____. *The Poet: The Life and Los Angeles Times of Jim Murray*. Washington: Potomac Books, 2013.

_____. *The Duke, the Longhorns, and Chairman Mao: John Wayne's Political Odyssey*. Lanham, MD: Taylor Trade, 2014.

Turner, Frederick: *Renegade: Henry Miller and the Making of Tropic of Cancer*. New Haven, CT: Yale University Press, 2011.

"Upton Sinclair, Author, Dead." *New York Times*, November 26, 1968.

"Upton Sinclair's Colony to Live at Helicon Hall. Luxury in Co-Operation and There May Be Some Compromises Just at First." *New York Times*, October 7, 1906.

Vanden Heuvel, Katrina. *The Nation 1865–1990*. Thunder's Mouth Press, 1990.

Wayne, Aissa, with Steve Delsohn. *John Wayne: My Father*. Lanham, MD: Taylor Trade, 1998.

Welch, David. *The Third Reich Politics and Propaganda*. London: Routledge, 1993.

Wells, H. G. *Mankind in the Making*. London (UK): Chapman & Hall, 1906.

_____. *The New Republic* ("Anticipations of the Reaction of Mechanical and Scientific Progress Upon Human Life and Thought, Final Chapter"), 1902.

White, Dana. *George Lucas*. Lerner Hardcover, 1999.

White, Theodore. *The Making of the President 1972: A Narrative History of American Politics in Action*. New York: Atheneum Publishers, 1973.

_____. *In Search of History: A Personal Adventure*. New York: Warner Books, 1978.

Williams, Raymond. *Television Technology and Cultural Form*. London (UK): Routledge, 1990.

Williams, Tennessee. *Memoirs*. New York: Doubleday, 1975.

Williams, Val. "Leni Riefenstahl." *The Independent* (UK), September 10, 2002.

Woodward, Bob, and Scott Armstrong. "Nixon Sheds Little New Light on Scandal." *Washington Post*, May 5, 1977.

Yakubovich-Yasny, *Odysseus*. Great Soviet Encyclopedia.

Yandex. Slovari. *The Cinema of Stalinism: 1930–1941*. Advameg, Inc.

Zajacz, Rita. "David Frost: British Broadcast Journalist/Producer." The Museum of Broadcast Communication, viewed January 2008.

Zakaria, Fareed. *The Future of Freedom: Illiberal Democracy at Home and Abroad*. New York: W. W. Norton, 2003.

Zito, Tom. "The News That Makes the Books: There's Big Money in the Jump from Front Page to Best-Seller List; the Big Book Push," *Washington Post*, May 6, 1978.

DVD/Documentaries

Breaking the Huddle. New York: Home Box Office, 2008.
Coach Paul "Bear" Bryant. New York: College Sports Television, 2005.
Fog City Mavericks. Directed by Gary Leva. Burbank, CA: Alpha Dog Productions, 2007.
Hearts of Darkness: A Filmmaker's Acopalypse. San Francisco: Zoetrope Studios, 1991.
In the Face of Evil: Reagan's War in Word and Deed. Santa Monica, CA: American Vantage Media, 2005.
Inventing L.A.: the Chandlers and Their Times. Los Angeles: KCET/Public Broadcasting, 2009.
Nixon/Frost: The Original Watergate Interviews (Digitally Remastered), 2014. *Songs of Our Success*. Hosted by Tony McEwen, 2003.
Tackling Segregation. New York: College Sports Television, 2006.

Websites

aber.ac.uk/media/Students/ram0202.html
aboutforesight.org
afrol.com/features/11116
amazon.com/Apocalypse-Now-Marlon-Brando/dp/B0045INOD8/ref=sr_1_1?ie=UTF8&qid=1413998347&sr=8-1&keywords=apocalypse+now
amazon.com/Kid-Stays-Picture-Robert-Evans/dp/B005EYF40I/ref=sr_1_1?ie=UTF8&qid=1414000739&sr=8-1&keywords=the+kid+stays+in+the+picture+instant+video
amazon.com/s/ref=nb_sb_noss_1?url=search-alias%3Dstripbooks&field-keywords=jeane+kirkpatrick
archive.newsmax.com/archives/articles/2001/4/11/174648.shtml
bartleby.com/79/1.html
boxofficemojo.com/yearly/chart/?yr=1985&p=.htm
conservapedia.com/Walter_Duranty
David Frost Show website, The.
en.wikipedia.org/wiki/Che_guevara
en.wikipedia.org/wiki/Heart_of_Darkness
en.wikipedia.org/wiki/Hyman_Ric
en.wikipedia.org/wiki/John_Milius
en.wikipedia.org/wiki/Robert_Evans_(producer)
en.wikipedia.org/wiki/Rock_music
goodreads.com/quotes/show/33210
google.com/#hl=en&sugexp=cqn%2Cconf%3D0.95%2Cmin_length%3D2&gs_nf=1&cp=18&gs_id=5&xhr=t&q=Ayatollah+Khomeini&pf=p&output=search&sclient=psyab&oq=Ayatollah+Khomeini&aq=0&aqi=g4&aql=f&gs_l=&pbx=1&bav=on.2,or.r_gc.r_pw.r_qf.,cf.osb&fp=bd74eeb444d882a5&biw=1024&bih=997
google.com/#hl=en&sugexp=cqn%2Cconf%3D0.95%2Cmin_length%3D2&gs_nf=1&cp=12&gs_id=1r&xhr=t&q=nicholas+romanov&pf=p&sclient=psy-ab&oq=nicholas+rom&aq=0&aqi=g4&aql=f&gs_l=&pbx=1&bav=on.2,or.r_gc.r_pw.r_qf.,cf.osb&fp=bd74eeb444d882a5&biw=1024&bih=997
guardian.co.uk/books/2011/nov/25/kerouacs-lost-debut-novel-published–The Guardian." London: Guardian.co.uk. Retrieved 2011-12-06
ihr.org/jhr/v21/v21n1p39_michaels.html
IMDb.com
individual.utoronto.ca/markfederman/article_mediumisthemessage.htm
infed.org/thinkers/alinsky.htm
latter-rain.com
lib.berkeley.edu/MRC/blacklist.html
library.thinkquest.org/11046/days/index.html
nationalreview.com/contributors/stuttaford051501.shtml
neatorama.com/2011/05/09/joe-stalin-vs-john-wayne/
nobelprize.org/nobel_prizes/literature/laureates/1949/faulkner-bio.html
nytco.com/company-awards-pulitzer-note.html
nytimes.com/2008/01/27/books/review/Oshinsky-t.html
online-literature.com/dickens/
progress.org
Robert Duvall (Apocalypse Now), "Bob Costas Interview" (https://www.youtube.com/watch?v=ZWAkTFoKcpE), 1991.
Screenwriter John Milius on Apocalypse Now—YouTube (https://www.youtube.com/watch?v=5v-G_c4f9RM), 2006.
seaofcortez.org/
Seven Minutes Film, The. https://en.wikipedia.org/wiki/The_Seven_Minutes_(film).
sfy.ru/?script=apocalypse_now_ts
sovereignty.org.uk/features/activistinf/morality.html
timeswatch.org/articles/2003/0310.asp#2
ucca.org/famine/
usatoday.com/news/nation/2003-10-22-ny-times-pulitzer_x.htm
Wikipedia.com. "Frost/Nixon Interviews."
wikipedia.org/wiki/Mark_Twain
weeklystandard.com/Content/Public/Articles/000/000/002/791vwuaz.asp?ZoomFont=YE
youtube.com/watch?v=-0OPtfm5sOc
youtube.com/watch?v=5vH7f__nCIQ
youtube.com/watch?v=EWIjnJbd-10
youtube.com/watch?v=H9f5amxkMC4
youtube.com/watch?v=H9f5amxkMC4-0
youtube.com/watch?v=HMzTcvXk1j4
youtube.com/watch?v=Isk-mJBK1tk
youtube.com/watch?v=iNx3OhZk9ZQ
youtube.com/watch?v=JSUIQgEVDM4
youtube.com/watch?v=JZswrVALi2M
youtube.com/watch?v=U8YYM_7KUpw
youtube.com/watch?v=X39evT9_onE
youtube.com/watch?v=yQljnlWW9j4

Index

American Zoetrope 4, 62; deal with Warner Bros. 63
Ashley, Ted 67
audience reaction 169

Blacker, Irwin 14
Bottoms, Sam 102
Brando, Marlon 101; arrives Philippines 139; weight 140; work ethic on set 140

Cannes 164
Conrad, Joseph 8, 83
Coppola, Eleanor 84, 105, 115, 133
Coppola, Francis Ford 1, 15; affairs on set 133; breaks into film industry 21; editing process 156; financial perils 158; forms American Zoetrope 63; on *Patton* screenplay 77; reaction to Martin Sheen's heart attack 125; relationship with George Luca 63; sanity on set 143; at UCLA 19; wraps filming 155
Coppola, Francis and Eleanor interview 208
Coppola-Milius interview 87, 120, 122, 213

debuts to general audience 167
description of film 188
difference in screenplay versions 192
Dolby stereo 159
The Doors 69; place in history 72
Duvall, Robert 120; interview with Bob Costas 121

"The End" 70, 118; during Ifugao animal massacre 149; meaning of song 153
ending of film 166
Evans, Robert 67, 159

filming shuts down 113
Fishburne, Laurence 102
Forrest, Frederick 102, 134
French plantation scene 137

Glenn, Scott 102
The Godfather 68
Goux, Marv 2, 81
Gray, Frederickson 106, 146

Hall, Albert 102
Heart of Darkness 8, 9, 10, 83
Hearts of Darkness 133, 143, 148
Hollywood 162, 203
Homer 122
Hopper, Dennis 102, 145
Hurricane Olga 110

Ifugao animal massacre 148
intellectual rights to *Apocalypse Now* 94

Jacob, Dennis 118, 155

Keitel, Harvey 5, 106

liberal bias 200
Lucas, George 1, 23; early attempts to make *Apocalypse Now* 91; enters USC 27; graduation from USC 36; relationship with Francis Ford Coppola 63; student films at USC 32, 36; youth in Modesto 25

Marcos, Ferdinand 110
Mathison, Melissa 133
Milius, John 1, 13, 32, 40; allegory of Homer 132; comes to Philippines 129; early versions of screenplay 97; influence of The Doors 150; influences 52; origin of *Apocalypse Now* 55; reaction to screenplay changes 150; reading Joseph Conrad 86; student films 54; upbringing 51; at USC 53; writing of working screenplay 96
Morrison, Jim 5, 41; fame of The Doors 71; legacy 202; sings "The End" 48-49; at UCLA 43, 45; use of rare sound audio 151
Murch, Walter 32

"Nirvana Now" 85

Palme d'Or 165
Patton 74; links to John Milius 82; origins 75
Pentagon 99; insists on changes in screenplay 108
Philippines 101; arrival of crew 103
Playboy bunnies 132
Psychedelic Soldier 190

Roos, Fred 141
Ruddy, Al 109

Schwary, Ron 82
Scott, George C. 78
Sheen, Martin 101; arrives Philippines 110; films scene on birthday 116; heart attack 124; as John Milius's literary Marlow 117; personal crisis 114; relationship with Marlon Brando 147; replaces Harvey Keitel 107
Spielberg, Steven 1, 34
Storaro, Vittorio 106, 109, 149

Tavoularis, Dean 111, 146

UCLA film school 1; legacy in Hollywood 211; student film festivals 37
United Artists 159
University of Southern California film school 1; legacy in Hollywood 211; role in *Apocalypse Now* 84; student film festivals 37

Vietnam 87; plans to film *Apocalypse Now* "in country" 87; progress of war 96
Vietnam War films 99

Warner Bros. 63; response to *THX 1138* 66
Wayne, John "Duke" 2
Welles, Orson 13, 84

Zanuck, Darryl 74

www.ingramcontent.com/pod-product-compliance
Lightning Source LLC
Chambersburg PA
CBHW081552300426
44116CB00015B/2851